CHURCHILL'S
SECRET
WAR

CHURCHILL'S

SECRET

WAR

THE **BRITISH EMPIRE** AND THE **RAVAGING** OF INDIA DURING **WORLD WAR II**

MADHUSREE MUKERJEE

A Member of the Perseus Books Group
New York

Published by Basic Books,
A Member of the Perseus Books Group

Designed by Pauline Brown
Typeset in 11.75 point Garamond

Library of Congress Cataloging-in-Publication Data

Mukerjee, Madhusree.
Churchill's secret war : the British empire and the ravaging
    of India during World War II / by Madhusree Mukerjee.
      p. cm.
   Includes bibliographical references.
   ISBN 978-0-465-00201-6 (alk. paper)
   1. India—History—20th century. 2. Great Britain—Foreign relations—India. 3. India—Foreign relations—Great Britain. 4. Famines—India—Bengal. 5. Churchill, Winston, 1874–1965. 6. Great Britain—Colonies—History—20th century. 7. World War, 1939–1945—Influence. I. Title.
   DS480.45.M794 2010
   954.03'59—dc22

                                                                        2010003803

10 9 8 7 6 5 4 3 2 1

To those who fell
so that I could be born free

Contents

Prologue:

Our Title to India

"No great portion of the world population was so effectively protected from the horrors and perils of the World War as were the peoples of Hindustan," Winston Churchill wrote in his 1950 history of the twentieth century's most lethal conflict. "They were carried through the struggle on the shoulders of our small Island." By Hindustan, or Land of the Hindus, Churchill meant India, which during the war was part of the British Empire. Britain's wartime prime minister did not discuss in his six-volume account the 1943 famine in the eastern Indian province of Bengal, which killed 1.5 million people by the official estimate and 3 million by most others. One primary cause of the famine was the extent to which Churchill and his advisers chose to use the resources of India to wage war against Germany and Japan, causing scarcity and inflation within the colony. In 1947, two years after the war ended, India attained independence—in part because the deprivation and anarchy of that fractious era had torn the fabric of its society and were erupting in violence that the United Kingdom could no longer subdue. Yet Churchill's efforts to retain the colony by means of divide and rule also contributed to its partition, and to the eventual establishment of the mutually antagonistic nations India, Pakistan, and Bangladesh.[1]

If the famine garnered little attention not just from Churchill but from twentieth-century historians, it also occasioned scant surprise, because Bengal had long been synonymous with hunger. Its modern incarnations, Bangladesh and the state of West Bengal in India, rank

among the poorest regions of the world: Henry Kissinger, the former
U.S. secretary of state, once described Bangladesh as a "basket case."
For two and a half centuries, the history of Bengal—which is in miniature the history of India itself—has featured relentless poverty. But
before 1757, when General Robert Clive founded the British Empire
by conquering Bengal, it was one of the richest parts of the world: "the
paradise of the earth," as Clive himself described it.[2]

Just as British sovereignty over India ended with a famine in Bengal,
it began with one. The famine of 1770 set the stage not only for the
British Raj (as the imperial era in India would eventually be called) and
the chain of famines that occurred throughout that reign but also, ultimately, for the emergence of impoverished and strife-torn South Asia.

IN LATE 1665, traveling eastward from the Mughal court in Delhi,
physician François Bernier arrived in Bengal to find a vast, populous
delta, its myriad channels lined with vibrant towns and cities interspersed
with fields of rice, sugar, corn, vegetables, mustard, and sesame. He declared it "the finest and most fruitful country in the world." Foreign
merchants worked the wholesale markets, offering to buy produce in
exchange for silver. They could not trade goods with the native businessmen, because Bengal was in need of virtually nothing. Its rice traveled
to Sri Lanka (called Ceylon by the British) and the Maldives, its sugar
to Arabia and Mesopotamia, and its silks to Europe; ships at its ports
were loaded with such exports as wheat biscuits and salted meats, opium,
varnish, wax, musk, spices, preserved fruits, and clarified butter. Bengal's
cottons, which supplied much of the world, were astonishing in variety
and quality: twenty yards of a delicate muslin could be stuffed into a
snuffbox. One can only imagine for what sublime piece of fabric another
seventeenth-century visitor, Mirza Nathan, paid 4,000 rupees, given that
a single rupee bought a score of chickens.[3]

Bengali merchants, whose ships plied south to Sri Lanka and west
to Gujarat, ate from gold plates and wore intricately wrought brocade
clothing and gem-studded gold jewelry. Nor were the lowly in want of
shelter or food. "The three or four sorts of vegetables which, together

with rice and butter, form the chief food of the common people, are purchased for the merest trifle," Bernier attested. Fish and meat were so plentiful, he added, that the region's many Portuguese immigrants virtually lived on pork. "Bengale abounds with every necessary of life," he wrote, concluding with a wink: "[t]he rich exuberance of the country, together with the beauty and amiable disposition of the native women, has given rise to a proverb in common use among the Portuguese, English and Dutch, that the Kingdom of Bengale has a hundred gates open for entrance, but not one for departure."[4]

At the time, Bengal was a part of the larger Mughal Empire, whose emperor in distant Delhi ruled weakly through his representative, known as the *diwan*. The rulers could not always provide physical security: Portuguese pirates raided the coastal villages and carried off tens of thousands of slaves, and marauders from central India routinely descended on horseback to lay waste to the western districts. But because the revenues from Bengal were vital to Mughal power, the diwan attended to the province's long-term prosperity.

In the early 1700s, a far-sighted diwan named Murshid Quli Khan reformed the administration. Sixteen powerful *zamindars*, or overseers, and about a thousand minor ones, ran the province under his watchful eye. The zamindars, who called themselves *rajas* if they were Hindu and *nawabs* if they were Muslim, maintained armies, collected taxes, and ran the courts, police, postal services, and often the schools. Villagers owned the lands they tended, and not even bankruptcy could evict them. Tax-exempt fields attached to temples and mosques aided the poor, whereas those who excavated ponds or made other improvements earned tax remissions. Agricultural taxes—a fifth of the harvest—could be paid in kind, without resort to moneylenders. The state, recognizing farmers, spinners, weavers, and merchants as the source of its wealth, tried to protect them. "The money in the hands of the people of the country is my wealth which I have consigned to their purses," explained Alivardi, a ruler in the mid-eighteenth century, cautioning his grandson Siraj-ud-daula to abstain from extortion. "Let them grow rich and the state will grow rich also."[5]

Soon, however, Bengal would descend into subjugation and ruin. Upon ascending to the Bengal throne, the impetuous Siraj-ud-daula confronted the British East India Company. In 1717 the Company had obtained from the Mughal emperor in Delhi the right to trade salt, opium, tobacco, and betel nut (a mild intoxicant) without paying customs duties, but many of its employees were claiming this right for their personal transactions and thereby defrauding the royal treasury. Moreover, in 1756 war broke out between England and France. The Company, fearing attack by French merchants, began to fortify its riverside trading post, Calcutta, and ignored the new diwan's order to desist. Siraj-ud-daula pursued a rival into Calcutta and took English prisoners, many of whom died of suffocation in an airless room that would become notorious as the Black Hole of Calcutta. This episode, embellished by Europeans and propagated as proof of native savagery, would retroactively help to justify what came next: the conquest of Bengal and, ultimately, India. General Robert Clive came to the rescue of Calcutta and defeated Siraj-ud-daula at the Battle of Plassey on June 23, 1757.[6]

Clive's victory was aided by his conspiracy with Siraj-ud-daula's general, Mir Jafar, who became the new nawab. As arranged, Mir Jafar paid the East India Company £2.2 million and its officers and troops £1.2 million, of which Clive took a lion's share. Two hundred barges carrying the first installment of the Company's booty set off from the capital city of Murshidabad on July 3, 1757, accompanied down the Ganga (or Ganges) River by the trumpeting of a British military band. It was a momentous occasion, for countless such tributes would thereafter flow from east to west. That day, another procession in Murshidabad displayed Siraj-ud-daula's body draped over the back of an elephant.[7]

Bengal now had a government beholden to the Company, but its treasury was empty. Mir Jafar's unpaid soldiers mutinied. The British East India Company's senior local officers, known as the Calcutta Council, soon replaced him with one of his rich relatives, Mir Qasim, claiming as a reward for his elevation to power another £200,000 for themselves and, for the Company, the revenues of the prosperous districts of Mid-

napore, Burdwan, and Chittagong. The Council put the task of collecting taxes up for auction, ceding it to whoever promised the greatest
returns for each of the contract's three years. "Thus numberless harpies
were let loose to plunder, whom the spoil of a miserable people enabled
to complete their first year's payment," related Harry Verelst, a later
British governor of Bengal.[8]

The new ruler, Mir Qasim, was not a weakling. Since the triumph
at Plassey, every Englishman had been trading without paying customs
duties, which not only pinched the treasury but undercut local businessmen as well. Bengal's towns began to empty out, bankrupt local
merchants moved to other Indian cities, and shopkeepers took to downing their shutters and running when British traders and their soldiers
approached. Some winders of silk cut off their thumbs for fear of being
forced to work in factories run by Englishmen. Mir Qasim protested,
complaining also that these British merchants "force the people to sell
their goods at a quarter the price and tyrannize over the common man
and the trader." In the noblest moment of his unhappy reign, he re-
scinded customs duties for everyone, native and foreign alike. Affronted
British merchants now demanded that the duties be restored, for all but
themselves. Mir Qasim conceded—provided the East India Company
remove all its troops from Bengal's soil.[9]

The result was war. Mir Qasim, soon defeated by the British, fled
westward, ultimately dying in obscure poverty, and Mir Jafar returned
to the throne, paying his British protectors another £500,000 for the
privilege. After his death in 1765, the Calcutta Council installed one
of his sons, in return for a payment of £230,000. Also during this year,
Clive rendered a final and momentous service to the British East India
Company. He gave its emerging empire a legal foundation and a lucrative source of income by obtaining from the ever-weakening Mughal
emperor in Delhi the right for the Company to collect the revenues of
Bengal province. (This vast administrative unit, larger than France,
comprised three segments, Bengal, Bihar, and Orissa—regions that were
differentiated by language.) In return, the emperor would annually receive £272,000, which left, in Clive's estimation, "a clear gain to the

Company" of £1,650,900 a year. As a result, the East India Company became de facto ruler of India's richest province.[10]

Within five years, Bengal became India's poorest province. The stream of treasure flowing to England had led to a boom in the Company's shares—a boom that was threatened now that Bengal had run out of money and its industries lay in ruins. The directors in London had come to expect enormous profits, even as they owed His Majesty's Government an annual payment of £400,000; so the Company proceeded to collect agricultural taxes with unprecedented rigor. It parceled out by auction the task of extracting revenue from the entire province. No longer were taxes a portion of the harvest, to be paid in kind: the Company operated on the principle that all land belonged to the state and fixed the tax at a specific monetary level, now called rent. This had to be paid in silver even when a crop failed, and farmers who could not pay lost possession of their land. The Company did make more money; for instance, the annual revenue from Bihar, which previously hovered around £200,000, shot up to £680,000. The tax collectors were so oppressive, wrote cloth merchant William Bolts, that farmers were often "necessitated to sell their children in order to pay their rents, or otherwise obliged to fly the country."[11]

For centuries, gold and silver had poured into Bengal; they now poured out. The East India Company no longer had to transport bullion to India to purchase goods for selling abroad. Instead, the tax revenues from Bengal supplied all the capital it had previously imported for investing in trade, and more. "If a district yielded, as in the case of [Birbhum], £90,000 of revenue, the Council took care that not more than £5000 or £6000 were spent in governing it," explained a nineteenth-century historian, William Hunter. "From the remainder, ten thousand pounds or so were deducted for general civil expenses, ten thousand more for the maintenance of the army, and the surplus of say £60,000 was invested in silks, muslins, cotton cloths, and other articles, to be sold by the authorities in Leadenhall Street." The revenue enabled the British East India Company to build on that London thoroughfare an expansive administrative center, called the India House. Often the Company's officials diverted the tax surplus to finance wars in Madras and to purchase tea in China; silver also flowed out when Englishmen sent their profits home. Between 1766 and 1768, Bengal imported £624,375 worth of goods and cash and exported £6,311,250—the amount going out ten times greater than what came in.[12]

Such an economic drain could not go on forever. By 1769, Bengal had no gold, silver, or other valuables left. A group of Armenian merchants—whose trade in the region long preceded that of the British—petitioned the Calcutta Council, complaining that the lack of currency had brought virtually all business to a halt, so that "not only a general bankruptcy is to be feared, but a real famine, in the midst of wealth and plenty."[13]

Then the rains failed. "The fields of rice are become like fields of dried straw," wrote a superintendent. Recognizing that the cost of rice would go up, British officers and their Indian agents, who enjoyed a monopoly on trading rice, bought up all that they could, often forcing peasants to part with the grain they had kept for planting. The British East India Company dispatched a shipload of grain for its forces in Madras, stocked up 5,000 tons for local troops, and, fearing that revenues would fall short, urged "rigor" in tax collection. By then the famine was in full force.[14]

"All through the stifling summer of 1770 the people went on dying," Hunter recounted. "The husbandmen sold their cattle; they sold their implements of agriculture; they devoured their seed-grain; they sold their sons and daughters, till at length no buyer of children could be found; they ate the leaves of trees and the grass of the field; and in June 1770 the Resident at [Murshidabad] affirmed that the living were feeding on the dead." A third of the people of Bengal, numbering about 10 million, perished.[15]

The British East India Company's policies had clearly aggravated the disaster. Despite repeated petitions, the Company had refused to march a brigade of troops out of a hard-hit district of Bihar, where they were appropriating all the available grain, to a region farther west that was better provisioned. (Calcutta's officials feared that if the troops were not close at hand, the French would take the chance to invade from bases in the Indian Ocean.) The Company also prohibited trade in rice among the districts of Bengal—unless the grain was destined for the cities of Murshidabad and Calcutta, the administrative centers of Bengal and the Company, respectively. In particular, the southern and eastern districts were permitted to export rice only to Calcutta. A contemporary observer would note that "as much grain was exported from the lower parts of Bengal as would have fed the number who perished for a whole year."[16]

Most important, during previous droughts agriculturists would have possessed grain, stored in anticipation of a bad year, as well as jewelry, coins, or other savings they could use to purchase rice. (Neighboring areas had a decent harvest. One zamindar bought rice in Benares, west of Bihar, had it transported down the Ganga in barges, and distributed it to famine sufferers on the riverbanks.) By 1770, however, rural Bengal had no currency left—even as, at the height of the famine, speculators were selling their hoards of rice at six times the usual price. Virtually every employee of the Company reaped huge profits in rice speculation. One Company clerk in Murshidabad, who could ordinarily scrape together no more than £200 a year in savings, allegedly sent £60,000 to England that year.[17]

The East India Company did spend £9,000 on famine relief, mainly by buying rice in the districts and distributing it in the cities of Murshidabad and Calcutta—even as it collected from Bengal that fiscal year a substantial rent of £1.4 million. Bihar, where many villages lost four-fifths of their population, yielded the Company a little above £400,000 for 1770, an amount that led the London directors to complain of being "deeply affected to see ourselves disappointed." Amazingly, at the end of that year a tremendous crop stood in the fields, planted by hands no longer alive to reap it. In February 1771, the Calcutta Council reported to the directors: "Notwithstanding the great severity of the late famine and the great reduction of people thereby, some increase has been made in the settlements [revenue collections] both of the Bengal and the Behar provinces for the present year." The revenue did not fall, commented a subsequent governor-general, Warren Hastings, "owing to its being violently kept up to its former standard."[18]

Large harvests appeared the next two years as well, and the Company's annual earnings continued to rise as its agents forced villagers to pay the rent owed by dead neighbors. "While the country every year became a more total waste, the English Government constantly demanded an increased land-tax," Hunter wrote—adding that the collections inevitably faltered. The villagers of Birbhum "were dragooned into paying the land-tax by Mussulman troops, but notwithstanding the utmost severities the receipts seldom amounted to much more than one-half of the demand."[19]

The level of taxes that the Company had grown to expect could not be met because there were now far fewer plantings of rice to tax. With no hands to tend them, a third of Bengal's fields returned to jungle. Most of the province was a fertile delta, formed over millennia by the Ganga and its distributaries: in the absence of cultivators its natural state was tropical forest. The impenetrable growth invaded formerly prosperous villages and shadowed tiny hamlets where the few inhabitants lived in terror of the jungle's rampaging elephants and man-eating panthers. In 1780, two battalions of sepoys—native soldiers in the employ of the British—trying to force their way through Birbhum (a district considered at one time to be "the highway of armies") found "all the way a perfect wilderness" infested with tigers and bears. Communications broke down throughout Bengal because the postmen began to get carried off by wild animals. Many of the surviving villagers deserted their lands and, led by Hindu sadhus or Muslim fakirs (men of religion), took to waylaying British consignments for grain or cash and looting any fields of rice they could find. The rebellion was the first of innumerable peasant and tribal uprisings that would harass the British Raj for the rest of its reign.[20]

Bengal's capital city of Murshidabad, where the dead had lain in piles on the street, fed on by dogs, jackals, and vultures, never recovered from the famine and its aftereffects. By 1771, Calcutta—which historian Narendra K. Sinha states "was well supplied with grain at a time when many places from which it was brought were destitute"—stood alone in all of Bengal as an island of wealth. Desperate people trekked to Calcutta in search of food. "I have counted from my bed-chamber window in the morning when I got up forty dead bodies lying within twenty yards of the wall, besides many hundred lying in the agonies of death for want, bending double, with their stomachs quite close contracted to their back-bones," wrote a correspondent who signed himself J.C. in *The Gentlemen's Magazine*, and who did not care to have the dying so proximate. "I have sent my servants to desire those who had strength, to remove further off."[21]

UNTIL THE FAMINE broke out, few people in the United Kingdom comprehended the source of the East India Company's profits. "Numerous fleets of large ships, loaded with the most valuable commodities of the East, annually arriving in England in a constant and increasing succession" had given rise to a misconception, a parliamentary committee subsequently observed. "This export from India seemed to imply also a reciprocal supply, by which the trading capital employed in those productions was continually strengthened and enlarged. But the payment of a tribute, and not a beneficial commerce, to that country, wore this specious and delusive character." The depopulation that resulted from famine eventually led to a steep drop in the Company's revenues, burst the speculative bubble in its shares, forced it to seek a loan from the Bank of England, and laid its affairs open to scrutiny. Clive, deemed by some to be the richest man in the United Kingdom, had become a member of the House of Commons—but was obliged to answer to Parliament for corruption. He was charged with having received in India valuable gifts that were deemed to belong rightfully to the Company. Although he was cleared of blame, for unknown reasons Clive took his own life in 1774.[22]

The British Parliament gave the East India Company a loan of £1.4 million and appointed Warren Hastings, a gifted protégé of Clive, as the first governor-general of India. Hastings instituted an English-style legal system in Bengal, basing certain of its aspects on what he understood to be local custom. He also sought to repair the Company's fortunes by canceling the portion of Bengal's revenues that were to go to the emperor in Delhi, and by subjugating Oudh, a prosperous kingdom west of Bengal, and subjecting it to rigorous tax collection. As a result, Oudh became "forlorn and desolate" and in 1784 underwent famine. Hastings returned to England a rich man, but he, too, had to answer for his foreign adventures.[23]

In an impeachment trial that dragged on for nine years, statesman Edmund Burke accused Governor-General Hastings of venality and brutality. The Company's revenue collectors, Burke charged in some of the most sensational testimony of the time, had stripped naked the wives of tax defaulters, dragged them from their homes, "put the nipples of the women into the sharp edges of split bamboos and tore them from their bodies." Although Burke's outrage was genuine, historian Nicholas Dirks argues that his crusade had a deeper motive. Burke hoped to cleanse the emerging empire of corruption and cruelty—and to ensure that its benefits flowed not just to employees, shareholders, and directors of the Company but, more broadly, to the people of the United Kingdom. He succeeded in his greater objectives. In the end Hastings was acquitted but, according to Dirks, "Empire emerged from the trial stronger than ever."[24]

IN 1793, AFTER a period of anarchy and intermittent famine that lasted two decades, Governor-General Charles Cornwallis reformed the land revenue system in Bengal. (He had earlier commanded the British forces that were forced to capitulate to George Washington's army in Yorktown, Virginia, in 1781.) Cornwallis returned to the zamindars their hereditary role of collecting taxes and fixed the annual revenue owed to the state (at £2.68 million) in the hope that such a permanent settlement would inspire them to tend their fiefdoms. Using the steady income from Bengal that Cornwallis's reforms assured it, the East India Company went on to conquer or otherwise annex kingdoms in central, southern, and western India. Compliant princes were permitted to continue ruling their kingdoms, as long as they paid a retainer for protection by the Company's troops. Bitter campaigns in the northwest ended with the fall of the Sikhs in 1849, bringing the border of the Raj to the edge of Afghanistan.[25]

In most of the newly conquered territories, the Company gathered its own land tax, which again it called rent. A levy of up to a third of the potential crop, which was often more than the harvest actually produced, ultimately became the norm for rent across much of India. As a result of the relentless benchmark of rent—in contrast to the Mughal tax, which varied with the harvest—land rapidly passed out of the hands of farmers and into the possession of moneylenders. An elderly peasant explained to a revenue official the essential insecurity of the system: "They told me that the river was passable at such and such a ford," he said, "and on their word I tried to cross it, but fell into a deep hole and was nearly drowned. They told me, when I struggled back to shore, that the average depth was quite safe. But that would not have kept me from drowning." To pay their rent after a poor harvest, farmers had to mortgage their future crops and eventually their plots, ultimately losing everything to usurers and ending up as laborers working for low wages in what had been their own fields. In the past, a peasant's land was secure even if he could not pay taxes. But British law in India invariably upheld the rights of creditors, who became critical cogs in the machinery of revenue extraction.[26]

A variety of economic traumas, ranging from the ravages of war and exactions of rent to natural calamity, led to a series of famines all over India. The Madras region, for instance, suffered famine in 1783, 1792, 1807, 1813, 1823, 1834, and 1854. Unlike the Bengal famine of 1770, the nineteenth-century calamities excited little comment in England, where influential scholars such as James Mill argued that poverty rather than wealth was India's intrinsic and unvarying condition. Hindu legal codes contained guidelines for helping ordinary people through "seasons of calamity," and Mill pointed to the existence of such regulations as evidence that "a state of poverty and wretchedness, as far as the great body of the people are concerned, must have prevailed in India" in the past, just as in the present.[27]

Mill asserted that the British conquest of India was ordained by the inexorable progress of humankind. Ascendant societies had many enemies; as a result, he wrote, "one of the first applications of knowledge is, to improve the military art." Superiority in the battlefield was a sign of cultural advancement. Muslims such as the Mughal emperors had ruled India for centuries, which indicated to Mill that their civilization was superior to that of Hindus—and the reins had naturally passed from them to Christians.[28]

The distinction between Hindus and Muslims, originally one of uncountable fissures in multifarious India, had sharpened with colonial attempts to classify the subcontinent's populace. Having encountered Muslims for centuries, the British believed that they knew them: a valiant, warlike, monotheistic people who, despite being occasionally savage, deserved respect. Indian Muslims were in truth far more varied and sophisticated than such a caricature would allow; Sufi saints, for instance, preached love rather than war. But once Muslims had been pegged, Hindus came to be defined by their perceived differences with their Islamic compatriots.[29]

Hindu was originally an ancient Arab or Persian appellation for anyone living east and south of the Indus River: it signified residence rather than religion. The myriad beliefs of Hindus, ranging from the extreme nonviolence of some to the human sacrifices by others, could scarcely be classified as a single faith. Nevertheless, Mill and others believed Hindus to be endowed with distinct characteristics, at the core of which lay effeminacy and its corollary, dishonesty. Unable to face what Mill called "the manliness and courage of our ancestors," the defeated Hindus with their "slavish and dastardly spirit" were wont to employ "deceit and perfidy" in achieving their ends. Over time, educated Indians came to internalize such distinctions between Hindus and Muslims—although the illiterate continued to worship at one another's shrines.[30]

A succession of nineteenth-century authors developed the argument that British rule conferred the benefits of a superior civilization to a people who had hitherto floundered in superstition and strife, and was justified thereby. In 1885, Tory politician Lord Randolph Churchill elaborated on the theme. "Our rule in India is, as it were, a sheet of oil spread out over a surface of, and keeping calm and quiet and unruffled by storms, an immense and profound ocean of humanity," he declared. "Underneath that rule lie hidden all the memories of fallen dynasties, all the traditions of vanquished races, all the pride of insulted creeds; and it is our task, our most difficult business, to give peace, individual security, and general prosperity to the 250 millions of people who are affected by those powerful forces; to bind them and to weld them by the influence of our knowledge, our law, and our higher civilisation, in process of time, into one great, united people; and to offer to all the nations of the West the advantages of tranquillity and progress in the East. That is our task for India. That is our *raison d'être* in India. That is our title to India."[31]

BENEATH THE SHEET of oil, the colony bubbled and foamed. Between 1760 and 1850 the Company's troops had to be diverted to suppress more than forty serious rebellions in different regions. In 1857, the hundredth anniversary of the Battle of Plassey, central and northern India erupted in unison, with thousands of villagers joining sepoys of the Indian Army and disaffected princes in violent opposition to British rule.[32]

A medley of social and economic grievances had combined to produce the Sepoy Mutiny, as the British called it, or the Rebellion of 1857, as historians know it today. Many of the sepoys were onetime farmers who resented the deprivations that had forced them to enlist as mercenaries, the racial discrimination that kept them from ever becoming officers, and the threats to religious purity entailed by certain army practices. Villagers hated the new revenue system, and royals feared the loss of their kingdoms. The most memorable of the rebel commanders was the Rani of Jhansi, who ruled a small principality in central India, and who led into battle not only her own forces but also those of two nawabs. Her death by gunfire, when she was about twenty, marked the end of the uprising. It was a bloody affair indeed. The rebels killed several hundred white men, women, and children; the 50,000 British soldiers imported to put down the uprising avenged these murders a thousand times over. Such at least was the claim of General Hugh Rose, who sacked the city of Jhansi.[33]

After suppressing the rebellion, the United Kingdom dissolved the East India Company and formally assumed the reins of government. On November 1, 1858, Queen Victoria proclaimed that henceforth the British Empire would be ruled for the benefit of all its subjects. In practice, control over India would rest with the British public, acting through their Parliament and a secretary of state for India based at the India Office in London. The governor-general in Calcutta acquired the title of viceroy, underlining his status as the Queen's representative. Loyal native princes retained their kingdoms but remained subservient to the viceroy. A "mutiny charge" of £50 million, the cost of importing British soldiers to put down the uprising, was deducted from the colony's account.[34]

Military strategists decreed that sufficient numbers of white troops should always be stationed in India to forestall further mutinies. And British officers painstakingly rebuilt the native portion of the Indian Army with "martial races"—mainly tall and light-skinned farmers from the northwest. They were Sikh, Muslim, or Rajput, the last group being Hindus who were believed to have retained fighting qualities possessed by their ancestors. Furthermore, because sepoys of diverse regions and religions had united in attacking their superiors, the generals segregated such groups and trained the regiments so that "Sikh might fire into Hindu, Gurkha into either, without any scruple in case of need." (Gurkhas are a mountain-dwelling people from Nepal.) By the end of the nineteenth century, the Indian Army was a formidable force called up in British battles from Africa and Afghanistan in the west to Burma and China in the east.[35]

EVEN AS THEY brought the recalcitrant sepoy under control, the British rulers of India came to perceive an even more potent threat: the educated Hindu male, or *babu*. Many of the babus were conversant with Western thought and were asking to be treated according to Enlightenment principles of liberty, equality, and fraternity. A few had entered the Indian civil service by traveling to London to take the requisite examinations, and their presence in the system emphasized the conflict inherent in the British Raj. Equality under the law was held by the conquerors to be one of the great benefits bestowed upon Indians, but native judges were not permitted to preside over cases involving whites. In 1883, Lord Ripon, one of the rare liberals who attained the office of viceroy, resolved to remove this discrepancy—only to provoke a furious outcry. For, as historian Thomas Metcalfe points out, it was "no easy matter at once to treat Indians and Europeans equally, and then to claim the right to rule a conquered India." All said and done, it was faith in racial superiority—the belief that natives were incapable of the supervisory tasks that whites performed—that supplied the theoretical foundation of the British Raj.[36]

English men and women, many of them based in Calcutta, penned furious attacks on the babu (often spelling it *baboo* to suggest a link with the primate). Mill had declared that "the Hindu, like the eunuch, excels in the qualities of a slave," and the popular historian Thomas Babington Macaulay had dwelt on the emasculation of Bengalis, who'd "found the little finger of the Company thicker than the loins" of the prince Siraj-ud-daula. Several authors now embellished these images. The writer Rudyard Kipling repeatedly portrayed the Bengali civil servant as a nincompoop who in a crisis fled the scene and left the real men to pick up the pieces. It was the Bengali male's "extraordinary effeminacy," as evinced by his diminutive physique, his flowing clothes, and his worship of goddesses, that best illustrated why he, and by extension India, had to be guided by the firm, benevolent hand of a supremely masculine race.[37]

Even as the babus realized with a shock how contemptible they were to the British, a popular novel suggested how they might prove their manliness. In 1882, a Bengali civil servant named Bankim Chandra Chattopadhyay had dramatized in the novel *Anandamath* the insurrection that followed the famine of 1770. In a conscious response to Macaulay's jibes, the writer imagined the rebels as warrior-saints who readily shed blood in defense of their motherland. The novel was a covert call to arms that offered visions of heroic self-sacrifice to angry youths and inaugurated an era of Bengali militancy.

A rather more sedate group of Indians, mainly lawyers and civil servants, came together in Bombay in 1885 to form the Indian National Congress. They hoped to articulate native grievances and seek redress from within the British imperial system, and over the next two decades they won greater representation for Indians on legislative councils. (These had negligible power but would form the basis of the more substantive legislatures of the future.) In 1905, when Viceroy George Nathaniel Curzon announced a plan to sever the large and unwieldy province of Bengal into two parts, the Congress initiated a mass public protest.

The province was to be divided into a predominantly Hindu western fragment and a largely Muslim eastern one. "Bengal united, is power, Bengal divided, will pull several different ways. . . . [O]ne of our main objects is to split up and thereby weaken a solid body of opponents to our rule," explained a British civil servant. Curzon, who regarded Muslims as potential allies against the largely Hindu nationalists, visited the city of Dacca in eastern Bengal to inform the region's Muslim zamindars how partition would enhance their influence. In 1906 the All India Muslim League came into being in Dacca and declared its support for the viceroy's partition plan.[38]

The Congress, which opposed partition, introduced a powerful weapon of Irish invention: a boycott of British goods. Thousands of students foreswore foreign fabrics. Bonfires flared on Calcutta's streets, consuming jackets, trousers, and other Western clothes. In the first year of the agitation alone, the importation of cotton goods fell by a quarter. Dadabhai Naoroji, a mathematician and businessman who headed the Congress, declared the greater goal of the movement to be *swaraj*, or self-rule. In 1911 a new viceroy succumbed to the persistent economic pressure and revoked the partition.[39]

The large province of Bengal was instead broken up along linguistic lines, with Bihar and Orissa becoming separate states. India itself would no longer be administered from Calcutta but from New Delhi, far beyond Bengal. "[I]t will be a very good idea to move the Government

offices away from the Bengali Babus, who now swarm in every office,"
noted a visitor to the city. "No Englishman has a good word for them:
they are said to have less character and backbone than any other Indians,
and to be intolerably conceited, besides being seditious." In 1912, when
the viceroy ceremonially entered the newly built capital city on a ca-
parisoned elephant, some revolutionaries lobbed a bomb that seriously
injured him. The chief conspirator, who escaped to Japan, turned out
to be a Bengali babu.[40]

"Bengal is the seat of bitterest political unrest—the producer of
India's main crop of anarchists, bomb-throwers and assassins," observed
American writer Katherine Mayo in *Mother India*, a 1927 travelogue
that described Hindu males as pedophiles enervated by excessive sex.
"Bengal is also among the most sexually exaggerated regions of India;
and medical and police authorities in any country observe the link between that quality and 'queer' criminal minds—the exhaustion of normal avenues of excitement creating a thirst and a search in the abnormal
for gratification." This book, the outcome of a tour organized by British
intelligence, would so captivate Winston Churchill that he would pass
it around among friends.[41]

ON AUGUST 4, 1914, the British Empire went to war against Germany. India presented £100 million to the United Kingdom as a contribution for war expenses and sent troops to the Middle East and
Europe; more than 60,000 of its soldiers would die fighting World
War I. In rural India, wartime inflation, the export of grain to the war
theaters, and drought made it difficult for the poor to afford enough
food. Epidemic forestalled famine: the Spanish flu, which soldiers
brought home from the icy trenches of Europe, thrived on emaciated
frames and killed an estimated 12 million.[42]

Mainstream Indian nationalists cooperated with the British war effort and expected political concessions as a reward. So when the Government of India hailed the end of World War I by enacting a repressive
law, Indian rage boiled over. Among other provisions, the Rowlatt Act
of 1919 allowed the government to imprison indefinitely and sentence

by tribunal—not trial—anyone suspected of sedition. A visionary leader, Mohandas Karamchand Gandhi, stepped to the fore and called for civil disobedience against what he termed a "devilish" law.

Gandhi was forty-nine and had returned to India a few years earlier, after a twenty-two-year sojourn in southern Africa. Born in Gujarat in western India in 1869, he had trained as a lawyer in England and moved to Natal, a British colony, to set up a practice. There Gandhi had come to identify with impoverished Indian laborers who worked on plantations and mines, and had championed their rights. In the process he had forged a political and moral weapon that he called *satyagraha*, transliterated as "passion for truth." Someone who offered satyagraha—by, for instance, refusing to obey an unjust law—had to follow a path "as sharp as the sword's edge," Gandhi wrote. He or she had to abjure violence and bear no animosity toward the opponent, no matter how intense the hardship: "Satyagraha postulates the conquest of the adversary by suffering in one's own person."[43]

Gandhi was sensitive to the charge that Indians were cowards. He recalled in his autobiography a ditty in his native Gujarati, which he and his schoolmates used to chant:[44]

Behold the mighty Englishman
He rules the Indian small,
Because being a meat-eater
He is five cubits tall.

As a child growing up in a strictly vegetarian family, he had secretly sampled meat because a friend had assured him it would make him brave enough to fight the English. Yet the adult Gandhi repudiated what he regarded as the Western definition of courage: a willingness to take life. In his view, true courage lay in upholding one's own values, and especially in enduring all manner of torment, without being provoked into violence.[45]

But India was not ready for satyagraha. During the civil disobedience movement, crowds took to rioting and many died in police firing, so

Gandhi called it off. He had yet to learn about the massacre in Amritsar, a city hallowed by Sikhs. On April 13, 1919, General Reginald Dyer had placed troops at the entrance of an enclosed park where men, women, and children had assembled, some to celebrate their New Year and others to listen to a speech. Gatherings of more than five were forbidden. Dyer had issued a warning and ordered the troops to open fire; the death toll was 379 by the official count, and more than 1,000 by the Indian reckoning.[46]

It was "an extraordinary event, a monstrous event, an event which stands in singular and sinister isolation," Winston Churchill declaimed at the House of Commons when it discussed the affair a year later. The elder son of Lord Randolph, Churchill was then the forty-five-year-old secretary of state for war in the British cabinet. He privately agreed with military officers on "the necessity to shoot hard," but he was also aware of the importance of Sikhs to the Indian Army. One needed to remember that the colony was not ruled by force alone, he continued in his speech, and that a sense of unity and cooperation "must ever ally and bind together the British and Indian peoples."[47]

It was too late for such sentiments. Muslims, who were also vital to the Indian Army, had been angered by the breaking of a British promise: to maintain the control of the Ottoman emperor over holy cities such as Mecca. After the war the victors proceeded to divide up that empire, with the United Kingdom acquiring portions of the Middle East—not so much for the oil as to secure the region around the Suez Canal. Leopold Amery, a Tory politician and a leading strategist, asserted that it was necessary to develop a contiguous British Empire that would run "from Cape Town through Cairo, Baghdad and Calcutta to Sydney and Wellington."[48]

After the Amritsar tragedy, when Gandhi was finally allowed to enter the Punjab, a vast and emotional crowd greeted him at the railway station. "The entire populace had turned out of doors in eager expectation, as if to meet a dear relation after a long separation, and was delirious with joy," he remembered. The official inquiry into the atrocity, he concluded after conducting his own investigations, was a "whitewash." Until then, Gandhi had believed that the British Raj, though liable to make mistakes, was fundamentally benign and just. Renouncing that faith, he cast about for ways in which to achieve swaraj.[49]

On August 1, 1920, the Indian National Congress, acting in concert with prominent Muslims, called for civil disobedience—and received a staggeringly positive response to their summons. Every corner of India erupted, each with its own cause. Peasants organized against landlords, laborers in tea plantations struck work, indigenous peoples defied the law to hunt and gather in forests, students walked out of schools and colleges, and prominent lawyers quit lucrative practices. A Bengali babu named Subhas Chandra Bose, who had just passed the Indian civil service examinations in London with high marks, abandoned his prospectively prestigious career and joined the Congress. A Muslim leader called upon Muslims to quit the Indian Army and was promptly arrested. Even the revolutionaries shelved their arms for a year to give Gandhi's method a chance. They were all to be bitterly disappointed. In a small town in northern India, policemen fired on a procession—whereupon the irate mob chased them into the police station and set it afire, burning twenty-three people to death. The incident horrified Gandhi, who persuaded the Congress to call off the movement in February 1922.[50]

Despite its abortive end, the protest revealed that, for the first time, overwhelming numbers of Indians were united under a single banner and inspired by Gandhi, who came to be called Mahatma, or "Great Soul." Gandhi's moral stature and popularity, even among some English men and women, made him the most baffling adversary that the British Empire had ever encountered. "I often wish you took to violence like the English strikers, and then we would know at once how to deal with you," a South African official had said to him, only half in jest. "But you will not injure even the enemy. . . . [T]hat is what reduces us to sheer helplessness." Gandhi was a contradiction in terms, fragility turned into strength, a "Dangerous Feminine Man." To Winston Churchill, who was profoundly committed to the British Raj, as well as to the knightly values of valor, honor, and chivalry, Gandhi came to represent Hindu guile—a "malignant subversive fanatic" and "a thoroughly evil force."[51]

WHEN WORLD WAR II broke out in September 1939, the people of the United Kingdom turned to Winston Churchill for leadership because he personified the British Lion, indomitable in adversity. "Let us therefore brace ourselves to our duty," Churchill declaimed, "and so bear ourselves that if the British Commonwealth and Empire lasts for a thousand years, men will still say, 'This was their finest hour.'" The prime minister's fierce determination buoyed Britons and helped them to rise above the tribulations to come. "One caught Churchill's infectious spirit that this was a great time to be alive in; that Destiny had conferred a wonderful benefit upon us; and that these were thrilling days to live through," remembered historian Robert Rhodes James.[52]

Churchill's utterances also indicated his dedication to the British Raj. He hoped at least "to see the British Empire preserved for a few more generations in its strength and splendour," as he had written to the viceroy of India. But in March 1942, three months after escalating the war with the attack on Pearl Harbor, Japanese forces smashed the empire's defenses and occupied Burma. They thereby cut off a vital source of rice imports for the Indian poor and simultaneously established themselves at the colony's mountainous eastern border. Fearing that India itself would be invaded, British authorities acted on a "scorched earth" order issued by the War Cabinet, the group of ministers and officials who made all the key decisions of the war. They removed provisions such as rice, and transport facilities such as barges, from coastal Bengal, where the enemy was expected to arrive by sea—creating another of several conditions that would culminate in famine.[53]

At the same time, India's people were reluctant to fight a war that held little promise of freedom for them. In August 1942, the Indian National Congress called for civil disobedience to protest the colony's forced participation in World War II. Gandhi and other nationalist leaders were swiftly arrested, unleashing what the viceroy would describe as the most serious rebellion since 1857. The authorities arrested more than 90,000, and killed up to 10,000 political protesters. India was "an occupied and hostile country," a British general declared. At the same time, the Indian Army continued to fight in theaters around the Mediterranean Sea, and Indian fields and factories supplied them and other troops with foodgrains, uniforms, boots, parachutes, tents, ammunition, and innumerable other necessities. Virtually all of India's industries had by now been redirected toward supplying the war effort, and the government was printing paper money to enable its purchases. The price of grain spiraled ever upward, a cyclone damaged Bengal's rice harvest, the local administration stocked up on rice to feed soldiers and war workers, and famine broke out in early 1943.[54]

According to an agreement drawn up three years earlier, a portion of India's war expenditure would ultimately be reimbursed by His Majesty's Government. The amount owed to India, called the sterling debt, swelled during the course of the war until it came to reverse the traditional economic relationship between colonizer and colony. For the past century, India had owed money to the United Kingdom—because of the mutiny charge, the investment for building railways, the pensions owed to British civil servants, and other loans and expenses. Now, for the first time ever, the United Kingdom owed money to India. The sterling debt worsened Britain's postwar economic prospects and became a source of immense frustration to the prime minister and his closest adviser, Lord Cherwell. Cherwell, a scientist of German aristocratic lineage who was so deeply racist that the presence of any black person evoked "physical revulsion which he was unable to control," aided Churchill with logistical matters such as the distribution of shipping and allocation of food supplies. Ominously, his recommendations almost always prevailed.[55]

Also in 1943, the nationalist Subhas Chandra Bose came to head a liberation army based in the Far East. The so-called Indian National Army comprised expatriate Indian laborers and captured soldiers of the (British) Indian Army, and was allied with Japan. It threatened India's eastern border with attack—while insurgents on Bengal's coast prepared to welcome Bose and his forces, should they arrive. With the empire at risk from a military invasion, and discord rife even as Bengal's people began to starve, Churchill was called upon to make a choice that would tilt the balance between life and death for millions: whether or not to expend valuable wheat and shipping space on providing famine relief to Bengalis.

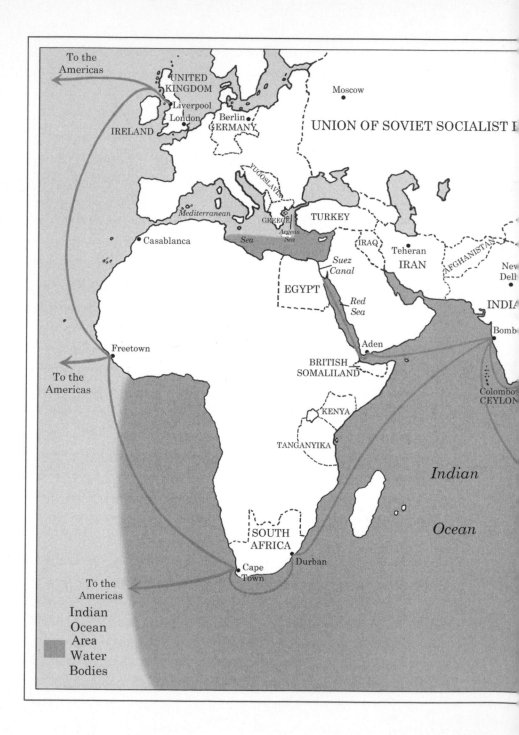

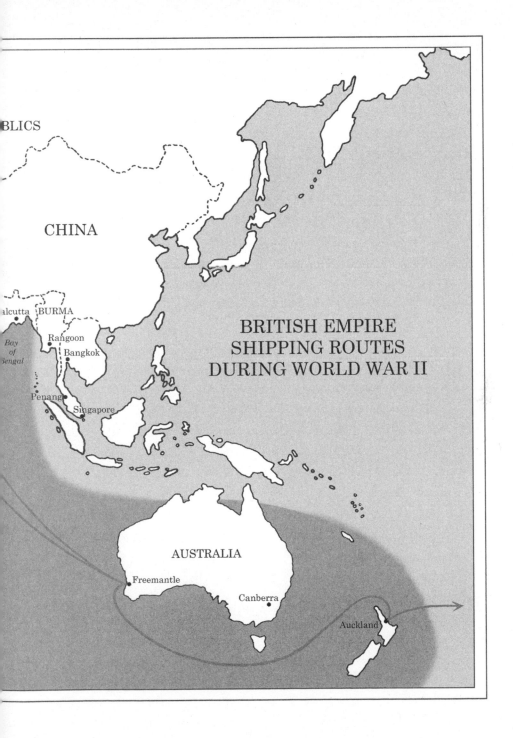

BLICS

CHINA

BURMA

alcutta

Rangoon

Bangkok

Bay of Bengal

Penang

Singapore

BRITISH EMPIRE
SHIPPING ROUTES
DURING WORLD WAR II

AUSTRALIA

Freemantle

Canberra

Auckland

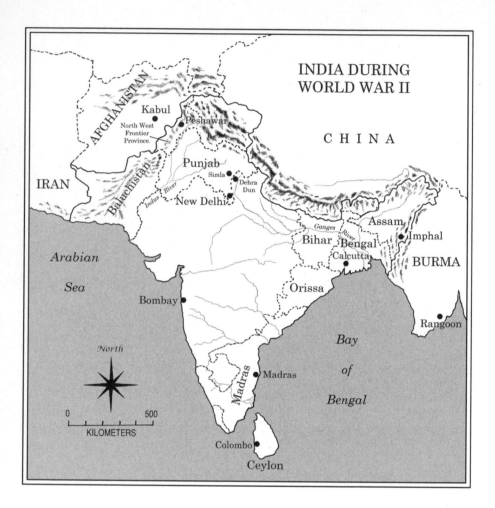

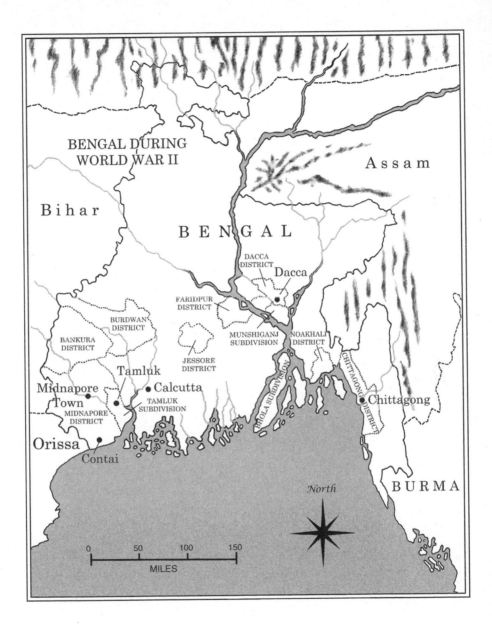

BENGAL DURING
WORLD WAR II

Bihar

Assam

B E N G A L

DACCA
DISTRICT
Dacca

FARIDPUR
DISTRICT

BURDWAN
DISTRICT

MUNSHIGANJ
SUBDIVISION

NOAKHALI
DISTRICT

BANKURA
DISTRICT

JESSORE
DISTRICT

Tamluk

Midnapore
Town

Calcutta

TAMLUK
SUBDIVISION

MIDNAPORE
DISTRICT

Orissa

Contai

CHITTAGONG DISTRICT

Chittagong

BHOLA SUBDIVISION

North

BURMA

0   50   100   150
MILES

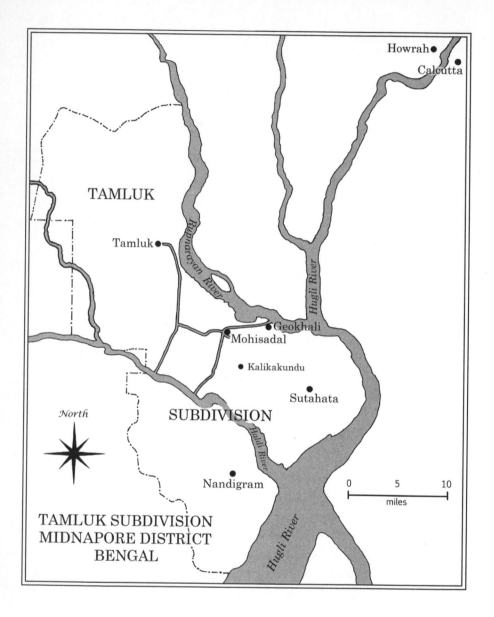

Howrah

Calcutta

TAMLUK

Tamluk

Rupnarayan River

Hugli River

Geokhali

Mohisadal

Kalikakundu

Sutahata

North

SUBDIVISION

Haldi River

Nandigram

0   5   10
miles

TAMLUK SUBDIVISION
MIDNAPORE DISTRICT
BENGAL

Hugli River

CHAPTER ONE

Empire at War

"In my view England is now beginning a new period of struggle and fighting for its life," Winston Churchill wrote in 1933, "and the crux of it will be not only the retention of India but a much stronger assertion of commercial rights." As the world began to edge toward war, none of the globe's other empires, such as the French or the Dutch, were about to relinquish their possessions; and Japan was already conquering new realms. According to Churchill, who was urging armament against a newly resurgent Germany, this crucial moment was no time to cede political powers to Indians, as the British government was planning to do. In the conflict to come, he believed the United Kingdom would need its huge and resource-rich possession as never before.[1]

Six years after Churchill's avowal and two days after the Nazis began their blitzkrieg into Poland, on September 3, 1939, the United Kingdom declared war on Germany. So did the viceroy of India, on behalf of nearly 400 million subjects of the British Empire. The colony was vital to the defense of British interests around the world. It sat in the middle of the supply and communication route that stretched from the United Kingdom, through the Suez Canal or around the Cape of Good Hope, and across the Indian Ocean to Singapore, Australia, and New Zealand. Throughout World War II, ships would transport food, armaments, and troops from the colonies and dominions on the periphery of the Indian Ocean to the United Kingdom, as well as to war theaters around the Mediterranean Sea or in Southeast Asia.

The Indian population would play a significant role in the war. Of the colony's prewar budget, a third went toward defense, and that fraction had increased to two-fifths by 1939. The Indian Army's primary domestic tasks were to guard the northwestern border against Soviet incursions southward across Afghanistan and to ensure internal security. Just as important, this army was ideally situated to defend British dependencies in the Middle East, Africa, and Southeast Asia, and could be dispatched to diverse theaters under direct orders from London. At the start of the war, it comprised 43,500 British and 131,000 Indian troops, some of whom had already been sent to Egypt and Singapore. Churchill, then a member of the War Cabinet, recommended that a further 60,000 British troops "be sent to India to maintain internal security and complete their training," while at least 40,000 trained troops be brought back. While being trained, the white soldiers would forestall any uprising among the increasingly restive population of Indians intent on independence.[2]

"I was kept for this job," Churchill confided to his doctor when he succeeded Neville Chamberlain as prime minister on May 10, 1940. Over his sixty-five years, Churchill had repeatedly placed himself in danger and had had several narrow escapes, which had bolstered his profound conviction that he was destined for a mighty task. It had taken him most of his life to discover what that something was: to lead The Island Race, as he would entitle his history of the British, in a great struggle. "I felt as if I were walking with destiny, and that all my past life had been but a preparation for this hour and for this trial," Churchill wrote of his accession to the most powerful position in the British Empire. Three days after his appointment he addressed the Parliament and the nation, promising nothing but "blood, toil, tears and sweat." The aim of the war, he declared, was "victory, victory at all costs . . . for without victory, there is no survival. Let that be realised; no survival for the British Empire, no survival for all that the British Empire has stood for, no survival for the urge and impulse of the ages, that mankind will move forward towards its goal." The prime minister would not only defend the British Isles from invasion and subjugation by Hitler's armies; he would safeguard its vast and sprawling empire. But India, like some of the other colonies and dominions, would sacrifice at least as much as the United Kingdom did in the defense of an empire from which it had long been struggling to break free.[3]

To make sure India obeyed him and did its part to support the war, Churchill needed a lieutenant with a record of firmness in dealing with colonies. The very day he gave his rousing "blood, toil, tears and sweat" peroration, the prime minister summoned the respected elder statesman Leopold S. Amery and asked him to serve as secretary of state for India.

Amery was bitterly disappointed by the request. He was sixty-six, a year older than Churchill, and up to that point his career had broadly paralleled that of the prime minister. Amery had covered the Boer War as a correspondent, had served in World War I, and had subsequently been appointed first Lord of the Admiralty and colonial secretary. At the very least, he had expected a significant role in the War Cabinet helping to direct the war effort. It was even said that if Amery had been "half a head taller and his speeches half an hour shorter" he might have become prime minister himself. Amery had also just played a central role in the Tory Party mutiny that had brought down Chamberlain and installed Churchill. A week earlier, he had denounced Chamberlain from the floor of Parliament: "You have sat too long here for any good you have been doing," Amery had declaimed, invoking the words of Oliver Cromwell, the seventeenth-century British leader who had deposed and killed King Charles I: "Depart, I say, and let us have done with you. In the name of God, go!"[4]

Amery protested to Churchill that he was "side tracking me from the real conduct of the war." Not so, the prime minister responded: it was important to ensure that India contribute as much as possible to the war, which might even move east. Amery was not persuaded, and believed that Chamberlain had urged against his appointment to the War Cabinet. Historian William Roger Louis holds, however, that by giving him a relatively subordinate role Churchill sought to contain a potential rival, one reputed to be "a man of integrity and judgment who had the courage to speak his convictions regardless of consequence." Eventually the patriot in Amery prevailed—even as he maintained a private hope that a cabinet reshuffle would bring him closer to power. He accepted the position.[5]

The new secretary of state for India rapidly put mechanisms in place "to utilize Indian supplies to the utmost," as he described in his diary, and moved to impart to the marquess of Linlithgow, the viceroy in New Delhi, emergency powers of arrest and detention, control of the press, prohibition of seditious groups, and so on. "My whole conception is that of India humming from end to end with activity in munitions and supply production and at the same time with the bustle of men training for active service of one sort or another, the first operation largely paying for the cost of the second," Amery explained to Linlithgow.[6]

The Indian Army was slated to play a crucial role in the war, and in June 1940 the prime minister directed Amery to ensure that additional divisions were shipped westward. "The fact that we are somewhat reducing the quality of our British garrisons [in India], makes it all the more desirable that a larger number of Indian troops should also be employed outside India," Churchill explained. That is, because recent recruits from the United Kingdom, who were in need of training, were replacing more experienced white troops in India (the latter were either returning home to defend Britain or moving to the war theaters), any mutiny by the native soldiers would be all the more difficult to quell. So India's internal security required that as many of the sepoys as possible should also be abroad. Moreover, Churchill continued, it appeared that the war would "spread to the Middle East, and the climate of Iraq, Palestine and Egypt are well suited to Indian troops." The prime minister's greater apprehension of a mutiny than of an external attack would mean that when Japanese forces suddenly and ominously arrived at India's eastern border in March 1942, the colony's most highly trained and best-equipped divisions would be on another continent.[7]

Apart from supplying soldiers for some of the toughest combat in countries around the Mediterranean Sea, India was designated to provide the bulk of supplies for those theaters. Starting in May, Amery oversaw the effort to ship from India around 40,000 tons of grain per month, a tenth of its railway engines and carriages, and even railway tracks uprooted from less important train lines. The colony's entire commercial production of timber, woolen textiles, and leather goods, and three-quarters of its steel and cement production, would be required for the war. Factories near Calcutta were soon turning out ammunition, grenades, bombs, guns, and other weaponry; Bombay's mills were producing uniforms and parachutes, while plants all over the country were contributing boots, jeep bodies and chassis, machine parts, and hundreds of ancillary items such as binoculars for which the need had suddenly swelled. Apart from the United Kingdom itself, India would become the largest contributor to the empire's war—providing goods and services worth more than £2 billion.[8]

Leopold Amery had not visited India since he had left it as a small child. He sought to travel there, to gauge first-hand the manifold problems with the war effort, but discovered that the viceroy was too protective of his turf to acquiesce. Lord Linlithgow was an acknowledged expert on India and had been viceroy since 1936; Amery, being far less familiar with the colony's affairs, needed his cooperation. Yet over a lifetime of service to the needs of the empire, Amery had acquired a special skill: devising constitutions that ceded power to colonies in small and careful doses. Resolving to maximize India's contribution to the war, he decided to apply this expertise toward breaking the prevailing impasse with the country's nationalists.[9]

AMONG INDIANS, THE advent of war had brought anxiety mingled with hope. Mohandas Karamchand Gandhi, now seventy, had retired from active politics because he was unhappy with the socialism propounded by younger leaders such as Jawaharlal Nehru and Subhas Chandra Bose. The attractive and erudite Nehru, who turned fifty in 1939, had long played a prominent role in the Indian National Congress. Early in his career Nehru had been emotionally and ideologically close to Gandhi, but they had since diverged on a number of issues. Bose, who was eight years younger than Nehru, was a passionate radical who had spent most of his adult life in prison or in exile because of his extreme antipathy to colonialism—which included, on more than one occasion, expressing a sympathetic interest in armed rebellion.

Both Nehru and Bose asserted that India needed to be industrialized along socialist lines, under the paternal guidance of a powerful state. Gandhi, in contrast, held that industrialization begat violence: it drew power away from individuals and toward large centralized entities, and it demanded the massive use of natural resources as well as expanding markets that could be acquired only by force. In the late 1930s, Gandhi had occupied himself with rejuvenating villages, believing that India's salvation lay in reviving cottage industries such as spinning, which would employ and thereby restore power to individuals in their homes. But World War II thrust upon him a moral challenge that would bring him back to the fore.[10]

In 1935, after a prolonged civil disobedience movement in India, a coalition government in London had granted limited powers of self-rule to the colony. Many members of the Labour Party were sympathetic to Indian aspirations, and even some Tory politicians held that Britain could not forever oppose some measure of self-government in the colony. But an earlier viceroy of India, Lord Irwin, had explained to Amery that Indians could probably be appeased, by "some façade which will leave the essential mechanism of power still in our hands." Accordingly, by 1935 London's socialists and conservatives had hammered out a compromise: a franchise of around 30 million voters would elect Indian ministers to run the provinces and send a few representatives to the viceroy's executive council in New Delhi. The viceroy, along with governors in the provinces, would retain ultimate control over defense, finance, foreign affairs, and internal security. As a colleague explained at the time to Churchill, this constitution would allow Indians to rule the provinces "as long as they do it properly, and leave the Governors absolutely free to take over the whole or any part of the administration themselves should the machine not function properly."[11]

The Indian National Congress contested the elections mandated by the 1935 act and won handsomely. Eight provinces (out of eleven) gained Congress ministries. But three years later the fiery Bose became president of the Congress and reiterated the call for independence. "Ours is a struggle not only against British Imperialism but against world Imperialism as well, of which the former is the keystone," he declared. "We are, therefore, fighting not for the cause of India alone but for humanity as well."[12]

As president, when Bose gazed at the thunderclouds of world war on the horizon, he perceived a silver lining: the conflict was a once-in-a-lifetime opportunity to wrest freedom for India. With the United Kingdom facing a mortal threat that left it utterly dependent on Indian men and materials, its leaders would be forced to give way to nationalists' demands. In early 1939, he trounced a candidate favored by Gandhi to win reelection as Congress president. Gandhi described the election as a personal defeat. At his instructions, on February 22, 1939, almost the entire senior leadership of the Congress Party resigned their positions, denying the president any way to implement his ideas.[13]

Bose was deeply hurt by this public repudiation and fell ill. In the 1920s, while imprisoned in Burma on unspecified charges, he had acquired a mysterious fever that recurred in times of stress. Undeterred, he urged at his inaugural address (which his brother had to deliver, Bose being too sick) that London be handed an ultimatum. If the United Kingdom did not liberate India within a specified time limit—he had in mind six months—the Congress should begin a nonviolent civil disobedience struggle with the objective of winning independence. Gandhi countered that civil disobedience would inevitably degenerate into civil war. "I smell violence in the air I breathe," he wrote to Bose. Communal tensions had escalated in recent years, and clashes between Muslim peasants and Hindu landowners, fueled by economic disputes, had already claimed many lives in eastern Bengal.[14]

At a meeting in September 1939, the differences among Gandhi, Bose, and Nehru broke into the open. Gandhi was horrified by the bloodshed unleashed by the Nazis and wanted to cooperate with aspects of the war effort. Bose asserted that both Germany and the United Kingdom were fighting for imperial stakes; he saw the war as amoral and urged that the Congress use it as an opportunity to wrest freedom. Nehru detested fascism—but he also felt that Indians had no compelling reason to participate in a war that would free others while leaving them colonized. His view prevailed, in that the Indian National Congress asked the United Kingdom to clarify the ends to which the war would be fought. "If the war is to defend the status quo, imperialist possessions, colonies, vested interests, and privilege, India can have nothing to do with it. If, however, the issue is democracy and a world order based on democracy, then India is intensely interested in it," the Congress announced. "A free democratic India will gladly associate herself with other free nations for mutual defence against aggression."[15]

In October, after consulting with the War Cabinet in London, Viceroy Linlithgow described British war aims as "laying the foundation of a better international system which will mean that war is not to be the inevitable lot of each succeeding generation." He did not mention democracy. After the war, he added, the 1935 act could be modified to incorporate progress toward the ultimate goal of dominion status—but only if the concerns of India's many minorities could be met. A dominion (such as Australia or Canada) was a self-ruling entity linked commercially and militarily with the United Kingdom, and in 1929 Viceroy Irwin had announced that His Majesty's Government desired such a status for India. Linlithgow's response now indicated to the nationalists that the British did not intend to fulfill this promise in the near future, if ever. "It became clear to us that they did not want us as friends and colleagues but as a slave people to do their bidding," asserted Nehru.[16]

In protest, on October 23, 1939, the Congress Party ordered its politicians to resign all the positions to which they had been elected. The Muslim League, which was headed by the lawyer Mohammad Ali Jinnah, celebrated the end of the Congress ministries with a "day of deliverance and thanksgiving." Jinnah also promised the Muslim League's support for the war effort—provided that the British recognized it as the only organization that spoke for India's Muslims.[17]

For decades the sixty-two-year-old Jinnah had played a leading role in the Indian National Congress. He had departed in 1920 because he disliked Gandhi's religiosity. Jinnah had since come to regard the Congress as a Hindu organization, because of the preponderance of Hindus in its leadership, which in his estimation made it insensitive to the concerns of Muslims. In the elections of 1937, however, the Muslim League had won only 4.8 percent of the Muslim vote, largely because some overwhelmingly Muslim regions, such as the North West Frontier Province, had returned Congress politicians. Subsequently, a triumphant Nehru had thwarted Jinnah's effort to get politicians from the Muslim League appointed as ministers in two provinces where the League had done relatively well. Indians would pay dearly for the resulting rift. The dual humiliation, at the polls and at Nehru's hands, had convinced Jinnah that the Muslim League could not coexist with the Congress; in an effort to boost the League's popularity, he began to appeal to Islamic nationalism.[18]

In February 1940 the marquess of Zetland, who was then the secretary of state for India, suggested to the War Cabinet that the cooperation of the Congress with the war effort be secured by an offer of dominion status at war's end. Churchill, then first Lord of the Admiralty and a vigorous presence on the War Cabinet, opposed the idea. He recommended instead a "firm course" that would keep the colony "quiet for the duration of the war." Nor did he "share the anxiety to encourage and promote unity among Hindu and Moslem communities": disharmony would be more conducive to retaining the British Raj. According to the minutes of the War Cabinet meetings, Churchill warned that if amity among Indians were somehow to be achieved, its "immediate result would be that the united communities would join in showing us the door. He regarded the Hindu-Moslem feud as the bulwark of British rule in India." Churchill's chain of reasoning hinged on the fact that the Indian National Congress, though it was secular in its principles, was nevertheless composed mainly of Hindus. If the Congress failed to agree to share power with the Muslim League, the British could claim that their relinquishing India was tantamount to abandoning a vulnerable Muslim minority to Hindu majority rule.[19]

Churchill had developed this argument during a prolonged campaign he had conducted in the early 1930s against granting partial self-government to Indians. In a 1931 speech, he had described a religious riot in India in graphic terms: "women and children were butchered in circumstances of bestial barbarity, their mutilated violated bodies strewing the streets for days." He had used the conflict to argue that only the British could keep the fanatics of India from one another's throats. By 1937 he had turned that argument on its head, stating in a letter to Viceroy Linlithgow that unity among Indians of different faiths was "fundamentally injurious to British interests."[20]

As Churchill explained it, the United Kingdom's task in India, an expansive land that comprised several feuding groups, was similar to its role in Europe: "to preserve the balance between these great masses, and thus maintain our own control for our advantage and their salvation." Therefore, Churchill continued, "I am not at all attracted by the prospect of one united India, which will show us the door." That the Government of India might incline toward promoting harmony between Hindus and Muslims was "to my mind distressing and repugnant in the last degree." Instead, Churchill hoped that the Muslims of the northwest would combine into a front to combat the "anti-British tendencies of the Congress." Strife between Hindus and Muslims would bolster the rationale that British rule over India, which Lord Randolph Churchill had described as a calming sheet of oil over turbulent waters, was as necessary as it had always been.[21]

Although Winston Churchill was not yet prime minister, his views on India were so vehement that they prevailed: the War Cabinet turned down Zetland's proposal. When in March 1940 the Muslim League introduced a fresh demand—a separate nation for Muslims, to be named Pakistan, or Land of the Pure—Churchill hailed "the awakening of a new spirit of self-reliance and self-assertiveness on the part of the different communities, of which the Moslem League's resolution was a sign." As the war dragged on, and financial and political circumstances indicated that the United Kingdom could not control India for long after it was over, Churchill would conclude that partitioning the colony to create Pakistan provided the best chance of retaining British influence in South Asia.[22]

LEOPOLD AMERY HAD his own, and if anything more carefully considered, ideas on the future of the British Empire. He believed that it had to be modernized so that it could continue to benefit the United Kingdom. Force could not forever hold the colonies, he maintained: loyalty to the Crown was necessary, and it could be bought only by economic solidarity. He saw the colonies not as possessions to be grasped in a fist but as extensions of England to be linked by handshakes. Amery was a leading advocate of Imperial Preference, a proposal by (the then late) statesman Joseph Chamberlain, who had envisioned a system of mutually helpful tariffs that would foster trade within the British Empire and fend off competition from the United States and Germany. As for India, Amery believed that it would sooner or later have to take its place in the imperial scheme as a dominion. But if Indians were to relinquish their stated goal of full independence and instead opt to remain within the empire as a dominion, their emancipation would have to be achieved without acrimony.

Accordingly, Amery suggested to Linlithgow that he probe Gandhi's views about the prospect of Indians designing their own constitution, while offering a guarantee of dominion status within a year after a successful resolution of the war. The Congress would also get greater representation on the viceroy's executive council. In return, the party would resume governing in the provinces and—most important—cooperate with the war effort. Linlithgow reported to Amery that Gandhi was responsive.

The initiative ran headfirst into an immovable roadblock: "Winston's passionately instinctive objection to anything that means giving self-government to India," as the secretary of state for India recounted in his diary. Churchill charged that matters so disruptive should not have been brought up "at a time when all our thoughts should be devoted to the defence of the Island and to the victory of our cause."[23]

Amery argued that it was essential to gain the support of at least the moderate Indians. "A feeling was abroad that we were relying on the continued absence of agreement between the two main communities to free us from the performance of our pledges," he had stated in his presentation to the War Cabinet. (He had yet to realize that this was indeed the prime minister's strategy.) Unless the British government acted to dispel this view, Amery continued, increasing resentment of colonial authorities and escalating hostility between the Congress and the Muslim League could ultimately lead to civil war. Should worse come to worst, he wrote to Churchill, "we could not hold India, even in wartime, for another year, certainly not for another five years." In the end—Amery warned with remarkable prescience—"a partition of India, like the partition of Ireland and just as fruitful of future trouble, may be the only immediate solution."[24]

The prime minister would not be placated. On July 25, 1940, he attacked Amery so furiously in the War Cabinet that one member, Sir Alexander Cadogan, walked out in embarrassment. The next day Amery went to 10 Downing Street to meet Churchill, who "said he would sooner give up political life at once, or rather go out into the wilderness and fight, than to admit a revolution which meant the end of the Imperial Crown in India," Amery wrote in his diary. It was "hopeless to try and point out to him that what I was suggesting was well within the four corners of pledges and statements made again and again and could hardly be so revolutionary if Zetland at the India Office had proposed it months ago." The prime minister demanded that Amery show him all the telegrams he had sent to Linlithgow—in which he had freely expressed himself about Churchill—and perused them carefully, showing signs of agitation. "I am afraid he will read and re-read the telegrams and get more and more angry as he does so and work himself up into a high mood of virtuous indignation," Amery sighed.[25]

His Majesty's Government could not accept just any constitution drafted by a group of Indians, the prime minister ultimately informed the viceroy. "We should have to know beforehand what this body was, and feel assured that it truly represented the broad masses of the leading Indian communities, including, of course, not only Hindoos and Moslems, but the Princes, the Depressed Classes, the Sikhs, the Anglo-Indians and others." (The so-called Depressed Classes, whom Churchill also referred to as Untouchables, were people of tribal origins or lower castes. Anglo-Indians were whites resident in India.) Nor could the War Cabinet tie the hands of a postwar British Parliament by promising dominion status: "under our free, democratic system," Churchill asserted, it was impossible to guarantee the attitude of a future House of Commons toward India.[26]

The prime minister's refusal to consider any move toward the colony's emancipation thwarted the possibility of meeting the wartime needs of the United Kingdom by the willing cooperation of Indian nationalists—and his determination to instead secure their compliance by divide and rule would disastrously deepen communal hostilities. "The whole basis of our policy, as you have laid it down yourself, is that it is Indian divisions and not our refusal to surrender authority that is holding back India's march towards the 'declared goal'," Amery wrote to the prime minister in April 1941. "On that ground I can continue to hold my own."[27]

THAT WINSTON CHURCHILL was for even an instant prepared to relinquish the post of prime minister, to which he had aspired his entire life, speaks to the depth of his attachment to India. A decade earlier, it had even induced Churchill to break with the Tory Party on its decision to permit limited self-government in the colony. "I have always said that the key to Winston is to realise that he is Mid Victorian, steeped in the politics of his father's period, and unable ever to get the modern point of view," Amery had written in 1929, after the two had had a long discussion on contemporary affairs. "It is only his verbal exuberance and abounding vitality that conceal this elementary fact about him."[28]

At the time, Lord Irwin's promise of dominion status for India had prompted Churchill to launch a forceful campaign to bolster his government's commitment to the Raj. "Dominion status can certainly not be attained while India is a prey to fierce racial and religious dissensions and when the withdrawal of British protection would mean the immediate resumption of mediæval wars," he had warned in an article in the *Daily Mail*. Should His Majesty's Government make any concessions at all, the nationalists would only be emboldened to ask for more. "The truth is that Gandhi-ism and all it stands for will, sooner or later, have to be grappled with and finally crushed. It is no use trying to satisfy a tiger by feeding him with cat's-meat." In 1935, when despite his furious five-year campaign the new constitution for India had passed into law, Churchill denounced it as "a monstrous monument of sham built by the pygmies"—the latter including the leaders of the Tory Party. A full third of the population of England "would have to go down, out, or under, if we ceased to be a great Empire," he warned in an oblique, if exaggerated, reference to India's importance for the British economy.[29]

Churchill's image of India as the fountainhead of British prestige, prosperity, and power derived in part from that of his own father. Lord Randolph had viewed the Taj Mahal by moonlight, "an unequalled sight," and bagged a tiger from the back of an elephant, "certainly the acme of sport." In 1885 and 1886 he had served as secretary of state for India, in which capacity he had ordered the invasion of upper Burma. Introducing his budget for India before the House of Commons, Lord Randolph had urged parliamentarians to take a more energetic interest in the colony, "that most truly bright and precious gem in the crown of the Queen, the possession of which, more than that of all your colonial dominions, has raised in power, in resource, in wealth, and in authority this small island home of ours far above the level of the majority of nations and of States—has placed it on an equality with, perhaps even in a position of superiority over, every other empire either of ancient or modern times." When his father died in 1895, the twenty-year-old Winston had resolved to "pursue his aims and vindicate his memory." As a cavalryman in India, Churchill had further pledged to "devote my life" to the protection of "this great Empire of ours."[30]

Winston Churchill had been bequeathed an imperial heritage simply by being born, in 1874, at Blenheim Palace. Featuring grand vistas, giant portraits of ancestors, and gory scenes of battle frozen into stone, the palace was Queen Anne's reward to John Churchill, the first Duke of Marlborough, for achieving a glorious victory in Bavaria in 1704. But Winston's upbringing was as parsimonious of warmth as his heritage

was opulent and intimidating. At the age of seven he was sent to boarding school, where he became a paradox to his teachers, devouring novels
meant for readers far older than he was but remaining resolutely at the
bottom of his form in virtually every academic subject. "Where my reason, imagination or interest were not engaged, I would not or I could
not learn," Churchill explained. At Harrow, an elite institution that
trained upper-class youths to become leading citizens of the empire,
Winston, judged unable to learn Latin and Greek, had to sit through
more English grammar than anyone else. "Thus I got into my bones the
essential structure of the ordinary British sentence—which is a noble
thing," he wrote in his autobiography, *My Early Life*. He would wield
the power of language with immense facility and force.[31]

At the military academy Sandhurst, Winston thrilled to the idea of
battle and wondered if he would ever get to apply in combat all the
martial strategy he was absorbing. "It did seem such a pity that it all
had to be make-believe, and that the age of wars between civilized nations had come to an end forever," he wrote in his memoir in the late
1920s, reminiscing about a time when war had still been glamorous.
The battles that had bloodied Europe for centuries seemed past; instead,
the continent's various powers were completing the conquest and colonization of Asia and Africa. "Luckily, however, there were still savages
and barbarous peoples" such as Afghans and Zulus to shoot at, Churchill
remembered thinking as a cadet. In between practicing cavalry charges,
the would-be officers would sit around hoping for at least an uprising
so that "we might have India to reconquer." In such an event, "we should
all get our commissions so much earlier and march about the plains of
India and win medals and distinction, and perhaps rise to very high
command like Clive when quite young!"[32]

Churchill traveled to India in 1896 as an officer of the 4th Queen's
Own Hussars, a cavalry regiment. After two days and a glittering banquet in Bombay, he had formed a "highly favourable opinion" of the
colony. He would write that he dropped off to sleep that second night
with "the keenest realization of the great work which England was doing

in India and of her high mission to rule these primitive but agreeable races for their welfare and our own."[33]

Churchill's cantonment in Bangalore was spacious, and the abundance of servants—one of whom would shave him at dawn while he lay half-asleep in bed—made military life luxurious. He found India sensual, exotic, romantic: "Snipe (and snakes) abound in the marshes; brilliant butterflies dance in the sunshine, and nautch-girls by the light of the moon." Between games of polo, the young man devoured books that his father had favored. "I revelled in his Essays"—he wrote of Macaulay's stirring histories of Clive, Hastings, and other conquerors. Churchill also learned about nature's hierarchy from Charles Darwin and about the perils of human fecundity from Reverend Thomas Malthus. And, as an act of filial piety and in preparation for a future career in politics, he read through every parliamentary debate in which his father had taken part.[34]

Even as he made up for the higher education he had missed, Churchill read only those works that reinforced his perspective on the world. He took straight to heart every sentiment that appealed, and was rarely forced to consider both sides of an argument. Churchill acknowledged as much. "I therefore adopted quite early in life a system of believing whatever I wanted to believe," he wrote, "while at the same time leaving reason to pursue unfettered whatever paths she was capable of treading." This habit of thinking was evident to his contemporaries. An acquaintance complained in 1921: "He does not want to hear your views. He does not want to disturb the beautiful clarity of his thought by the tiresome reminders of the other side." Throughout his life, on India and myriad other topics, Churchill would cling to certain convictions with the tenacity of a bulldog, the figure that would long be associated with him. Only "some lucky phrase, some form of words, some vivid image," as his friend Violet Asquith put it, could loosen its jaws.[35]

In 1897, a two-thousand-mile train journey took Churchill to the foothills of the Himalayas. "Those large leather-lined Indian railway carriages, deeply-shuttered and blinded from the blistering sun and kept fairly cool by a circular wheel of wet straw which one turned from time to time, were well adapted to the local conditions," he would recount three decades later. "I spent five days in a dark padded moving cell, reading mostly by lamplight or by some jealously admitted ray of glare." Perhaps because he was so absorbed in his reading, Churchill did not describe the landscapes he traversed or the famine raging at the time, described as the worst of the century (although that appellation would pass to the famine that began in 1899). Instead, the young man's upbringing, the tomes he perused, and the skirmishes to which he was headed would combine to frame his ideas about India. Malthus, Darwin, Macaulay, and pride in paternal inheritance would fuse into a comprehension of human destiny that would nowadays be called social Darwinism.[36]

Churchill stopped for a night at a military camp where he had a friend. Fellow officers inspired him with "noble sentiments" by singing:[37]

Great White Mother, far across the sea,
Ruler of the Empire may ever she be.
Long may she reign, glorious and free,
In the Great White Motherland.

Churchill was going to the North West Frontier Province, British India's border with Afghanistan. "From the level plain of the valleys the hills rise abruptly. Their steep and rugged slopes are thickly strewn with great rocks, and covered with coarse, rank grass," he wrote in his first book, *The Story of the Malakand Field Force*, which described expeditions of the Indian Army against Pakhtun farmers. "The rice fields along both banks of the stream display a broad, winding strip of vivid green." If the young man looked up from his books, that was because this stark paradise—with its "splendid butterflies, whose wings of blue and green change colour in the light, like shot silk"—was a setting for strife.[38]

British strategists had ordered an advance to the north, so as to claim mountain passes by which Russian forces might threaten the borders of India. Several tribes made their homes on this route, however, and they resisted the incursions on their territory. Writing of the Pakhtun tribesman, Churchill declared: "Not because he is degraded, not because we covet his valleys, but because his actions interfere with the safety of our Empire, he must be crushed." He was at the front line as a correspondent for the *Daily Telegraph*, but he took enthusiastic part in skirmishes: "there is no reputation I cherish so keenly as to gain a reputation of personal courage," he wrote in a letter home. The twenty-three-year-old had also surmised that his blow-by-blow accounts of the empire's battles would give him the visibility necessary to establish a career in politics.[39]

Churchill would always carry with him certain lessons he learned in the frontier wars. He could be magnanimous in victory: after the fighting ended in the tribes' appeal for a truce, he pronounced the Pakhtuns to be "a brave and warlike race." While the conflict raged, however, his hostility was absolute. "These tribesmen are among the most miserable and brutal creatures of the earth," he had opined about Pakhtuns just a week earlier. Insofar as "these valleys are purged from the pernicious vermin that infest them, so will the happiness of humanity be increased." He recounted in violent detail how the British commanding general, Sir Bindon Blood, ordered reprisals after an enemy attack on a military camp: "We proceeded systematically, village by village, and we destroyed the houses, filled up the wells, blew down the towers, cut down the great shady trees, burned the crops and broke the reservoirs in punitive devastation." Churchill offered a defense of such scorched earth tactics in *Malakand*, arguing that "it is only an unphilosophic mind that will hold it legitimate to take a man's life and illegitimate to destroy his property." Economic warfare was destined to become a key weapon in his arsenal of military tactics.[40]

In a sense, Churchill found his fortune in India: *Malakand* became a spectacular publishing success. "I had never been praised before," he would recall; now, even the Prince of Wales wrote to congratulate him. Having conquered many of his own deficiencies in India, Churchill soon left for other fields of battle. In South Africa, he helped save a trainload of soldiers from a Boer ambush, got captured by the enemy, and managed to escape. That adventure made him a household name, while the royalties accumulating from *Malakand* allowed him to support himself during his preparations to enter public life. At age twenty-five, in September 1900, he was elected to the House of Commons.[41]

To Winston Churchill the empire, won by the valor of heroes such as General Robert Clive, would always remain "worth the blood of its noblest citizens." In his autobiography, he exhorted English youths to meet the challenge. "You must take your places in life's fighting line," he wrote. "Enter upon your inheritance, accept your responsibilities. Raise the glorious flag again, advance them upon the new enemies, who constantly gather upon the front of the human army, and have only to be assaulted to be overthrown." The world could not really be harmed by conquest—only renewed. "She was made to be wooed and won by youth. She has lived and thrived only by repeated subjugations."[42]

IN AUGUST 1940, after Churchill torpedoed Amery's proposals for granting India dominion status within a year after the war, the viceroy issued a long statement to the effect that a body of suitably representative natives would be permitted to draw up a constitution at some unspecified point following the war. No minority group would be obliged to accept a government of which it disapproved. In effect, His Majesty's Government was giving the Muslim League the power to determine the nature and pace of political advancement in India. Nehru described the offer as "fantastic and absurd," and to no one's surprise the Congress rejected it.[43]

Several of the party's leaders now urged Gandhi to sanction a civil disobedience movement protesting India's induction into the war. Gandhi refused: the Muslim League had signaled its intention to support the war, so he surmised the danger of clashes between independence-minded Hindus and pro-government Muslims to be high. Instead, and in "fear and trembling" at the horrors he envisaged erupting around him, Gandhi began nominating tried and tested individuals to offer satyagraha, or nonviolent resistance, by means of seditious statements. Nehru was arrested on October 31, 1940, after giving three speeches urging the public to refuse to aid the government's war. It was "monstrous," Nehru declared when he was brought before the court, that hundreds of millions of Indians should be commandeered into a war not of their choosing, and "amazing and significant that this should be done in the name of freedom and self-determination and democracy." He was sentenced to four years' rigorous imprisonment. As the circle of those nominated for satyagraha expanded into the villages, the number of people convicted of sedition would rise to 25,000 by the summer of 1941.[44]

Gandhi himself remained free—an indication that the government considered this restrained protest to be insignificant. Should he have to be arrested, however, Churchill suspected he might resort to a hunger strike, a political weapon with which the British government had long experience. One standard procedure for thwarting the protestors (called Cat and Mouse) was to release them, only to rearrest them when they resumed eating. Churchill determined that Gandhi would not get this treatment. Amery wrote in his diary on November 21, 1940, that the prime minister was "particularly anxious that I should ask Linlithgow to convey privately to Gandhi that we had no objections to his fasting to death if he wanted to."[45]

Subhas Bose was already in prison, having been arrested in July 1940. After failing to resolve his dispute with Gandhi, he had resigned the presidency of the Indian National Congress and returned to Calcutta, where he had once served as mayor. There he had planned a march on the Holwell Monument, which commemorated the Englishmen who had suffocated to death in 1756 after their imprisonment by nawab Siraj-ud-daula. To many of the city's white residents, the monument recalled the brutality that had preceded and thereby necessitated the British Raj. To Bose it was "the symbol of our slavery and humiliation," and he resolved to tear it down.[46]

Gandhi's strategy of satyagraha rested on the belief that an adversary would respond with pangs of conscience to evidence of the suffering he caused. Bose, in contrast, maintained that Britons were more likely to respond to material weapons than to spiritual ones. Bengalis had been excluded from the army "on the ground that they were not sufficiently warlike or brave," Bose declared; and Viceroy Curzon had added injury to insult by summoning armed police to disperse peaceable protestors. "In sheer despair, young men took to the bomb and the revolver," Bose asserted. The offspring of upper-class families had begun to assassinate British officials and, on the streets of Calcutta, youth responded with their fists to racial insults. And slowly an "impression gained ground that for the first time the Bengalee was being respected by the Britisher," Bose concluded. Violence demonstrated that the people of Bengal were not "a race of cowards."[47]

On July 2, 1940, the day before the announced march, Bose was arrested under the Defence of India Act and taken to a Calcutta prison. After four months of watching political developments from behind bars, he resolved to not spend the rest of the war thus incapacitated and devised an escape plan. On November 29, he started fasting, and in a few days grew dangerously weak. "One individual may die for an idea but that idea will, after his death, incarnate itself in a thousand lives," he wrote Bengal's government. "Today I must die, so that India may live and may win freedom and glory." Taking the warning that Bose's death in custody could make him a highly inconvenient martyr, on December 5 local authorities released him to a loose house arrest.[48]

Once at home with his family, Bose disappeared from view for two weeks, pretending to be sick while secretly growing a beard to use as a disguise. His attempts to free India by political means having been thwarted, he had formulated a fresh goal: to seek military aid from Britain's enemies, the Axis powers. Such an opportunity as a world war was not to be squandered, he was certain. Early on January 17, 1941, Bose left his house dressed as a Muslim insurance agent, and a nephew drove him all the way to Bihar province, west of Bengal, where he boarded a train. After changing trains near Delhi, Bose finally disembarked in Peshawar in the North West Frontier Province. There he met up with a Pakhtun associate and, decked in flowing turban and pajamas and hastily trained in tribal etiquette, he trekked with a guide over frozen mountain passes into Afghanistan.

That nation, cursed by cartography, sat neutral and uneasy between two warring powers, the British Empire and the Soviet Union (which at the time was allied with Nazi Germany). Arriving in Kabul on January 27,

Bose approached the Soviet embassy, which demonstrated no interest in him; the German embassy, which cabled to Berlin and awaited instructions for what seemed like forever; and finally the Italian embassy. An official there informed Rome that the newcomer was "intelligent, able, full of passion and without doubt the most realistic" of the Indian leaders. Bose was insisting that "if 50,000 men, Italian, German, or Japanese could reach the frontiers of India, the Indian army would desert, the masses would uprise and the end of English domination could be achieved in a very short time." According to the Italian cable, India was the secret fount of British military power, and therefore it was essential that Bose be rendered all the help he needed to realize his grand plan. In early April 1941, Subhas Chandra Bose arrived in Berlin in the guise of an Italian diplomat.[49]

Bose had taken a car and a train into the Soviet Union and flown to the German capital from there. He was fortunate in this choice of route, because in March, after learning of his whereabouts and guessing his intentions, Britain's Special Operations Executive (SOE) had issued orders to assassinate him. The agents had assumed, however, that he would travel through Iran, Iraq, and Turkey to reach Germany. The War Diary of the SOE noted that Amery "was also interested" and would no doubt lend his support "to Bose being liquidated on Turkish territory" if necessary. Such a venture was diplomatically risky, because Turkey was neutral, but the Foreign Office consented to Bose being killed there. Given that the SOE was created by Churchill and was headed by Desmond Morton, one of his close associates, the order to kill Bose must have emanated from the very top.[50]

IN HIS PRISON barracks in Midnapore, a coastal district in the southwestern corner of Bengal, twenty-nine-year-old Sushil Kumar Dhara thrilled to the news of Bose's escape. "I was convinced that he'd gone toward Japan or Germany," Dhara wrote in his autobiography. "If only he could get there, surely he would secure India's freedom." Like many others immersed in the independence struggle, Dhara regarded the enemies of Britain as his friends.[51]

A village-level Congress worker like Dhara planned and executed acts of civil disobedience while otherwise living his life and pursuing a calling in social service. Dhara had been attending college in Calcutta when Gandhi had launched the satyagraha movement. He was on Gandhi's select list of participants and, in the fall of 1940, had returned to Midnapore to await the word to launch his protest. In the meantime, one of Dhara's duties was to beg for money from shopkeepers, collecting a coin here and a coin there until, at the end of an exhausting day, he might have a rupee to pay for food for himself and his co-workers. A rupee could buy a *maund*, or 37.4 kilograms, of coarse rice, and Dhara's cell survived on around 25 rupees a month. Dhara did the cooking himself, boiling rice and lentils together and flavoring the mixture with a bit of clarified butter or a donated vegetable. Soon after his arrival in Midnapore, his seniors had begun to visit marketplaces and give anti-war speeches. One by one they had been arrested. When it was his turn, Dhara earned himself half a year in jail.[52]

LIKE MANY OF his comrades, Sushil Dhara had joined the Congress Party a decade earlier, during the protest movement known as the Salt Rebellion. In the spring of 1930, Gandhi had embarked on a long, winding trek that had taken him to Dandi, Gujarat, on the west coast of India. Reaching the sea on April 6, he had waded into the surf, picked up a handful of water, and set it onto the beach to dry—symbolically defying the law. The Government of India had the exclusive right to manufacture and trade salt; and this monopoly, along with taxes, made the product hundreds of times more expensive than it would otherwise have been. The burden fell hardest on the poor, who lived by performing manual labor under a tropical sun, sweated profusely, and needed around fifteen grams of salt a day to stave off heatstroke.

In the early eighteenth century, the coastal district of Midnapore had supplied salt to all of eastern India and Nepal, but it had since become dependent on salt imported from England. The teenage Dhara, sitting cross-legged in the dust near an old temple, just before the salt uprising, had listened wide-eyed as a Congress speaker had detailed the economic misadventure of India under colonial rule—and had been among the first to sign up. On April 6, 1930, thousands of protestors walked from the crumbling red-brick palace at Tamluk, the region's most ancient town, to an inlet of the sea, there to boil water and make salt. From the second day onward, the police began to beat and jail the leaders of the movement, and Dhara, too, was soon under arrest.

Prison turned out to be instructive. The indulgent Indian jailor permitted Dhara to visit restricted areas in the facility, where members of a revolutionary outfit gave the youth books on armed insurrection and spent hours indoctrinating him. "Gandhian thought had yet to leave much of a mark on me," Dhara recounted. "So their message of power mesmerized me." Everyone, including the English superintendent of the jail, seemed to treat these men, described as "terrorists," with a respect that bordered on reverence—especially after the events of April 18, 1930. On that day, sixty-five rebels who called themselves the Indian Republican Army had seized control of a police armory and other strategic sites in Chittagong town in eastern Bengal. They had eventually retreated to a forested hill that the authorities had surrounded with troops and raked with machine-gun fire. An unknown number of the rebels had died there, while others had escaped into surrounding villages and were being hunted down.[53]

Within weeks after the salt movement began, all of Midnapore's nationalist leaders were behind bars. But Bengal's officials reported to the viceroy that every villager was making salt in his home: the entire populace had lost its fear of the law. The police took to punishing dissidents by setting fire to huts, cowsheds, and the occasional *gola* (mini-silo) full of grain. An Indian civil servant protested to his superior, District Magistrate James Peddie, that the local people were behaving in a nonviolent fashion. "This way, you will be provoking them into violence."[54]

"That's what I want," replied Peddie, who had the power to adjust the level of force used by the police. "As long as they remain nonviolent it is very difficult for us. If they become violent, we can crush it in a day." Eventually, however, he developed misgivings about the strategy he was meant to implement. One incident illustrated his doubts. When his train stopped at a station, a boy on the platform caught sight of him and called out a freedom slogan. Peddie rushed up and punched him in the face, shouting, "Will you now stop?"

"Wait, let me catch my breath," the boy gasped. "Then I'll do it again."

"I never felt so small in my life as I did then," Peddie confided to a friend. Soon after that encounter, the viceroy summoned all district officers to meet with him in Calcutta—but Peddie refused to go. "Ask his Excellency," he instructed a colleague, "what more he expects me to do for his British Raj."[55]

In April 1931, James Peddie was shot dead by a revolutionary from a secretive cell in Midnapore town. Two other white district magistrates were also killed in quick succession. As a result, for the next decade only native civil servants, selected for loyalty to Crown and career, were appointed by the Raj to the most senior position in the district.

Elsewhere in India, the uprising of 1930 surpassed that of 1920 in its pervasiveness and force. Peasants fled into neighboring princely states to avoid paying rent; women picketed liquor shops, from which the government earned a hefty revenue; and the middle class boycotted imported luxuries such as cigarettes, whose sales halved. In the North West Frontier Province, a charismatic pacifist named Khan Abdul Ghaffar Khan inspired nonviolent protests, including a refusal to pay taxes. More than 200 of his followers were shot dead—but Hindu soldiers in a regiment from the Himalayan foothills refused to open fire on these unarmed Pakhtun farmers. On January 25, 1931, Viceroy Irwin released Gandhi from prison (where he had been for eight and a half months) and subsequently summoned him for discussions. In return for certain concessions, such as the right of villagers living near the coast to make salt, the liberation of nonviolent political prisoners, and a promise to invite the Congress for talks, Gandhi called off the movement.[56]

In London, Winston Churchill charged the viceroy with craven capitulation. "It is alarming and also nauseating to see Mr. Gandhi, a seditious Middle Temple lawyer, now posing as a fakir of a type well-known in the East, striding half-naked up the steps of the Viceregal palace, while he is still organising and conducting a defiant campaign of civil disobedience, to parley on equal terms with the representative of the King-Emperor," he told a conservative association in February 1931. As the chief spokesman for the Indian Empire Society, an association devoted to the preservation of the British Raj, Churchill would write and speak extensively on the topic over the next few years. The crux of his argument was that granting any power to a tiny "oligarchy" of Hindu politicians—the leaders of the Congress—would be a dereliction of duty to ordinary Indians. In his view, native politicians were incapable of rising above the confines of the communities to which they had been born; it took the distant Briton, who stood far above the fray, to adjudicate impartially among India's quarreling castes. For the British Raj to abandon its responsibilities would be "an act of cowardice, desertion and dishonor," Churchill argued, as well as "a hideous act of self-mutilation, astounding to every nation in the world."[57]

His furious efforts bore fruit. Gandhi, arriving in London in September 1931 to attend the promised conference, found himself facing princes, landlords, merchants, and representatives of various religious and ethnic groups from his homeland—all of whose concerns would have to be met before His Majesty's Government could be confident that Indian self-government would not degenerate into a Hindu dictatorship. Virtually every representative demanded a separate electorate for his constituency, a privilege already enjoyed by Muslim politicians. (That is, every minority Indian would be forced to vote for someone of the same religious or ethnic persuasion.) Gandhi refused: the entrenchment of such divisions was anathema to the secular Congress.[58]

"Chief concrete result of the human Mahatma's visit is that in London the price of goats and goat's milk has gone up," quipped *Time* magazine (after noting a goat whose milk Gandhi drank, and who had been labeled "Mahatma" at an agricultural show). By the time Gandhi returned empty-handed to India and called for a renewal of civil disobedience, Lord Irwin had been replaced by a new viceroy, Lord Willingdon, who took a harder line. Gandhi was rearrested on January 4, 1932, and within four months around 80,000 protestors would be jailed. As if to underline their power, the authorities increased the tax on salt, which during fiscal year 1932 yielded a record revenue of 102 million rupees. The Government of India had finally "begun to act sensibly," Churchill noted with satisfaction. "I always said how easy it would be to crush Gandhi and the Congress."[59]

Dhara had been released from prison, thanks to Gandhi's understanding with Irwin; he began to hide out with other Congress agitators in the countryside. They were well protected—by the conch shells possessed by many Hindu women in nearby villages. The women blew the shells during their evening *pujo*, or prayer, sending a long, melodious call resonating through the dusk. But when one of them spotted policemen passing by, she would blow the shell then, prompting mothers, wives, and daughters for miles around to relay a cacophonous warning. Except in the dead of night, the police had no hope of catching anyone by surprise.[60]

In 1932, in a fresh act of resistance to the Raj, Midnapore's householders started refusing to pay a small tax that maintained the village *chowkidar*, or watchman, who often doubled as a police informer. In response, parties of police—usually Muslims from northwestern India in largely Hindu Midnapore, divide and rule being the principle by which keepers of the law were assigned to different regions—established camps alongside the villages. In lieu of the tax of a few rupees, they confiscated cattle and jewelry worth thousands. The government also imposed a punitive tax to fund these police outposts. Villagers unfamiliar with English called it the *pituni*, or "beating," tax because of how it was extracted.[61]

Also in these years, the Great Depression overcame rural India. High grain prices in the 1920s had allowed some cultivators to accumulate savings in the form of gold or land, which had prompted an increase in taxes. Although the prices of wheat and rice began to slide in 1930, slashing farmers' incomes, cultivators still owed taxes and other dues. Moneylenders (who, through a chain of refinancing arrangements, were ultimately beholden to banks) ran out of cash, refused additional credit, and instead forced peasants to pay up their debts—which they did by confiscating the gold bangles, earrings, and necklaces belonging to the family's women. (The alternative was to sell land, which for a peasant was the last resort because it deprived the family of its cheapest source of food.)

The secretary of state for India and the governor of the Bank of England controlled the colony's monetary policy. They ensured that as much as possible of this "distress gold" flowed to the United Kingdom. In the United States, President Franklin Delano Roosevelt stopped the export of the metal and used the country's gold reserves to support the value of the currency, allowing him to inject money into the economy to revive it. Historian Dietmar Rothermund has written that had the British government in India been more responsive to the needs of the people, it similarly would have collected the distress gold and used it to finance projects to alleviate rural suffering. Instead, banks melted down 3.4 billion rupees (£255 million) worth of gold jewelry into bars and shipped it to London, helping to buttress its threatened position as a financial capital of the world. As a result, rural India was drained of its savings, leaving peasants defenseless against future economic shocks.[62]

By the end of 1932, the civil disobedience movement was petering out. Also that year, the Government of India announced a so-called Communal Award: along with reserved seats in Parliament, every significant minority group would have a separate electorate. Gandhi, who was in prison, embarked on a fast until the leader of the Depressed Classes agreed to merge his constituency with the general Hindu electorate, in exchange for a larger number of reserved seats. When in 1935 His Majesty's Government enacted into law the colony's new constitution, Nehru charged that it "petrified" British rule in India by playing off different constituencies against one another. "The Act strengthened the alliance between the British Government and the princes, landlords, and other reactionary elements in India; it added to the separate electorates, thus increasing the separatist tendencies; it consolidated the predominant position of British trade, industry, banking, and shipping and . . . retained in British hands complete control over Indian finance, military, and foreign affairs," Nehru would write in a history of India. The new political arrangement gave elected ministers certain responsibilities, such as in agriculture and education, but posed no bar that would keep India from being inducted, with or without its acquiescence, into World War II.[63]

AFTER HAVING SERVED six months for his satyagraha against the war effort, Sushil Kumar Dhara emerged from prison in the spring of 1941 to find that the leader of his local Congress cell, a dedicated Gandhian named Kumar Chandra Jana, was still in prison. Jana's wife was running the cell, and around this motherly figure had gathered a cluster of young women who were eager to join the fight. Most of these recruits had very little schooling, and it became Dhara's pleasurable task to teach them poetry, the history of rebellions around the world, and the political ideas of Gandhi, Nehru, and Bose.[64]

Dhara became entranced with one of the women: Kumudini Dakua was dark-skinned, sweet-faced, and quick-witted, with almond eyes that "held an inexplicable allure." It was just as well that a few years earlier, when his mother had pressed him to get married, Dhara had sworn to remain celibate until the land became free. Kumudini was the wife of his close friend Khudiram Dakua, with whom he had played pranks on unsuspecting elders when both had been in school and later in the same prison. She found Dhara attractive as well. His deep voice "had a magical ability to entice," Kumudini Dakua would recall decades later, and his impassioned recital of the poem *Bidrohi* (Rebel) "made revolutionaries of us all." Soon the women were touring the countryside, exhorting everyone to help the movement in any way they could. With Dhara around, "none of us felt any fear at all," Dakua remembered. His high spirits, his patriotic songs and poetry recitals, and his attention to the trainees' every need made it fun to become a *sadhinawta songrami*, or fighter for freedom.[65]

As they trekked around the villages, urging the people to refuse help to the government, Dhara and his fellow rebels often found shelter in the homes of ordinary villagers. "We were very young, would run around a lot," Dakua related. "Once, we were all sleeping on the upper floor of a mud hut, and we were so many and so rowdy that the roof fell. We were terribly embarrassed. The lady of the house came up and said, 'That's okay—the old roof fell so we'll build a new roof. Why should you be upset?' The villagers loved us so much, they'd keep piling food on our plates even when we were stuffed."

During 1941—as Churchill crossed the Atlantic Ocean to seek help for the war from the United States, Amery dispatched Indian troops to secure the oilfields of Iraq and Iran, Bose strove to gain German assistance for Indian liberation, Hitler attacked the Soviet Union (unknowingly sealing his own fate), Nehru languished in prison, and Gandhi fretted about the scarcities stalking the land—a suppressed but powerful surge of excitement was mounting in rural Bengal. No matter what their imperial rulers believed, "slowly the people were realizing that the era of the British was coming to an end," Dhara wrote. At the same time, war-related shortages of food, cloth, and kerosene (used for lighting lanterns—rural Bengal had no electricity) were making survival ever more difficult. In every villager's heart a small flame of rage was spontaneously coming alive. "We began to fan the flames," Dhara recalled, "in the hope of uniting them all into one gigantic conflagration."

CHAPTER TWO

Harvesting the Colonies

"Shoot Gandhi, and if this doesn't suffice to reduce them to submission, shoot a dozen leading members of Congress; and if that doesn't suffice, shoot 200 and so on until order is established," Adolf Hitler had advised the viscount of Halifax (formerly Lord Irwin, viceroy of India) when they met in November 1937. "You will see how quickly they will collapse as soon as you make it clear that you mean business." Hitler esteemed Britons and Germans as superior races that nature had designed for hegemony over lesser peoples. Divining the British Raj to be the source of English pride and affluence, he sought to bestow a similar empire on his compatriots. As he saw it, Britons could continue ruling over Indians, while Germans would subjugate Slavs; the labor of the vanquished races, and the natural resources of their former territories, would nourish and enrich the victors.[1]

Hitler's determination to carve the Third Reich out of the countries on Germany's eastern border would place him on a collision course with the United Kingdom—even as the conviction of shared destiny would complicate his attitude toward the British, the adversaries he could not but admire, and undermine his prosecution of the war. Perhaps because of his racist worldview, Hitler did not comprehend the extent to which the Indian freedom movement, along with other developments of the twentieth century, had weakened imperial controls over the colony. The days of formal empires were numbered—and, ironically, the conflict he initiated would deal the fatal blow. To commandeer Indian manufactures and produce for the war, His Majesty's Government would have to deploy inflationary monetary policies in preference to straightforward

31

confiscation of the colony's products or revenues, which would have
met with resistance from the colony's business elites and politicians. In
the short run, the United Kingdom's wartime financial arrangements
with India would set the stage for famine, and in the long run they
would hasten the disintegration of the British Empire.[2]

Hitler had been influenced in his thinking about Indians by the eu-
genicist Houston Stewart Chamberlain, whom he dubbed the Prophet
of the Third Reich. Chamberlain admired India's caste system as having
been engineered to preserve the purity of Aryans—but he nonetheless
considered modern Indians to be a bastard people hopelessly contam-
inated by inferior blood. During the nineteenth century, tomes from
ancient India had been translated into European languages, revealing
a prehistory of colonization of that subcontinent by whites. Around
2000 B.C., Caucasian nomads on horseback who called themselves *arya*
had poured into the Indian plains through passes in the northwestern
Himalayas. They had settled on the banks of western rivers, adopted
agriculture, and founded a civilization. Their earliest text, the Rig Veda,
spoke of battles against the aboriginal *dasyu*, or dastards. The Aryan
god of storms, with his bolt of lighting, "flays the enemy of his dark
skin, kills him and reduces him to ashes," the Rig Veda proclaimed of
the dastards. Many of the dasyu were expert farmers and city-builders,
but in defeat they became the *dasa*, or slave. They were inducted into
the lowest ranks of a severely hierarchical and patriarchal social structure
called *caste*, over which reigned priests—Brahmins—and warriors.[3]

Western eyes could still discern the Aryans' stock in the northwest
of India, where the men were tall and light-skinned. But as the invaders
had penetrated the subcontinent, bedding native women, their pure
warrior blood had succumbed to dilution, according to Herbert Risley,
a late-nineteenth-century anthropologist. Every successive tribe of conquerors "became more or less absorbed in the indigenous population,
their physique degenerated, their individuality vanished, their energy
was sapped, and dominion passed from their hands into those of more
vigorous successors." In the distant east, where the influence of aboriginal
women had been strongest, the ancient miscegenation had resulted in

the feminized Bengalis, whom "no necessity would induce to fight," another British scholar commented.[4]

According to Hitler, if anyone had asked Lord Robert Clive by what
right he had seized the riches of Bengal, he would have replied, "I am
an Englishman!" Racial superiority entitled the British to the possession
of India, Hitler informed a student body in Munich. Accordingly, the
führer considered the anti-colonial movement—"a rebellion of the lower
Indian race against the superior English-Nordic race"—to be as futile
as it was contemptible. "The Nordic race has a right to rule the world
and we must take this racial right as the guiding star of our foreign policy," he said in 1930. Hitler had only a secondary interest in regaining
the German colonies in Africa that had been confiscated by the Allies
after World War 1. What he wanted most of all was to conquer an extended backyard that could be defended by a land-based army. Germans
would thus realize their inherent eminence and restore their prosperity
by acquiring *Lebensraum*, or room to live, toward the east.[5]

In two books (the second of which was published long after his
death), in prewar speeches, and in wartime after-dinner monologues,
Hitler laid out a blueprint for the economic regeneration of Germany
that drew on the British Empire as a prototype. White men, he stated
in a 1932 address that won him the support of leading German industrialists, had exercised their "extraordinarily brutal right to dominate
others" (which they possessed by virtue of their race) in order to reorganize
the economy of lesser peoples, in India and in the Americas—thereby
procuring their own prosperity. The English, in particular, had achieved
a "wonderful marriage of economic conquest with political domination"
that had given rise to "a remarkable development: instead of expanding
in space, instead of exporting men, they have exported goods and have
built up an economic world-system." Thanks to such a process, white
nations had come to possess "gigantic world-central-factories" for which
"the rest of the world provides enormous markets for the disposal of
goods and enormous sources of raw materials."[6]

This state of affairs, Hitler maintained, could persist only "so long
as the difference in the standard of living in different parts of the world

continues to exist." The imperial lifestyle required lesser races to be preserved in poverty. Different countries had safeguarded their economic superiority in different ways, he continued, "most brilliantly of all perhaps England who has always opened up for herself new markets and immediately anchored them through political dominance." Germans—having been, in Hitler's view, idealistic rather than pragmatic in their approach to colonies—had failed to make adequate use of them and thus had been unable to guarantee an adequate standard of living for the fatherland's domestic industrial workers, laying themselves open to the specter of communism.[7]

The führer would repair German fortunes by creating sources of cheap food and raw materials, as well as expansive export markets; this would necessitate acquiring fresh territories. The Ukraine would supply the ruling race with bread, the Black Sea with an inexhaustible supply of fish, the Crimea with oranges, cotton, and rubber; and the crowning glory, Russia, would be an insatiable captive market for German "cotton goods, household utensils, all the articles of current consumption." (The Slavic areas would also provide fields for Germans rendered "superfluous" by industrialization—an aspect of Hitler's dream that was inspired not by India but by the colonization of North America by white farmers.) Such expropriations of the colonies' resources and products would result in the deaths of tens of millions of Slavs by famine and disease, estimated a Nazi policy paper formulated in 1941.[8]

Because Germans would deploy divide and rule to retain control, only a few selected officers would be needed to administer the vast new territory. "The Russian space is our India," Hitler elaborated. "Like the English, we shall rule this empire with a handful of men." His favorite movie, the 1935 Hollywood production *Lives of a Bengal Lancer*, depicted the adventures of a few such valiants: English cavalry officers at India's northwest frontier. The movie illustrated the feats that the warriors of an inspired race could perform in service of their homeland, and Hitler made it compulsory viewing for SS guardsmen. A great deal about Hitler remains mysterious, but his daydreams of world conquest were transparently inspired by what might be called Empire Envy.[9]

"ENVY IS ONE of the less pleasing features of the German character, and there is a peculiar German word [Brotneid], envy of another for earning the bread that might be yours, which conveys tersely what Germans felt about our wealth and the vast resources of our Empire," wrote Leopold S. Amery in his autobiography. "Looking back on the costly struggles and sacrifices of their own history they felt that our Empire had been far too cheaply won; largely won, indeed, by utilizing Germany as a pawn in our long struggle with France. Not only cheaply won, but cheaply held; not by the kind of sacrifice which conscription imposed upon Germany's manhood to maintain her frontiers, but by a Navy."[10]

In 1934 Amery had read *Mein Kampf* and found it "very interesting and stimulating," as he wrote in his diary. Hitler's "intense sincerity and clear thinking on some points, as well as really careful study of propaganda methods, attracted me very much." On the other hand, the author was clearly "quite insane about Jews and Socialists," Amery observed. The next year, when he was holidaying in the Bavarian Alps, Hitler had invited him for a meeting. The führer looked unprepossessing, rather like a salesman in a gent's clothing store. Amery did not find "the hypnotic charm I had heard of, and no attempt to exercise it, but liked his directness and eagerness to let his hearer know his mind." Amery judged that Hitler had a "grip on economic essentials and on many political ones, too, even if it is crude at times and coloured by deep personal prejudice."[11]

Like Hitler, Amery believed that less developed parts of the world, such as India, should provide raw materials and markets for the highly industrialized centers of imperial power. Amery did not regard Indians themselves as greatly inferior, however: his confidence in their abilities underlay his later attempts, as secretary of state for India, to secure the assistance of native politicians and manufacturers in provisioning the war effort. In part because of personal experience, he was aware that political disadvantage did not necessarily indicate feebleness in character or intellect. Historian William D. Rubinstein has discovered that Amery's mother came from a distinguished Jewish family, many of whose members had converted to Christianity. Amery himself had a deep-seated empathy for Jews and was one of the architects of modern Israel. But he kept his origins a close secret throughout his life and dropped not a hint of his Jewish ancestry in three portly volumes of autobiography (which he could not complete).[12]

Given this background, Amery's rather positive appraisal of Hitler is astonishing. Like many others, he may have assumed that Hitler could not possibly carry out the exterminations that he had hinted at in *Mein Kampf*. Nor could Amery have foreseen a bizarre personal tragedy: his troubled elder son, John, would turn into an anti-Semite and, finding himself in Europe in 1942, would travel to Berlin to assist Hitler with his war effort.[13]

LEOPOLD S. AMERY was born in northern India in 1873, to an English forester and a woman of east European extraction. When Leo was three, he went to England with his mother and younger brother, and in their absence his father abandoned the family and moved to Canada. Leo's mother was forced to live in boardinghouses while she spent all her money educating her sons. "Nobody could ever give herself over so helplessly to laughter, and laughter was a large ingredient in our childhood's atmosphere," Amery remembered. Leo was precocious and spoke Hindi fluently when he left India. From his father's side he inherited a diminutive frame (he was five feet four) and from his mother's a gift for languages, of which he would learn fifteen. He read parts of the *Mahabharata* in Sanskrit and once astonished a London audience by reciting the first book of the Koran in classical Arabic.[14]

At Harrow the brilliant youngster garnered most of the prizes—and encountered a bumptious redhead by the name of Winston Churchill. During Winston's first summer at Harrow, he spent hours by the swimming pond, eating buns and sneaking up behind unsuspecting boys to push them in. One day he saw a student standing right on the edge of the pond and gave him a shove. "I was startled to see a furious face emerge from the foam, and a being evidently of enormous strength making its way by fierce strokes to the shore," Churchill recounted. He ran, but his pursuer easily caught him and flung him into the pond. It was Leopold Amery of the Sixth Form: "He is Head of his House; he is champion at Gym; he has got his football colours." Mortified, Winston approached the "potentate" the next day and explained: "I mistook you for a Fourth Form boy. You are so small." Since Leopold did not seem at all calmed, Winston brilliantly improvised: "My father, who is a great man, is also small." Leo laughed and indicated the end of the episode. Neither ever forgot this introduction, however.[15]

Amery went on to Oxford University and eventually became a fellow of All Soul's College—in whose lounges not only scholars but also "cabinet ministers, bishops, Members of Parliament, civil servants, lawyers, journalists and businessmen" conversed on equal terms. It was the intellectual soul of the empire, and Amery, one of its brightest lights. He served on several fronts of World War I as an intelligence officer, went on to hold important positions in the British government, and drafted the Balfour Declaration of 1917 that promised Jews a home in Palestine. By 1938, Amery understood the ferocity of Hitler's ambitions and joined Churchill in attacking the British government's policy of appeasement. Listening to a broadcast of one of the führer's speeches, he found it terrifying: "It was the most horrible thing I have ever heard, more like the snarling of a wild animal than the utterance of a human being."[16]

IN APRIL 1941, a week after his arrival in Berlin, Subhas Chandra Bose submitted to the German foreign ministry a couple of detailed memoranda on how the goals of Indians could mesh with those of the Axis. In *Mein Kampf,* Hitler had described India's nationalists as "a coalition of cripples" and asserted that he could not link "the destiny of my people" with that of such an inferior race. His contempt for the Indian independence movement indicated a reversal of German policy, which during World War I had been strongly supportive of Indian insurgents. In 1915 German agents, acting in concert with Sikh émigrés in Canada and the United States, had sent a shipload of arms to Bengal's revolutionaries. (The plot was foiled by the British.) Aware of Hitler's attitude, Bose anticipated resistance from the German government; he nevertheless hoped that rational self-interest would prompt the Nazis to take him seriously.[17]

"It is one of the cardinal principles of British diplomacy to adopt a sanctimonious role when she is fighting in reality for her own selfish interests," Bose wrote in his proposal. His Majesty's Government had, for instance, allowed several European nations to set up governments-in-exile and thereby acquired credentials as a champion of freedom. "Why should not the Axis Powers adopt the same policy and pay England back in her own coin?" Germany should shelter a free Indian government and—through broadcasting incendiary messages, sending weapons and other supplies to revolutionaries, and other means—incite the subcontinent to rebellion. Moreover, he asserted, if the Axis powers publicly committed to liberating British colonies, they would prompt defections among Indian soldiers fighting in the Middle East and Africa. And once the loyalty of the Indian Army was shaken, the arrival of "a small force of 50,000 men with modern equipment" on the colony's border would be enough to topple the British Raj.[18]

Whereas Bose was exaggerating the chances of success of such a rebellion, historian Milan Hauner has argued that the Nazis could have significantly disrupted the British war effort by providing prompt and substantial assistance to anti-colonials in India, Iraq, and elsewhere. It was not to be. The German government granted Bose a beautiful house in Berlin and permitted him to violate the Reich's race laws by living with, and later marrying, an Austrian woman with whom he had fallen passionately in love while exiled from India in the mid-1930s. (Reuniting with her was no doubt a motive for his desperate escape.) The Nazis also permitted Bose to recruit thousands of Indian soldiers captured in northern Africa for a liberation army that he dreamed would march into its homeland via the Afghan border. But although the Italians and the Japanese urged a joint declaration in favor of Indian independence, Hitler refused to go along. He feared that any open threat to the Raj would strengthen the British resolve to fight on against the Germans.[19]

Despite overwhelming evidence to the contrary, Hitler still fancied he could reach an accommodation with the United Kingdom. The previous summer, in July 1940, the führer had announced to horrified generals his determination to eventually attack the Soviet Union. He nursed a fond hope that when Russia had been crushed and Britain stood alone, it would accept the position of Germany's junior partner in world domination. "During the whole of my political activity I have always expounded the idea of a close friendship and collaboration between Germany and England," Hitler had declared in April 1939. Surely, he said, the British could understand that just as the Raj gave meaning to their lives, the vision of a thousand-year Reich gave purpose to Germans. Hitler had made several peace offers to Britain, at one point putting forth "an assurance to the British Empire of German assistance regardless of where such assistance should be necessary."[20]

But the United Kingdom had rejected Hitler's overtures. Instead it had sent troops to defend France and, in the summer of 1940, had dispatched bombers over Germany, some of which had dropped their payloads on residential areas. On September 4, 1940, Hitler announced that his patience had run out: he would force the United Kingdom into submission. Starting three days later, some 200 bombers at a time, escorted by hundreds of fighters, attacked London and other towns almost every night for two months straight.[21]

CHURCHILL VISITED A shelter at Bristol in April 1941, where an old lady who had lost everything to the bombs saw him and cheered, waving the handkerchief with which she had been wiping her eyes. The prime minister choked up and remained sunk in thought on the train home. When he broke his reverie, it was to announce that he would ensure that Britons got all the nutrition necessary "to protect them from the strain and stresses that they may be subjected to in this period of great emergency." Although a "Grow More Food" program had boosted domestic production of wheat, potatoes, and other staples, vast quantities of provisions would nevertheless have to be acquired abroad and transported to the British Isles.[22]

If the United Kingdom had an Achilles' heel, it was the stomach. Two-thirds of the island nation's food was imported, which made its very sustenance vulnerable to disruptions in shipping. During World War I, German U-boats in the Atlantic had threatened the delivery of imported wheat and provoked panic hoarding, causing temporary shortages. After that war, civil servants had formalized plans for feeding Britain in wartime. In a crisis, the government immediately would have to demonstrate that it was on top of the situation—or else people would build personal stockpiles, depriving others. The cost of living, in particular the prices of bread and potatoes, should be tightly regulated so that no one went short of calories; and the more nutritious foods should be rationed to ensure adequate proteins and minerals. In 1936, a government committee had recommended that the United Kingdom build a stockpile of at least three months' usage of food and animal feed in order to guard against wartime disruptions of supply. By the time World War II broke out, the entire machinery for feeding the country was in place.[23]

To watch over the care and feeding of Britons, Winston Churchill recruited a trusted old friend, the physicist Frederick Alexander Lindemann. Known as the Prof to admirers (because of his academic credentials and his brilliance) and as Baron Berlin to detractors (thanks to his German accent and aristocratic tastes), Lindemann was responsible for the government's scientific decisions. He also headed a Statistics Division, or S branch, with whose help he scrutinized the performance of the regular ministries and prioritized the logistical machinery of warfare. Lindemann attended meetings of the War Cabinet, accompanied the prime minister on conferences abroad, and sent him an average of one missive a day. He saw Churchill almost daily for the duration of the war and wielded more influence than any other civilian adviser.[24]

On most matters Lindemann's and Churchill's opinions converged; and when they did not, the scientist worked ceaselessly to change his friend's mind. "He spoke *sotto voce*, but with complete self-assurance, as though stating facts that must be obvious to every schoolboy," related Roy Harrod, an S branch employee who later became one of Britain's premier economists. All those who disagreed with his views Lindemann dismissed as "perfect fools." To create the ten lines of text for the prime minister's benefit that summarized weeks of S branch research, he wielded the final scalpel, taking out "redundant words, unnecessary sentences, inessential parts of the argument and many qualifications," according to Donald MacDougall, Lindemann's right-hand man at the S branch. "At first this last type of shortening worried me—and my colleagues—quite a bit," MacDougall confessed in a memoir. Soon, however, the S branch staff realized that the Prof was merely anticipating the prime minister's wishes. "The normal machinery of government churned up certain proposals, which finally came to the Prime Minister; it was our duty to counter-brief him on what we knew to be the lines of his own thinking," wrote Harrod. In other words, the mission of the S branch was to provide rationales for whichever course the prime minister, as interpreted by the Prof, wished to follow.[25]

Other department heads were at first furious that the Prof had access to their figures and used these to criticize their performances and overrule their decisions even as they were prohibited from seeing the S branch's calculations and so could not defend themselves. But soon they "began to realize that, like it or not, the Prof. was the man whom Churchill trusted most, and that not all their refutations, aspersions, innuendos or attempts at exposure would shift Churchill from his undeviating loyalty to the Prof. by one hair's breadth," wrote Harrod. So it was that the Prof would pronounce judgment on the best use of shipping space, the profligacy of the army, the inadequacy of British supplies, the optimal size of the mustard gas stockpile, the necessity of bombing German houses—and, when the time came, the pointlessness of sending famine relief to Bengal.[26]

THEIRS WAS AN unlikely friendship. Churchill was a self-described "Beefeater" who relished multicourse meals washed down with whisky, whereas Lindemann was a vegetarian, teetotaler, and nonsmoker who lived on salads, egg whites, olive oil, and a specific variety of cheese. Churchill cared, if fitfully, about the troubles of the poor, but Lindemann made no secret of his contempt for social and intellectual inferiors and, according to an acquaintance, "looked upon poverty as a fault." His accent tended to arouse suspicion in wartime Britain. Yet the mutual loyalty of the two friends was total. "Love me, love my dog, and if you don't love my dog you damn well can't love me," muttered a furious Churchill in 1941, after a member of the House of Commons had raised questions about the Prof's influence.[27]

Lindemann's father was a wealthy entrepreneur of German origin who lived in the United Kingdom. Frederick was sent to Germany for gymnasium, and at the University of Berlin he studied physics with a pioneer of thermodynamics. He eventually landed a professorship at Oxford and, when World War I broke out, joined an aircraft factory. He learned to fly and, by repeatedly putting an aircraft into a downward spiral while memorizing measurements such as airspeed, he formalized recommendations for bringing an aircraft out of a fatal spin. This feat of nerves and skill would save the lives of many pilots, and it endeared Lindemann to Churchill when they met in August 1921 at the residence of a duke.[28]

Lindemann boasted a count for an uncle and possessed a chauffeured Rolls Royce, which eased his passage into the aristocratic circles he cherished. (A joke at Oxford ran thus: Why is Professor Lindemann like a Channel steamer? Because he runs from peer to peer.) The physicist impressed the highborn with ridiculous ease, such as when he suggested to a duchess that they sit diagonally on a couch because it would "make an improvement of 41.42%" in space. Churchill declared that the Prof had "a beautiful brain" and came to seek his assistance with practically everything that needed research.[29]

Lindemann had been to India once. In 1929, he visited an Indian mountain resort to serve on a panel on forestry. He was repelled by blacks, but he took along his English valet and did not have to be touched by native hands. On the strength of this two-month tour, he would aid Churchill with the colony's affairs for the next two decades. In 1931, Churchill asked him to study the constitution the British government was devising for India, to "show up its weak points," and to ferret out the background and funding of the Indian National Congress.[30]

Apart from a distaste of dark-skinned foreigners and working-class Britons (the latter being insufferably "stupid"), Lindemann had a horror of ugly faces. These "set up a violent prejudice, which only the most supreme intellectual merits could counterweigh." He also possessed an ingrained anti-Semitism, which his reverence for genius could similarly overcome. Nonetheless, Lindemann's links with the Continent made him one of the first outsiders to comprehend the reality of life under Hitler, and in the 1930s he rescued a number of Jewish scientists from Nazi persecution by offering them positions at Oxford. And when Churchill began to warn about the terrific pace of German rearmament, it was the Prof who analyzed the figures that bolstered his arguments.[31]

By 1942, Lindemann had the title of paymaster-general and had also achieved a peerage; he was now known as Lord Cherwell. His reputation was such that lines of verse inspired by *The Pirates of Penzance* were passed around ministerial offices:[32]

> *My secretariat scrutinizes memoranda topical,*
> *Elucidating fallacies in detail microscopical;*
> *I plumb the depths of strategy, I analyze ballistics;*
> *Reform the whole of industry, or fabricate statistics;*
> *My acumen's infallible, my logic irrefutable,*
> *My slightest proposition axiomatic, indisputable;*
> *And so in matters vegetable, animal and mineral,*
> *I am the very model of a good Paymaster-General.*

Lord Cherwell repaid his friend's patronage by adopting his causes as his own—and nowhere was this synergy more evident than in matters vegetable, animal, and mineral. One of the prime minister's abiding concerns was that the British people should get enough meat. "Have you done justice to rabbit production?" he asked in one of numerous memos on the topic. Another time he inquired if a ship returning from the Middle East might swing by Argentina to pick up some beef. The Prof did not touch flesh, but when it came to feeding Britain he became "an extreme anti-vegetarian." No one "fought harder to keep up the war-time ration of good red meat for the British people," attested MacDougall.[33]

Chocolates and candy were also close to Churchill's boyish heart, and the Prof brought his persuasive powers to bear against their rationing.

He waxed eloquent about the significance of tea to the overworked char-woman, so that when the food ministry eventually rationed tea (which came from India), it ensured that everyone could get her favorite blend. Lord Cherwell did not smoke, but he argued that tobacco rationing would impose undue hardship on those who did. Nor did he touch al-cohol, except when dining with Churchill, who insisted. Yet the Prof strove to ensure that the working class was kept in adequate supplies of beer, which he believed it downed in the prodigious quantities of ten pints a night per man and five per woman. (A pint is a little less than half a liter.)[34]

Nutritionists at the Ministry of Food had nursed a quiet hope that the war would allow the government to improve the eating habits and opportunities of the populace. That dream came true. Milk became free for the poorest mothers and children. The ministry maintained large stocks of wheat and flour, which it released as required to keep down the price of bread. And in the spring of 1941, copious quantities of high-protein foods such as cheese and egg powder began to arrive from the United States under the Lend Lease program, which allowed re-sources to be shared among friendly nations on easy terms. Despite the casualties of war, by 1942 such vital statistics as life expectancy were recording their best levels ever.[35]

There were two problems. First, meat arrived on refrigerated ships that could serve instead as troop carriers; keeping Britain in an ample supply of meat meant that tens of thousands of troops could not reach the front. Wheat, sugar, and farm-animal feed similarly competed with steel that could be turned into tanks and weaponry. To his astonishment, Harrod was repeatedly asked to figure out how resources might be shifted from soldiers to civilians. "It may be noted that the great words with which Churchill called upon the nation, 'blood and toil and tears and sweat' did not include the word 'austerity,'" Harrod pointed out. "He was against it." The prime minister derided suggestions for austerity as "self-strafing proposals" while the Prof referred to them as the Death of a Thousand Cuts. Everyone in the S branch took for granted that "victory would go to the nation in which civilian morale was the better sustained," according to Harrod, and putting tasty food on the table was half the battle won.[36]

The second issue was Britain's incipient pennilessness. The United Kingdom's industries having been redirected toward supplying the war, the nation had had to cut down on exports. So the considerable imports of food and industrial raw materials, as well as the war effort in the Middle East and North Africa, were being paid for with borrowed money. The debts would become due after the war. And unlike past economic crises, when India had bailed Britain out, this time the colony was becoming, after the United States, the primary creditor. "India is piling up sterling credit so fast that, having bought back all her Government and railway indebtedness she may want to buy out every British interest in India," a colleague warned Amery in January 1942. Provisioning the war would enable India to pay off its debts to the United Kingdom, reducing its usefulness as a colony and enhancing its prospects for independence. While the war raged, however, the economic stress induced by such contributions would build inexorably to the point of precipitating famine.[37]

IN APRIL 1940, the United Kingdom had agreed to share the costs that India would incur for the war. The colony would pay for expenditures that could be construed as "purely Indian liabilities by reason of their having been undertaken by India in her own interests"—which would come to mean all costs incurred within its borders and to its east. The United Kingdom would pay for soldiers and supplies used elsewhere (except for the cost of one division, which accrued to India). But as long as the war lasted the Government of India would pay the United Kingdom's share, which would be counted as sterling credits to be remitted from London after the war was over.[38]

The agreement secured the enthusiastic cooperation of native industrialists and contractors. In the meantime, however, the Government of India needed cash to pay for its purchases. Taxes and bonds failed to raise enough, so the presses went to work and printed paper money. World War I had demonstrated that India, as a major source of war

materials, was vulnerable to inflation. Cash supply had more than doubled and, flowing to war industries, had induced a kind of internal
export—from the villages where food was grown to the factory towns
and cantonments where it was consumed—and led to severe scarcities
in rural areas. During World War II, however, defense expenditure in
India would balloon by seventeen times and the money supply by between six and seven times.[39]

The Indian Army was hiring up to 50,000 soldiers each month.
Most of the new recruits suffered from anemia, and even those hailing
from the more prosperous northwest gained five to ten pounds after
four months of eating a standard army ration. The most highly trained
and best-equipped divisions were shipped westward. Under General
Archibald Wavell they led the way to early victories against Italian forces
in Egypt and Eritrea, while under the direction of General Claude
Auchinlek, commander-in-chief in India, they took control of oilfields
in Iraq and Iran. The bulk of the grain these soldiers ate continued to
derive from India.[40]

In 1941 Bengal had a poor harvest and several districts witnessed
hunger marches. The authorities dismissed these as having been organized by "designing persons" to create political unrest and strove to ensure
that no rumors of shortages leaked out. A British soldier wrote in his
diary about an army wife who was stationed with her husband in India.
She had told friends in Ceylon that she was pregnant but soon discovered that she was not. Hoping to forestall the gossip, she sent off a
telegram—"No bun in the oven"—and got a call from irate censors demanding to know "why she was spreading alarm and despondency in
that there was plenty of food in India!"[41]

Through his newsletter, *Harijan*, Gandhi warned Indians on January
19, 1942, that scarcities would worsen as the war continued. "There
are no imports from outside, either of foodstuff or cloth," he observed.
He advised peasants to grow banana, beetroot, yam, and pumpkin,
which "can take the place of bread in time of need." And the finance
member of the viceroy's executive council, Sir Jeremy Raisman, informed
the War Cabinet in August 1942 that inflationary financing had led to

the possibility that Indians would lose all faith in the currency. If farmers chose to store their grain instead of selling it for the suspect cash, that "might give rise to famines and riots."[42]

FAMINES WERE INTEGRAL to India's colonial experience, having been several times more frequent during the Victorian era, when tens of millions died of hunger, than during the Mughal period that had preceded the British. Although often triggered by drought, the famines were so lethal because India was exporting grain—some 10 million tons annually by 1900. Since the earliest days of imperial rule, the colony had sent abroad goods of greater value than it had received in return. (Only in the period 1856 to 1862, when investment for building railways entered India, did this flow reverse.) By the end of the Victorian period, India's export constituted almost exclusively the products of its fields.[43]

General Robert Clive's victory in 1757 had drastically altered India's economic relationship with the United Kingdom. "Very soon after Plassey, the Bengal plunder began to arrive in London, and the effect appears to have been instantaneous; for all authorities agree that the 'industrial revolution,' the event which has divided the nineteenth century from all antecedent time, began with the year 1760," wrote nineteenth-century American historian Brooks Adams. The tribute from India, which amounted to almost a third of Britain's national savings for the last three decades of the eighteenth century, financed trading networks, serving as lubricant for the new economic engine. It also enabled suddenly wealthy merchants to wrest power from the monarchy and stabilize the British parliamentary system, which would thereafter provide consistent support for their ventures. Ironically, the lack of liberty in the colonies subsidized the increasing political freedom in the United Kingdom.[44]

Its head start in industrialization meant that "for nearly fifty years Great Britain stood without a competitor," Adams continued. During this period British banks, loaded with colonial spoils, lent to and traded with North America, Europe, and Australia, thereby helping them industrialize. These continents imported British machines and erected tariff barriers behind which they nurtured their infant industries. The pace of advancement in the United States and Germany ultimately left the United Kingdom behind, but Indian revenues would allow the imperial nation to retain its financial primacy well into the twentieth century. "Under English domination, India became a key foundation of the emerging worldwide capitalist edifice," wrote historian Eric Wolf.[45]

"India is your great free market," Lord Randolph Churchill reminded Parliament in 1887. "Every kind of British goods flows into India without the smallest obstacle, and the possession of India is of incalculable value on that account to the British working man." During the preceding century, however, while its own economy industrialized, the United Kingdom had sheltered it from Indian imports, especially textiles. The new spinning machines were initially banned in the colony, and by around 1800 Indian cotton and silk products were either banned in Britain or subject to import duties of 30 to 80 percent. "[H]ad not such prohibitory duties and decrees existed, the mills of Paisley and Manchester would have been stopped in their outset, and could scarcely have been again set in motion, even by the power of steam," remarked historian Horace Hayman Wilson. Between 1790 and 1830, textile exports from Bengal fell by 95 percent, while those from the rest of India were reduced by 30 percent.[46]

Instead, bales of raw Indian cotton and silk came to feed Lancashire mills, which churned out cloth cheaper than many an Indian artisan could. Targeted tariffs ensured that not only would Indian textiles fail to sell in England; they would often be more expensive than English textiles sold in India. English cottons paid at most 3.5 percent duty upon import into India, whereas native products were subjected to internal duties of up to 17.5 percent. As a result, Calcutta, which had sent to London £2 million worth of cotton goods in 1813, instead imported the same value of similar British goods in 1830. Dacca, whose translucent muslin had once evoked awe, became ghostly as its specialized craftsmen deserted or died of starvation. Around 1848, spinning machinery was allowed into India, but tariff barriers continued to hinder the rise of a domestic industry until the 1870s, when a few mills came up near Bombay.[47]

By the mid-nineteenth century, half of the United Kingdom's exports came from cotton manufactures and virtually all of India's from its fields. The colony had been reduced "from the state of a manufacturing to that of an agricultural country," as a director of the East India Company had predicted in 1823. In many villages of India, spinning wheels, which women had operated between bouts of housework, and weaving looms, which men had worked in slack seasons, were stilled. Bereft of income from their cottage industries, villagers became ever more dependent on the crops of the fields.[48]

The paucity of manufactures also meant that agricultural exports had to bear almost the entire burden of India's permanent financial obligation to the United Kingdom. The most visible portion of this payment, the Home Charge, met the expenses of overseas wars in which the Indian Army fought; the interest on mutiny charges, railway investment, and other debts; the pensions of British citizens who had been employed in the colony; and all expenses, including salaries and banquets, associated with the India House in London. The Home Charge, which Her Majesty's Government regarded as fair payment for services rendered and capital employed, came to £20 million per year by the end of the Victorian era. Indian nationalists such as Dadabhai Naoroji argued that because virtually all of India's foreign exchange earnings were used for paying the Home Charge, and for remitting to the United Kingdom the earnings of British citizens stationed in India, those profits could not be invested in domestic agriculture and industry. Most Indians thus remained so poor that they could not compete with foreign consumers in buying grain—with the result that a significant portion of the crop ended up abroad. Nationalist historian Romesh Chunder Dutt calculated that to meet its foreign exchange requirements India had to annually export rice, wheat, cotton, tea, jute, indigo, opium, and other produce of the land, equal in value to a year's cereal for 25 million people.[49]

Such was the turn of the screw: to pay their rent, interest, and other dues, cultivators had to surrender their harvest, part of which was exported, thereby earning foreign exchange to pay for the charges, remittances, and imports (such as silver to maintain the flow of currency). The tax and interest demanded of the grower meant not only that his produce would be extracted and placed on the market but also that after meeting his liabilities he would have little money left with which to buy food for the family—which in turn boosted grain exports.

The advent of railways in the late 1850s had made matters worse. The Government of India guaranteed British financiers a 5 percent return on railway investment, compared with the 3 percent interest that banks offered. As a result, more than 25,000 miles of railway track, connecting every corner of the country, would be laid by 1900—"an impressive achievement indeed, but a very costly one too," comments historian Dietmar Rothermund. He found that each mile of railway track cost Indian taxpayers 10,000 rupees for annual debt service, at a time when their average income varied from 20 to 30 rupees a year. As promised, trains helped to bring grain into famine-stricken locales, but that merely spread high grain prices over a broader area: whereas in an earlier era a famine would have killed many in a small region, now all the poorest in a larger region died.[50]

To top it all, the Suez Canal opened in 1869, halving the shipping time from India to the British Isles. A few years later, export duties on wheat were eliminated and rail freight charges to the ports were reduced well below those for transport within the country. In consequence, a greater portion of the crop ended up abroad. During the last three years of the 1870s, a time of famine when millions starved to death, India sent abroad seven times more grain than during the first three years of that decade. The colony's wheat crop was exported at such cheap rates that it determined international overall prices between 1870 and 1900.[51]

Historian William Hunter observed in 1874 that in Bengal, if the price of rice after the winter harvest was twice that in a normal year, it foretold a famine—and a price three times the normal, later in the year, indicated that the famine had already set in. Yet even a tripling in the

cost of rice, enough to depopulate hundreds of villages, was of little financial significance to a consumer in the United Kingdom. Whereas
the colony and the colonizer probably had the same level of prosperity
in the mid-eighteenth century (with Bengal having been richer than
this average), by the end of the Victorian era the per capita income in
the United Kingdom was twenty times that in India. The industrial
revolution and imperial policy had plugged India smoothly but asym-
metrically into the global economy, such that the high incomes abroad
siphoned off a good part of the grain that the land revenue system ex-
truded onto the market. Because the grain was free to follow the cash
out of the country, this forced-feedback loop went by the name of
free trade.[52]

Nationalists invariably demanded that cereals not be allowed to be
exported in times of famine. But the authorities pleaded the virtues of
free trade, and local administrators who curbed exports or otherwise
interfered with market forces were severely chastised. Even during dev-
astating famines, the government rigorously collected agricultural taxes,
thereby feeding whatever harvest there was into the free market. If the
revenue collectors could not gather all the tax due during a famine, they
recovered it the following year, along with that year's dues. "The one
good harvest that stood between the famine of 1897 and 1899 had to
pay the famine revenue and the revenue for the current year," observed
journalist Vaughan Nash, so that "when the moneylenders had taken
their share, the cultivator had nothing left for a rainy, or, rather, a rain-
less day."[53]

The crux of the matter was that India's agricultural exports had become crucial to the United Kingdom's economy. The imperial nation
settled more than a third of its trade deficit with the United States and
Europe by means of India's export surplus. Prohibiting the export of
food from India would make it more affordable within the colony, admitted economist Fred J. Atkinson in 1909. Yet such a measure would
adversely affect India's trade balance, reduce the value of the rupee, and
make the Home Charge (which had to be paid in sterling) effectively
more expensive. Moreover, Atkinson continued, "if the food supply

from India ceased, unless the gaps could at once be filled from elsewhere, food prices outside India would rise, and this, owing to the existence of unions and their methods of enforcing their wishes by means of strikes . . . might affect wages outside India and thus indirectly all prices." Should Indians eat their grain instead of exporting it, they would destabilize the economy of the United Kingdom.[54]

The death toll from the nineteenth-century famines is difficult to estimate, because starvation and disease fed off one another. Civil servant William Digby calculated a famine toll of 28.8 million for the latter half of the nineteenth century, but this number is probably too high. For instance, Digby obtained 10.3 million as the famine mortality from 1876 through 1878, whereas demographer Arup Maharatna calculates 8.2 million. Part of the discrepancy arises from contemporary observers having added up all starvation deaths, whereas modern scholars subtract from this total the deaths expected in a normal year. Because starvation was widespread even in so-called normal years, the modern method does not include all fatalities from hunger. A more meaningful measure is life expectancy, which can be calculated from after 1871, when the first nationwide census took place. The years of life a newborn Indian could expect hovered at about twenty-four until 1920, after which the age slowly increased.[55]

In contrast, life expectancy in Great Britain improved throughout the Victorian era to reach forty-seven years by its end, in large part because of better nutrition. In 1905, arguing in favor of free trade, Winston Churchill observed: "The harvests of the world are at our disposal, and, by a system which averages climatic risks, we secure not merely a low but a fairly stable price. With that marvellous operation by which the crowded population of this island is fed, we cannot take the responsibility of interfering." During his 1930s campaign against Indian self-government, Churchill went so far as to warn of famine engulfing the United Kingdom if, "guided by counsels of madness and cowardice disguised as false benevolence, you troop home from India." He feared that a full third of the English population would perish if the empire was lost.[56]

By then, however, India was no longer a net exporter of grain; the outflow of depression gold would instead enable the colony to temporarily meet its financial obligations to the United Kingdom. On the contrary, India imported cereals. Whereas in the nineteenth century it had been producing more than required to feed the people (had the grain stayed in the country), the population's needs had since overtaken food production. But the depression slashed the net earnings of Bengali peasants, the vast majority of whom needed to buy some rice for their families, by 90 percent—with the result that they could not import enough. A 1933 survey revealed that 41 percent of India's inhabitants were "poorly nourished" and another 20 percent "very badly nourished," with the statistics for Bengal being worst of all: 47 and 31 percent, respectively. The province underwent serious food scarcities in 1934 and 1936; mass migration, the most egregious sign of famine, was averted thanks to rice shipments from Burma.[57]

By the time World War II hit, India was importing between 1 and 2 million tons of rice a year from Burma and Thailand. That lifeline would be cut by the Japanese occupation of Southeast Asia—just when India had again become an exporter of grain, this time for the war effort.[58]

"I WOULD GO to the political gatherings to listen," said Chitto Ranjon Samonto, recalling his teenage experiences in rural Bengal of 1941. "They would say, leave school, come join us, we'll free the country. But in school we sang the praises of the British." Not until someone handed him a copy of the nationalist novel *Anandamath* did he make up his mind. "It inspired me to get rid of the British," Samonto said.

Samonto hailed from Kalikakundu village in southeastern Midnapore. According to legend, Kalikakundu received its name from an image of the goddess Kali, carved out of black rock, that was discovered in a local pond *(kundu)* in the distant past. Two thousand years ago, this coastal region belonged to the glittering port city of Tamralipta, which berthed ships from as far off as the Roman Empire and China. Old fragments of terra-cotta testify to a cultural and spiritual melee. They depict harvesting scenes, copulating couples, and festivals with musicians and dancers; scenes from the mythology of Jains, many of whose descendants worship the god Krishna; heads of the Buddha, who attained enlightenment in neighboring Bihar; figures of the sun god and other Aryan deities; phalluses of the fertility god Shiva; portraits of the goddess Durga felling the buffalo demon; and others. Tamralipta has since metamorphosed into the dusty and impoverished town of Tamluk. But Midnapore's villagers exhibit an easy tolerance of other ways of life whose origins probably lie in that distant, cosmopolitan tumult.[59]

Kalikakundu in modern times is a collection of hamlets separated by expanses of low-lying rice fields. Coconut palms, banana groves, and ponds cluster around the mud or brick huts of each hamlet, while rice plants of day-glo green stick out of the flooded fields everywhere else. Raised ridges, paved with crumbly red earth, radiate across the fields to link the hamlets, each of which is home to a specific religious group or a single extended family. Chitto Samonto knew individuals in every hamlet—whether worshippers of Kali, Krishna, or Allah—well enough to merit a cup of tea and intimate details of life and death.

Samonto was born in 1926, the youngest of four children. His father was one of the most educated men of the locale, boasting a master's degree, and he taught Bengali and arithmetic in several high schools at some distance away, which meant he came home to Kalikakundu only once or twice a month. "I feared my father," Samonto said. "He had elevated tastes. If I spotted him coming across the fields, I would have to run home, lay out a reed mat, put out water to wash his feet, pour drinking water into a cup, and be ready to offer his pipe stuffed with his favorite aromatic tobacco." The patriarch had tutored the princes of Mohisadal—the sons of the local zamindar—and they had once invited the teacher to the palace to play chess for a full week. For all that, he earned a pittance. The teacher's annual salary was around 150 rupees, whereas every year the Mohisadal rajas collected 1.3 million rupees in rent alone.

Cornwallis's reforms of 1793 had transformed zamindars, who used to be tax collectors and administrators, into English-style landlords who owned fields, rivers, pastures, ponds, and groves that were once collectively held by villagers. The landlords maintained private security forces that assisted them in collecting rent and in wresting fields from the ownership of defaulters. Often the farmers who lost their land continued to cultivate it, supplying the seed, plough, bullocks, and fertilizer and bearing the risk of natural calamity while being entitled to at most half the crop. In a lean year the cultivators had to borrow grain or cash in order to stay alive, and either repay the debt with interest or work without wages to pay it off—thereby entering a state of ever-deepening subjugation.[60]

Chitto's mother was beautiful but illiterate, hailed from a neighboring village, and grew rice on the small plot of land the family owned in Kalikakundu. With help from her children, she also cultivated a large field belonging to the Mohisadal zamindars. "My mother worked all the time," Samonto recalled. "It is very hard work, transplanting the rice plants into flooded fields, bent over all day, come sun or rain. You can't stop when it rains." The managers of the Mohisadal estates usually claimed three-quarters of the crop. In consequence, all this effort gained the Samonto family enough rice for only three or four months a year, and the rest had to be bought or borrowed. Each sackful of rice borrowed had to be repaid by one and a half sackfuls from the next harvest. It was a no-win game, yet his mother somehow pulled the family through. "I still dream of her," Samonto confessed. "She is feeding me, taking care of me."

Chitto's sisters had finished primary school, after which they were married, and his brother had gone on to middle school. But by the time Chitto was old enough to study, the economic depression had arrived and the family could barely eat. The boy desperately wanted an education: "My father was a teacher—I didn't want to let him down." He managed to attend a primary school in a nearby village. It had perhaps sixty students, three or four teachers, and a huge portrait of King George V to which everyone had to render *pronam*, a gesture of obeisance. But the only way Chitto could afford to study was by living with and working for a better-off family in that village.

"They gave me food and I went to the school. I did everything for them—cooking, cleaning, washing clothes, scrubbing dishes, you name it," Samonto said. The boy had to get the groceries, make meals, spoon-feed the family's feeble old patriarch, clean up drunken messes left by his bachelor son, and run errands for the other son and his wife (who, fortunately, were often away in Calcutta). Chitto had no books, and in any case his chores left very little time for study. "It took me years to get through primary school. By the time I finished I was twelve or thirteen."

Thereafter the boy had wandered from house to house in other villages, begging to be allowed to stay, work, and study at a nearby middle school. "I was willing to do anything for them, even then it was impossible." Giving up, he had hung out at home, helping his mother in the fields or making flattened rice and carrying almost 40 kilograms of it, stuffed into a sack and balanced on his head, to sell at Geokhali town, eight miles away. After two years he was lucky to be admitted with free board to a school run by a Hindu charity. Chitto emerged with good grades—and immediately suspended his studies. It was August 1942. British forces had departed Southeast Asia, the Japanese were at India's border, Gandhi had just been arrested, India had erupted into the most concerted rebellion since 1857, and the teenager wanted to help make history.

CHAPTER THREE

Scorched

"If, after India has made the very great material effort in defence of the Empire which she has already made, she should be attacked and find herself without any of the necessary materials and equipment for defence, the political effect would be disastrous," General Archibald Wavell had warned in September 1941, two months after arriving in India as commander-in-chief of the Indian Army. Earlier that year, British forces sent to defend Greece had been routed by Germans, a debacle that had led the prime minister to remove Wavell as general officer commanding-in-chief of the Middle East Command.[1]

Wavell's new command was to prove at least as challenging as his old one. The Indian Army numbered almost a million at the time, but the majority of troops were poorly trained and had no equipment to speak of. The seven best Indian divisions—the only ones with up-to-date weaponry, functioning vehicles, technical expertise, and experience— were fighting in the deserts around the Mediterranean. Not a single armored car or modern tank, bomber, or fighter plane was to be found on the entire subcontinent. India's cities and military installations were defended by only 30 anti-aircraft guns but required at least 520. General Claude Auchinlek, who had preceded Wavell as commander-in-chief in India, had asked the War Cabinet for tanks in order to prepare at least one armored division in India, to which the prime minister had replied: "But General, how do you know that they wouldn't turn and fire the wrong way?" Amery, for his part, had been consistently urging aircraft production in the colony, and had been just as consistently turned down. "Winston," he observed in his diary, "hates the idea of Indians producing anything for themselves in the way of defence."[2]

India was unprotected from Axis attack for several reasons. The prime minister believed that the Japanese would not dare to take on the fabled Royal Navy and, in any case, that the fortress of Singapore would halt any significant advance toward India. Moreover, he worried that if Indian troops with contemporary weapons were on home ground, they would turn on their superiors—just as they had in 1857. After that rebellion, the Indian Army had been remade with men from the so-called martial races; it was meticulously structured so that ties of kinship and ethnicity translated into loyalty to commanding officers and, thence, to the Crown. But by the time World War II arrived, the army had expanded so much that officers of diverse origins—even Bengalis—had had to be inducted. Being educated, the officers were more politicized than rank-and-file soldiers, and 60 percent of them expected independence for their homeland as a reward for their services in the war. To make matters worse, Axis propaganda, engineered by Subhas Chandra Bose in Berlin, was urging nationalists to join the army and subvert it from within.[3]

Churchill's suspicions of the Indian Army were well founded. Nevertheless, leaving India without the means to defend its eastern flank would prove to be an error—as fatal to the stature of the British Empire as to the security of its subjects.

PRESIDENT FRANKLIN D. Roosevelt could scarcely believe that their two nations were fighting a war against fascism but would not also try to free the world of colonialism, as he remarked to Winston Churchill in August 1941. The comment made Churchill apoplectic. The prime minister had traveled to Placentia Bay in Newfoundland in order to woo his benefactor and inform him of the United Kingdom's vital needs. For the president, the Atlantic Conference was a chance to size up his ally—and to impose his own democratic views.[4]

Also present was Elliott Roosevelt, the president's fourth son, who later published a controversial account of his father's wartime conferences. "The cigars were burned to ashes, the brandy disappeared steadily," he wrote of Churchill after one dinner. But the tongue remained lucid, and the president provoked it by bringing up the empire's economics. No stable peace was possible, he suggested, if the colonies remained poor—and dated methods of taking out raw materials and giving nothing back made progress impossible. According to the younger Roosevelt, Churchill's neck reddened and his sentences lengthened into paragraphs—and the president, having said his piece, let him talk. After 2 A.M. Elliott was finally able to help his wheelchair-bound father to his cabin and sit awhile to share a smoke. The prime minister was an old-fashioned Tory, the president said, but they would be able to work together just fine. They would, his son warned, as long as the two men stayed off the topic of India.[5]

The conference resulted in an inspiring statement of war aims, known as the Atlantic Charter. The document offered the first hint of the president's goal of a United Nations to police the postwar peace. It also asserted that the United States and the United Kingdom would "respect the right of all peoples to choose the form of government under which they will live; and that they wish to see sovereign rights and self-government restored to those who have been forcibly deprived of them." Leopold Amery—who worried that the Americans would use the war to undermine the British Empire and turn it into "a lebensraum for their exports"—was disgusted by the charter. "We shall no doubt pay dearly in the end for all this fluffy flapdoodle," he confided to his diary. At his urging, the prime minister clarified to the House of Commons that the Atlantic Charter applied only to those countries conquered by the Axis powers. The colonies were exempt.[6]

ON DECEMBER 7, 1941, Japanese bombers devastated the American fleet in Pearl Harbor, Hawaii, bringing the United States into the war. That night Churchill slept the sleep of the saved, because he believed the entry of the United States into the war meant ultimate victory. The United Kingdom immediately declared war on Japan, as did India. For the moment, however, things got worse.

Churchill had earlier dispatched two battleships, the *Repulse* and the *Prince of Wales*, toward Singapore in the hope of deterring an Axis advance toward the British Empire. But within days "an army of highly trained gangsters," as Wavell described the Japanese invaders, landed in Siam and Malay and sped toward the city of Penang—on bicycles. Japanese bombers flattened Penang ahead of the army's advance and torpedoed the two British battleships, which were bereft of air cover, and sank them. It was the single worst day of the war for Churchill, who had traveled on the *Prince of Wales* for his meeting with Roosevelt.

If the Japanese reached India, the natives might welcome them in. So when Churchill visited Washington later that December, Roosevelt broached the prospect of political reform in the colony. "I reacted so strongly and at such length that he never raised it verbally again," the prime minister would write in his history of the world war.[7]

Churchill's defiance could not conceal the grave threat to the British Empire. Singapore was indeed impregnable if approached by sea, but in January 1942 Japanese soldiers traversed seemingly impenetrable jungles on foot and arrived at the city's vulnerable northern side. "India had been sucked dry of trained troops by the requirements of the Middle East, Iraq, and Iran," Wavell would later note, and most of the British, Indian, and Australian soldiers who were rushed to face the enemy were rookies. Worse, the invaders had air cover, whereas the defenders had none. "There must be at this stage no thought of saving the troops or sparing the population," Churchill cabled. "Commanders and senior officers should die with their troops. The honour of the British Empire and the British Army is at stake."[8]

Singapore fell on February 15, 1942. At an extraordinary ceremony the following evening, Indian soldiers and officers who had defended Siam and Malay watched as a commander, Colonel Hunt, formally surrendered them to the Japanese before embarking with his compatriots for safety. With surgical precision, the white men in an army that had hitherto trained and fought as a unit separated themselves from the brown. Fujiwara Iwaichi, a Japanese commander unusual in his belief in liberating colonies, encouraged a personable Sikh officer, Captain

Mohan Singh, to recruit the captive soldiers into an Indian National Army that would eventually march back to their homeland to fight the British. Of the 67,000 soldiers who surrendered, more than 20,000 would join this liberation army.[9]

Next in the line of attack was Burma—defended by a Burmese division and an Indian division that had been partially trained and equipped for desert warfare, and possessed no tanks or anti-aircraft guns. During the awful retreat, a commander precipitously ordered a bridge to be blown up, leaving thousands of his own troops on the wrong side of a mile-wide river. On March 8 Rangoon fell, and the Japanese were at India's border.[10]

The evacuation of Burma was chaotic. White administrators and civilians commandeered all available transport and piled in, leaving everyone else to seek his or her own way. Some 600,000 Indians who worked in Burma, and who also feared the Japanese, took to the sea on horribly overcrowded ships or trudged over rain-sodden Himalayan passes in an attempt to reach their homeland. Around 80,000 would die on the way. Women and children sank into ferocious mud; feces and bodies mingled in campsites with living, starving people; and cholera became endemic.

Congress leaders imprisoned in the fall of 1940, during Gandhi's satyagraha movement against the war effort, had been released just before Pearl Harbor, after a prolonged argument that Amery had won in the War Cabinet. ("A most unnecessary waste of time and generation of heat owing to Winston's refusal to accept things as they are and not as they were in 1895," he commented in his diary.) Nehru toured transit camps in the northeast and found that white evacuees had food but the brown ones had none—yet the native peoples were being prevented from leaving the camps lest they carried their germs further. The catastrophic exodus devastated the myth of the brave Briton standing firm in defense of his charges.[11]

WITH THE BURMA Road to China closed, American forces began pouring into Calcutta and traveling northeast into the Indian province of Assam. They constructed runways and flew thousands of tons of war supplies, brought by rail from the western ports of India, over the Hump: the perilous eastern Himalayas. As long as China kept resisting them, the Japanese could field fewer forces in the Pacific. India became a beneficiary of Lend Lease, with the United States providing tanks, jeeps, aircraft, and other war equipment in exchange for clothing, services, and food. India was also set to provide shelter and supplies to troops from China, the United Kingdom, Africa, and Australia—around a half-million foreign soldiers in total.[12]

If Calcutta fell, the supply route to China would be cut off. An anxious Chiang Kai-shek, the leader of the Chinese nationalists, visited India in early 1942 to ask for the support of Congress leaders and was shocked to find them indifferent to the Japanese threat. At his urging, President Roosevelt instructed a representative in London, Averell Harriman, to suggest to the prime minister the desirability of reaching a settlement with Indians that would rouse them to fight for the Allies. Churchill responded that he could not alienate the Muslims, who, he stated, constituted three-quarters of the Indian Army. (In reality, the fraction was one-third.) He also sent the president a letter that the government had received from Mohammad Ali Jinnah, reiterating the demand for Pakistan as the price for Muslim cooperation.[13]

The stunning reversals of Allied fortunes in Southeast Asia had made Churchill politically vulnerable, and critics in the Labour Party were also insisting that the Indian National Congress be won over to the war effort. As a result, that February the prime minister came up with an astonishingly liberal scheme for India: an enlarged viceroy's council consisting mainly of elected members to assist in the war effort and, subsequently, to formulate a constitution. This time, it was Viceroy Linlithgow who protested, declaring that Muslims would "refuse to serve on any body in which they would be an ineffective minority." An army general further warned that "any concessions to Congress" could anger Muslim soldiers and result in "the ruin of the Indian Army as at present constituted." Such concerns convinced Amery, who ended up telling Churchill, "we must reassure the Moslems that they are not to be outvoted over a constitution."[14]

A year earlier, Amery had expressed concern about the deepening division between Hindus and Muslims, to which Churchill had replied, "Oh, but that is all to the good." Amery had since become sensitized to Muslim sentiment, possibly because he had helped dispatch Indian troops to take control of oilfields in the Middle East. During World War I, some Muslim soldiers from India had mutinied upon being ordered to battle the Turks, and once again the British Empire was asking Muslims to fight Muslims. The last thing Amery needed was for Jinnah to inflame any incipient Muslim anger. Amery even wondered whether, with the Japanese at India's door, "it would not be better, for the moment at any rate to go back more to the spirit of Mutiny days and revive British Rule in its most direct and, if necessary, ruthless form."[15]

IF THE JAPANESE invaded, they would probably land on the coast of Bengal, which adjoined Burma. Because of the inadequate defensive installations, they would be impossible to resist; worse, they might even be welcomed by the locals. On January 21, 1942, Linlithgow had warned Amery: "Recent reports from military authorities in eastern India [are] to the effect that there is a large and dangerous potential fifth column in Bengal, Assam, Bihar and Orissa, and that, indeed, potentiality of pro-enemy sympathy and activity in eastern India is enormous." Many Bengalis, including Sushil Dhara of Midnapore, were elated by news of Japanese successes—and the events to follow would only increase their disaffection with the British.[16]

On November 14, 1941, the prime minister had urged a "scorched earth" policy involving "ruthless destruction in any territory we have to surrender." The following January the War Office ordered such measures in colonies on the periphery of the Indian Ocean, which were at risk of seaborne Japanese attack. Amery relayed the instructions to India. The army was to destroy industrial, military, and transport facilities, while the civil administration should deprive the enemy of sustenance.

"Water supplies and minimum stocks of essential foodstuffs should be left for local inhabitants but latter should as far as possible be distributed to population before withdrawal takes place to avoid bulk supplies falling into enemy hands," the order elaborated. If some resource could not be burned or blown up, "dumping in sea or rivers may suffice."[17]

In Bengal the winter crop had just been harvested, so scorched earth would not mean literally burning the fields. Instead, the rice would have to be removed from traders' storehouses and landowners' *golas*, or miniature silos. In the confusion and panic, the vital caveat of leaving enough food for the people would be disregarded.

Wavell hoped to retake such regions as the Japanese might occupy, and he protested the demolition of industrial facilities. Amery cabled back on March 27: "it is essential that destruction should be ruthless and should achieve without fail total denial of such resources as would assist enemy operations." Removal of river craft, which the Japanese might use to advance along Bengal's waterways, "should commence now repeat now," he urged. The viceroy sided with the commander-in-chief, however. Demolition along a coastline as long as India's would "give handle for agitation," the viceroy wrote; and with "enormous population in threatened areas any scorched earth policy will mean that we will have millions on our hands who it will be quite impossible to feed."[18]

Thus scorched earth was reduced in scope and limited to coastal Bengal, where it went by the less incendiary name of Denial Policy. The province was selected because it adjoined Burma, and perhaps also because its populace was deemed treasonous: one War Office memo warned that in Bengal saboteurs and provocateurs could "gravely impair the efficiency of Indian defence." Military planners drew on the map a line that ran east to west some twenty miles south of Calcutta. South of that line, the Japanese would be denied transport and food. Civil servant Olaf M. Martin, who was posted in eastern Bengal, recalled that army chiefs were demoralized and "temporarily obsessed with the supposed necessity of 'denying transport' to any invading force." Vital records and white women were swiftly moved out of the demarcated region. The government advised "wise men" to keep two months of rice in stock—amounting to a confession that the public would be left to its own devices. The viceroy sent his private secretary, Leonard George Pinnell, to Bengal to implement the Denial Policy.[19]

Hardly any defense existed in eastern and southern Bengal, Pinnell would subsequently state to a Famine Inquiry Commission that was set up in 1944. Nobody knew "whether, by the next cold weather, Calcutta would [be in] the possession of the Japanese." To prevent anyone from potentially hearing Axis broadcasts, the authorities confiscated all the radios they could find. Allied forces established observation posts, linked by wireless sets to the old fort in Calcutta, every ten miles along the seacoast and on the banks of major rivers. Military authorities had already requisitioned all serviceable trucks and cars, as well as most buses; now the officials confiscated from southern and eastern Bengal virtually all other forms of conveyance. Bicycles, steamers, boats carrying more than ten passengers, bullock carts, and even a few elephants were commandeered, destroyed, or forced to move north of the denial line. From Midnapore alone, the police removed close to ten thousand bicycles.[20]

Boats were the primary form of transport in riverine Bengal. Most villagers were so poor that they either walked or boarded a ferry. Boats took traders to the market, fishers to the sea, potters to their clay pits, and farmers to their plots, which were often marooned between vast swathes of river. Demolishing boats meant destroying livelihoods: as Pinnell confessed, "for anyone who knows the Bengal cultivator it was a completely heart-breaking job." Of 66,500 registered boats, more than two-thirds were rendered inoperable in coastal Bengal. Pinnell said that in fact nine-tenths of the larger boats that could be found were taken out, and he could not be sure how many still plied within the denial area. Of the surviving vessels, many would be used for transporting jute (needed for sandbags, a necessity of war), of which Bengal was the world's only significant source. As a result, the rice crop harvested at the end of 1942 could be moved from regions of surplus to those of scarcity only with great difficulty. When a member of the famine commission asked if "boat denial" had ended up "killing" the economy of certain locales, Pinnell replied: "I do not think a consideration of that sort would have been of any weight at all."[21]

Boat denial "completely broke the economy of the fishing class," he further testified. In December 1943 a journalist visited Faridpur in eastern Bengal and was told by an elderly survivor that in his fishing village of 200 households, 50 had perished in entirety. The 35,000 families that lost their homes and fields to military barracks and aerodromes would also feature prominently among the victims of famine.[22]

ANOTHER ASPECT OF the scorched earth policy, called "rice denial," would impact the economy of Bengal just as fiercely. Just when the authorities began to remove rice stocks from the coastal and eastern parts of the province is unclear. When civil servant Asok Mitra arrived in Munshiganj in eastern Bengal in early February 1942, he found less than 10 tons of rice in riverside storehouses that should have held thousands of tons. The police, he was told, had gone around destroying or seizing the stocks. Journalist Sukharanjan Sengupta alleges that thousands of tons of rice stored at three river ports of eastern Bengal were thrown into the water, while a villager told radio correspondent Nazes Afroz that he saw soldiers setting fire to stacks of rice.[23]

Bengal's elected chief minister, Abul Kasem Fazlul Huq, further charged that in April the governor of Bengal, Sir John Herbert, ordered a British official to remove "excess rice from three districts within 24 hours." Since the Bengal administration did not have the staff to enforce such a drastic order—its only village-level employees were chowkidars, or night watchmen—the official had advanced 2 million rupees to a merchant to buy up rice. The businessman was Mirza Ahmad Ispahani, a key financier of the Muslim League. Herbert described his political adversaries in the province as "Caste Hindus" and regarded members of the Muslim League as "enemies of our enemies" and thus as natural allies in his task of committing the productive capacity of Bengal to the war effort. The Ispahani Company would become the government's principal buying agent, with the power to commandeer rice if the owners refused to sell.[24]

"At the moment we are facing a rice famine in Bengal" because of the governor's policies, Huq protested in August 1942. Just as worrisome, brokers from Ceylon and other Indian provinces were also buying rice in Bengal. After the fall of Burma, the Government of India had undertaken to do without the usual rice imports from the east—and moreover to supply rice to those parts of the British Empire that could no longer obtain it from Southeast Asia. As a result, whereas Bengal had imported 296,000 tons of rice in 1941, it would export 185,000 tons in 1942. The price of rice soared.[25]

EVEN AS INDIA waded into an economic morass, the president of the United States had been trying to throw a bridge across the ideological chasm between the Indian National Congress and His Majesty's Government. The prevailing political stalemate was embittering nationalists and endangering the prosecution of the war against Japan. On March 11, 1942, Roosevelt had written to the prime minister, likening the Indian predicament to that of the thirteen American colonies facing the War of Independence. The colonies had joined to form a stopgap government in order to fight the British, he pointed out. During the war, confusion had prevailed among the "separate sovereignties"—but then "the experiment was still in the making and any effort to arrive at a final framework would have come to naught." Roosevelt asked Churchill to similarly allow a temporary government, headed by representatives of the various political groups, to be set up in India.[26]

The United Kingdom's left-wing politicians had also upped the pressure on the British government, which in March led it to dispatch to New Delhi Sir Richard Stafford Cripps, a socialist committed to the cause of Indian emancipation, to negotiate with the nationalists. But Cripps had been sent merely "to prove our honesty of purpose and to gain time," the prime minister privately assured the viceroy, while Amery further clarified that Cripps would probably fail. "We shall have shown our good will to the world and India," he informed Linlithgow.[27]

Cripps presented to the Indian National Congress the proposal he had brought. During the war all matters pertaining to defense would remain in British hands; afterward India would get dominion status. But nestled within the offer lay "the Pakistan cuckoo's egg," as Amery put it: any province that wished to could break away. Amery did not believe that partition was practicable or desirable but had inserted the egg to please Jinnah. Furthermore, he anticipated that "most of the Hindus will set up a howl of protest against the thought of dividing Mother India"—and sure enough, Gandhi balked at dismemberment. He dismissed the offer as "a post-dated check" and, leaving detailed negotiations to Congress politicians, departed New Delhi for his ashram in western India.[28]

On April 3, 1942, Colonel Louis Johnson arrived in the city as President Roosevelt's personal representative. Johnson had fought in World War I and had helped organize the American Legion; he understood military matters and hoped to facilitate a speedy settlement so that Indians would wholeheartedly support the war. Johnson worked tirelessly with Cripps and Congress leaders, and ultimately told the latter that they would get control of a new defense ministry, which would oversee India's war effort while leaving all military decisions to the commander-in-chief. But Viceroy Linlithgow, who resented his powers being negotiated away, informed London of the "Johnson offer"—which the Congress had indicated it would accept.[29]

Churchill was incensed. He cornered Harry Hopkins, Roosevelt's friend and emissary in London, who calmed him down by saying that Johnson was "not acting as the representative of the President in mediating the Indian business." That was not quite true, but in effect it withdrew American backing from the Johnson offer. On April 9 and 10, Cripps received forceful telegrams from London. When he next met Congress leaders, he told them that the Johnson offer was off the table; instead of directing the domestic war effort, their role in defending India could stretch to running army canteens and implementing scorched earth. Stunned and upset, Nehru and others turned him down. "I fancy most of us feel like someone who has proposed for family or financial reasons to a particularly unprepossessing damsel and finds himself lucky enough to be rejected," Amery confessed to his diary.[30]

The American representative concluded that the War Cabinet had intended its overture to the Indian National Congress to fall through. "Cripps is sincere, knows this matter should be solved," Johnson cabled to Roosevelt. "He and Nehru could solve it in five minutes if Cripps had any freedom or authority. London wanted a Congress refusal." One last time, the president tried. On April 11, 1942, he cabled Churchill requesting that Cripps stay on in India for another attempt. Americans felt that "the deadlock has been caused by the unwillingness of the British Government to concede to the Indians the right of self-government, notwithstanding the willingness of the Indians to entrust technical military and naval defense control to the competent British authorities," Roosevelt wrote. He asked Churchill to instead make "a real offer and a fair offer" to the Indian people.[31]

No suggestion that the president made to the prime minister was "more wrathfully received," as biographer Robert E. Sherwood would recall Hopkins saying years later. Although it was 3 A.M. on a Sunday when the cable arrived, Churchill summoned Hopkins and stormed at him. A national government like the one the president proposed would "almost certainly demand the recall of all Indian troops from the Middle East," he charged. Hindus would conspire with the Japanese, allowing them to cross the country in exchange of military support against Muslims, princes, and Untouchables. If it would help with American opinion, the prime minister would give up his position and "retire to private life," but nothing whatsoever would change British policy.[32]

Hopkins was a man of frail health, and when the president heard of his late-night trial he ordered a general to put him to bed under armed guard for twenty-four hours. Roosevelt also received a telegram from Churchill, indicating that Cripps had already left India. In any case, the prime minister stated, he could not take responsibility for defending the colony against Japanese attack "if everything has again to be thrown into the melting pot at this critical juncture." The president's views meant a great deal to him, however. "Anything like a serious difference between you and me would break my heart and surely deeply injure both our countries at the height of this terrible struggle."[33]

The threat of discord that could harm the Allied effort finally silenced Roosevelt. A few months later, when a senior official urged the president to guarantee Indian independence, he replied: "You are right about India but it would be playing with fire if the British Empire were to tell me to mind my own business."[34]

In his memoir *The Hinge of Fate*, written after the war (which Roosevelt did not survive), Churchill described the president's proposal on India as "an act of madness" that fate had fortuitously rendered impossible to implement. "The human race cannot make progress without idealism, but idealism at other people's expense and without regard to the consequences of ruin and slaughter which fall upon millions of humble homes cannot be considered as its highest or noblest form," he wrote. The British could not have deserted the Indian people in their hour of need, "leaving them to anarchy or subjugation."[35]

IN EARLY APRIL 1942, Japanese airplanes showed up over Calcutta, dropping a few bombs and thousands of leaflets urging Indians to rise up against their overlords. Japanese bombers also attacked several coastal towns in southern India, which had no air protection at all, and sank two cruisers, a light carrier, a destroyer, and possibly twenty merchant ships in and around the Bay of Bengal. The colony possessed fourteen outdated bombers, which were useless against the aircraft carriers from which the Japanese were operating. "India can not repeat not be held against likely scale and method of Japanese attack," Wavell warned in a series of cables demanding immediate consignments of military equipment and trained troops.[36]

The prime minister perceived no such urgency. The Japanese would not be so foolish as to take on the subcontinent while still engaged in subduing China, Churchill told Wavell on April 18, 1942. Did the commander-in-chief "really think it likely that Japan would consider it worth while to send four or five divisions roaming about the Madras Presidency?" he asked. "What could be achieved comparable to the results obtainable by taking Ceylon or by pushing north into China and finishing off Chiang Kai-shek?" On May 4, Churchill remarked at a

War Cabinet meeting that the Japanese already had all the territory that their plans called for. Hence, the enemy was "unlikely to make a heavy attack either on Australia or on India. For why hasn't he done it earlier?"[37]

Unconvinced, Wavell protested that it was "sheer madness" to leave him with so little by way of men and materials: "India parted with all her trained troops for Mideast and Iraq and then sent half-trained troops to try to save Malaya and Burma and will take time to recover." He further requested that the few Indian officers who commanded British troops be permitted to discipline them—provoking a Churchillian outburst on the "poor much harassed British soldier having to face the extra humiliation of being ordered about by a brown man," as Amery recorded. Notes on the War Cabinet meeting of July 27 show that a War Office representative concurred with Churchill. The "face of white man in East is low enough and this is not the time to do it," he said, and cited "Gandhi's likely movement" as a further argument against enhancing the powers of Indian officers.[38]

At the Battle of Midway on June 4–6, 1942, American bombers had devastated the fleet of aircraft carriers from which the Japanese were operating in Southeast Asia, and days later Churchill had written that a Japanese invasion of India "seems extremely improbable at the moment." Within a few months, the British Raj had shifted its sights from a Japanese threat to India to a Congress uprising within India.[39]

CHURCHILL WAS CORRECT in his assessment that Japan was not interested in a full-scale invasion of the colony. China alone had proved indigestible to the python (as Hitler described his ally) and India was too large for it to tackle without help from other forces. Crucially, Axis strategists could not agree on how the colony fit into their long-term plans. The Japanese envisioned India as an independent, if subordinate, country at the periphery of their empire, which they called the Co-Prosperity Sphere. Should Japan have to invade India, in order to oust the Allies from a vital base, it would need an influential nationalist backed by a declaration of independence to reassure the highly politicized natives of Axis intentions. Germany held "the supreme trump card in the person of S. C. Bose," as historian Milan Hauner put it—and it refused to play along.

A linkup through Russia and Afghanistan with Japanese forces in India did feature among the German flights of fancy. Not Hitler's, though. He had mixed feelings about the Japanese triumph in the Far East, so much so that a German diplomat recorded that the führer would "gladly send the British twenty divisions to help throw back the yellow men." The Nazi boa was in any case choking on the Soviet Union, which it had attacked in June 1941.[40]

So for the remainder of 1942 and, as it would transpire, all of 1943, India was safe from attack. Instead of the experienced Indian divisions, which were still needed abroad, the War Office estimated that the colony could use thirty-four British battalions made up mostly of half-trained recruits. They could train in India to take on the Japanese sometime in the future, and meanwhile would uphold "internal security"—which meant combating Congress agitators. The Indian Army numbered 900,000 at the time, of whom a third were abroad, with 50,000 men being hired each month. The War Cabinet nevertheless expended valuable shipping resources to transport to the colony British soldiers who resembled their Indian counterparts in being inadequately trained to fight the Japanese. Those soldiers' immediate objective was to deal with the rebellion that everyone could see coming.[41]

IN MAY 1942, soldier Clive Branson arrived in India with the Royal Armoured Corps. He felt "very fit, and in good spirits," he wrote to his wife. Born in India to an army officer, he had been taken to England as a baby and now was returning at the age of thirty-five. In letters written over the next nine months, Branson would describe to his wife much that he saw and felt, providing a chronicle of the war in India through the eyes of a soldier with an acute sense of compassion.[42]

Branson's squadron was sent for training to the arid west of India. Gazing at the landscape, he was enthralled. "The other evening the sun was just setting making the whole sky a brilliant hard yellow. A labourer came past, his skin a brown black; round his head the folds of gleaming white cloth. The road, the dry earth, a pale mauve with strips of lemon-green sugar patches," Branson wrote. In the 1930s he had become a communist and volunteered to fight fascists in Spain, where he had spent eight months in a prison camp. By the time he was called up for World War II, Branson, a gifted painter, had a family. An aristocrat's daughter had given up a life of luxury to share his quarters in the poorest section of London and had also borne him a girl. But Branson hated fascism and did not regret going to war again.[43]

To his annoyance, all that his unit seemed to do in India was hang around waiting. At least Branson had time to explore his surroundings. Virtually all the other British soldiers were getting their first glimpse of the colony, and they were "filled with amazement at the appalling conditions in which the people live." Branson made friends with the few natives he met: the *chicko* or little kid who brought in hot tea many times a day and the laundry boy who returned his clothes clean and pressed. The food was excellent, the fruit plentiful; the Englishman enjoyed the dry heat and even, when it came, the rain, which gave the countryside "a lovely rich earth and green look."[44]

Not having the wherewithal to paint, Branson spent his free time learning Hindi. He chafed at the restrictions that prevented soldiers from visiting villages or getting to know ordinary people. And many of his compatriots treated Indians "in a way which not only makes one tremble for the future but which makes one ashamed of being one of them." Branson often had cause to defend a chicko, as when one boy burst into tears after being struck for not having understood a command in English.[45]

Most of the British soldiers came from working-class or rural backgrounds and, to their astonishment, were treated with contempt by white expatriates in India. Here they were, ordinary soldiers expected to lay down their lives for civilization, but when they were on leave in a city they had no hope of landing a room in one of the better hotels, all of which seemed to be owned by whites. Only officers were entertained there. Such discrimination had its positive side, Branson felt: it gave the newcomers a hint of what the natives had to put up with. He was surprised and pleased when, after an Indian soldier was killed in an accident, a sergeant opined that the man should be thought of not merely as "another black bastard out of the way" but as a human being with, perhaps, a wife and child.[46]

One night the squadron left for a two-day outing. Because the moon was full, the truck drivers switched off their headlights and coasted silently. Driving through a village, Branson caught a glimpse of peasants, the men all in white and the women "in brilliant colours, lit up by the moon," sitting in front of a stage with a painted backdrop and watching a play by the light of two lamps. That was all he could see. "But what ideas crowded through my brain as we went on through the night. Of Indian student youth going to the peasants of Bengal, showing them in plays how to unite against Japanese Fascism. . . . How I wanted to stay, to see the play through, and talk to the peasants about it! But our worlds are different, so I had to go on with the white sahibs in lorries."

When day dawned, Branson got his first extended look at the countryside of western India. "Oh, why am I here as a soldier and conqueror, and therefore the prisoner of my conquest?" The trucks drove by an endless expanse of fields, tilled only by bullocks, with not a tractor in sight. "Past village after village where human beings live in hovels; a bit of roof resting against an old stone wall, with mud floor; a shelter of matting laid over sticks, improved with bits of tin, old carpet, some tenting, perhaps; just high enough for the occupants to sit up in on their haunches." He had read in an armed forces' magazine about the benefits that Empire had brought. But to see is to believe, wrote Branson. "Let our imperialists boast . . . never will any of us who have come to India for this war forget the unbelievable, indescribable poverty in which we have found people living *wherever* we went, and in millions." If those at home knew the truth, surely "there would be a hell of a row—because these conditions are maintained in the name of the British."[47]

AS SOLDIERS POURED into India, and reports of forced evacuation of villages and destruction of boats flowed into his ashram, Gandhi became increasingly alarmed. "I see no Indian freedom peeping through all this preparation for the so-called defence of India," he commented in *Harijan* on April 26, 1942. "It is a preparation pure and simple for the defence of the British Empire, whatever may be asserted to the contrary." The abortive Cripps mission had convinced him that the United Kingdom was not about to relinquish its "stranglehold" on India, and the preparations for war indicated that this grasp was instead being tightened. Gandhi knew of Japanese atrocities in China and had no wish to exchange "one form of slavery for another possibly much worse," he wrote. He believed, however, that if the Japanese were being drawn to India that was because it was an Allied base: removing the British would eliminate this "bait."[48]

The Indian National Congress was also receiving alarming accounts of the scorched earth program in Bengal; in July it exhorted the people to defy the requisitioning of boats and vehicles unless they received adequate compensation. Amery saw the proclamation as a petty ploy to obstruct the war effort and wrote to Churchill urging prompt action:

> *Twice armed is he that has his quarrel just;*
> *But thrice armed he who gets his blow in fust.*

The viceroy notified British army and air force units to stand by for a crackdown. Not wanting to strike before he had a provocation, he waited until spies could confirm that the Congress was planning a program of civil disobedience.[49]

Meanwhile, Chiang Kai-shek heard from Gandhi and informed Roosevelt that an uprising could still be averted if he would persuade the United Kingdom "to restore to India her complete freedom." Roosevelt forwarded the letter to Churchill, asking only how the president should respond. The prime minister replied angrily that the president should "lend no countenance to putting pressure upon His Majesty's Government." From then on, a resigned Roosevelt ignored pleas to intervene that came from several quarters, including a cable from American writer Louis Fischer, who had interviewed Gandhi and who now warned that a "terrible disaster may be impending in India."[50]

ON AUGUST 8, 1942, the Indian National Congress, with much hesitation and doubt, adopted what came to be called the Quit India resolution. It was in part a last-ditch appeal to the United States. British rule, the document stated, was "degrading and enfeebling India and making her progressively less capable of defending herself." If granted independence, Indians would eagerly throw in their lot with the Allies; but if this plea were denied, the Congress would sanction a nonviolent struggle "on the widest possible scale." The party asked the people to hold together under Gandhi's guidance "as disciplined soldiers of Indian freedom." Should a time come when the leaders could no longer lead, everyone who desired liberation "must be his own guide urging him on along the hard road where there is no resting place and which leads ultimately to the independence of India."[51]

Early the next morning, all the senior Congress leaders were swept off to jail. Gandhi managed to call out the words "karenge ya marenge," meaning Do or Die, as a final message to his countrymen before he was imprisoned. That evening, Amery spoke over BBC radio. In addition to the usual strikes and demonstrations, he said, the Congress had envisaged cutting telegraph and telephone lines, picketing army recruitment centers and government offices, and otherwise paralyzing the government. Such actions amounted to sabotaging the war effort. The broadcast successfully turned American and British public opinion against Gandhi and the Congress.

Amery's statement was in accordance with a War Cabinet resolve, from as early as September 14, 1940, that "if conflict with Congress should arise, it should appear as an outcome of war necessity rather than as a political quarrel unrelated to the war." Although the radical action of paralyzing the government had indeed been suggested at a regional Congress meeting, the national party had not endorsed it. But Amery's broadcast had an unintended effect. The sudden arrest of Congress leaders had left them with no opportunity to decide, let alone explain to their subordinates, exactly what form civil disobedience should take: Amery did it for them. Every Indian who heard the tactics he detailed took them as instructions direct from the Congress—and the very next day the country exploded in a seemingly coordinated rebellion. Enraged crowds attacked government offices, destroyed telegraph poles, and damaged railway tracks. In Bihar two Canadian airmen were lynched, leading to a retaliatory attack in which aircraft strafed crowds of protesters, killing several hundred.[52]

Clive Branson followed all of this unrest closely. "Discussions go on night and day with views expressed ranging from two extremes: (a) I came to fight the Japs not the Indians, to (b) It would be all right to have a go at Gandhi and his Hindus; we should get some practice like the Japs got in China," Branson related to his wife. Being a communist, he dismissed Gandhi as bourgeois and saw no virtue in pacifism; but when it came to the Quit India movement he felt that the problem was not so much Gandhi as his absence. The Labour Party had asked the Congress to call off civil disobedience—"how *brilliant*!! Doesn't the Labour Party know that the Congress leaders are in jail, and that is why the rioting is going on, anarchistic because without leadership," he railed.[53]

On August 20, 1942, when soldiers from his squadron were dispatched to "maintain law and order" in a nearby town, Branson stole off to a canteen to be by himself. "This sort of warfare is so distasteful to me that I take every care not to be detailed," he explained to his wife. Perusal of the newspapers soon convinced him that British imperialists had deliberately provoked the rebellion, which offered "the long-sought opportunity to smash the nationalist movement." To prohibit the Indians from fighting the war as free Allies was to damage the war effort, he opined, for now the natives cared not at all about the aggressor at the doorstep but only wanted to be rid of the one in the room. "We English fellows came out here to fight the Japs and face the possibility of finding a grave," Branson continued. "We did not come here to be killed by Indians provoked by the insane reactionary policy of Amery and Co."[54]

Figuring that the viceroy would "need as much British strength as possible in these difficult times," Churchill stopped a division from being moved out of India as per an earlier schedule. There was no chance of the Japanese arriving during the monsoon, which allowed six weeks for 222,000 policemen and 57 battalions of soldiers to contain an uprising by essentially unarmed civilians. By May 1943, as many as 105 battalions would be involved—all of which were fed, clothed, sheltered, remunerated, and largely equipped at the expense of Indians. Meeting Churchill at a train station, Amery found the prime minister "looking very fit and in capital spirits," as he wrote in his diary. "His only remark to me was 'We've got them on the run.'"[55]

SOON AFTER, HOWEVER, an Indian member of the viceroy's council met Churchill and found him rumbling with rage. "What have we to be ashamed of in our Government of India? Why should we be apologetic or say that we are prepared to go out at the instance of some jackanapes?" the prime minister fumed. "If we have ever to quit India, we shall quit it in a blaze of glory, and the chapter that shall be ended then will be the most glorious chapter of that country, not merely in relation to the past but equally in relation to the future, however distant that may be. That will be my statement on India tomorrow. No apology, no quitting, no idea of weakening or scuttling." That very day, while discussing his forthcoming speech with Amery, Churchill exclaimed, "I hate Indians. They are a beastly people with a beastly religion."[56]

The prime minister's euphoria had rapidly soured into resentment because of the vital concession he had been forced to make: India would get dominion status after the war. With the American president prodding him, the offer would be hard to rescind. And once India became a dominion, it would likely opt for full independence—the ferocity of the repression had ensured that much. The tighter he grasped, the more surely the prize slipped away.

In his broadcast on September 10, 1942, the prime minister announced that the Congress had finally thrown off its cloak of nonviolence. The conspirators, he asserted, had received help from "Japanese fifth-column work on a widely extended scale and with special direction to strategic points." But there was no cause to worry, in part because "the numbers of white soldiers now in that country, though very small compared with its size and population, are larger than at any time in the British connection." The speech infuriated Branson, who wrote home that it was "just filth," without even the virtue of invented evidence to support the case. Despite Churchill's insistence, the secret service had failed to turn up any links between fascists and Gandhi or other Congress leaders—there were none.[57]

Summing up the Quit India movement in *The Hinge of Fate*, Churchill wrote: "What was at one time feared to become the most serious rebellion in India since the Sepoy Mutiny of 1857, fizzled out in a few months with hardly any loss of life." In Midnapore district of Bengal, however, the uprising would lead to a lethal confrontation with authorities. It would also give birth to a secret government that would endure for two tortuous years, through famine of an intensity not seen since the Victorian era.[58]

CHAPTER FOUR

At Any Price

The news of Gandhi's arrest left the nationalists of Midnapore stunned. That August of 1942, after much discussion in their rural hideouts, the top leaders of the district's Congress—brawny, mustachioed Satish Chandra Samanta and his close friend, the small and sharp-witted Ajoy Kumar Mukhopadhyay—decided on a course of action. On September 29, 1942, the people of Tamluk subdivision, where the Congress organization was strongest, would take over all government offices in the locale. Unarmed crowds would have to face down armed police and perhaps even soldiers.

Sushil Dhara, the insurgency's designated warrior, had built up a cadre of youths who seemed ready to risk their lives at his behest. But Dhara had been trying hard to live by Gandhian precepts, and he demanded to know how the planned program squared with a policy of nonviolence. So the elders sent him on a risky trip to Calcutta to meet a respected Gandhian educator. If enormous crowds approached government buildings, the guru postulated, the occupants might surrender without a fight. He also showed Dhara a publication in Hindi: in Gandhi's absence, those of his disciples who had evaded capture were freely interpreting his enigmatic instructions—Do or Die—and their readings of their leader's injunctions leaned increasingly toward allowing violence as a means of moving toward independence. Dhara returned to Midnapore "with a cloudless mind" and threw himself into planning the day of liberation. "I searched within my mind and found in it no fear," he would write. From among his recruits he selected fifty whom he judged were also ready to face death.[1]

On September 8, Dhara heard that police shootings had claimed
three lives at a riverside rice mill at Donipur, near Tamluk. Arriving at
the site, he found a few thousand agitated people surrounding the building. The small police force was inside, as were the bodies of the slain
men. The day before, villagers had resolved to stop a barge loaded with
30 tons of rice from being dispatched upstream to the Ispahani Company, and women had used their conch shells to summon hundreds of
people to the riverbank. The mill owners had sent for help, and an
officer with five armed policemen had arrived the next morning. The
villagers had asked to buy two kilograms of rice each, but the mill owners
had refused. When the angry crowd entered the mill, the police had
fired in panic. Dhara advised the villagers to distribute the rice among
the needy but to let the officer and the other policemen go. Leaving a
few subordinates at the site, he walked back to his hideout.[2]

Dhara's route lay through the town of Mohisadal, and past the home
of the very police officer whose life he had just saved. It was 11 P.M.
when he was striding by, and he spied a forlorn woman, clearly the officer's wife, staring out of the window. She called to him, asking if he had
seen any trouble on the road. "A wicked idea came into my head," Dhara
related later. Pretending to be just a passerby, he told her of having
seen a large crowd holding a police officer hostage and threatening to
burn him alive. A Congress leader named Sushil Dhara, he said, had
been firing up the crowd by saying all kinds of angry things. Leaving
the poor woman close to tears, he went on his way. Whatever the morals
of this prank, it was the last time Dhara would do anything playful. As
for the villagers, thirteen of them would serve up to two years of hard
labor each, on charges of looting.[3]

ON THE NIGHT of September 28, thousands of men armed with
spades, shovels, saws, and axes slipped out of their huts to gather in
darkness on the arterial roads of southern Midnapore. According to a
history of the insurgency written by one of its participants, Radhakrishna
Bari, they dug gaping holes in the road surfaces, broke through culverts,
and sawed laboriously through ancient roadside trees—dropping them,

branches and leaves and all, onto the path. "One guy told me he was bitten by a snake, but he threw it off and just kept on felling," recalled Kumudini Dakua. "Fortunately it wasn't poisonous." There were no electricity poles to worry about, but the men snapped telegraph and telephone poles and slashed all wires within reach.[4]

Through a network of informers, word reached the local police that the people were about to take back the government. Discovering that all communication lines were down, they used the wireless set at a military observation post outside Tamluk to warn the district magistrate in Midnapore town, to the northwest. Two truckloads of troops set off toward Tamluk, only to find the road impassable. Soldiers descended from the trucks, got people out of nearby hamlets, and set them to work at gunpoint, repairing breaches and removing trees.[5]

Dawn found three processions, from the north, northwest, and south, making their way toward Tamluk town. (The Rupnarayan River flowed along the eastern side of Tamluk, blocking approach from that direction.) The people sang, shouted slogans, and waved green, white, and orange Congress flags; no one had weapons. "We'd hoped that the soldiers wouldn't make it. If so, we had word that the police would surrender," Bari would later recall. The son of a poor farmer, he had just left his Calcutta college to join the Midnapore insurgency and would become its chronicler.

But when the crowd from the northwest detoured into a soccer field to listen to instructions, the military trucks pushed past it to reach Tamluk at 2:30 P.M. The demonstrators, arriving at the town's police station half an hour later, found themselves facing rows of constables with *lathis*—bamboo rods, lethal in trained hands—and, behind them, soldiers with guns. The police charged into the crowd, but because it continued to edge forward, the soldiers fired, killing three. At about the same time, the southern procession reached a twenty-foot bridge spanning a canal, and sepoys stationed on the north side fired without warning. Many of the wounded started crying out for water: most of them were Hindu, and they believed a sip of holy water before death ensured salvation.[6]

From a lane to the right came a prostitute, Sabitri Dasi, with a *ghoti*, or small brass vessel, from which she began pouring water into the mouths of the injured and dying. Sepoys raced forward and shouted at her to stop. Dasi withdrew to her hut and emerged holding aloft a *boti*, a fearsome two-foot knife set into a wooden board, which she normally used to chop straw for her cow. *"Ek hatey ghoti, ar ek hatey boti"*—in one hand she held a bowl, in the other hand a blade—remembered Krishna Chaitanya Mahapatro, a teenager who was jammed into the panicked crowd at the back. Dasi looked like an avenging goddess. Behind her came a train of fisherwomen brandishing their own bloodstained botis. Perhaps stunned at the apparition, the sepoys left them alone.[7]

The third procession, from the north, had set its sights on Tamluk's courthouse, which the marchers regarded as a seat of institutionalized oppression. They approached the building by a narrow road, between the steep bank of a pond on one side and a row of shops on the other. The policemen and soldiers raised their lathis and rifles and charged. Seeing the youths ahead hesitate, a woman in the middle of the procession, seventy-three-year-old Matongini Hazra, took charge. An ardent follower of Gandhi, she had once spent six months in jail for displaying a black flag of protest to a visiting viceroy. Now Hazra grabbed the largest tricolor Congress flag and climbed onto a nearby porch. "Cowards!" she shouted at her compatriots. "Return home, I will go on alone. I will not look back to see if anyone came." Then she strode forward, along with several women who were blowing conch shells. Their summons reminded the crowd of its mission, and it re-formed. Those at Hazra's side would later report that the first gunshot hit her left hand, and that she took the flag in her right and kept on walking; a second shot hit her right hand, and she grasped the flag against her chest with both arms and kept on walking; the third shot passed through her temple. She died along with several others, including three teenage boys.[8]

AT SUTAHATA, TWENTY miles southeast of Tamluk, the protesters arrived at the small police station to find three constables standing in front, their hands folded in supplication. Their superior officer had left for Tamluk to seek reinforcements but had failed to return, so the three had decided to surrender, while three other constables had gone off to hide. The leaders of the march took them into custody along with their guns, while the people set fire to the straw-thatched station, its records, and the bundles of cash they found inside.

"As we were leaving, two fireballs suddenly appeared in the sky," Kumudini Dakua remembered. The authorities, unable to send reinforcements by road, had dispatched two aircraft to drop incendiary bombs on the crowd. "We were so excited at that moment, we didn't care," she said. The bombs passed over the police station and fell into a flooded field nearby, exploding in a shower of fire and water. Later that day the elders gave their police captives homespun cottons to wear, handed them a little money for passage, and put them on a ferry toward Calcutta.[9]

At Mohisadal, ten miles southeast of Tamluk, Sushil Dhara led his fifty youths, uniformed but unarmed, toward the police station. A crowd of people followed the cadets—as did volunteers marked with red crosses on their white garments, who were to aid any people who might be wounded by gunfire and convey them on makeshift stretchers to a schoolroom where two doctors waited with supplies. Dhara had heard that the small police force in Mohisadal expected to be overwhelmed and planned to surrender. But when he was still a mile away, he learned that a smaller procession from the east side had already neared the station and was being shot at.[10]

Sixteen-year-old Chitto Samonto of Kalikakundu was in the front lines of the eastern procession. He had signed up with the Congress six months earlier, and had been asked to round up the people of Kalikakundu and its small neighboring village, Boksichawk, for the march. Chitto's mother came from Boksichawk, so the youngster was de facto nephew to all of its male residents, whether they were related or not. A villager named Bholanath Maity had offered to come along. "Don't know what emotion came over him; he said, 'Nephew, I will go,'" recalled Samonto. "He was a very poor man, quite illiterate. Some days he got some food, other days nothing. He bought and sold bananas in local markets." Srihorichandro Das, from the border of Kalikakundu, "said, 'I too will come. Who cares what will happen!' As if, living in such hardship, he didn't place much stock in life. Sometimes he'd lie around drunk" on date palm brew, Samonto remembered.

Most of the two villages had marched, including Chitto's mother, elder sister, and uncles. His brother was attending the march in Sutahata (southeast of Kalikakundu), while his father had stayed home. People from several other villages had joined them, so that a procession of about 2,000 had passed the elephant stalls of Mohisadal's palace and approached the police station from the southeastern side. They were about one hundred yards away when the first bullets hit.

Bholanath Maity fell. "He was right in front of me. I saw he was all bloody," said Samonto. "We were terrified, ran off in all directions. I hid inside a bamboo thicket by the lane." Sheikh Surabuddin, Sheikh Kumaruddin, and Sudam Chandra Das of Kalikakundu got bullets in the knees and thighs. Seeing that his flock had fled, one of the leaders, Manoranjon Bhoumik, somehow obtained tin roofing sheets from the bazaar and called to the youths to try again. Chitto and others emerged from the bushes and, holding the sheets ahead like shields, tried to move forward. He was scared, Samonto confessed, but he felt obliged to obey his leader: "I was a cadet by that time, not like the other villagers."

Bhoumik exhorted his forces, shouting, "Look, the police station is taken, see they set fire to a building there!" Smoke was indeed curling into the western sky, over Mohisadal town. A few of the cadre tried to press forward, but the bullets pierced the tin. "Only one person was shooting at us," Samonto said. "You could see him—he was running this way and that." It was the commander of the Mohisadal raja's private force. As a staunch supporter of the British Raj, the zamindar had bolstered the police with his personal guard of Gurkha soldiers, led by a retired military man known as G Sahib.

After they heard of the shooting, Dhara and his boys sprinted a mile until they were close to the police station, approaching from the south. Immediately they came under fire from the Mohisadal palace guards, and a few of the youths fell. Someone brought doors and tin roofs; hiding behind these, the unarmed attackers tried to crawl forward. But the guards continued to fire, and G Sahib himself shot at Dhara several times. Through all this, the volunteers—marked with their red crosses—gathered the wounded and bore them away, although they, too, came under fire.

Dhara knew that police records had been secreted at the home of the same police officer whose life, just three weeks earlier, he had used his influence to save. Now he did not feel generous. He ordered that the house be burned, and an enormous flame rose into the sky. The bizarre battle at the police station lasted until sundown, when the rebels retreated, having failed to occupy the building. The crowd had managed to unfurl the tricolor at other government offices in Mohisadal. But twelve had died, and at least two people were unaccounted for—left behind where they had fallen, in front of the police station.[11]

One of the wounded, Subhas Samanta, fought all night to regain consciousness. A bullet had entered his chest and emerged through his arm without killing him, but he had lost much blood. Hearing his groans, a police sepoy lifted him off the pile of bodies outside the station, splashed water on his face, laid him on a cot, and fed him some bread. In the morning the sepoy's shift ended. A police officer arrived to find Samanta on the cot and kicked him off onto the dirt, where he lay all day without food or water. That night the sepoy again tended his patient. Three days and nights thus passed, after which Samanta and another wounded man were removed to the hospital in Tamluk. The other man died, but Subhas Samanta would recover and spend two years in jail. Astonishingly, the sepoy, Sinhara Singh, was transferred to work as a guard at the same prison, where he continued to protect the man whose life he had saved.[12]

After the debacle, stretcher-bearers had borne a grievously injured boy, Bonkim Maity, to the makeshift clinic in a schoolhouse. A bullet had entered through his belt into his lower stomach and lodged against his spine. It would take a major operation to save him but the police could be coming at any moment. Volunteers carried the rebel to a village, where the clinic doctor operated to remove the bullet. For a week the schoolboy bled heavily through the anus; but then, almost by a miracle, he started to recover. He was spirited from hut to hut for months to evade the police, who never caught up with him or his rescuers. As a result of his injuries, he would suffer from cramps and complications for more than a decade.[13]

Chitto's uncles brought the banana-seller's body back to Boksichawk. "He had a wife and two small sons, they had a terrible time afterward," remembered Samonto. "Later, after independence, they got some pension. Srihorichandro Das, how he died I don't know, we never found him. He went missing. We heard some bodies were lying around and the police dumped them into the Rupnarayan." Sheikh Surabuddin, made lame by his injuries, could no longer earn a living and begged for his food until, after independence, Samonto was able to get him a freedom fighter's pension. Sheikh Kumaruddin never received that pension, and he would beg for the rest of his life.

Nandigram, in the southwest corner of Tamluk subdivision, had been in turmoil since the middle of September 1942, because police teams searching for Congress volunteers had killed six villagers. To give tempers a chance to cool, the region's leaders had put off the march until September 30. On that day, a procession tried to approach the town's police station, and five fell to bullets.[14]

The events of the two days were disastrous, not just for the rebels themselves but also for the credibility of their creed of nonviolence. Just several dozen soldiers and guards with guns had easily upheld the British Raj against perhaps 100,000 marchers—15 percent of the Tamluk subdivision's population. At least 36 villagers had died, and hundreds had been injured. Nonviolence could perhaps take credit for keeping the death toll down: no doubt the defenders would have fired more rounds, or aimed more carefully, if the people had targeted them rather than the institutions they guarded. Surely it was also true that if the crowd had harmed the sepoys and officers, most of whom were their own countrymen, the fight for freedom would have degenerated into a civil war, which in turn would have portended a bitter future for India's people. And even as people mourned their dead, counted their blessings, and pondered the next move, their situation was about to get very much worse.[15]

THE POLICE ESTABLISHED camps in rural Midnapore and began to hunt for fugitives and set fire to their homes. Rather than determining the innocence or guilt of certain individuals, the government imposed fines on entire Hindu communities for political subversion. Often, when they were raiding better-off Hindu households, the police encouraged poor Muslims from neighboring villages to come along with them and loot—with the apparent intent of stirring up communal hostilities. All over the country, criminals were being released from prison to make room for Quit India activists. According to Kumudini Dakua, many violent offenders returned to their former village homes and began to prey on the people and inform for the police.[16]

Nature, too, began to prey on Bengal. One morning in October 1942 it started raining fiercely. Sushil Dhara, who had been lazing with friends under a flimsy open-air thatch, attempted to seek refuge at a nearby house. The wind lifted him and deposited him in a pond. He tried crawling along the path. Alternately flattened and knocked sideways by the gusts, he had ventured some ninety yards when "it was as if someone picked me up and smashed me" against a massive tamarind tree that had fallen earlier. Dhara clung to the trunk, dazed and shivering, until he gathered enough strength to sprint to safety. He could not return to fetch the others from under the thatch, who included an elderly couple who were not strong enough to brave the cyclone.

At midnight the wind abated, and Dhara emerged with a lantern to find that his earlier shelter had been pounded into the ground. His companions were safe; they had submerged themselves in a ditch to evade the wind and had waded and swum to a neighbor's house. But the banks of the Rupnarayan River had burst and the ocean had swept in. Salt water covered the entire landscape. The cyclone had destroyed virtually every tree and house on the horizon.

THE DAY AFTER the Mohisadal palace guards shot up his cadre, Dhara had organized a retaliatory looting of one of the royal storehouses, five miles north of Kalikakundu. Chitto Samonto and his brother had each managed to carry off a sack of rice. From part of this stash their mother had made *muri*, or puffed rice, for the festival of the goddess Durga. During the storm, they stored the muri in a tin, placed Chitto's six-day-old nephew inside a trunk (so that if water overwhelmed their two-story mud house, the boy would float away), and huddled with the baby on the attic floor. Chitto and his brother tied the beams with thick rope and took turns holding the roof down against the wind. "We had a knife to cut a hole in the straw thatch if the house collapsed," Samonto recounted. "Then we would all climb onto the roof and float to safety."

The neighbors came over after their hut had collapsed. "So much screaming and wailing, it was awful. Someone was saying, 'My cow was swept away'; someone else was saying, 'Where is my mother-in-law, I couldn't find her!'" All through the night they had tried to see how high the flood had reached. "You could tell it was sea water—it was glittering in the dark," Samonto said. In the morning dead cows and uprooted trees floated by, as well as a wooden bridge; strangers had fought the brothers for it and taken it away. They had all eaten the muri and "caught a huge carp right there, off the porch." After the ponds over-flowed, the fish the villagers reared were enjoying a brief spell of un-bounded freedom.

A few days later the water receded—revealing a layer of sand that squashed the rice plants. The new crop, due to be harvested that winter, was gone. People began to loot, Samonto said: "Forty to sixty of them would go to a landowner's house and demand rice." The Samontos' own plot was small, but the family also cultivated a large field belonging to the Mohisadal rajas, receiving a share of its yield. Still, the landowner's minions took away all that could be salvaged. "We managed to sweep up some scattered grains and keep it for seed," Samonto remembered. The rice from the looted storehouse lasted them another month.

No more cereal was going to be available for upward of a year—until the next crop could be sown in the monsoon of 1943 and harvested at the end of that December. Everyone in Midnapore dates the famine from the day of the cyclone, October 16, 1942.

ON THE NIGHT of the storm, villagers of coastal Midnapore had sheltered the wounded pilot of a small aircraft that had fallen near Sutahata, as well as soldiers whose encampments had been devastated by the cyclone. But the subdivisional officer in Tamluk, the most senior civil servant present, had refused to lift the town's nighttime curfew so that refugees from the flood could seek shelter there, or to release government boats for rescuing people stranded on rooftops and in trees. In the following days, Midnapore's district magistrate asserted that any cyclone relief should be "withheld from the disaffected villages until the people hand over the stolen guns and give an undertaking that they will take no further part in any subversive movement." A British police officer protested that prompt government aid might win back an estranged populace. But the first relief workers to arrive, from a Calcutta-based private charity, were arrested and no other succor came for weeks—on orders, it seemed, from Sir John Herbert, the governor of Bengal.[17]

In Calcutta, an army general summoned Ian Stephens, editor of the city's leading newspaper, *The Statesman*, and asked him not to report on the devastation, in case the Japanese should guess that the coast was undefended. (The cyclone was scarcely a secret to the Japanese, who were repeatedly broadcasting that it had killed more than 100,000 in its first hour alone.) And the Bengal government reported to New Delhi that the calamity had left the "rebel spirit unbroken"—implying that the task remained to be finished. Two weeks after the storm, a group of ministers from Calcutta arrived in Mohisadal to survey the damage and, from the palace rooftop, saw plumes of smoke rising in the distance. The police had been hunting for fugitives in Kalikakundu; having failed to find them, the keepers of the law had set their homes on fire.[18]

At the time of the storm, Nirmala Kuila of Kalikakundu and her family were better off than most and had grain stored in two golas, she recalled. The rice had escaped the flood. But on October 30, 1942, a police team led by a feared superintendent named Nolini Raha had arrived in search of Kuila's nephew. They had not found him, and had instead arrested her husband and brother-in-law. Wartime shortages of fuel allowed few villagers to light lanterns at night, but the police had kerosene, which they had sprayed onto the thatch and fired with flaming torches. They burned down all fourteen huts of the extended Kuila family—the entire hamlet of Kuilapara—along with all the rice.[19]

At the time Kuila had an infant, less than six months old. With the men gone to prison, her sisters-in-law saved her and the baby by finding enough food to allow her to produce milk. They had continued to live in the charred remains of their hamlet, which was open to the sun and rain. "Where else will we stay?" she asked. "When there were storms, I would clasp my baby in my arms and cry." Not until the politicians who toured Midnapore had returned to Calcutta and threatened to publicize the extent of cyclone damage did the government relent. Eighteen days after the event, on November 3, 1942, *The Statesman* briefly noted that a storm and tidal wave had killed an estimated 11,000 in Bengal. The unofficial count was 30,000. Most of the dead were from a coastal area of Midnapore known as Contai, southwest of Tamluk subdivision, which had borne the brunt of a twenty-foot storm surge.[20]

"Hundreds of us insurgents could easily hide in the ravaged countryside," Dhara would write, "but when I contemplated the suffering that the people faced, I felt utterly overwhelmed." Satish Samanta organized villagers to repair the banks of the Rupnarayan, somehow procuring *muri* and *chire* (flattened rice) to feed everyone while they worked. "We built eight miles of embankments out of mud," recalled Radhakrishna Bari. After a month or so the government set up relief centers in the towns, but some who collected rice there complained that the police followed them home to smash pots and trample on the cooked food. A government relief worker charged that by day he was expected to provide succor, and by night he had to indicate to the police and the military the villages that had received food, so that the communities could then be punished.[21]

In response to these actions, on December 17, 1942, the rebels set up their own government for the region. Drawing inspiration from a happier past, they called it the Tamrolipto Jatiyo Sorkar, or the Tamluk

National Government. In the future it would merge with a free government of India, a newsletter announced, but for the time being the
president was Satish Samanta.[22]

The teenage Bari began to compose the government's newsletter,
called *Biplabi* (Revolutionary), using news that couriers brought from
diverse corners of the district. His elders provided the editorials. Late
at night, on the attic floor of a mud house, Bari would print the sheets
on an old hand-operated Roneo duplicator. Most copies were distributed
in the villages, but local businessmen smuggled some to Calcutta in
consignments of betel leaf. The renegade government also set up civil
courts that operated with the consent of all parties. More menacingly,
it boasted a "national militia" headed by Sushil Dhara—who would also
come to run secret tribunals that tried, convicted, and sentenced informers and other allies of the British, usually in absentia.

Ajoy Mukhopadhyay, the finance minister of the rebel government,
instructed Dhara to serve notices on selected landowners, demanding
cash in amounts commensurate with the extent to which they were
deemed to collaborate with the authorities. Most paid right away, and
Mukhopadhyay ordered the "arrest" of those who did not. (Among the
leaders of the Tamluk government, he was probably the least committed
to Gandhian values.) Dhara also forced landowners to share any excess
rice with the villagers.[23]

The Tamluk government's officials got no pay, but they did get food.
"We went on strict rations, only a little rice and lentils, and as much
vegetable as we liked," related Bari. "Our leaders gave away most of the
rice we could get. They also thought of other kinds of food, encouraged
people to grow pumpkins. The silt that the flood had brought was very
fertile—I never saw such a crop of pumpkins in my life. Only the runners who brought the mail were allowed all the rice they could eat, for
they had to go far. It was very hard work."

Sushil Dhara could eat staggering quantities of food—on one occasion he downed 150 *pithe*, or filled crepes. Having to trek tens of
miles each day, he found the ration very painful and debilitating, and
would sometimes be discovered by his soldiers leaning on his stick in

the middle of a path, fast asleep. If there was a benefit to their deprivation, it was that the rebels became as skinny as everyone else, the
easier to blend in.

"YOU KNOW THAT Calcutta is being bombed," Clive Branson wrote
to his wife in early January 1943. "But do you know that an acute food
crisis is raging throughout Bengal?" Branson was on leave in Bombay,
where his hotel served ample food: "breakfast, lunch and dinner are all
five course meals." But reading the newspapers made him melancholy.
"I fear that we may again be called out to maintain law and order—
don't misunderstand me—not to shoot the speculators, landlords, government officials, but to deal with the angry people" who were rioting
for food.[24]

The price of rice in Bengal had jumped after the cyclone, and in
February 1943 official policy gave it a further, lethal boost. Leonard G.
Pinnell headed the Bengal government's Department of Civil Supplies,
which was charged with acquiring rice for Calcutta's "priority classes"—
employees of the government and of firms deemed essential to the war
effort. His task, supported by requisition from northern Bengal, had
begun well enough. But at Christmas of 1942, Japanese aircraft bombed
Calcutta, causing suppliers to down their shutters and laborers to pile
their bundles on their heads and stream out. Pinnell had to do something
drastic. "It had become a fight for survival, for collapse in Calcutta—
not only the headquarters of Government, but with its port, its railways,
and its industrial area—would have been a disaster for the Province as
a whole, and for the successful prosecution of the war," he wrote in an
unpublished memoir. He forcibly acquired stocks of rice in the city—
inadvertently driving all remaining supplies underground.[25]

What happened next is best told in the words of another civil servant, Binay Ranjan Sen, who was entrusted with overseeing cyclone
relief in Midnapore. (A decade later, Sen would head the United Nations
Food and Agriculture Organization.) Pinnell was supposed to provide
Sen's operation with grain, but cyclone relief was getting only a quarter
of its requirements, Sen told the famine commission: "I could not pos-

sibly carry on with such meager supplies." On February 13, 1943, however, he was instructed to no longer rely on Pinnell but instead to buy what rice he could on the market. The Civil Supplies Department could not fulfill even its primary task of feeding the war effort, Sen explained. When that department's officials found their reserves to be critically short, "they instructed their agents to go to any place and purchase at any price" and store the rice on behalf of the government. The alternative to such desperate acquisitions was to use the police to seize grain from rural areas, which would "probably lead to much violence," Pinnell confirmed in his memoir.[26]

Because there were no limits to what the administration would pay, rice prices immediately escalated. Worse, several other bodies—the Bengal Chamber of Commerce, the railways, the Government of India, and the army—were also told to fend for themselves. (The Bengal Chamber of Commerce comprised mainly British-owned firms, dealing in ordnance manufacture, jute, coal, banking, tea, tobacco, and other industries, all of which were deemed essential for the war effort.) Armed with vast quantities of paper money, these entities began to vie with one another to buy up the winter crop. Sen joined the competition.

"Every morning one or two of my men came to me to say that Mr. MacInnes"—a former bank employee who was working for Civil Supplies—"had offered say about Rs. 22 and why should I not buy at Rs. 21 per maund," Sen related. (A maund is equivalent to 37.4 kilograms.) Just a few days earlier, a man from central Bengal had offered Sen rice at 13 or 14 rupees a maund. But the "same afternoon he found that the price went up to Rs. 15 and he could not keep up the contract," Sen continued. "This shows that the prices in the morning were not the same as the prices in the evening. In that way the prices went up within a few days to nearly double." Civil servant Olaf Martin confirmed, in his unpublished memoir, that the authorities were asking agents to buy rice and store it for the government in private warehouses, and that "every large Government purchase helped to raise prices still further." The middlemen were playing the bureaus and firms against one another to extract enormous profits.[27]

The absence of boats hampered the trade in grain, but the railway carriages that took troops and their equipment out of the city could bring rice on the return trip. That meant that the sky-high prices in Calcutta vacuumed rice out of rural marketplaces and into storehouses, where it awaited transport to the city. In Bengal, half the crop went to rice mills and thereupon to the rural or urban market; the other half, which village women husked by hand, stayed mainly with landowners. By the spring of 1943 almost all the machine-milled rice seems to have ended up with the government and its agents, as well as some part of the hand-milled rice. A district official would subsequently tell the commission investigating the famine that even the larger landowners had very little rice left early that year: "Whatever stock was available had been bought up at fantastic prices by military contractors and speculators." Of the 10.5 million Bengali families that depended on agriculture for their livelihood, four-fifths owned too little land to feed themselves in a normal year, earning what more grain they could by working on plots owned by wealthier families. With the landowners carefully husbanding the remnants of their stock, the landless would starve.[28]

Later that February, Sen could find only two men, each with a maund of rice, selling their wares in Geokhali, a market town that normally supplied much of Tamluk subdivision (including Kalikakundu). Quite possibly some rice still remained in Midnapore, a cyclone relief worker would later tell the famine commission, but if so the Ispahani Company controlled most of it. In December 1942, this relief worker had seen close to 20,000 tons of rice stacked at a rice mill near the railway station at Contai. But the mill owners had refused to sell him any because they were under government orders to store it for the agents. Every grain of rice that made it to that mill through normal channels of trade was earmarked for Calcutta, the relief worker would charge. Over the two months during which he had seen the grain stacked at the rice mill, the price of rice in Contai had risen by three times.[29]

In a replay of the famine of 1770, rice was being extracted from the countryside to feed the army and the city of Calcutta. If instead the harvest had been distributed evenly, the epidemic of widespread hunger would have been deferred to late 1943—at least in those districts of Bengal that were unaffected by scorched earth or cyclone. But the lifting of price controls and the panicked purchases precipitated famine right away, and everywhere. The authorities had been faced with a stark choice, as Pinnell would confess to the famine commission. It was either "death of a large number of people in the rural area," he said, or "chaos in the city," which would have impaired war production and services. "The first choice was taken."[30]

By the end of February, district officials were reporting widespread starvation in the villages of eastern Bengal and urging immediate relief measures. *Biplabi* listed seven starvation deaths and a hunger-related suicide that occurred in March in Tamluk subdivision. During a tour that he undertook at the time, Sen concluded that "famine was in the offing and its character would be overwhelming."[31]

A DETAILED SURVEY conducted in 1944 by statistician Prasanta C. Mahalanobis and his team would find Bhola, in eastern Bengal, to have been the region worst affected by famine—no doubt because of rice and boat denial, which most severely impacted the east. Among the regions studied, however, Tamluk subdivision ranked second worst, with 13.2 percent of the population having perished in 1943 alone. Since Contai had been much harder hit by cyclone but suffered slightly less from famine, some other factor appears to have increased the mortality in Tamluk. That was probably repression—in particular, the destruction of food reserves in the many hamlets that were suspected to shelter rebels. Although by March 1943 famine had set in, the authorities continued to burn down homes and rice supplies. And increasingly they targeted the most vulnerable supporters of the insurgency: women.[32]

Kumudini Dakua's husband was in prison, having been arrested for protesting rice denial, but on November 1, 1942, she had trekked with a colleague to the remote village in Sutahata where her in-laws lived. The neighbors warned her not to stay for long, but her mother-in-law was so happy to see her, and it was such a rainy day, that she took the risk. At midnight, police and soldiers surrounded the two-story mud house. (Soldiers on internal security duty were assisting the police, as authorized by the district magistrate.) "Sepoys came in, knocked the lamp over, hit my father-in-law," Dakua recalled. "They aimed rifles at us, but we refused to leave the house at night. There were many reports of rapes."[33]

The police officer restrained his men, told the captives they could leave in the morning, and withdrew. He must have retired somewhere, for after a while two or three sepoys suddenly broke in, ran up the stairs, and grabbed the young women. But because police and soldiers were perpetrating many rapes, Dhara had supplied his female recruits with daggers. They pulled out the weapons and attacked the assailants, who fled, bleeding but not seriously hurt, down the stairs. Early the next morning the police handcuffed the women and walked them to Tamluk. Kumudini was seventeen but small, and a senior police officer scolded his subordinate for having arrested a child. "He said to me, you stay here tonight, tomorrow you can go home," Dakua recalled. "But I was in prison for fifteen months."

The first night, in a cell that stank of urine, she stayed awake listening to an unknown man in another cell singing: "Those whose lives are made of sorrow, what is more sorrow to them?"

A WEEK AFTER the flood, the police were searching for Anil Kumar Patro, an eighteen-year-old member of Sushil Dhara's band, and burned down Patropara, the hamlet of Kalikakundu in which his extended family lived. Their stash of rice was also destroyed. "My father was furious with me," Patro recalled, but Dhara visited and somehow managed to pacify the paterfamilias.

Soon after, Patro helped the Tamluk militia kidnap a local zamindar and release him for a ransom of 7,000 rupees. The dreaded police officer Nolini Raha hunted furiously for the perpetrators. "He would come with his men and burn down our shelters—he burned some seven or eight of them," Patro said. But the chowkidar (watchman) who informed Raha of the rebels' whereabouts also told the insurgents when to run, so the officer could not catch them. In his frustration he decided to teach the villagers who sheltered the fugitives a lesson.

On January 9, 1943, Dhara heard that the police were raiding the village of Masuria, seven miles north of Kalikakundu, and sent a couple of youths to investigate. Reaching a canal that bordered Masuria, they saw on the other side two sepoys, each dragging a woman by her long hair. The women were Behula Burman and Satyabala Samanta, according to one of the witnesses, Basudeb Ghora. They screamed that several women had been raped, and they feared that they would be, too. "We could do nothing—they had guns. We had to run in case they got us," Ghora recalled.

The police used to come often, recalled a Masuria villager, Kanonbala Maity. They would beat the men up and, not being able to find whomever they were looking for, would eventually go away. Her husband, she attested, still bore the scars of a whip on his back. That day, when he heard all the commotion and knew the police were coming, he had hidden in a hole that he had dug just for the purpose. Maity, who was nineteen, had a one-year-old who was playing in front of the house, and she had run out to bring him in. She could not find him—because, it later turned out, her sister-in-law had picked up the child and raced with him to safety. But as Maity hunted frantically for her boy, a sepoy had caught her. She was fortunate that he was the only one to have raped her.

The police and soldiers scoured the houses, took all the men they could find at gunpoint to the bank of a nearby canal, and beat them. Maity's father-in-law was also rounded up. "Not a grown man was left around," she said, and as for the other women, Maity could only hear them: "The whole village was screaming, the terror of it!" For weeks afterward she had hidden in the house, too ashamed to emerge in the daylight. "I never lied to anyone, I never quarreled with anyone," Maity would say, wondering why she had suffered so.

According to testimonies subsequently compiled by Bari and others, forty-six women were raped that day in Masuria and its two neighboring villages of Dihi Masuria and Chondipur. Most victims, including a fourteen-year-old, were each raped by two or three uniformed men, and one woman by four. A twenty-one-year-old, Sindhubala Maity, had already been gang-raped by the police and was suffering from internal injuries; she died after the second assault. Hundreds of police or soldiers were estimated to have taken part in the affair, some to round up the men and the others to rape. The scale of the attack suggests the complicity of the district magistrate, Niaz Mohammad Khan (if not a more senior official), who had assigned this sizeable force for an operation against unarmed villagers.[34]

THE GANG RAPE in the three villages of Midnapore would have a far-reaching political outcome. It contributed to the downfall of Chief Minister Fazlul Huq as well as to the induction of a Muslim League ministry in Bengal that would enable Governor Herbert to run the province as he chose.

In late January 1943, Shyama Prasad Mookerjee, a politician with a Hindu nationalist party, received from the Tamluk government's courier, Krishna Chaitanya Mahapatro, an issue of *Biplabi*. Mookerjee had served as Bengal's finance minister but had resigned his post on November 16, 1942, citing official callousness in the response to the cyclone that he said had possibly "no parallel in the annals of civilized administration." According to Mahapatro, when Mookerjee read about the gang rapes, he wept. He subsequently wrote to Chief Minister Fazlul Huq, informing him of the assaults.[35]

A few days later, on February 2, Governor Herbert reported to Viceroy Linlithgow that the situation in Midnapore had improved. "Even from Tamluk hope to be able to release troops first week of March if improvement maintained," he declared. In another few weeks, however, Herbert wrote to complain that Mookerjee had made a "most venomous statement" in the Bengal legislature. Worse, Huq had responded by promising "an impartial enquiry by persons of the status of High Court Judges into the alleged excesses by officials in Midnapore!" It was all very annoying, given that the governor had recently flown to that district to reward policemen who were rendering "loyal service" in the combat against Congress rebels. Herbert opposed any special investigation into the events in Tamluk and demanded of the chief minister that he explain his "failing to consult me" before promising it.[36]

Fazlul Huq and John Herbert had already clashed over alleged gang rapes and murders by soldiers posted in Noakhali, along the coast of eastern Bengal. And the upcoming famine was yet another source of friction. Huq was a peasant leader. He could not fail to observe that rice denial had removed the remnants of 1942's stock from villages, that the cyclone and subsequent pests had damaged the vital year-end crop, that no imports were in sight, that rice exports continued unabated, and that the government's purchases had precipitated an ominous price rise. Huq had repeatedly warned that pervasive hunger was about to worsen into outright famine, which meant that instead of dying quietly in their huts, millions of skeletal, wild-eyed people would drag themselves out of their villages in a conspicuous search for food. But Herbert believed that Huq's alarms had prompted cultivators to hang on to their stocks—an explanation for why the government could not procure enough rice for the war effort.[37]

The governor resolved to remove the chief minister. On March 28, 1943, the night before the budget for Bengal was to be discussed—a critical matter given the anarchic economy—Herbert summoned Huq to the governor's palace. He presented the visitor with a typewritten resignation letter and browbeat him into signing it. "Huq, and Huq's Ministry, were a menace to good government and security," the governor subsequently explained to the viceroy. A ministry minus the "Caste Hindus" who constituted a number of Huq's associates would in Herbert's view be "infinitely better than the Ministry which has gone if it is to be remembered (as it hardly ever is in Bengal politics) that the war has to be won and the Congress rebellion kept under."[38]

For Herbert, retaining firm control over Bengal's policies meant working with the Muslim League, which was eager to supplant Huq's coalition. In Bengal, Muslims formed 55 percent of the population, with almost all the remainder Hindu. The 1935 Indian constitution had, however, given 119 seats in the legislature of Bengal to Muslims, and only 80 to Hindus. The seats confiscated from Hindus had gone to Europeans, who, although comprising only 0.04 percent of Bengal's population, held 10 percent of the seats. Fazlul Huq, a moderate Muslim, had scraped together the numbers for a ministry with the help of Hindu politicians left over after those belonging to the Congress had gone to prison. With Huq out of the way, the so-called European Group of legislators (mainly representing British business interests) could help loyalist Muslims form a government. In three weeks Bengal was being governed by a Muslim League ministry headed by Sir Khwaja Nazimuddin, advertised as "undoubtedly a friend of the British." While bemoaning the governor's unorthodox methods in having forced Huq's resignation, the viceroy trusted that Nazimuddin would "lend much more effective support to [the] war effort than we were ever able to get from Huq."[39]

The rare British administrator who empathized with the natives was also eased out of power. The most senior civil servant in Bengal, Chief Secretary James Richard Blair, asked for early retirement, reportedly because he could not stomach the repression in Midnapore. Blair had related some of his concerns about Bengal's governance to Amery. Still, when the viceroy decided in another few months that the governor himself was incompetent and needed to go, the secretary of state for India demurred: "Herbert had handled a difficult Ministry well on the whole and given good support to the Military authorities."[40]

Each link in the command chain—Churchill-Amery-Linlithgow-Herbert—was welded to the others by a grim resolve: "the war has to be won and the Congress rebellion kept under," as Herbert had put it. The care and feeding of the populace was not a priority. "The authorities worried only about how to keep the soldiers and war workers safe, didn't think about keeping the people safe," related social worker Ashoka Gupta. "Fish, eggs, fruit, everything was being collected and fed to the army. Big rice banks were formed. They told everyone, give us your rice, we'll give it back to you when you need it, but they didn't give any, even after people started dying."

CHAPTER FIVE

Death of a Thousand Cuts

"I am glad to learn from the Minister of War Transport that a strict line is being taken in dealing with requests for cereals from the Indian Ocean area. A concession to one country at once encourages demands from all the others," the prime minister commented in a memo on March 10, 1943. "They must learn to look after themselves as we have done. The grave situation of the U.K. import programme imperils the whole war effort and we cannot afford to send ships merely as a gesture of good will."[1]

For three months, Viceroy Linlithgow had been warning about a food crisis in India, and earlier that March a member of his council, Sir Ramaswami Mudaliar, had told the War Cabinet's shipping committee of "some danger of famine conditions, particularly in Calcutta and Bombay." Wheat was available in Australia, but all Indian ships capable of the round trip were engaged in the war effort. Moreover, in January the prime minister had brought most of the merchant ships operating in the Indian Ocean over to the Atlantic, in order to bolster the United Kingdom's stocks of food and raw materials. He was reluctant to release vessels to carry grain to the colony, because lowered stocks at home would compromise the British economy and limit the War Cabinet's ability to pursue military operations of its choice—and because his hostility toward Indians was escalating.[2]

THE CHANCELLOR OF the Exchequer, Sir Kingsley Wood, had long been warning that India had erased its traditional debt to the United Kingdom and was instead becoming a major creditor. The sterling debt owed to the colony was mounting at a million pounds a day. It would fall due right after the war, just when a ravaged if liberated Europe would have to be fed. Food in the postwar era would be scarce worldwide and expensive to import—and His Majesty's Government would already be bankrupt from paying for the war. In consequence, maintaining British food stocks had become crucially important to the War Cabinet, and the debt to India a source of profound frustration.[3]

On September 16, 1942, Amery had recorded in his diary: "Winston burbled away endlessly, the general theme being that it was monstrous to expect that we should not only defend India and then have to clear out but be left to pay hundreds of millions for the privilege." The secretary of state for India strove to explain that the debt had little to do with the defense of the colony, but arose from its contributions in manpower and materials to the war in the Middle East and North Africa. "It is an awful thing dealing with a man like Winston who is at the same moment dictatorial, eloquent and muddleheaded," Amery wrote eight days later. "I am not sure that I ever got into his mind that India pays for the whole of her defence including the British forces in India, or that there is no possible way of reducing these accumulating balances except by stopping to buy Indian goods or employing Indian soldiers outside India."[4]

The prime minister announced at a War Cabinet meeting that the sterling debt should be neutralized by a counterclaim: a bill presented to India for its defense by the United Kingdom. At the very least, he insisted, the financial agreement forged in April 1940 should be revised to make the colony pay more of the costs of the war. Viceroy Linlithgow had already warned against this course of action: "if any suggestion were made that it was doubtful whether India would in due course receive value for her sterling balances, the reaction on India's war effort could not fail to be disastrous." Should the United Kingdom signal its desire to renege on its financial commitments, then industrialists, contractors, and even peasants would anticipate a drop in the value of the rupee and balk at supplying goods for cash.[5]

The sterling debt arose from the fact that commodities were being continually drawn from India with no recompense beyond the promise of payment in the future. The indiscriminate printing of paper money was enabling the Government of India to acquire supplies for the war effort, both within the country and without. But the situation was volatile: inflation was poised to combine with a shortage of every necessity of life to bring disaster to the colony's poor. Amery did not anticipate that the Government of India's warning of August 1942—that inflationary financing might lead to "famines and riots"—would actually come to pass. He was, however, cognizant of the risk posed by such a method of war financing to the war effort itself. Should Indians come to believe that His Majesty's Government would not keep its promises, the torrent of supplies from the colony would dry up.[6]

"Winston cannot see beyond such phrases as 'Are we to incur hundreds of millions of debt for defending India in order to be kicked out by the Indians afterwards,'" Amery confided to his diary. "But that we are getting out of India far more than was ever thought possible and that India herself is paying far more than was ever contemplated when the present settlement was made, and that we have no means of making her pay more than she wants or supplying goods unpaid for, is the kind of point that just doesn't enter into his head." The prime minister was aware that the sterling debt was inverting the economic relationship between colony and colonizer. After the war, money would flow from Britain to India, not as investment to be repaid with interest but as remittance. Whatever the romance of empire, a colony that drains the Exchequer is scarcely worth having—and that reality, notes historian Dietmar Rothermund, would make it easier for India to be finally released.[7]

ANOTHER SOURCE OF irritation to Churchill was the 1940 U.S. Republican presidential candidate, Wendell Willkie. In an October 1942 broadcast, he reported to Americans what he had learned on a world tour. "When the aspirations of India for freedom were put aside to some future unguaranteed date, it was not Great Britain that suffered in public esteem in the Far East," Willkie said. "It was the United States."

The inhabitants of Asia "cannot tell from our vague and vacillating talk whether we really do stand for freedom, or what we mean by freedom." Willkie's criticism induced President Roosevelt to reiterate that the Atlantic Charter applied to the entire world and to appoint a seasoned diplomat, William Phillips, as his "Personal Representative with the rank of Ambassador" to India.[8]

Apparently stung by the disapproval emanating from the United States, Churchill made on November 11, 1942, what would become his most quoted pronouncement on India. "We mean to hold our own," he declared in Parliament. "I have not become the King's First Minister in order to preside over the liquidation of the British Empire." According to Amery, the next day he "went off the deep end in a state of frantic passion on the whole subject of the humiliation of being kicked out of India by the beastliest people in the world next to the Germans."[9]

IT WAS AT this inopportune juncture that the viceroy had begun to press the secretary of state for India to arrange for imports of wheat. He further cautioned: "I think it probable that until our own position becomes clearer we shall have to stop all exports of foodgrains." After the fall of Rangoon in March 1942, the Government of India had undertaken to supply Ceylon and Arabia with the rice that they used to import from Burma. But in a series of telegrams starting that December, Linlithgow warned Amery that cyclone and subsequent pest infestations in Bengal, and a failure of monsoon rains in Madras, had caused a "serious deterioration in food situation in India." The rice crop was hardest hit, and what with ongoing exports, it would fall short by "something over two million tons." Wheat and other cereals would possibly be in excess, but the war effort in India and abroad would absorb much of that surplus, leaving a worrisome overall shortage of a million tons of cereals. The stringency anticipated for later in the year was causing many people to stock up on grain, making matters much worse than might be gauged from the numbers alone.[10]

The Government of India would subsequently calculate a gap between rice production and consumption of 2 million tons in Bengal alone, with a 3.5 million ton shortage in India overall (including export and defense requirements) for the fiscal year that ended on March 31, 1943. That implies a shortfall of the same order for 1943 as a whole. The actual extent of the rice shortage in Bengal remains controversial to this day.[11]

"I am very uneasy about position that is rapidly developing," the viceroy cabled to Amery on December 13, 1942. Requests for grain were pouring in from the provinces, and the governor of Bombay had threatened to disperse the entire city in the countryside if he did not get 50,000 tons of wheat within a month. The effects of shortages, the viceroy (erroneously) believed, would be confined to urban and industrial areas. "But those, as you know, are precisely the most inflammable areas in some ways from the political point of view," he continued. A new crop of wheat would be harvested in May, but until then the situation would be acute and he urgently needed 600,000 tons of wheat to arrive by the end of April 1943.[12]

The Government of India had been caught unawares by the Japanese occupation of Southeast Asia. Any threat to India had been presumed to emanate from the borders of the Soviet Union, the British Empire's traditional rival in the region—which was why vital ammunitions factories had been placed as far east as feasible, around Calcutta. Worse, the authorities had failed to anticipate that rice imports might be cut off by Japanese conquest and had not planned for any stringency in its supply. Instead they had encouraged jute cultivation in Bengal, reducing the fields available to rice by 2.7 million acres.[13]

Although aware of the significance of wheat, which grew in the cooler climes of the northwest and was essential for feeding the army, the government had failed to control the supply of that grain as well. In December 1941, for instance, the authorities had imposed ceilings on the price of wheat. Even in meticulously managed Britain, however, the food ministry could keep down bread prices only by maintaining adequate stocks of wheat and releasing it to the market as required. The Government of India did not have the stocks to enforce price controls. Sellers had refused to accept the new prices, so that little wheat could thereafter be found on the open market. Subsequently, the authorities had decided that India was too large to administer in its entirety and, instead, had empowered each province to protect its own people. That had frozen the grain trade among the provinces. "It is only human nature that if you give a province power to prevent grain going out of its border, that province will look to its own safety," Robert Hutchings of the Department of Food would explain to the famine commission. The government next undertook to purchase grain from "surplus" provinces such as Punjab in the northwest and to send it to "short" provinces such as Bengal, but failed to procure enough.[14]

The problem was that cultivators of the northwest were enjoying a double windfall: their soldier sons were remitting paychecks, and their wheat was more in demand than ever before. Instead of selling, farmers were holding out for higher prices. Indeed, many preferred to keep their savings in the form of grain because they had come to distrust the value and security of cash. An intelligence report noted a widespread fear that after the war the United Kingdom would revise the exchange rate between the rupee and the sterling, thereby slashing the wartime earnings of Indians—as had happened after World War I.[15]

Nor could officials use coercion to extract wheat from the northwestern province of Punjab, as they had forcibly claimed the produce of Bengali villagers: maintaining army morale meant pleading with, rather than threatening, the families of Punjabi soldiers. As Linlithgow would subsequently explain to Amery, he did not want to antagonize the helpful ministry that held power there, or to upset cultivators whose sons were in the army. One had to consider, he wrote, "the reaction on the very large numbers of the Punjab soldiers of every religion and community who are serving overseas of the receipt of letters from the Province representing that their houses were being invaded, and their families insulted, under the pretext of requisitioning, and that their legitimate claims out of food profits were being taken from them."[16]

On January 2, 1943, Governor Herbert warned the viceroy that his province was desperately short of wheat. "Bengal's normal demand is 18,000 tons a month and we are short of nearly twice this amount over last quarter alone. Amount of 110 tons mentioned by you therefore represents only few hours supply." If factory workers who ate wheat did not get it, they would either riot or leave, so the shortage threatened the production of ammunition. Herbert urged Linlithgow to get hold of a ship "for large-scale import of wheat which might prove palliative for the whole situation" involving both wheat and rice.[17]

AMERY HAD ALREADY responded, on December 15, 1942, that ships were in such short supply that the United Kingdom's own imports were "cut to bone and involve serious inroads into stocks both of food and of materials." The War Cabinet wanted assurance that, if it acceded to the viceroy's request, India would continue monthly exports of 30,000 tons of rice to Ceylon. It also desired confirmation that all ships registered in India were "under full control so as to afford maximum utilisation for war effort." For the time being, Linlithgow responded, he could spare 12,000 tons a month for Ceylon, and some more for Arabia. Of India's larger ships, seventeen had been requisitioned and the remaining nine, although still in private hands, were plying military stores and the most essential civil supplies along the Indian coast or to the Red Sea. But Commander-in-Chief Wavell was so concerned about food shortages that he would forgo up to 180,000 tons of war materials if the shipping space could instead be used to bring wheat.[18]

So in early January 1943, Amery wrote to Lord Frederick Leathers, the minister of war transport, arguing the urgent necessity of sending to India 600,000 tons of wheat within the first quarter of the year (over and above 30,000 tons already promised to the army). The imports would enable the viceroy "firstly to maintain supplies to the Army, secondly to feed the urban population on whose labour the war effort mainly depends, thirdly to maintain supplies to those areas where for one reason or another there is an unsatisfied deficiency of food grains, and fourthly to convince holders of supplies that holding for a major shortage is not good business."[19]

Amery was talking to the wrong person. Leathers was a former shipping magnate who had been brought in by Churchill to run the British

Empire's merchant shipping during the war. He was reputed to be very competent; but he lacked the authority, and by all accounts the inclination, to release ships for any purpose that the prime minister had not approved. Nor was the timing propitious. Gandhi, who remained in custody, appeared to be embarking on a fast—sparking anxiety in London because of the likelihood that it would influence opinion in Washington. According to Amery, Churchill began the War Cabinet meeting of January 7 "with a terrific tirade against apologising for the Empire, appeasing the Americans, etc."[20]

On January 10, 1943, Amery received an even more desperate plea from India's Department of Food. The army's wheat reserves would run out in a month. The remainder of the wheat promised to the army was waiting in Australia and must be brought in by February; and if shipping could not right away be found for 600,000 tons, at least 200,000 tons must come by April. "The vital necessity for expedition cannot be exaggerated as we have to carry on with practically no supplies for civil population till some of these shipments arrive," the officials warned.[21]

IT WAS TOO late. On January 5, 1943, the prime minister had slashed the number of ships operating in the "Indian Ocean area." The term, used in connection with wartime shipping, referred to the entire span of water rimmed by Australia, Arabia, and Africa (as well as the British Empire territories and dominions surrounding this composite body of water). The United Kingdom controlled the merchant ships there, whereas the United States ran the Pacific. Of the forty vessels that remained in the Indian Ocean area after the cut, the lion's share would go toward supplying Operation Torch, an invasion of French colonies in North Africa, leaving only a handful of ships to ply to and from India—just enough to collect whatever goods the colony could still provide to the outside world.[22]

Churchill seems not to have mentioned this crucial decision when, at a War Cabinet meeting on January 12, 1943, Amery brought up India's serious food problem. Instead of wheat shipments, the War Cabinet offered to send to the colony an official who had experience, from a stint in the Middle East, of prying grain out of cultivators. Unusually for the prime minister when India came up, he was "full of internal glee"—because, it turned out, he was shortly to depart for Casablanca to meet the U.S. president.[23]

At the Casablanca Conference, a misunderstanding between American and British planners precluded a realistic allocation of shipping to different theaters. The British wanted to focus their war initiatives on the Mediterranean region and persuaded the Americans to participate in an attack on Sicily in July. American generals, in contrast, wanted a cross-Channel assault on France by September, to which Churchill nominally agreed. But the battles around the Mediterranean would absorb so many resources that the landing in Normandy would have to be postponed until 1944. The Allies also agreed upon Operation Anakim, a plan involving a sea-borne assault on Burma—although the cut in vessels in the Indian Ocean would deprive the forces based in India of essential war materials and had doomed the invasion even before it could be launched. Anakim would eventually be canceled, so that India ceased to be an important war base until the very end of 1943. But the colony remained responsible for feeding 2 million troops, whether or not they fought.[24]

While Churchill and Cherwell were away in Casablanca, Amery described India's plight to a shipping committee and warned of "dissident elements" gaining leverage from the food shortages. The committee determined that ships with a carrying capacity of between 40,000 and 50,000 tons, then loading for the United Kingdom at foreign ports, should instead take wheat to India. Cabling the viceroy, Amery suggested that Indian ships supplying the war effort in the Middle East might also be released to ferry a total of 130,000 tons. (These ships were not in fact made available.) "H.M.G. regret that they find it impossible at this stage in view of the heavy sacrifices already assumed on behalf of India and of the present pressure from all sides on our shipping, to consider your further request" for 400,000 tons, Amery concluded.[25]

Four days later, on January 20, the Government of India informed the secretary of state for India that it was dispensing with price controls on wheat, and in another few days it approved the Bengal government's decision to do the same with rice. An official paper attributed the action to the desperate straits in which the authorities found themselves. The viceroy explained to the provinces' governors on February 3 that although some wheat was on the way, with regard to "the rice problem no help can be expected from outside the country and we are forced back on our own resources."[26]

The timing of the decision to lift price controls is significant. It indicates that a sudden realization of the stranglehold on shipping, along with supplies being set to run out within weeks, prompted the Government of India to give up on trying to control the economy and instead buy up all the grain it could get. So the cut in shipping—or more broadly put, the prioritization of the United Kingdom's needs over those of the colonies—motivated the February 13 order to "go to any place and purchase at any price" that detonated the famine in Bengal.

THE ALLIED SHIPPING crisis had built up slowly but inexorably. During 1942 German U-boats, operating mainly in the Atlantic Ocean, had taken a heavy toll, sinking 1.3 million gross tons of British-controlled shipping in the last quarter alone. The buildup of forces for Operation Torch, in North Africa, had also absorbed many more shiploads of supplies than had been anticipated. The minister of war transport had met that contingency by withdrawing ships from the Indian Ocean and from the United Kingdom's civilian program, so that the rate at which imports reached the island nation had fallen to less than half of what it had been before the war.[27]

The United Kingdom intended to bring in 27 million tons of food and raw materials in 1943, plus around 15 million tons of liquids (mostly petroleum). In November 1942, British representatives had approached President Roosevelt with a request for 7 million tons of American shipping toward the dry-cargo import program. The president had acquiesced—but told them that some of the ships were in use and might not be released for three months.[28]

At the S branch, Lord Cherwell's most trusted assistant, Donald MacDougall, became concerned that imports were not arriving fast enough. (Roy Harrod, the more experienced economist, had left by that time.) MacDougall was convinced that if the United Kingdom did not get more shipping for civilian needs, stocks of food would "quite possibly fall to dangerously low levels before very long." He figured that stocks could, however, be adequately protected by cutting the number of ships serving the Indian Ocean area down to 60 percent and bringing the rest over to the Atlantic to serve the import program. "I told Prof he would never get away with such a dramatic reduction and had better suggest 80," MacDougall related in his memoir. "He replied that, on the contrary, he would put in 40–50, which would be argued up by the military to my figure of 60, which he believed."[29]

Thus was born one of Churchill's most far-reaching decisions. On January 2, 1943, the Prof informed the prime minister that the United Kingdom's imports would increase by a million tons if the ninety monthly sailings to the east were cut to fifty during January, February, and March; and by 1.25 million tons if the cut were to forty sailings. Moreover, the "gain would be increased to 3½ millions if the cut were prolonged up to the end of June." (A more nuanced calculation, taking into account the delay in transferring ships from the Indian Ocean to the Atlantic, would find that the last cut actually yielded 2 million tons of imports.) Failing such strong action, "factories will have to close down for lack of materials, with all the political repercussions this involves," Cherwell asserted.[30]

Although the first option seemed enough to meet the United Kingdom's needs, the memo did not state that; nor did it mention any negative consequences of such cuts. Accordingly, Churchill circled the most drastic, last option, marked it "A," and wrote on the memo "We must go for A." Thanks to the Prof, MacDougall's suggestion to cut Indian Ocean shipping down to 60 percent ended up as an even deeper cut, to 44 percent—and for twice as long.[31]

Ships that went to the Indian Ocean generally made loops, going from port to port within the region before heading back to the United

Kingdom or the United States. Combined with the imperative to supply troops in North Africa, the shipping cut meant that very few vessels would be available on the run between Australia and India. The shipping cut "must portend violent changes and perhaps cataclysms in the seaborne trade of large numbers of countries," the Ministry of War Transport warned the prime minister.[32]

As ships gradually left the Indian Ocean, the cessation of trade deranged the economies of the colonies on its rim. They were already reeling from wartime inflation and scarcity, and "the menace of famine suddenly loomed up like a hydra-headed monster with a hundred clamouring mouths," related C.B.A. Behrens in the official history of wartime British shipping. Desperate appeals began pouring into colonial offices. Several British possessions bordering the Indian Ocean, such as Kenya, Tanganyika, and British Somaliland, suffered famine that year. Historians attribute the calamities to a combination of drought, wartime inflation, acquisition of grain for the armed forces, and hoarding by Indian traders. That all the famines, including the one in Bengal, occurred in 1943 suggests, however, that the shipping cut also played a role. "In the Indian Ocean area the burden of paying for victory, shifted from place to place to ease the weight, finally came to rest," summarized Behrens.[33]

ON JANUARY 6, 1943, the viceroy of India relieved his hectic schedule with a duck shoot in a princely state. The party boasted fifty-two guns and bagged 2,310 birds on a single winter's day.[34]

A political crisis was flaring up at that time, and it too involved starvation. Gandhi was depressed. His personal secretary had died shortly after having been arrested; his countrymen were in desperate straits and, because he was in custody, he was unable to help them. Moreover, "palpable departures from the truth" in the government's portrayal of recent events were adding to his distress. Gandhi asked for an audience with the viceroy to explain his reasons for having launched the Quit India movement. If he was not granted even a meeting, he wrote, he might "crucify the flesh by fasting."[35]

In response, the viceroy accused the captive of having unleashed a "sad campaign of violence and crime." That Gandhi himself advocated nonviolence was "no answer to relations of those who have lost their lives, and to those themselves who have lost their property or suffered severe injury as a result of violent activities on the part of Congress and its supporters." Gandhi responded that the authorities had "goaded the people to the point of madness." Still, the viceroy's allegations rankled him, and he announced a fast of three weeks. He wished "not to fast unto death, but to survive the ordeal, if God so wills," and to that end he would drink water, with a little citrus juice to make it palatable.[36]

Gandhi held twenty-one days to be the limit of his endurance and appears to have seen the fast as a trial before God. The viceroy charged that it was "an easy way out" and "a form of political blackmail." The War Cabinet had long decided that if Gandhi chose to fast he would be allowed to die. But some Indian members of the viceroy's council worried about Gandhi's perishing in prison, and Linlithgow fretted that they might resign their seats if he were at risk of dying. Such weakness infuriated Churchill, who raged on February 7, "what did it matter if a few blackamoors resigned! We could show the world that we were governing." If indeed Gandhi died, "[w]e should be rid of a bad man and an enemy of the Empire." His anger persisted into the next day's War Cabinet meeting. The British had scored victory after victory in North Africa, the Soviets had fought the Nazis to a standstill, and the Americans were pounding the Japanese—"and this our hour of triumph everywhere in the world," he said, "was not the time to crawl before a miserable little old man who had always been our enemy."[37]

The viceroy nevertheless proposed to release Gandhi from prison for the duration of his fast, an offer he declined. So the ordeal began, and as each excruciating day crawled by, Indians came to besiege the new American envoy with pleas for help. William Phillips once arrived at his office to find twenty-five agitated schoolgirls camped in the hall outside. He asked the viceroy for permission to visit Gandhi and was turned down. But when Indians realized "that I could not intervene without instructions and that the President would not intervene with Churchill, American stock in India fell rapidly," Phillips recounted in a memoir. On February 19 he was finally able to hand Linlithgow a telegram from Cordell Hull, the American secretary of state, expressing the president's alarm at the prospect of Gandhi's death.[38]

Linlithgow explained to Phillips that if Gandhi should die, the worst would be "six months unpleasantness steadily declining in volume; little or nothing at the end of it." After it was all over, India would be "far more reliable as a base for operations." The prime minister instructed Lord Halifax, the ambassador in Washington, to leave no doubt that any interference from the United States would "cause great embarrassment between the two Governments."[39]

Gandhi's moral stature nevertheless posed a serious problem to the British. Since he was holding out longer than expected, the prime minister asked the viceroy to check if he was sneaking some glucose with his water: "Would be most valuable [if any] fraud could be exposed." Gandhi had refused glucose, Linlithgow responded. On February 21 the old man's condition suddenly worsened, but the crisis passed. A British doctor attested that one of the Indian doctors might have panicked when Gandhi appeared to be on the verge of death and secretly given him a dose of glucose, but the old man could not have known and so could not be exposed as a cheat. No matter: Churchill would write in *The Hinge of Fate* that it "was certain however at an early stage that he was being fed with glucose whenever he drank water."[40]

The viceroy thanked the prime minister for standing firm against "a wicked system of blackmail and terror" practiced by "the world's most successful humbug." Churchill had meanwhile come down with pneumonia and was on his own irksome diet. "I do not think Gandhi has the slightest intention of dying," he complained in a letter to Prime Minister Jan Smuts of South Africa (who, three decades earlier, had had his own share of troubles with the Indian). "I imagine he has been eating better meals than I have for the last week."[41]

AS LUCK WOULD have it, while the prime minister was down with pneumonia and irascible over Gandhi's fast he received a complaint from Cherwell about the transportation of grain to India. Upon returning from Casablanca, the Prof had vehemently protested the shipping committee's promise to send the colony at least 40,000 tons of wheat. The consignment would cost the United Kingdom dearly in terms of shipping, Cherwell argued, and India's annual output of cereals was so enormous (a little above 50 million tons) that even the 600,000 tons that the viceroy wanted could make no conceivable difference to its food supply. He trusted that "no further gestures of this sort will be encouraged."

Churchill concurred. "I am much concerned about these heavy inroads into your shipping due to the improvidence of the various Governments in the East concerned, and the failure of their crops," he wrote to Leathers, the minister of war transport. "I hope you will be as stiff as you can. There is no reason why all parts of the British Empire should not feel the pinch in the same way as the Mother Country has done."[42]

In his January memo to Leathers, Amery had noted that the food stringency in India was a result of high prices, arising from the cessation of Burmese imports, crop failure, and the demands of the army and of Ceylon, all of it compounded by hoarding. With prices on the rise, cultivators were refusing to sell while traders and householders were buying grain and storing it for future use, forcing prices even higher. Imports would render the army and part of the urban population less dependent on open-market purchases of grain until the summer wheat was harvested, reducing prices and greatly alleviating the problem.[43]

Compared to Amery's incisive analysis, Cherwell's drop-in-the-bucket argument was shallow. Indeed, India's harvest was large. The problem lay in distributing it so that everyone got enough—which was more likely to happen if everyone was confident of getting enough. For instance, the people of the United Kingdom knew that their government would take care of them and felt no need to stockpile essentials. The residents of Bengal, in contrast, knew that famine was impending and were equally sure that the government would *not* take care of them.

That awareness had led landowners to store grain for survival, unscrupulous agents to hoard for speculation, and the government itself to stockpile for the war effort. Had the War Cabinet sent significant consignments of grain, it would have demonstrated a resolve to not let the colony starve and signaled that hoarding would be unprofitable. Those holding stocks in excess of their immediate needs would therefore have released them to the market, reducing prices and saving many lives.[44]

As it happened, the Government of India had already announced that wheat was coming, so Leathers felt obliged to send some. But after arranging for ships to carry 26,000 tons from Australia to India, he found that amount adequate to meet the United Kingdom's immediate needs from the colony—and became reluctant to assign any more vessels. (During 1943, the United Kingdom continued to draw tea, oilseeds, and cotton from India.) Soon after, the Government of India reported that the lifting of price controls had enabled it to procure enough grain for the time being. In view of the simultaneous grain crisis in eastern Africa, the secretary of state for India asked the viceroy to forgo the shipments already promised.[45]

Linlithgow protested that India's grain reserves were so low as to threaten disaster in the near future. "Rice crisis [inevitable] later in the year and additional shipments of wheat will be essential to help to meet this," he wrote to Amery on February 21, 1943. "India's own need is so acute that I must press for retention of all tonnage allocated to us already and repeat that further substantial allocations will be necessary later on." But on March 2—after hearing a member of the viceroy's council warn of famine—the shipping committee asserted that "no further diversions of ships from the United Kingdom import programme could be contemplated at present." [46]

THE INDIAN OCEAN shipping cut saved the United Kingdom from impending calamity, at least as Donald MacDougall of the S branch told the story. The "imports—after falling to a terrifyingly low level for about four months—started arriving in increasing quantities just in time; our stocks—after plummeting in an equally alarming way—

levelled off just above the minimum safety level before starting to recover slowly," he wrote in his memoir. MacDougall was referring to civilian stocks having reached their lowest point in March 1943—when they were still 3.1 million tons above the level (of 11.5 million tons) considered essential by the shipping committee, and 4.8 million tons above the level (of 9.8 million tons) considered essential by the Ministry of Production. And as it happens, even these so-called safety levels of stocks were inflated. "It is clear in retrospect that minimum food requirements were considerably, and raw materials requirements wildly, overstated," historian W. K. Hancock and economist M. M. Gowing would comment in their official history of the British war economy. The shipping transferred from the Indian Ocean would add 2 million tons of supplies by the end of the summer. That is, the shipping cut that contributed to the outbreak of famine in Bengal merely added to the margin by which stocks were in excess in Britain.[47]

Stocks had originally been viewed by the Ministry of Food as a way to tide over the early difficulties of the war, until the dividends were apparent from the Grow More Food program, which expanded the area under cultivation in the British Isles. But as the war wore on, the purpose of the stocks, and the stipulated size, had altered. Cherwell, for instance, saw these food reserves, along with stocks of raw materials needed by factories, not so much as insurance against hard times but as savings that would enable full use to be made of strategic opportunities. "[W]e should strive to build up our stocks so as to be in a position to divert large masses of shipping for military purposes if the occasion arose," he wrote in a memo. In his view—which prevailed—stocks should be maintained at levels well above those stipulated by the ministries, so that the War Cabinet could retain "flexibility for meeting emergency needs in a period of large scale military operations."[48]

In June 1942, for instance, the shipping committee had formulated a plan to run down existing reserves. It "thought that, between January 1942 and June 1943, stocks could be reduced by six million tons before they reached the level estimated for indispensable working stocks," wrote Hancock and Gowing. By the summer of 1943 the United States would be producing an abundance of ships, supplies could be swiftly ferried across the Atlantic Ocean, and stocks should no longer be so necessary. But the War Cabinet worried that the Americans might not provide the necessary shipping. If so, food reserves might never be rebuilt to former levels, and "the Government would have no elbow room for strategic operations to take advantage of any sudden weakening of the enemy." The prime minister inveighed against "tightening the belt," while the Prof demanded at least 27 million tons of imports in 1943—more than ever before.[49]

Another reason for maintaining large stocks, and the corresponding claim on shipping, was the prime minister's distaste for austerity. In the summer of 1940, for instance, the Ministry of Food had estimated that it needed 15 million tons of imported food and animal feed each year, but at the urging of Churchill and Cherwell it had asked for almost 19 million tons. British rations would come to include red meats, butter and other fats, cheese, tea, sugar, jam, and other preserves. Prices were controlled for bread, milk, eggs, poultry, rabbits, frozen cod, canned salmon, herring, canned pork and beans, spreads made of fish and meat, preserved vegetables, potatoes, onions, rice, lentils, tapioca, sago, biscuits, macaroni and other noodles, canned soups, pickles, sauces, relishes, coffee, cocoa, honey, custard powder, jelly, dried fruit, nuts, oranges, and lemons. Rations and price controls required that stocks of at least the nonperishable commodities be maintained. Despite all this effort and expense, however, Americans had access to more meat, eggs, and fresh fruit than did Britons, a disparity that irked the prime minister.[50]

Sensitivity to the public's tastes consumed additional tonnage on Allied vessels. Nutritionists argued, for instance, that the fraction of wheat grain used for bread flour, called the *extraction rate*, should be increased so as to enhance the intake of iron and vitamins. Raising the extraction rate would also cut wheat imports and thereby save shipping. But Britons preferred soft white bread, baked out of no more than 80 percent of the flour that whole wheat could yield, so it was not until the spring of 1942 that the extraction rate was increased to 85 percent. The Ministry of Food banned a further increase to 87 percent. That economy would save shipping space and thereby "weaken our bargaining power in that we should immediately be called upon to surrender an equivalent amount of shipping," one official argued. American officials at the Combined Food Board, an agency based in Washington, D.C., that coordinated the Allies' distribution of food, had grown suspicious of British import requirements—which meant that every ton of shipping had to be fought for, sometimes for its own sake.[51]

The Ministry of Food also resisted the rationing of bread, which it regarded as "the last resort of a starving nation." The prime minister himself had spoken for such rations in July 1942: he fretted that people might feed chickens with the cheap and plentiful bread. Rationing would reduce such wastage and save a large quantity of shipping. Lord Woolton, a businessman whom Churchill had appointed the minister of food, responded at a War Cabinet meeting that he could save 800,000 tons of shipping by other means if he chose to, and he would prefer that to rationing bread. (Bread rations were introduced only after the war.)[52]

Diluting the wheat flour used for baking bread with flour from home-grown barley and potatoes would also save shipping and improve nutrition. But barley was needed for beer, which was necessary for morale, and officials "unanimously recoiled" at the prospect of pubs closing for two days a week. Instead, brewers were persuaded to supplement their barley with oats. These deliberations and negotiations took time, so it was not until January 1943 that the order went out to replace 5 percent of the wheat flour used for bread-making with flour made out of potatoes, oats, barley, and rye. The 5 percent was subsequently increased to 10. It saved 284,000 tons of shipping over nine months—although most of the saving came after the summer, when ships became more available again. The sole sacrifice that ordinary Britons were asked to make in response to the shipping crisis of 1943 was to eat multigrain bread.[53]

Historian Kevin Smith maintains that the War Cabinet's panic over food and other reserves was nevertheless understandable, in light of the heavy and ongoing losses of Allied merchant vessels to German U-boats. In January 1943, no one could have foreseen that three months later the battle against the submarines would be won, and ships would there-after ply in relative safety across the Atlantic. Be that as it may, the re-markable rate at which the United States was producing ships had been expected to render the shipping losses to U-boats irrelevant by the sum-mer, and by that count alone stocks were ample—more than 4 million tons higher, at the end of 1942, than the quantity of food and raw ma-terials the British economy would consume during the next half-year.[54]

In retrospect, it is clear that the threat to British rations posed by the shipping crisis was exaggerated. Take, for instance, the discrepancy between the stock estimates that the S branch provided to the War Cabinet and the figures that the War Cabinet provided to the U.S. gov-ernment. On January 8, 1943, Cherwell stated in a draft paper that do-mestic reserves "are now only 3 million tons above the minimum working level absolutely required, and would continue for several months to dwindle by ¾ million tons a month unless remedial steps were taken." On March 9, in a draft paper prepared for use by the for-eign secretary in his dealings with American authorities, Cherwell again asserted, "by April it seems likely that we shall be down to about ¾ mil-lion tons above the minimum safety level." This estimate is consistent with the previous one if the gains from the cut to Indian Ocean shipping are ignored. But the final version of this paper stated: "by April it seems likely that stocks will be nearly 1 million tons below the minimum safety level." This was an extraordinary claim, given that in March stocks were 2 million tons *above* the minimum (of about 12.5 million tons) implicit in the S branch calculations of January. The War Cabinet went on to warn of "living from hand to mouth. Any further drop and the wheels would cease to turn and rations would be jeopardised."[55]

If the food reserve situation was not as critical as claimed, what con-tingency actually motivated the Indian Ocean shipping cut? In internal documents, the Statistics Division and the Ministry of War Transport cited the real reason as operational flexibility. As Smith explains, an at-mosphere of distrust between British and American shipping authorities had made the War Cabinet uncertain of whether the president would keep his promise of extra ships for the United Kingdom import program.

In addition, much acrimony prevailed around which of the desired military operations would actually take place. In such circumstances, it made sense for Churchill and Cherwell to hold on to as much shipping and stocks as they could, so that the War Cabinet could pursue military objectives for which the Americans might decline support.[56]

Indeed, when in March 1943 General Charles P. Gross, who determined shipping allocations for the United States armed forces, learned of the president's promise of 7 million tons for the British civilian import program, he expressed himself in such forceful terms that his remarks were left off the record. Such a large call on shipping threatened the entire strategic program agreed upon at Casablanca. Gross alleged that the United Kingdom could get by on 16 million tons of imports for 1943 instead of the 27 million tons that it demanded as the "first charge" on Allied shipping. Furious about what it regarded as British deviousness in having directly approached the president, the U. S. military resisted the handover of ships.[57]

THE NOTES ON War Cabinet meetings that were released in 2006 point also to an economic factor as having bolstered the need to retain ample stocks: the extent to which the United Kingdom's indebtedness threatened its postwar well-being. After the war, Europe would need large infusions of food, world prices would be high, and for the United Kingdom to be importing food at that time would prove costly. Rather than let domestic food stocks run down as the war turned in the Allies' favor, in July 1942 Churchill had resolved to build them up by accepting Cherwell's formula of requiring 27 million tons of civilian imports in 1943. Whatever reserves happened to be left at the end of the war would help feed the United Kingdom.[58]

Surplus stocks would also be worth a lot on the world market. On January 5, 1943, the War Cabinet discussed an American plan to create stockpiles for feeding liberated Europe. Gathering these supplies without provoking a price rise would require the United States to extend rationing, and officials had asked for a British gesture to help "[put] this across to their people." An S branch memo composed the day before the meeting noted that the Chancellor of the Exchequer had cautioned against making promises to the United States "about the disposal of any stock-piles of commodities we may hold at the end of the war, as these will be our only liquid assets."[59]

At the meeting, Lord Woolton said that the United Kingdom might have to continue rationing after the war, but Americans would still be enjoying more ample portions. "Why shd we bind ourselves to rationing more severe than U.S. impose upon themselves?" Churchill retorted. (The transcripts are abbreviated.) "We have done our share already." Nor was it wise to promise contributions to Europe: "Do we want to pledge ourselves in advance to give away our only liquid assets?"

"Don't want to promise free gifts. Many countries cd. pay," countered an official.

"We can bld. up stocks of some commodities here and in Empire. We can promise contributions from those stocks," added the minister of production.[60]

On that very day, the prime minister instituted the shipping cut in the Indian Ocean. Unless the Americans provided a great deal of extra shipping, the goal of 27 million tons of imports could not be met, the Prof warned on January 8: "restriction of shipping to the Eastern theatres will therefore have to be maintained to a very considerable extent throughout the year." That would be well after the stock stringency anticipated for the spring had passed. So it was concern about the United Kingdom's postwar finances, not just about wartime food supply or operational flexibility, that motivated the determination to build domestic stocks by cutting Indian Ocean shipping. In making their decision, the Prof and the prime minister exported as much as possible of Britain's future economic risk to the colonies—where it precipitated immediate catastrophe.[61]

DURING THE FIRST half of 1943 the United Kingdom would receive two-thirds of the goods that were loaded at North Atlantic ports. British stocks of food and raw materials, after dipping to a low of 14.6 million tons in March, increased steadily to reach an all-time high of

18.5 million tons in December. Such levels of reserves had to be repeatedly justified to American officials who questioned British appetites. The explanations involved elasticity in the definition of a key quantity: the working stock. As R. J. Hammond described in the official history of Britain's wartime food supply, the most essential stocks were of the "working" or "distributional" type, needed to maintain the smooth flow of commodities. For instance, a dockside warehouse needed to be sufficiently empty that it could absorb goods whenever a ship arrived to unload, but also full enough that it could disgorge goods to trucks anytime they showed up to load. Working stocks were the sum total of such reserves. The exigencies of war required, in addition, "contingency" stocks to allow for sudden difficulties.[62]

In practice, the Ministry of Food lumped working stocks together with contingency stocks to define a quantity that it insisted was an absolute minimum. This figure was actually much higher than necessary. Hammond noted, for instance, that although in the first months of war the stocks of wheat available to mills had fallen to 260,000 tons, the vast majority of mills had kept on going. But in 1943 the ministry insisted that it needed 850,000 tons of working stocks alone. And although 1942 saw a record harvest of wheat (2.5 million tons) and 1943 topped even that, the ministry ignored the home crop in its calculations— almost doubling its secret margin of safety. Nor did estimates of bread consumption allow for the gigantic output of potatoes (10.1 million tons in 1942), large quantities of which would be fed to pigs. The Ministry of Production similarly inflated the stock requirements of industrial raw materials and defined a "distributional minimum" that it put forth as irreducible. The Prof referred to an analogous, but even higher, quantity as the "minimum safety level" or "danger level"—at once rendering it sacrosanct. In truth, had stocks fallen below even "the real minimum working level, there still remained some additional economies the Government could impose," noted Hancock and Gowing.[63]

Unfortunately, "every ton of food unnecessarily earmarked for [working stocks] was condemned to uselessness only less surely than if it had been destroyed," commented Hammond. Millions of tons of supplies had to be held in storage in the British Isles and could not be consumed even during the shipping crisis of early 1943. In December 1942, for instance, 1.8 million tons of wheat grain and flour were at hand, enough for more than six months' consumption, with record harvests of wheat expected for, and reaped in, the summer of 1943. Overall, the stocks of imported food and raw materials held at the end of 1942 were around 4.5 million tons higher than those consumed during the next six months—after which the shipping stringency was over.[64]

On March 9, 1943, Leathers reminded the shipping committee that the second half of 1943 should see a "large increase" in available shipping because of the phenomenal rate at which Americans were producing ships. The president should be persuaded to transfer some vessels to British control, Cherwell suggested: "Only if we can build up our stocks to something like the 1942 level shall we be in a position to seize our opportunities in the summer and autumn." Losses of vessels to submarines fell steeply that spring, because bombers recently assigned to the convoys of merchant ships were picking off the enemy's U-boats in unprecedented numbers. So Roosevelt reiterated his promise of 7 million tons. Even if all this shipping should come in, the Prof argued in April, "it would still leave us short, unless shipments to the Indian Ocean remained at their present low level."[65]

As it happened, in April 1943 a bumper wheat crop was being harvested in the northwest of India, so the Government of India agreed to do without further shipments. But it then proceeded to buy such vast quantities of grain—the armed forces alone would consume 650,000 tons that year—that by May prices had resumed their upward trend.[66]

In the circumstances, it was inevitable that London would later accuse New Delhi of having sent conflicting messages about its need. The Ministry of War Transport pointed out that the estimated cereal shortage had fallen from 2.5 million tons before the wheat harvest to 1.3 million tons after it, "which suggests that these paper calculations are rather an unreliable basis" for the Government of India's requests for substantial help. Defending the government against the charge of unreliability, Robert Hutchings of India's food department stated to the famine commission that he and others had "always tried to recognize the appalling strain on His Majesty's Government and the United Nations over shipping. We never felt justified in asking for a ton more than we really believed to be necessary. Sometimes, when our crop prospects seemed good, we have stated: 'All right, we could do with a little less or you could slow up imports; let us have them later in the year.' . . . [W]e never at any stage adopted what is sometimes described as bazaar tactics—that is, asking for a lot in the hope that we will get something less."[67]

British officials in India were understandably alarmed by reports of food stringencies back home. The prime minister had warned of living "hand to mouth"; the secretary of state for India had stated that British rations, which were "already cut to bone," might have to be further trimmed to meet the colony's demands; and the viceroy of India had informed provincial governors that home rations might have to be reduced in order to send wheat to India. In late December 1942, the Ministry of War Transport had congratulated the India Office on dealing "so firmly" with the colony's request for cereals, and expressed a hope "that the demand is at least watered down, if not eliminated." According to the ministry, meeting the Indian need would have reduced U.K. imports by a million tons in 1943.[68]

Even when they hit bottom in March, however, U.K. stocks were between 2 million and 5 million tons above the various estimates of necessary minimum levels. Thus the Indian cereal requirement posed no actual threat to British rations. The warnings had nevertheless suggested to expatriate civil servants that their shortcomings were adding to the troubles of their beleaguered countrymen. "I am fully confident you will agree that if we can save, by our own efforts in India, even one of the ships [diverted to bring grain], then we shall have made a significant contribution to easing the burden on those responsible for directing the war," the viceroy had exhorted.[69]

So it was that the Government of India came to measure the food problem by the yardstick of the United Kingdom's needs. When officials could feed the army and the industrial population for some months, and thereby keep up the war effort, they figured they had enough. Rather than importune the War Cabinet for ships, they chose to ignore the distress in the eastern villages. In late spring, the viceroy informed Governor Herbert that little could be done about the food shortage, which would likely persist for the duration of the war.[70]

In any event, India received a little less than 30,000 tons of wheat by July 1943 (plus the 30,000 that had been previously promised to the army). That is, of the 600,000 tons that the viceroy had requested in December 1942 as being essential to avert disaster, it received less than 5 percent. As a result, only a quarter of the wheat that the Government of India had promised to send to Bengal in the first half of 1943 could arrive in that province. Most of that, in turn, remained in Calcutta for use by the priority classes, with small quantities being sent to the districts for official use. In April, an intelligence summary observed that "large numbers of starving people" were emigrating from the province—a marker of famine as given in the Bengal Famine Code, the official manual for the region.[71]

Curiously, the Government of India chose not to explain to the Bengal administration why it was unable to help out in supplying wheat. Instead it insisted that the province had more than enough rice. "This shortage is a thing entirely of your own imagination," Justice Henry B. L. Braund of Bengal's Department of Civil Supplies said he had been told by officials of the Government of India in March 1943. "We do not believe it and you have got to get it out of your head that Bengal is deficit. You have got to preach that there is sufficiency in Bengal and if you wait you will find that there is sufficiency in Bengal." Civil servant Pinnell was similarly instructed, by Major General E. Wood of New Delhi's Department of Food, that if only he would "preach the gospel of sufficiency" and hint that large imports of grain might suddenly arrive and drive down prices, he would draw out hoarded stocks. Meanwhile he should battle any misconceptions about shortages "by attacking and confining on a large scale those who were likely to be its exponents." A food minister was appointed for Bengal—Huseyn Shaheed Suhrawardy of the Muslim League—and although he believed a famine to be approaching, "he was not allowed by the Government of India to say so." On the contrary, he announced that the province faced no shortages.[72]

If the brokers who were hoarding could be persuaded of abundance or of impending shipments, they would certainly release hidden stocks; but they were not deceived. A witness to the famine commission offered another reason for the Government of India's assertion of sufficiency: "We were told that they were insisting on this in order to purchase rice for export." In December 1942, Pinnell wrote in his memoir, Bengal had been "pressed to agree to export rice" in exchange of receiving wheat for the war effort. Viceroy Linlithgow met Chief Minister Huq in January 1943 and told him that he "simply *must* produce some more rice out of Bengal for Ceylon even if Bengal itself went short!" The chief minister "was by no means unsympathetic," Linlithgow reported to Amery, "and it is possible that I may in the result screw a little out of them."[73]

New Delhi had come under "very heavy pressure" from London to continue sending rice to Ceylon, another official confirmed. The source was Winston Churchill. At a meeting of the War Cabinet in November 1942, for instance, the prime minister had demanded "fresh pressure" on India to send an additional 20,000 tons per month (for the next two months) to Ceylon, where rubber tappers were deserting the plantations for lack of rice. The quantity demanded was small compared to India's total crop, Churchill had argued, ordering that his "[very] strong wish [that] further help be given" be conveyed to India.[74]

Pinnell charged that rice was sometimes exported from Calcutta without his knowledge and that it had a "disastrous" impact on prices. By way of example, in about November 1942 "suddenly it was heard that a ship was available and that it must be loaded the very same day," he related to the famine commission. "You can quite easily buy two or three thousand tons in different places quietly without upsetting the market, but if one man runs round [the market in Howrah, across the river from Calcutta] for the whole quantity to be obtained in the course of the day the effect of that is very severe. As a matter of fact rice disappeared from the Howrah market and prices rose in Calcutta; this had far reaching effect, the Calcutta market dominating the rest of Bengal." The quantity being exported did not matter as much as the modality, Pinnell felt, for "the very sight of loading a ship with rice in the Calcutta port was certain to create panic in the middle of a crisis."[75]

Nor were the quantities small. Whereas India annually imported at least a million tons of rice and wheat before the war, it exported a net 360,000 tons during the fiscal year April 1, 1942, to March 31, 1943. Of this quantity, 260,000 tons were rice. Gross exports of foodgrains (including lentils) in that fiscal year totaled 465,600 tons. The exports took place after the war had reached India's borders, imports of rice from Southeast Asia had been cut off, invasion appeared imminent, and hunger marches and food riots had become routine. The exports continued even after the cyclone had damaged the vital winter crop of rice. On April 22, 1943, more than a month after it had been warned of famine, the Ministry of War Transport recorded with approval "continued pressure being brought upon India to persuade her to release more than the previously agreed quotas of rice and, more recently, cargoes of wheat." Between January and July of 1943, even as famine set in, India exported 71,000 tons of rice, an unknown fraction of it through Calcutta's port.[76]

Shiploads of food departing a captive and stricken land recall the Indian famines of the Victorian era and the Great Irish Famine of the 1840s, when crop failure combined with colonial policy to fell millions. The exports of 1942 and 1943 were far smaller than those of earlier times, but just as damaging given the substantial imports that were needed to keep native souls from departing their bodies. Ceylon, Arabia, and South Africa, where the rice ended up, were already better supplied with grain than was India. But if distributed at relief camps in Bengal at the average rate of a half-kilogram per person per day, 71,000 tons of rice would have kept 390,000 people alive for a full year. The 360,000 tons of wheat and rice, if similarly used, would have saved almost 2 million.[77]

On July 21, 1943, the Government of India once again asked Amery for immediate imports, noting that "famine conditions have begun to appear" in parts of southern India and in Bengal.[78]

CHAPTER SIX

An Occupied and Starving Country

Ambassador William Phillips was alarmed at what he saw of India. The Muslim League was gaining in influence, which to his mind made future strife in India more likely. He met Mohammad Ali Jinnah and "felt attracted to him personally but not to his dream of severing India into separate nations," Phillips wrote later. Another source of worry to him was scant evidence of British interest in the war against Japan, although he noted that the Indian Army was remarkably large: "Was this necessary for the preservation of internal peace I wondered, or were the British hesitant to send this untried army to the battle fronts?" Indeed, the War Cabinet had shifted its subsidiary military focus from India to the Balkans. During the fall of 1943, the United Kingdom would build a stockpile in the Mediterranean region for feeding the Greeks and Yugoslavs it intended to liberate. That meant shiploads of Australian wheat would pass by famine-stricken India, destined not for consumption but for storage.[1]

In April 1943, shortly before he was to return to the United States for consultations, Phillips visited Linlithgow at the Himalayan resort of Dehra Dun, where the viceroy was engaged in hunting tigers from elephant-back. The envoy again asked if he might meet Gandhi: he was concerned about rumors that Gandhi was planning a fast, this time to the death. Linlithgow refused Phillips's request, informing him that if the war effort could be aided "by the holding of Gandhi to death then I would so hold him without the least hesitation."[2]

As it happened, Gandhi regarded his survival through the fast as a divine blessing and was energized by it. Instead of attempting another fast, on May 4 he wrote to Jinnah asking if they could meet to try and reach an understanding about the future political integrity of India. The Government of India referred the matter to the War Cabinet. "Surely a letter from an interned person seeking conference for the purpose of 'uniting and driving the British out' should not be delivered while war-time conditions prevail," Churchill advised, and the missive did not reach the addressee. (Gandhi had not of course written in such terms, knowing full well that the authorities would read the letter.) The government did, however, make the message public to forestall news of it leaking out— and Jinnah dismissed the possibility of any such encounter unless Gandhi first accepted the prospect of a Muslim-majority Pakistan.[3]

Back in Washington, Phillips warned the president that it was high time to press the War Cabinet for a conciliatory gesture in India. The people were seeing the war as one between fascists and imperialists, he said, and had no stake in its outcome. "Lassitude and indifference and bitterness have increased as a result of the famine conditions, the growing high cost of living and the continued political deadlock," he told Roosevelt. The president seemed reluctant to deal with the matter, but he asked Phillips to meet with the prime minister, who happened to be visiting the United States.[4]

Ambassador Phillips told Churchill on May 23, 1943, that if indeed the transfer of power to Indians was being held up by disagreement between Hindus and Muslims, the government should try to bridge the gap and, to that end, arrange a meeting between Gandhi and Jinnah. The prime minister did not respond kindly to the suggestion "Take India if that is what you want! Take it by all means!" he raged. "But I warn you that if I open the door a crack there will be the greatest blood-bath in all history; yes, a blood-bath in all history. Mark my words," he went on, shaking his finger at the envoy, "I prophesied the present war, and I prophesy the blood-bath."

Phillips took his leave. Churchill followed him to the top of the stairwell and "repeated once more his certainty of a 'bloodbath.'" The ambassador was bemused, for he did not have in mind the precipitate withdrawal that Churchill assumed he was proposing. "It was only too clear that he had a complex about India from which he would not and could not be shaken," Phillips concluded. He had a long talk with Roosevelt, who was an old friend, and told him that his returning to New Delhi would be pointless.

In his memoir, Phillips would hold British policy responsible for the partition of India that transpired after the war. By the time the war ended, he wrote, "the situation had crystallized"—in that the prolonged incarceration of Congress leaders had enabled a single personable actor, Jinnah, to command the Indian stage. As a result, the idea of Pakistan had captured the imagination of Muslims.[5]

A RELIGIOUS BLOODBATH and its possible outcome—the partitioning of India—had been on Churchill's mind for some time. In March 1943, when a relatively liberal Tory politician, Richard A. Butler, had gone to dinner to the prime minister's country residence, the conversation turned to India. According to Butler, his host had "launched into a most terrible attack on the 'baboos,' saying that they were gross, dirty and corrupt." He would like to "clear out of India," he reported Churchill as saying: "Our army is going to be kept there only to prevent one section of the population mauling and murdering the other." The answer to *that* problem, the prime minister continued, was Pakistan.

Surely the British Raj stood for unity among Indians, Butler protested, to which his host responded: "Well, if our poor troops have to be kept in a sweltering, syphilitic climate and lice-infested barracks for the sake of your precious unity, I'd rather see them have a good civil war." Upon which the prime minister's wife chided him, prompting Churchill to declare that he liked to rile people who disagreed with him. He went on to explain, however, that he saw the United Kingdom presiding over a "tripos" consisting of a Hindu India, the princely states, and Pakistan. The problem was that "in India we shall be bound by the Americans, if by nobody else, to all the promises we have given"— including the 1942 Cripps offer of dominion status after the war. Which somehow reminded him of Madame Chiang Kai-shek, the wife of the leader of the Chinese nationalists fighting alongside the Allies, who, he lamented, was rather too influenced by Nehru—but that was all "offly-toofly; they are in love with one another."[6]

Over the next years, the word *Pakistan* would turn up in the prime minister's verbal and written communications with increasing frequency. This suggests that Churchill was becoming fearful that the Indian colony could not be retained for long after the war and was speculating about alternatives. A new nation of Pakistan, beholden to the power that assisted in its birth, would possibly enable the United Kingdom to retain influence in South Asia and perhaps even provide a military base for future operations against the Soviet Union. And which fragment of India could be more desirable for such a stronghold than the rugged northwest, amidst whose "scenes of savage brilliancy" he had spent some of the most exhilarating days of his youth?[7]

As nationalists of the Congress festered with impotent rage and religious radicals of the Muslim League flexed their muscles, communal strife in India was indeed becoming more likely. During the monsoon season, Governor George Cunningham of the North West Frontier Province exulted at the Muslim League's triumph in local elections. "It would not, I think, have been possible had not the ground been prepared by the propaganda which we have been doing almost since the war started, most of it on Islamic lines," he wrote to the viceroy. British authorities were arguing that Muslims and Christians were natural allies because they each had a holy book, unlike the idolatrous Hindus; and they were describing the region's most popular leader, Khan Abdul Ghaffar Khan, as anti-Islamic because he was a believer in Gandhian nonviolence. That the charismatic pacifist—and devout Muslim—was behind bars, along with 6,000 of his followers, had also helped the elections deliver the outcome desired by British authorities. By the time "the Frontier Gandhi," as Ghaffar Khan was known to admirers, would emerge from prison, it would be too late for him to curb the religious furies that imperial policy had unleashed in his homeland. The same would be true of Gandhi himself.[8]

Yet throughout 1943, all remained quiet—because tens of millions of people in the rice belt that stretched from Bengal in the east to Cochin in the south had begun to starve. Bereft of physical and mental strength, they could no longer rebel, and the Quit India movement petered out. India was no longer in revolt but simply "an occupied and hostile country," a British general stated. In July the viceroy wrote an assurance to the secretary of state for India: "politically the position is very easy here at the moment. The fact is that none of these people know what to do. The Moslem League have no wish to do anything, the Congress are completely at a loss."[9]

DEFIANCE PERSISTED IN a few areas, among them Midnapore. The orchestrated violation of so many of the region's women in January 1943 had so humiliated the rebel leaders that they had publicly renounced their former reluctance to kill for their cause. The newsletter *Biplabi* instructed women to grab any implements at hand and gather in a prearranged place to resist attackers, should any enter a village when the men were away. The demand for daggers was such that the Tamluk government distributed more than seven thousand of them to village women.[10]

Soon after the announcement recanting nonviolence, Sushil Dhara shed blood for the first time. The victim was a high school teacher who had shown the police the homes of several students who had participated in the September 1942 assault on the administration. One night Dhara dressed in an overcoat over a flowing *dhuti*, just as the government's agents did, and along with an associate in a fake police uniform went to the teacher's house and asked him in Hindi to step outside. A senior officer of the Intelligence Bureau, he said, was waiting in the school's playground and needed help with an arrest. The man readily followed them. He was taken to a river at the point of a dagger, stabbed there, and his body carved up and thrown into the water. Dhara's autobiography is reticent about his actions and emotions during this, the most violent, period of his life, as if he had walked through a door that shut behind him.[11]

On April 29, 1943, he got caught. Acting on a tip, plainclothes policemen and officers from Calcutta surrounded a village home that Dhara was visiting. He ran out the back door, flipped over two men who came at him, jumped a ditch, landed his foot on a patch of cow-dung, and fell flat on his face. Several men piled on him. The sepoys did not recognize Dhara, for unknown to them he had grown a beard as part of his disguise, but the officer to whom they took him was better informed. Satish Samanta had already been arrested, which left Ajoy Mukhopadhyay as the only significant leader not in custody. Mukho-padhyay needed his right-hand man and hatched a plot to free Dhara before he could be dispatched to a distant prison.

The captive had been taken to Tamluk jail, where he had a warm reunion with other rebels, including his elder brother. One night Dhara came down with violent stomach cramps. Two friends sat by with wor-ried faces—while his brother, who was not in on the plot, became frantic with anxiety. The prison doctor had been paid off. He ordered that Dhara ingest nothing but milk and barley, which ensured that the patient became progressively more haggard. He also took away a stool sample and, in a few days, announced that the prisoner had a potentially lethal internal hemorrhage. The jail superintendent came to check on the pa-tient, by which time Dhara looked suitably awful.

A Congress worker now applied at Tamluk court for Dhara's bail, and as expected it was refused. That meant bail could next be sought at a higher court in Midnapore town, where Mukhopadhyay had bribed the public prosecutor. The judge perused the medical report, said that he could not let a man die in prison, and with the prosecutor not utter-ing a squeak of protest granted "town bail"—release into Tamluk. A go-between raced back to Tamluk prison and presented the order be-fore the police got wind of what was going on. Dhara hobbled out, leaning heavily on the friend, clambered into a rickshaw, and vanished into the night.[12]

The police put a reward of 10,000 rupees on his head. Dhara had shaved right after getting out of prison but the mug shots had him heavily bearded, so that false sightings were reported from everywhere.

Still, with the police perpetually on the lookout, it was hard for him to get around. So Radhakrishna Bari was dispatched to Calcutta with the task of obtaining proof of Dhara's death. He got hold of an emaciated volunteer who suffered from gastric ulcer, admitted him to a hospital under the name Sushil Dhara, and withdrew him after the doctor had supplied a fearsome medical report. Subsequently an unclaimed corpse—there being many on the city's streets by that time—was cremated, with Dhara's name being entered in the "burning register," which the police subsequently checked. Word went out that Dhara had died.

Soon after Dhara's escape, Ajoy Mukhopadhyay got caught. The loss of the Tamluk government's two top leaders almost broke its back. Partly out of desperation, Dhara increased his reprisals on informers, so that in a few months the authorities could no longer find anyone to spy for them.

At this time, two of Dhara's female subordinates asked him if they could participate fully in the movement—if, that is, they could also kill. Both women had spent time in jail for their political activities but had hitherto been used only as decoys. To test their mettle, Dhara had them first observe slayings, then dissect bodies and throw the pieces into a river at high tide, so that all traces of the crime would disappear. "I saw no distress even when they were covered in blood," he reported in his autobiography. Next the women were assigned to commit executions, which they performed flawlessly: "Either of them could walk thirty or thirty-five miles by night, accomplish her task and be found asleep in the morning in her bed—such a thing happened many a time." All this the women did for love of liberty, Dhara attested.

In such manner the Tamluk region became a *muktanchal,* or free zone, where members of the renegade government could carry out their duties without always having to look over their shoulders.[13]

"I CONFESS TO being somewhat disturbed about the continuance of Congress troubles in Western Bengal and can only hope that Nazimuddin's Government will tackle the Congress miscreants in the Midnapore District with greater vigor than its predecessor," Amery wrote to Linlithgow on May 25, 1943. The Bengal administration had more pressing problems, however. In March, Governor Herbert had requested permission to use special wartime ordinances to dismiss Bengal's cabinet, which he felt would enable him to deal directly with the food problem. Linlithgow replied that these coercive laws were for containing political subversion, not for solving problems of food supply, which might "disappear entirely"—after the war was over.[14]

Linlithgow did lift provincial barriers so that Bengal could purchase rice in Bihar and Orissa. This time the food minister, Huseyn Suhrawardy, appointed the Ispahani Company the principal buyer of grain, giving it an advance of 30 million rupees and instructions to buy at any price. (An exhausted Leonard George Pinnell had departed for a district posting.) Prices in Bihar and Orissa immediately rose, and starvation deaths were reported there, so the administrators of those provinces defied the Government of India's orders, arrested the purchasing agents, and held up grain shipments to Bengal. They suspected fraud—and, indeed, a subcontractor of the Ispahanis was later proved to have cheated the government out of millions of rupees.[15]

On May 27, 1943, Linlithgow advised Amery that he was "unable to guarantee" the stability of the Indian economy. Every necessity of life—food, fuel, drugs, cloth—was "approaching the scarcity limit." The manifold causes included the lack of shipping for imports and the diversion of every industry to war production, which had left a dearth of products for civilian use. As a result, all the cash in the economy was being used to buy up grain, the only commodity at hand. Thus far, the viceroy continued, the Government of India had "succeeded in holding the fort: in producing the men and material needed for the war and in keeping the vast majority of the population quiescent." But the "real resources of the country are already strained almost to breaking point: on the psychological side, we are within sight of a collective refusal to accept further paper currency." The time had come when the United Kingdom needed to choose between "utilising India as a base for operations and utilising India as a source of supply for overseas theatres and countries."[16]

"Bengal is rapidly approaching starvation," the governor of Bengal wrote to the viceroy on July 2. Unless he received immediate help, Herbert could not "guarantee two indispensable requirements of the war effort, internal security and war production." (At no recorded instance did either the governor or the viceroy express concern for their subjects: their every request for grain would be phrased in terms of the war effort. Contemporaries attested that Herbert did care about the starvation in Bengal; so prioritizing the war effort may reflect his and Linlithgow's estimation of which concerns might possibly have moved their superiors.) Hunger was widespread in the districts, Herbert wrote three weeks later, and masses of ticketless beggars were boarding trains in the hope of finding food in the towns. The U.S. Board of Economic Warfare reported in July: "Famine has been a real and ever present threat, and it is now reliably estimated that unless substantial quantities of food-stuffs are forthcoming from outside sources, hundreds of thousands of deaths from starvation will occur in India during the current year."[17]

Also that July, a committee headed by economist Sir Theodor Gregory reviewed the food problem in India and urged a ban on grain exports, in particular those of rice, in order "to stop the crop of rumours which have exercised a dangerous effect on the country." Rather, the committee called for imports: a half-million tons to create a grain reserve and thus stabilize the market, and another million tons a year to meet the country's continuing needs. Such imports were all the more urgent, the committee stated, because eastern India, which was suffering the most from shortages, would also be the base for future military operations.[18]

The Government of India warned Amery that the food shortfall was so large that "it will be physically impossible to bridge the gaps entirely with India's own resources." On July 23, possibly because the Gregory Committee report had been leaked to the press, the Government of India announced a cessation in rice exports. At about the same time, it asked the India Office for 80,000 tons of wheat to be imported every month for six months, for a total of almost a half-million tons. Half of that quantity would support the army for six months, while the remainder would go toward feeding laborers and otherwise shoring up industrial production. The mere knowledge of impending imports would have a decisive effect on prices, the viceroy wrote, because it would squeeze out hidden hoards. Indeed, he wanted to be able to make a public announcement that His Majesty's Government had guaranteed "shipping sufficient to import into India enough wheat to satisfy all reasonable requirements of the population."[19]

LORD LINLITHGOW'S TERM as viceroy was to be over on October 30, 1943, and in June the prime minister had decided upon Field Marshall Wavell as his replacement. Churchill had never thought much of Wavell—he had once remarked that the general would make a decent manager of a golf club—and had hit upon this way of easing him out of the military command chain. Meanwhile, General Claude Auchinlek had also incurred the prime minister's displeasure and had reverted to his former position as commander-in-chief in India.[20]

In London on July 30, the War Cabinet's shipping committee considered Viceroy Linlithgow's request for grain. An India Office representative stated that "famine conditions" were appearing in Bengal and in parts of the south, and relayed Auchinlek's opinion that India might not be usable as a base until the food problem was solved. The committee was divided in its response. Some members argued that meeting the colony's need "could hardly do more than involve some degree of interference with the re-establishment of stocks in the United Kingdom" unless some large military need showed up in 1943. The minister of war transport objected, however, that providing the ships to lift any more than 30,000 tons of grain a month from Australia would involve "a serious dislocation of our plans." In the end, the shipping committee noted a "wide divergence of opinion as to the part which the import of cereals should or could play in solving the Indian economic problem" and left the decision to the War Cabinet.[21]

It was the Prof who questioned the role that "the import of cereals should or could play," as evident from a memo he prepared for the prime minister the day before the War Cabinet took up the problem. Despite India's urgent demands during the previous winter, he wrote, "the emergency vanished." (The India Office was now reporting the outbreak of famine, but Cherwell perceived no link between current events and the earlier crisis.) On top of that, the Indian harvest was massive. "Yet we are told that failure to provide half a million tons of cereals will result in a reduction of national output, refusal to export food [to Ceylon], famine conditions, civil disturbance and subversive activity among the troops in the Indian army." Imports were being regarded as a means of extracting stocks from hoarders, Cherwell complained. "This seems a roundabout way of tackling the problem. In any event, it is a little hard that the U.K., which has already suffered a greater drop in the standard of life than India, should be mulcted because the Government of India cannot arrange its affairs in an orderly manner."[22]

One draft of this memo ended with the sentiment that, since shipping would be needed to feed Italian civilians if the Allied invasion caused Italy's fascist government to collapse, expending it on famine relief in India "scarcely seems justified unless the Ministry of War Transport cannot find any other use for it." The sentence was eventually changed to a straightforward recommendation against sending grain.[23]

According to minutes of the War Cabinet meeting of August 4, 1943, the secretary of state for India began the proceedings. (The transcripts released in 2006 are more candid than the minutes, but they unaccountably stop in mid-July, just before this crucial meeting.) The Indian economy "was being strained almost to breaking-point" by the demands of war, Amery stated, and the direst effects could be countered only by meeting the viceroy's request. The War Cabinet took the view, however, that the problem "could not be dealt with simply by the importation of grain." Lord Leathers argued that it would be "extremely difficult" to find ships to get grain to India. If the War Cabinet felt that something needed to be done, he would suggest sending "not more than 50,000 tons as a token shipment. This should, however, not be earmarked for India but should be ordered to Colombo to await instructions there." It might also be possible to send up to 100,000 tons of barley from Iraq.[24]

Lord Leathers owed his position and peerage to the prime minister, and took his cues from him. In his diaries, Field Marshal Alan Brooke accused Leathers of "trimming his sails to the wind"—adjusting the availability of ships to suit the War Cabinet's predilection. Lord Moran, Churchill's doctor, likewise described Leathers as a weak man who did whatever Churchill told him to. The prime minister, in contrast, was all praise for Leathers's efficiency. "It was very rarely that he was unable to accomplish the hard tasks I set," he would write. On several occasions, when no one could solve a pressing problem such as finding the ships to transport an extra division, "I made a personal appeal to him, and the difficulties seemed to disappear as if by magic." In any debate over sending grain to India, Leathers would invariably state that the shipping could not be found, in the right quantity or at the right place, and no personal appeal on behalf of Indians was forthcoming from the prime minister.[25]

Breaking the bad news to the viceroy, the secretary of state for India could offer scant comfort. He suggested that Linlithgow anyhow announce imports, but "without disclosing figures." The viceroy replied (and a note of desperation broke through his usual bureaucratese): "A firm promise of 100,000 tons of barley and the possibility of small additional quantity of wheat will go nowhere in meeting our essential demands." Whereas substantial imports of wheat would have broken the famine, barley was of little help because it had a negligible effect on prices.[26]

The situation was worse than Amery and Linlithgow realized. A Ministry of War Transport paper declared that "[t]he War Cabinet directive [of August 4] is not a precise instruction as no decision is taken whether any wheat is, in fact, to go to India and no time limit is laid down beyond the implication that the requirements of Ceylon and the Middle East for cereals are to receive priority." In point of fact, the War Cabinet had not scheduled any relief at all for India.[27]

IN DEFENDING CHERWELL'S role in the decision to deny India famine relief, Thomas Wilson, the S branch economist who assisted him with Indian matters, would make several points. First, as he wrote in a book on the Prof's wartime achievements, the United Kingdom could not have added substantially to total supplies in India. That was correct—and irrelevant, because the relatively modest quantity of grain being requested by the viceroy would have brought considerable relief. Second, he declared that no one "could possibly say how much would be required" to make an impression on speculators. On the contrary, the Government of India had a good idea, based on the wheat required to feed the army and part of the urban populace until the next harvest; so also did the Gregory Committee. Third, the situation with available ships and where they could be deployed "was acutely critical at the time."[28]

In truth, perhaps at no other period during the war than in the summer and fall of 1943 did the number of ships at hand so greatly exceed those already committed to Allied operations. The war against U-boats was won and American production of ships was increasing steeply; the net gain for the Allies had been 1.5 million tons of shipping in May alone. That month the president had transferred to British control fifteen to twenty cargo vessels for the duration of the war. By the summer of 1943, the British shipping crisis had given way to what historian Kevin Smith calls a "shipping glut" and the S branch would refer to as "[w]indfall shipping." Lord Arthur Salter, who had headed the British shipping mission to Washington, returned to London to find that instead of worrying about the scarcity of ships, his colleagues were now concerned about the impact on postwar trade of too many ships in American hands. So many vessels would present at North American ports that autumn to be loaded with supplies to add to the United Kingdom's stockpile that not enough cargo could be found to fill them. If ever during the war a window had opened for saving lives in Bengal—at no discernible cost to the war effort—this was it.[29]

The prime minister had other uses for the surplus ships, however. He had observed in mid-July that the "immense saving" in shipping had been "partly allowed for in our calculations and plans, but if maintained should require a further drastic re-examination of these in a favourable sense." He urged that some of the extra ships be used to restore white bread to the United Kingdom. With the remainder, the War Cabinet would continue to bolster the United Kingdom's stockpile—

and it would create a second one in the Mediterranean region, in preparation for a British liberation of the Balkans.[30]

As First Lord of the Admiralty during World War I, Churchill had pushed through a seaborne attack on the Ottoman Empire. The Gallipoli (or Dardanelles) campaign had ended in dismal failure, with more than 40,000 Allied troops killed, and Churchill's superiors had forced his resignation. He had retained an interest in the region—and an apparent desire to prove, by means of a successful reprise, that his strategic concept had been sound. Churchill hoped that military successes in the vicinity of Turkey would induce that nation, which remained neutral, to join the war on the Allied side and provide an unconventional route for attacking Germany and supplying the Soviet Union. Historian A.J.P. Taylor would describe Churchill's strategy as a "strange fantasy." The venture was doomed for several reasons, including mountainous terrain in the Balkans that was easy for the enemy to defend, the Turkish determination to stay out of the war, and American hostility to the plan—which would lead the president and his generals to withhold vital military equipment.[31]

As a prelude to what he envisioned as a full-scale campaign in the region, on August 3, 1943, Churchill had instructed his military chiefs to prepare for an occupation of islands in the Aegean Sea (which lies between Greece and Turkey). Australian wheat and the surplus ships would meanwhile be used to build up a substantial stockpile for feeding the civilian population of southeastern Europe—just in case these inadequately supported but prospectively heroic efforts in the eastern Mediterranean led to freedom for Greece, Yugoslavia, and other Balkan countries. By December, German forces would have routed the British Empire's soldiers and sailors from their island outposts, in what Stephen Roskill, the official historian of the United Kingdom's naval war, would describe as "the Aegean fiasco . . . a tragic, and one may feel a wholly unnecessary ending to a year which had brought important and long-awaited successes."[32]

In the fourth part of his defense of the War Cabinet's policy toward the Indian famine, Wilson stated that rice was hard to get hold of, and no grain other than rice would have sufficed to forestall mass fatalities.

Some rice was actually available in 1943. That year, around 150,000 tons of rice were exported from Egypt, most of it going to Ceylon, and the United Kingdom imported 131,000 tons from unknown sources. British authorities would also turn down offers of rice for Bengal, as will be discussed in later chapters. And it was mistaken to maintain that starving Indians would eat only rice. This untruth appears so regularly in British accounts of the Bengal famine, in one of three forms—that Bengalis "would sooner starve to death" than eat wheat, had difficulty digesting wheat, or did not know how to prepare wheat—that it deserves special scrutiny.[33]

Wheat was one of the ancient crops of Bengal and is one of the nine plants symbolically offered to the goddess Durga. When Bengalis worship her in October, they eat a wheat paste as a sacral offering. They have no trouble digesting it; on the contrary, better-off Bengalis use cream of wheat to wean infants. Chitto Samonto said that rather than shun wheat, he and other villagers regarded it as a luxury food to be enjoyed at certain festivals. Those who could not afford to buy wheat would visit wealthier homes, where they would help prepare, and subsequently feast on, *pithe* (filled crepes) or *luchi* (fried bread). All that it took to make *ruti*, or flat bread, out of wheat flour was to knead it with water into dough, roll it out, and toast it.

However, when people have been starving for a long time, their bodies would have partially consumed themselves, rendering the intestines paper-thin. At that point in starvation, the ingestion of any solid food—including rice—could be fatal. Famine victims would not have possessed griddles, so the ruti would have turned out crusty and possibly risky to eat. But there was another option. Civil servant Olaf Martin, who was later pressed into famine relief, fed rescued orphans with a concoction of whole-meal wheat flour, butter, and molasses. "This was boiled up into a sweet porridge which all children would eat eagerly and digest easily," he wrote in his memoir. "And about 10 days of this diet put them in a condition to eat ordinary cooked rice and vegetables. These children recovered very rapidly in our orphanages, mental and physical condition improving simultaneously."[34]

Bengalis did have trouble digesting coarse grains, and relief workers came to believe that even the gruel made out of these was causing diarrhea. "One of the extraordinary features of Bengal is that although all this time they have been talking of shortage of supplies, they practically refuse to use either millets or gram [small chickpeas]," stated Robert Hutchings in 1944. "This year they have told me 'For goodness sake stop sending millets.' Now they say stop sending gram because we cannot use it. They are quite willing to take wheat." The famine commission ignored such testimonies and thus abetted the they-won't-eat-bread theory, claiming that commission members saw wheat rotting in warehouses because Bengalis did not want it. But that argument is inconclusive, because the Bengal government held stores of rice for the war effort that were also rotting.[35]

The only problem in feeding wheat to Bengalis was that the people lacked the means to grind it, which meant it would have had to be milled into flour before distribution. Australian wheat was mainly exported as flour, however; and in any case the Government of India had asked for wheat shipments not so much to feed Bengali villagers but to unburden the people of the demand to fill the stomachs of soldiers. Because of the wheat shortage, the army would eat 115,000 tons of rice during 1943—twice the quantity it had consumed the year before. An assurance of receiving enough wheat to feed the war effort might have prompted the authorities, if not others, to release to the starving some of the rice they had stockpiled.

AN ALTERNATE VIEW of the August meeting on famine relief can be found in Amery's diary. After propounding the urgent Indian need for food "in as strong terms as I could," he fended off a counterattack. According to Amery, the War Cabinet treated the demand for rice "as a bluff on India's part aimed at loosing existing hoards with less trouble than by other methods, while the discussion rapidly developed into an attack on India's failure to deal with the inflationary position." The S branch regarded inflation as an instrument by which Britons were "being exploited" by Indians. Because the real value of the rupee had fallen steeply since 1940, when it had been pegged against the sterling, Cherwell believed that the money being expended in India was buying less than it should, which left the sterling debt three times too high. Amery, in contrast, held that the enormous demand for Indian goods would normally have led to the rupee *rising* in value instead of falling: had it not been pegged down, the sterling debt would have been three times greater than its already high amount. He pointed out that "nothing could counteract the immense amount of our purchases, not repaid in any amount by consumer commodities. I fought hard and expressed myself very freely about the nonsense talk by Professor Cherwell whom Winston drags in on every subject and who obviously knows nothing of economics, but, like Winston, hates India."[36]

By then, the prime minister's several sources of anger with Indians had fused into one fury. In May 1943 he had accused Field Marshal Wavell of "creating a Frankenstein by putting modern weapons in the hands of sepoys" and had brought up the specter of 1857. In June he had warned that native troops might "shoot us in the back," demanding that suspect peoples, including Bengalis, be purged from the Indian Army—an action that had turned out to be unfeasible. The prime minister "hates India and everything to do with it," Wavell observed in his diary on July 27, after witnessing an outburst in the War Cabinet. "Winston drew harrowing picture of British workmen in rags struggling to pay rich Indian millowners; and wanted to charge India the equivalent of our debt to her for saving her from Japanese invasion." The field marshal pointed out that "India had defended us in the Middle East for the first two years of war" rather than the other way around. Amery, for his part, noted that it was not a good idea "when driving to catch a train for life or death, to lean through the window and tell the taximan that you do not mean to pay the fare at the station because you have a moral counter-claim against him." Because it was patently counterproductive to seek a revision of the financial agreement at that juncture, the prime minister had been frustrated in his resolve to abolish the balance owed to India.[37]

It became clear during the August 4 meeting on famine relief that the sterling debt was still embedded in the lion's paw. Instead of sending relief, the War Cabinet recommended "forceful propaganda" and curbs on inflation as measures against famine. It also used the session to set up a committee for studying Indian inflation and finding ways to reduce the sterling debt.[38]

Lawrence Burgis, a secretary who attended that meeting, took sketchy notes that point to yet another factor prompting the denial of relief. After Amery spoke of the famine, Churchill's associates questioned the necessity of meeting the Indian demand for wheat. Leathers argued that Ceylon's needs should receive priority, while Cherwell suggested an attempt to "bluff Indian hoarders" by announcing that enough grain was being imported to bring prices down. Sir Percy James Grigg, the secretary of state for war, said that bluffing would not help—in his view, not even the half-million tons of wheat that the viceroy sought would actually help, because the shortage was of rice. (Grigg appears to be the source of the myth that wheat would not suffice to thwart the famine.) Churchill opined that the food crisis pointed to the "failure of Indians" in higher echelons of government. At least the essential war workers should be fed, he felt; but although shipping 50,000 tons posed no difficulty, sourcing wheat from Australia could be a problem. As for barley from Iraq, India could have "as much as [possible]."[39]

That fall, Ceylon and the Middle East were to receive each month 75,000 tons of Australian wheat to meet the regions' continuing needs, according to the Ministry of War Transport. In addition, building a stockpile required "to meet potential demand for re-occupied S. Eastern Europe" would consume 70,000 tons of wheat by the end of October and a further 100,000 tons by the end of 1943. Churchill must have had the Balkan stockpile in mind when he commented on the necessity of conserving Australian supplies: because Europeans, if and when they were liberated, would need wheat, Indians would have to make do with barley. Cherwell, Leathers, and Grigg must also have known that the surplus shipping and Australian wheat were to be used for building the Balkan stockpile, and could not be spared to relieve famine in India; these most loyal of Churchill's aides were no doubt looking for reasons to reject the viceroy's request.[40]

Churchill did say that if the situation in India got worse Amery could bring it up again. The next day, August 5, the prime minister boarded the *Queen Mary* for a conference in Quebec. The following week, a committee disbursed the shipping in the Indian Ocean for the next two months. In September, ten vessels would be required to load in Australia with wheat flour, and two with other foodstuffs, but none would be going to India. In October, ten vessels would have to load in Australia with wheat and other food, but again none would be destined for India. War-related cargo would instead fill the ships traveling to that colony. As for the Iraqi barley, at most 30,000 tons could be transported per month; negotiations on price, being the province of Lord Woolton, were incomplete when the War Cabinet again discussed the famine on September 24, 1943.[41]

As long as food could be exported from India for use in the war theaters, the imperial administration had exported it. But while the colony itself suffered from famine—in no small part because of the scarcity and inflation resulting from such extractions of supplies—shiploads of Australian wheat would pass it by, to be stored for future consumption in southern Europe. "India's need is absolutely urgent and immediate," Amery would remonstrate in late October. "Relief for the Balkans, badly needed as it is, cannot be delivered in any quantities for many months to come for the simple reason that the enemy still control the situation. As for depleting our stocks here to danger point, that is a pretty remote consideration, especially now that we have got so effective a whiphand over the U-boats."[42]

IN MARCH 1943 the Bengal government had extended over several districts the relief operations originally intended for cyclone victims. "A large famine relief organization could not however be set up without a great deal of publicity," explained Nihar Chandra Chakravarty, a civil servant employed with the effort. "This publicity could not very well be done when propaganda was being made that there was no fear of serious shortage for keeping up the morale of the people." The Government of India surely knew of the dire situation, he testified, because in

July a minister had written to New Delhi warning that "we were going to starve by the millions."[43]

With the Department of Civil Supplies keeping all the grain it could get hold of, or distributing it to priority industries, little was left for even these circumscribed relief operations. Around July or August, Chakravarty and others "had the feeling that it might not be possible to save all people," as he said later to the famine commission. "We simply wanted the people to keep going on, on something like half or one-fourth ration for a few weeks," until supplies arrived. As a result, the gruel offered at the relief kitchens got thinner, so that a pound of rice a day was feeding three people. Sometime after that, the portion was further reduced, to four ounces per person per day. That came to 400 calories, at the low end of the scale on which, at much the same time, inmates at Buchenwald were being fed.[44]

CHAPTER SEVEN

In the Village

"In Sapurapota village of the 17th Union of Panskura Thana a Muslim weaver was unable to support his family and, crazed with hunger, wandered away," recorded *Biplabi* on August 5, 1943. "His wife believed that he had drowned himself in the flooded Kasai River. Being unable to feed her two young sons for several days, she could no longer endure their suffering. On 7/23 she dropped the smaller boy torn from her womb, the sparkle of her eye, into the Kasai's frothing waters. She tried in the same way to send her elder son to his father, but he screamed and grabbed on to her. The maddened mother had lost all capacity for love and compassion. She discovered a new way to silence her child's searing hunger. With feeble arms she dug a small grave and threw her son into it. As she was trying to cover him with earth a passerby heard his screams and snatched the spade from his mother's hand. A *kagmara* (low-caste Hindu) promised to bring up the boy and the mother then went away, who knows where. Probably she found peace by joining her husband in the Kasai's cold torrent."[1]

Such killings were not rare. "Kironbala the Acharjo girl threw her baby into the canal," attested Bhawbanibala Samonto of Kalikakundu. After Kironbala's husband died, she had returned to her father's home with her one-and-a-half-year-old girl. Dependent on her father and hungry, Kironbala had gotten angry over some careless words. She dropped her toddler into the water and came home. Her father went to look for the child but the tide had come, and he returned empty-handed.

Often, the murderer—or mercy killer—was the father. A "man with a female child requested everybody he met to buy the baby. As nobody

151

agreed to his proposal, the man threw the baby into the well and fled away," reported the *Hindustan Standard* on November 28, 1943. Another newspaper mentioned that Bhogurdi Mandal of central Bengal was tried in September and sentenced to deportation for life (presumably to a penal colony on the Andaman Islands) for killing his three-year-old son Mozaffar, whom he could not feed. *Biplabi* wrote that on September 15, Gyanendranath Panda of Chongra village, having become crazed with hunger, slew his father, mother, grandmother, grandfather, wife, son, and daughter—everyone in the house. Suicides were so common that the newsletter took to listing these by name, place, and rough date, providing no further details. Another press report related that on October 22, in a suburb of Dacca, a fisherman, his wife, and their small daughter threw themselves in front of a train. The child miraculously survived, but what then became of her was not stated.[2]

The effect on the psyche of prolonged hunger is profound. An American experiment that enrolled conscientious objectors to World War II in a study of starvation revealed that it leads to an obsession with food, intolerance for loud sounds, and sudden bursts of irrational rage. A parent in such straits may well be impelled to do violence to an importuning child. An anthropologist in Calcutta at the time described a mother and son who had received some morsels from a relief kitchen. After eating his portion the boy took a piece of potato from hers, and she began to beat him so mercilessly that the onlooker had to intervene.[3]

Stories of abandonment during the Bengal famine—of a small child found wandering alone in a field, or of a woman who continued to eat at a relief camp while her baby died untended in her lap—are also common. An actress in Calcutta reported that once when her cook poured onto the pavement some *phyan*, the starchy water in which rice had been boiled, a shriveled-up woman who nevertheless seemed young caught it in her clay pot. Her four children ran up, but the mother ferociously slapped them away and drank up most of the phyan in quick gulps. Then she stopped and looked into the pot, which she must nearly have emptied, peered up at her crying children, and, horrified at what she had done, burst into sobs. At Faridpur in eastern Bengal, some workers were removing a corpse when a woman huddled nearby threw a bundle in their direction, saying, "Take that also." It was the body of her child.[4]

FAMILIAL BONDS DID, however, persist even amid calamity. The husband of Fatema Bibi had plied a ferryboat on a river not far from Kalikakundu, but died of vomiting and diarrhea sometime after the 1942 cyclone. She was then perhaps sixteen and had a baby, Sopi. Her mother had died long before, but Fatema brought Sopi home to the Muslim hamlet of Kalikakundu. The famine then took her father and elder brother, leaving her with a younger brother to bring up alongside her son. Asked sixty-two years later how she and her son had survived, she replied simply, "I lived by looking at his face." She made it through for her son's sake, by working as a servant and begging to bring home what food she could. "It was a very hard time," she said and stopped, too overcome with emotion to elucidate.

Abdul Rahman was thirteen or fourteen at the time of the famine. Telling his story six decades afterward, he recounted how he had trailed along with an elder brother the day everyone converged on the Mohisadal police station and was lucky to escape the bullets. Later he ate at a nearby soup kitchen, along with perhaps a thousand others, many of whom came from far away. But no one could get more than a ladleful. "It was a thin gruel. How could it be enough?" he asked. "Even that some people would divide up and eat. Lots of people died. Sheikh Khurshed, Intiaz, Latul . . . and many children. We couldn't bury them or anything. No one had the strength to perform rites. People would tie a rope around the necks and drag them over to a ditch."

Gunodhar Samonto, who was living by a canal in Kalikakundu at the time of the cyclone, named the men he knew who died during the famine: Behari Das, Gobindo Das, Bhuson Jit, Hori Jit, Pawnchom Jit, Haradhon Khan, Madhob Khetua, Nityanando Pramanik, Pawnchom Pramanik, and Madhob Rai. Among the female fatalities he recalled Poribala Acharjo, Saroda Acharjo, Surobala Acharjo, and Sagori Giri. Almost all the able-bodied of Kalikakundu had left their homes and trekked to Calcutta to look for employment, he said. Saroda Acharjo's three sons found jobs in the city's wartime factories, and Moni Giri's sisters Gyanoda and Kulobala also got work, in the brothels.

Gourhori Majhi of Kalikakundu was eight at the time of the cyclone and living in another village. The family's hut had fallen, but they had forded the floodwaters to reach a higher house. The starvation started right away, for there was no rice to be had. "Everyone was crazed with hunger," he said in 2005. Whatever you found, you'd tear it off and eat it right there. My family had ten people; my own stomach was wailing. Who is your brother, who is your sister—no one thought of such things then. Everyone is wondering, how will I live?" For months the boy fed on boiled *patalawta* (leaves and vines), *kochudata* (yam stems), and seeds of *durbo ghas* (lawn grass). "There was not a blade of grass in the field," he said, because everyone was searching them out for their tiny grains. While Gourhori's body grew skeletal his stomach had ballooned, a marker of approaching death.

He would eat at the gruel kitchen, where "the food was like water." The family had sold its utensils and would accept the soup in cupped leaves, but others would snatch even these out of their hands. The child was fortunate, though, in that his swollen belly caught the eye of a gentleman with the relief operation, who called him aside. "He gave me a few grains of rice and watched me eat them." Day after day for months the man had fed him, in secret and a little at a time, so that the boy slowly recovered. Tears coursed down the cheeks of the seventy-one-year-old Majhi as he remembered this unknown savior.

Mani Bhaumik lived in a village near Tamluk. His father, Bhaumik would write in an autobiography, was a former schoolteacher who had become a nationalist and therefore rarely dared to come home. Sometimes the police would show up instead, to search for the fugitive and to ransack the house. Once an officer smelling of sweat and cologne called Mani a "wog" and hit him in the face. But the eleven-year-old was fortified by the love of two remarkable old women.

One of them was Matongini Hazra, who lived alone in a nearby village. Married at twelve to an old man and widowed at eighteen, she used to eke out a precarious living by husking rice. Many years earlier, when Mani was only a year old, his father had led a procession that had wound by Hazra's hut, and she had run out to join it. Since that day she had been a freedom fighter and a friend of the family, and would sometimes bring the boy some pithe, or crepes with sweet fillings, that she had made.

One evening in September 1942 Hazra arrived with a plateful of pithe and, seating the boy on the doorstep, fed them to him by her own hand. Her eyes had a strange fire in them. She told him not to worry about his father, to trust in God, and to always do what he most fervently believed in. When he grew up he would live in a land that was free, even if there would still be a lot of struggle, because "nothing comes just because you want it . . . you have to fight for it. And you have to stay on the right path." She blessed him and walked into the night. The next day, September 29, she died in a hail of bullets.

The other woman who profoundly affected Mani was his grandmother, Saroda Devi. After the famine began, the family started receiving mysterious bundles of food—millets, yams, *kolai* lentils. His father must be sending these, Mani presumed. Still the provisions were not enough for him, so his grandmother began to give him her portions. Each evening she would lie down, enervated, and stare "listlessly at the light coming through the cracks in the door," wrote Bhaumik. "I knelt by her side and clasped her bony hand, sharing in her secret plot to make one life from two." Someone must have told Mani's father that the old woman was doing badly, for he managed to visit just before she died. Bhaumik went on to finish school and college, get a doctorate in physics, migrate to the United States, co-invent a laser used for corrective eye surgery, and live as a millionaire in Malibu, California.[5]

"AFTER THE FLOOD we started a vegetable garden," said Chitto Samonto. His family owned less than a half-acre of land, but because many of the local people had died or wandered away, fields all around now lay fallow. There the brothers sowed pumpkins, squash, and watermelons. In three months they started to get fruit, which they boiled and ate, long before it could ripen. "Otherwise we had coconuts and some boiled kolai," he said. These lentils, which when freshly picked resemble tiny green peas, are a valuable source of protein but contain few calories. "We would gulp everything down with water," Samonto remembered. They also boiled and ate stems of yam, fleshy stems of vine, leaves and seeds of tamarind and other trees, seeds of grass, and stringy whole kolai plants, which were normally fed to cows. Occasionally they drank palm sugar mixed with water. Finding and processing food often took more energy than one could get out of eating it.

For much of that time the family had an extra mouth to feed. Chitto's elder sister was married to a postal officer in Calcutta. But after her ten-year-old daughter had died of some illness, her husband had taken to abusing her, so her father had brought her back to Kalikakundu. Many of the poor were selling their land *jawler damey*—as cheap as water—in order to buy rice, so the husband then bought almost twenty acres in a village not far away. He carried a badge that kept him safe from the police, and he would sometimes visit his estranged wife. "He praised the British all the time, said they were civilized," recalled Samonto. "One time he was coming along the fields to our house, cursing Gandhi loudly. Our boys from the underground government"—here Samonto grinned—"caught him and took away his watch, ring, and bicycle." Chitto's father recovered the valuables and sent them back to his son-in-law, who never ventured that way again. Near the end of the famine the sister was fortunate to get a nurse's job in a faraway town.

"My mother wouldn't eat—she would feed us," Samonto recalled. "Still, we were like skeletons. Sometimes I would just sit around and cry." About five months after the flood a gruel kitchen opened in a neighboring village, but its soup "wouldn't fill your belly." Later some relief materials were distributed at Geokhali, eight miles away, and Chitto and his brother trekked there to collect it. "Some days it would take me two and a half hours to get there, I was so weak. They gave us rice, half rotted and with worms inside—it had been sitting around in a storehouse. The two of us brothers would come back with five kilograms for a week. But there were four of us in the house, it wasn't enough." In normal times a youth such as Chitto, who worked in the fields, would eat a kilogram of rice a day.

One night in the rainy season, the police surrounded their house. Chitto and his brother were not involved in politics at the time, but they had been in a crowd who watched while the Tamluk militia had taken away a local bandit, Kalo Khan, alleged to be one of the violent criminals who had been released from jail when the Quit India movement began. Many of these ex-convicts informed the police about fugitive nationalists, which may have been why Kalo Khan had been targeted—Samonto did not know. But the police investigation into the death named forty-four perpetrators, including the two brothers.

The first time the police came it was daylight, and the brothers had seen them and hidden in the fields. The second time it was night, and the police were suddenly at the front door and also at the back: they could not run. In any case, Chitto's brother was in bed with inflamed tonsils, and something in his throat had burst, filling his mouth with blood. Fortunately, in place of the dreaded Nolini Raha were two gentlemanly police officers, and Chitto's parents had pleaded their sons' innocence. "My father had been a well-known teacher, everyone respected him," said Samonto. So the policemen removed Chitto's name from the charge-sheet, but said that his brother should surrender when he recovered.

Later that year Chitto trekked with other village youths to Geokhali to excavate canals for a food-for-work program that gave them wheat and a little money. On the way he would pass many bodies dumped by the canal, with dogs and jackals feasting on them, a grim reminder of what awaited him should he falter. Sometimes the beasts attacked the living, and not everyone had the strength to fend them off. In November 1943 a journalist took a boat seven miles down a canal in coastal Midnapore and counted on its banks at least five hundred skulls and skeletons, most picked clean by dogs and jackals. "The entire place looked like an abandoned battlefield," he wrote.[6]

"My father was old—he stayed at home," Samonto said. "My mother would work in the fields, in pouring rain or blinding sun, tending to the vegetables or planting the rice she had saved. It was extremely hard labor." Somehow she found the resolve to refrain from delving into the seed grain while her son sat around sobbing with hunger: she would have been able to plant it only after the monsoon arrived in the middle of 1943. "A mother's love is unstinting," Samonto concluded. "Her care is what allowed me to grow up."

IF IT TOOK love to save a boy, it often took sex to save a girl. Innumerable families in Bengal survived by means of what one social worker, speaking at a meeting in Calcutta in January 1944, described as "mass prostitution among village women." Some mothers, wives, and daughters remained in their homes, feeding their families on rice they exchanged for sex with anyone who had access to the grain. Others went, or were trafficked, to brothels in the cities or near military encampments, where they serviced war profiteers or soldiers waiting to be sent to the front. As Clive Branson noted with disgust, army cantonments featured officially sanctioned brothels. A 1944 survey found that 90 percent of the 30,000 women serving in the military labor corps at Chittagong in eastern Bengal, ostensibly digging ditches and building runways for the war, were suffering from venereal disease.[7]

Saday Maity and his wife, three daughters, and two sons were Chitto Samonto's neighbors on the west side. They possessed very little land. The storm had broken their small hut, after which the family had built a shack on a nearby mound. "One day a well-dressed city man came by—he was looking for the Maitys' house," Samonto said. "I pointed it out, and asked who he was. He replied that he was their relative, come for a visit." The man was in fact a pimp, and he bought one of the daughters. Not seeing her around, the neighbors later asked Maity what became of her. "He said he couldn't get anything to eat and had sold her." What the neighbor had obtained for his daughter Samonto did not know. "She was very pretty," he said quietly.

During the famine of 1943 Pawnchanon Das was living in the same hut where he had been born, some 150 yards from Samonto's. His father had died in the spring of 1935, soon after selling the family's one-and-a-third acres of land, and his sister had perished soon after, leaving only him, his mother, and a younger brother. On the night of the flood, when the waters rushed in to collapse their hut, the family had fled to their cowshed—but one wall of that structure also fell down. Two of their six cows were washed away, as well as a big earthen pot in which the family stored salt. Times were hard, Das said: "My mother was begging around."

Pawnchanon, sixteen at the time, patched up the hut with bamboo. An influential local man arranged for the family to get relief materials from a Hindu mission: some rice and wheat, pots and pans, a metal spatula for cooking, and matches. Even better, his mother secured all the half-rotted rice salvaged after the flood from a small plot belonging to a landowner. "My mother would husk rice at a zamindar's home five miles away," Das explained. "One of the landlord's sons said, 'See if you can get anything out of this wasted rice, take it, and go.' We got the rice stalks crushed under cows' hooves to release the grain, and swept up six sacks. Me and my brother carried it away before the old man got home. He might have objected." They stretched the rice out through the famine year, while his mother continued to husk rice in better-off homes and bring back her small portion.

"In this village forty or fifty people died of hunger," Das remembered, qualifying that he knew only of what had happened in the southern and western regions of Kalikakundu, not in the northern or eastern ones. "My relative Bhim Das died. He had some illness, the 'doctor' here said he needed a hundred grams of rice daily. Of course there wasn't any. I had a large pumpkin ripening on my roof. One morning I saw part of it was gone. He'd eaten it." Bhim Das had left a wife and young children; what became of them Das did not know.

Their neighbor Saday Maity had indeed sold his daughter, Das said, and not just one daughter but two. He had three to begin with, Das added. The eldest he had married off to an old man sometime before the flood; but the two other girls, of perhaps fifteen and ten, he sold during the famine. The agent was a poor local, Gokul Jana, who had a sister in Calcutta's red-light district. According to Das, Jana brokered the sale of eight or ten girls from Kalikakundu.

One of Maity's daughters subsequently visited her parents, accompanied by a well-dressed man she said was her husband. "She had jewelry on, and a fine sari," Das remembered. The couple stayed for two or three days. The trafficked girls were likely the only members of the family to have made it through the famine, because sometime after that visit the Maitys left and never returned.

OTHER LOCAL GIRLS survived because they were adept at housework and childcare, and so had several uses in the desperate village economy.

At the time of the famine Giribala Malakar was teenaged and married, living in a nearby village. "I was innocent when they married me off, unknowing," she said. Her husband was a chowkidar (watchman) and helped carry sacks of grain for the relief operation, but even then he earned next to nothing. "We sold everything to buy food," including their utensils, she recalled. The couple would eat boiled spinach, when they could, off plates made of baked clay. After her husband died, Giribala fled home to her original village of Bilaspur, only to find that her father, too, had perished of hunger.

Giribala's mother managed to marry her off again—"so I would live"—to a man in Kalikakundu. There were no gifts: only the bride changed hands. The groom's first wife had just died, leaving two small daughters, and it was Giribala's task to look after them while her husband searched for work. Soon the new husband also died; and back home in Bilaspur, her mother and elder brother succumbed to starvation. "It saved my life, getting married," Malakar said. "If I'd stayed at home I wouldn't have survived. Things were worse there than here—all the neighbors were suffering and dying." Of the family she had left behind, only a younger brother made it through the famine. Malakar herself survived by living in people's homes to work as a maid and even managed to save her two stepdaughters.

She was only eleven or twelve at the time of the flood, said Tukibala Das Odhikari, who lived in a Vaishnav hamlet of Kalikakundu. Although her sect worshipped Krishna and rejected the dehumanizing barriers of caste, it was evidently subject to other perversions of the time. For Tukibala was then already married, to a man she described as "having grown old." That was how things were in those days, explained her neighbor in 2005: once a girl turned ten, she had to be married to whoever would take her, or villagers would ostracize the family.

At the time of the flood Tukibala was with her husband, in a village not far away. The two lived alone, for he had no relatives. Water poured in through their window that night but failed to bring down the hut; nor did it spoil their grain, because they had none. The hut was built on land owned by a wealthy family: the husband and wife were therefore *proja*, she said, using the word for king's subjects. They were required to work for the family as servants. Sometimes they got rice in return, stretching out a kilogram to last two or three days. At other times, when her husband was gone, either working or looking for work, Tuki would be alone at home. Then the girl would breakfast on boiled spinach, gulped down with water—"even spinach I couldn't find on some days"— and trek to a gruel kitchen for a mugful of soup, bringing it home for a late lunch. At least she found food often enough to stay alive. Her sister, she later learned, also managed to survive, by trekking with her baby to Calcutta.

A family with the surname Bera, which lived to the east of Chitto, had sheltered with the Samontos on the night of the flood. Their hut destroyed, Haradhon Bera decided to move, with his mistress, his two grown sons, and their wives and children, to the immense mangrove forest south of Calcutta known as the Sunderbans. Some zamindars were trying to reclaim the land and were inviting migrants to chop down forests and settle down. But a cholera epidemic had broken out. Doctors were in demand and, boasting some knowledge of medicine, Haradhon Bera hoped to find employment there.

Virtually all the Beras died of cholera in the Sunderbans. Only the old mistress and one of the sons' wives returned one day in the middle of the famine. "They arrived with their pots and buckets tied up in rags, back to their old home, and started wailing," recalled Samonto. "Everyone gathered to hear what had happened." The younger woman had lost her husband and daughter but was pregnant; she soon gave birth to a boy she named Kangal, meaning destitute. (The word may derive from *kankal,* for skeleton.)

"I was married when I still had my milk teeth," related Nayontara Bera, who had become Kangal's child bride. Her father had been wealthy but gambled most of his possessions away. At her childhood home, her mother would seat the siblings for their scant midday meal and say, "Eat up what you have—what else can you do? Eight mouths you brothers and sisters are. They gave me here in marriage seeing your father has twenty-five acres, but he has destroyed everything." Nayontara, then seven, would complain that she had been served too little food and would willfully refuse to eat. One day when her mother was away, an aunt talked to her father. Her relative in Kalikakundu was bringing up a little son alone and could use another pair of hands around the house. Could she have Nayontara? The father agreed, and the aunt talked the little girl into a trip.

"They said they'd take me to the fair, and to my mother, but they brought me here instead. I was crying for my mother. They gave me puffed rice and sweets to keep me quiet." Nayontara was forced to stay and a year later was married to the much younger Kangal, with whom she would play in-between housework. "We'd get rice once in two or three days," she related, weeping throughout the telling of her story. "My mother-in-law would go to people's homes to make puffed rice and earn something. If we got an egg we couldn't eat it—had to sell it."

NEWSPAPERS IN CALCUTTA wrote horrified accounts of the moral degeneracy that the famine had induced. Mothers had turned into murderers, village belles into whores, fathers into traffickers of daughters. But why had the millions of starving people refrained from looting food from the shops, most of which were unguarded? Surely, opined some experts, it was due to that inexplicable eastern trait known as fatalism.

The evidence suggests otherwise. Initially, what had kept the villagers from committing robberies was the ferocity with which they clung to their values. And by the time they became desperate enough to consider crime, most were too weak to strike at anyone who was better fed. Relief officer Binay R. Sen explained to the famine commission why there were no food riots in later stages of the calamity. "When there is a famine on that scale people are devitalised to such an extent that by the time they come to an area where there is supply they have no physical reserve left in them to take to violence," he testified. One man reported seeing a beggar in Geokhali who grabbed a handful of kolai from a pile stacked in a storefront and stuffed it into his mouth: "The shopkeeper hit him, and he just fell there and died."[8]

Hori Das of Kalikakundu remembered another man who had died for eating food that was not his own. "Binod Jana would steal others' yams," said Das. "He stole from Umesh Maity, got killed for it." Hearing this story, Chitto Samonto nodded in agreement, and explained: "Perhaps they just hit him and he died. In those days everyone was so weak a slap could kill you."

Hori Das's sister Rasi had died on the night of the cyclone, buried under a falling wall. She was about eleven then, while her brother was two years older. Some days afterward the police came by, looking for fugitives. "They hit us, stomped their boots, demanded we show them where the Kuila boys were hiding," Das said. Sepoys—whether soldiers or police he did not know—would often harass the family. They would take bananas and coconuts, and once forced him to throw a net into his own pond to catch a fish. "They took it, hit me with the gun, and went off."

The family owned no rice land but had cultivated a wealthy neighbor's fields. The landlord would put the entire harvest into his storehouse, and "we would have to borrow to eat," Das recalled. But during the famine no one would lend rice, so Hori, his father, and his brother went to the gruel kitchen. "You were still hungry after you ate there," said Das. "I looked for food all day. We ate leaves of all kinds, stems of yam, whatever. There was nobody to give us any work. Lots of land was left fallow that year." What little food the family could find they would measure and divide up, with Das's mother often abstaining from eating anything. Still, "my younger brother would complain that I got more and he got less. We all looked like skeletons anyhow."

KRISHNA CHAITANYA MAHAPATRO, or Kanu for short, was the seventeen-year-old courier of the Tamluk government. While in Calcutta he would distribute copies of *Biplabi*, and from time to time he would travel from the city to hideouts in Midnapore. One day, carrying a consignment of sensitive documents, Kanu started off for his home village of Donipur, near Tamluk. From Calcutta he took a train and a bus to Tamluk, reaching the town at 9.30 P.M., and began to walk the remaining five miles along the banks of the Rupnarayan River to his house. He had to keep hiding behind shrubs or trees, because soldiers seemed to be everywhere that night, and his white city clothes made him conspicuous. Around midnight a farmer came up to him. He must have guessed who Kanu was, for he had a warning. Just ahead, where the road bifurcated, one branch crossing the river by a bridge—the very route that Kanu would have to take—a group of soldiers was camped. "It was dangerous on the road too, with the military roaming around," Mahapatro recalled. So the farmer invited him to spend the night at his hut.

"He was clearly very poor," Mahapatro said. The one-room shack was made of mud plastered onto slivers of bamboo: it was not even a real mud hut whose thick walls would stand strong against wind. The roof was constructed out of leaves and extended some ways in front of the hut, sheltering a kind of yard. A bamboo screen split the yard: on one side stood a cow, and on the other hung a hammock where Kanu was to spend the night.

"I sat on the hammock, but I saw that he was restless, hovering around," Mahapatro recalled. "Won't you eat something?" his host asked. It was the famine time, and the youth could see that the farmer was too poor to have anything in the house. "In those days the people in our villages were very hospitable to us—they loved us," Mahapatro explained.

By *us* he meant the members of the renegade government. "Whatever the villagers had in the house—some fermented rice, some puffed rice—they would offer. But he was so poor he had nothing." Kanu asked him not to worry. It was the middle of the night; he should just go to sleep. The farmer went inside, but soon emerged. "Babu, you had nothing. I'm feeling bad," he said wringing his hands. Kanu tried again to reassure him, but to no avail. In a little while the man got a small brass pot out of the hut, washed it in a nearby pond, and milked the cow. "Please have at least this," he offered.

"I drank the warm milk, and his love brought tears to my eyes," Mahapatro said. Early the next morning he saw that inside the house the man's wife and a child, three or four years of age, had been sleeping. "If he'd been caught sheltering me, they would have been in real danger." The farmer walked to the riverside to see if the military camp was still there. He returned to say that the coast was clear, and the young courier left.

WHAT WAS IT like to have no real food in the house, day after day for more than a year? Bengalis commonly use the phrase *payter jala*, meaning burning of the belly, to describe hunger. One stage of starvation appears to be a kind of physical torment—not nausea, not pain, but a violent craving. The things that famine victims have been known to ingest demonstrate that the suffering of acute hunger easily beats the misery of nausea. A schoolteacher in Mohisadal reported seeing children picking and eating undigested grains out of a beggar's diarrheal discharge. Hunger can also eclipse all fear of pain: during the wartime American study of conscientious objectors enduring profound hunger, one subject found starvation so hard to endure that he chopped off three fingers with an axe in the hope of getting out of the experiment. Elie Wiesel, a chronicler of the Holocaust, wrote of being "tormented with hunger" and witnessed a starving man plunge his face into a cauldron of steaming soup, which killed him.[9]

Almost everywhere in the world, famished people have resorted to eating human flesh. Amazingly, not a single case of cannibalism was reported during the Bengal famine of 1943, although tens of millions of villagers suffered from acute hunger. A religious lawmaker named Manu, writing in about the second century A.D., had forbidden Hindus to eat human flesh even for self-preservation—but neither did Muslims resort to it, although they were poorer than Hindus and perished in greater numbers. Chances are that Manu's text and other scriptures merely codified a prehistoric taboo that still persists in rural Bengal. Indeed, given the frequency and intensity with which famines hit nineteenth-century India, accounts of anthropophagy are so rare that they point to a prohibition that prevailed across the subcontinent. (One such act was reported during the famine of 1770, but it occurred in a city, where moral codes seem always to have been more pliable than in villages.)[10]

How could a deeply ingrained culture prove so powerful as to over-come the animal instinct to preserve one's life? The question remains a mystery. George Orwell would write of Gandhi: "There must, he says, be some limit to what we will do in order to remain alive, and the limit is well on this side of chicken broth." Gandhi was possessed of phe-nomenal will power, as evidenced by his twenty-one-day fast—but the tens of millions of famine sufferers in Bengal also accepted as a moral norm that they would go only so far to stay alive.[11]

Nor did the vast majority of people eat dogs, cats, or other creatures forbidden by custom, but that was probably because the starving were too debilitated to catch any prey. One man in Mohisadal described pass-ing on a road a group of old people whose feet had gotten stuck in the mud—and who had consequently died there. Instead, it was humans who became prey. By a roadside near Dacca, a nun found a groaning woman, her ravaged eye-sockets full of maggots: they had consumed her eyes while she had lain there, too weak to move away. "It was not an uncommon sight at Contai to see dogs and vultures waiting beside dying children for their share of human flesh," commented another ob-server. The scavengers were not usually so merciful as to wait for death. On the contrary, the uncommon physical weakness of humans provoked the usually inoffensive village dogs to morph into creatures of nightmare. They wandered in packs around the countryside, snatching babies, attacking and bringing down the feeble, gorging on them while they still lived, and tripping brazenly in and out of homes as they searched out cozy corners in which to gnaw the body parts they carried in their mouths.[12]

Despite the horrific ways in which they met their ends, those Bengalis who perished of hunger in the villages did so in obscurity, all but unnoticed by the national and international press. Not so their relatives and neighbors who trekked to the cities. Accounts and photographs of the skeletal figures who swarmed into Calcutta to fall and die on its pavements would travel around the world, prompting offers of relief from several Allied countries, as well as from an Axis collaborator.

CHAPTER EIGHT

On the Street

"The food is good here," Clive Branson had written to his wife in March 1943. "I shall have to take great care not to grow into a tub." But an Indian who had tried to steal a head of lettuce, apparently from the vegetable patch of a European residence, was wounded by a bullet, which led a sergeant major to opine, "Pity it didn't kill the bastard. One out of 400 million wouldn't be missed. Shoot the bloody lot of them." Branson was relieved to find that for once he did not have to argue against the sergeant major; two officers did instead.[1]

Branson was still stationed in western India. "You have no idea how deeply angry the men are at the fact of thousands of soldiers sitting around both here and at home," Branson complained. He sketched with charcoal, scrutinized the papers, got reprimanded for his subversive letters, and fended off bouts of depression. He was among the few in his unit who truly wanted to fight fascism but was not promoted to officer, Branson suspected, because of his anti-imperialism. The papers were full of the famine in the east. Why could a government that had dealt so easily with Congress protestors not arrest speculators, he wondered? Six students who had handed a hoarder over to the police had themselves been arrested, while the offender had been advised to "quietly remove his stocks." And the army had been called upon to quell food riots. "The ordinary, decent people in England *must* do something—this is *their* Empire," Branson wrote.[2]

Rather to his surprise, in October he was given his stripes and put on a train toward Bengal. Branson surmised that he was being sent away because his views made his superiors uncomfortable. At a party just before he left, an officer who had never deigned to speak to him came up and said that he'd hated reading Branson's letters home. (He was a censor.) The only people sad to see him go were the Indians—an artist who had become a friend and whose wife baked cakes for Branson's journey, and a boy who had served as his factotum and who upon his departure garlanded him with flowers.[3]

The ride was pleasant enough, until the train entered Bengal. "The endless view of plains, crops, and small stations, turned almost suddenly into one long trail of starving people. Men, women, children, babies, looked up into the passing carriage in their last hope for food. These people were not just hungry—this was *famine*. When we stopped, children swarmed round the carriage windows, repeating, hopelessly, 'Bukshish, sahib'—with the monotony of a damaged gramophone. Others sat on the ground, just waiting. I saw women—almost fleshless skeletons, their clothes grey with dust from wandering, with expressionless faces, not *walking*, but foot steadying foot, as though not knowing where they went. As we pulled towards Calcutta, for *miles*, little children naked, with inflated bellies stuck on stick-like legs, held up empty tins towards us. They were children still—they laughed and waved as we went by. Behind them one could see the brilliant fiendish green of the new crop."[4]

AMONG THOSE ON the move was Chitto Samonto of Kalikakundu. His brother had gone to Howrah, a congested city across the river from Calcutta, to look for work, but had not returned. His mother had become so anxious that she had sent Chitto after him. From somewhere she had produced three-quarters of a rupee to pay for the ferry from Geokhali to Howrah, along with the address of a merchant from whom his brother had hoped to get a job. Samonto had a motive for the trip beyond finding his brother: "I also wanted to see if I could get anything to eat in the city," he confessed.

But when he finally located the merchant's house, the person who opened the door said he had never heard the brother's name and shut the door in Chitto's face. "They treated me like I was a good-for-nothing,"

Samonto said indignantly, and did not even offer him a glass of water. It was the time of *Durga Pujo*, or festival of Durga—a year had passed since the terrible cyclone. The merchant had an altar by his house, and Chitto spent that night at the feet of the goddess, along with many homeless people. For the next five or six days he wandered the streets looking for his brother. Discussing his sojourn decades later, Samonto would only reluctantly reveal how he had managed to eat: by begging. "Many people were surviving that way," he said, but the humiliation still smarted.[5]

He did not have the money to return home. Eventually Chitto decided to visit an uncle who worked at a village some eight miles from Howrah. He trudged along the Grand Trunk Road under a blazing sun, reeling with hunger and exhaustion, and was thrilled to find that at the temple of Belur the monks were running a gruel kitchen. After eating his fill he went on to his uncle, who earned a meager living building bamboo huts with tiled roofs. The uncle fed Chitto for a few days and then gave him the fare for the steamer to Geokhali. "My mother was overjoyed to see me," Samonto said. Her joy overflowed when a few days later his brother also returned—having failed to find work or any real food.

Asked if he had seen the awful sights that were reported in the metropolis, such as a baby trying to drink from its dead mother's breast, Samonto looked away. "There were such scenes here too," he said sternly. "The people who went to the city came from places like this. They were hoping they would get food. But there too they suffered, gained nothing."

"WE WOULD CLOSE doors and windows when sitting down to eat," said Calcutta resident Gita Mukhopadhyay, who was then a college student. "Phyan dao ma"—give me phyan, mother—"they would call, I'll never forget it." On her walk to college or back, Mukhopadhyay would often pass a baby on the pavement, lying abandoned "like a stray cat. Our elders would say, 'Don't pick it up, you'll get involved in a police case.'"

"WE SAW WAVE after wave of women and children coming, and some old people. They came along the road, falling, limping, getting up, falling again," social worker Ashoka Gupta related. "There was a hospital behind our house, and every morning some mothers would have left their babies on the steps, in the hope that they would be saved." Gupta's husband, a civil servant, had been posted to Bankura in southwestern Bengal in the fall of 1943. The region was hit not by denial or cyclone but by acquisition of grain for the war effort: the villagers had eagerly sold whatever rice they had at the high prices they were offered and could not buy any of it back.

Gupta was then a housewife, but faced with "such a terrifying reality" she could not remain aloof. She enlisted friends in the All India Women's Conference, obtained rice through government connections, and started a relief kitchen that fed a hundred people once a day. Later Vijaylakshmi Pandit, sister to Nehru, visited and promised to help with funds, leading the women to found orphanages to rescue as many of the children as they could.[6]

"We discovered that whenever we also let the mother stay, the child survived," Gupta said. "I saw one mother feed her baby with such infinite patience, drop by drop, a sugar and salt solution. She saved the child." Dehydration was a major problem; people who had taken to the road had few serviceable utensils or containers. According to Gupta, they would try to carry water in cupped hands or leaves, or in rags stretched tight, back to loved ones who had fallen by the wayside—but it would all dribble through. After a woman's own child was safe, Gupta would give her others to nurture: "We found that those who could save their own children could save others' children, too."

One morning a boy named Gora was resting by Gupta's house. His two sisters had fallen far behind on the road, and Gora insisted on going back to find them. The parents never turned up. Given their first food, the three children ate so frenziedly that they were in danger of getting diarrhea, but they slowed down when they were told that they would get more meals. "We found that siblings were tremendously attached," Gupta said. "As they grew older we separated girls and boys into different schools, but they always stayed in touch." She had also restored many lost children to their families. "They'd say things like, 'My village is behind the big banyan tree near the grocery store.' We would try to figure it out. One said, 'If you take me to Triveni train station, I can find my house.' She was at most five, but we did manage to get her home."

One boy, Nitai Sawrkar, believed his original home to be near Dacca in the east of Bengal. "My mother died perhaps two years before the famine, when I was two or so," Sawrkar said in 2003. "My father came to Bankura for work, and brought me with him." Unable to feed the boy during the famine, Nitai's father had left him at Gupta's orphanage. The home held only ten children then; by the end of the famine it would have fifty. "I missed my father," Sawrkar said, "but when I was with the other kids we'd forget our troubles." After about a year, a friend of his father had visited him. A supervisor subsequently informed the boy that his father had died: that was what the friend had come to tell Nitai, but had been unable to do.

"We rented a large house for the children, with wide verandahs," Gupta remembered, "and got a retired school headmistress to run it." The curriculum, inspired by Gandhi, emphasized basic education, handwork such as spinning—and democracy. The children elected a "Prime Minister" who appointed a council of "Ministers" to execute all the jobs at hand: budgeting, planning menus, serving food (cooked by an adult), cleaning, tending to vegetable gardens, taking care of visitors, and so on. Once a month, at an open meeting, everyone would voice his or her complaints. As the children got older they trained for future jobs, and Nitai had learned to be a tailor. "If they hadn't saved me, I would have been washed away," Sawrkar concluded. "That I have become a man, stand on my own feet, is her blessing."

Nitai Sawrkar was one of the exceedingly lucky few. One observer witnessed, in Munshiganj town in eastern Bengal, lost or abandoned children "of all ages—a child of seven carrying another child of three. They were to be found in every corner, standing, sitting and sleeping. It was almost impossible to ascertain where they had come from and what had become of their parents."[7]

Near the bridge that connected Howrah with Calcutta, a journalist saw a boy eating out of a dustbin. The child said that he had walked from his village in Midnapore along with his mother, in the hope of finding food in the city, but she had died of a fever. Another observer described the crazed cries of a wild-haired, half-naked woman who, while wandering the city in search of food with her four children, had lost a daughter. "She was rushing madly making her way out of the crowd crying, 'Purana! Purana! Where have you gone Purana!' She entered lane after lane, hunting desperately, and finally hit her head against something and fell down unconscious."[8]

One of Gita Mukhopadhyay's aunts started a relief kitchen, and Gita would help line up the destitutes who gathered there. "One woman with a baby kept saying, 'Please give me milk now, right now,'" Mukhopadhyay recalled. "But we couldn't put her ahead of the others, who were also desperate. When she finally reached the head of the line, she said, 'I don't need milk any more.' Her baby had died."

IAN STEPHENS, CHIEF editor of *The Statesman*, could not be sure just when it dawned on him that a disaster of major dimensions was at hand. In April or May 1943, he had watched Pinnell and Braund of the Department of Civil Supplies at a press conference, striving to assure the public that the food situation was under control. Stephens had been a public relations officer for the Government of India and felt sure that he was seeing "two unhappy but not dishonest men working to a brief they didn't believe in." Over the next months the mortality on Calcutta's streets became disconcerting enough that cocktail conversations had turned to the need for a "corpse disposal squad." Yet officials continued to dither over what was becoming indistinguishable from an old-fashioned famine.[9]

Where did his duty lie? Stephens had been appointed the newspaper's editor precisely because he could appreciate the official point of view. His predecessor, an Irishman named Arthur Moore, had been forced out soon after the Quit India movement began and his editorials had gone from being "most mischievous" to "pestilent," in Amery's words. Stephens was conservative enough to have viewed Gandhi's three-week fast as "a mean device by a politician" seeking the limelight—but famine was another matter. As an Englishman, he reasoned, he enjoyed a security and credibility not enjoyed by his Indian rivals, which gave him a particular responsibility to speak out.[10]

Starting in the summer of 1943, *The Statesman* began to publish editorials excoriating the government for the spreading famine. Stephens pointed out the official confusion, indifference, subterfuge, and buck-passing, and every day his voice became more strident. The response was disheartening: "Write, write, write, but nothing came of it," he wrote in a memoir. On Sunday, August 22, the newspaper came out with close-up photographs of children with protruding rib cages and panoramas of stick-like beings huddled in vast numbers. Despite a warning from censors, the next week *The Statesman* printed more photographs—and another editorial.[11]

Until Stephens publicized it, the calamity in Bengal had been unknown to most of India and utterly unheard about in the rest of the world. In a bid to keep the news from leaking out, the Government of India had allegedly destroyed all but one of five thousand printed copies of *Hungry Bengal*, a collection of sketches and reportage on the Midnapore famine—but it could not suppress *The Statesman*. In New Delhi, storefronts displayed the pictures of famine victims, and in Washington the State Department circulated them among policymakers.[12]

On August 14, 1943, the Indian Independence League, an association of expatriate nationalists, announced over Axis radio that it was accepting the help of Japan, Thailand, and Burma to send rice to India. "Though it is normally impossible to send rice to India from Japanese occupied territory the league is prepared to do so if the British Government approves the proposal and gives an undertaking that the food so sent will not be reserved for military consumption or exported from India" went the message, as translated from Tamil by British intelligence. Over the next months Subhas Chandra Bose repeated the offer, because he had instigated it, in speeches and broadcasts, such as this one from Singapore: "100,000 tons of rice are waiting to be sent to

India to alleviate the famine. The rice is stored in a suitable port near India. As soon as the British Government shows its readiness to accept delivery, I will announce the name of the port and the competent authority from whom the rice is to be collected. I will then also ask the Japanese Government to guarantee a safe convoy for the transport. Further deliveries for the starving population of India can be made as soon as the offer has been accepted. I hope that the British Government will accept without hesitation, as it is a humane offer, the acceptance of which will save hundreds of thousands of men, women and children in India."[13]

Ripples of hope stirred in his prostrate homeland. According to one intelligence report, the "latest Bose rumour is to the effect that he has written to the Viceroy asking him to send two ships to enable Bose to send rice to the starving people of Bengal."[14]

FOR TWO YEARS, Subhas Bose had resided in Berlin. He had married the woman he loved, fathered a daughter—and utterly failed to arouse German enthusiasm for the cause of Indian independence. The Nazis were mired in the Soviet Union, so the army that Bose had raised from the ranks of captured Indian soldiers had no hope of reaching their homeland via Afghanistan. And although the Japanese and the Italians urged a joint Axis declaration promising freedom to Indians and Arabs, Hitler continued to refuse. According to historian Milan Hauner, he was still concerned that if the United Kingdom perceived its empire to be threatened by Germany, its will to resist would be increased. He did, however, agree that Bose should travel to Asia, where he would be of more use.[15]

On May 27, 1942, Bose had an audience with the führer. In response to his request for more substantive support, Hitler launched into an interminable lecture, the essence of which was that he could do nothing. Bose then asked him to repudiate passages in *Mein Kampf* that were contemptuous of Indians. That prompted another monologue—ending with the assertion that Indian natives would take one or two centuries merely to achieve unity among different factions. By the time the interview was over, any illusions that Bose had entertained about the führer's rationality were gone. He told colleagues that Hitler reminded him of the Fakir of Ipi, a Pakhtun warlord he had met on his trek to Kabul, "with whom it was practically impossible to have a discussion on any topic even for a few minutes." All that Bose got out of the long-awaited meeting was a cigarette case.[16]

Traveling to Asia from Europe had become very difficult for an Axis sympathizer, and Bose's three guardians—Germany, Italy, and Japan—could not agree on which route was safest. Eventually it was decided that he would travel by German submarine to a point near Madagascar and switch in mid-ocean to a Japanese one. After three months of under-sea travel he surfaced in Sumatra on May 6, 1943.[17]

Bose flew right away to Tokyo, where he insisted on meeting Prime Minister Tojo Hideki. Again he had to cool his heels, but when they did confer, Tojo was impressed enough to pledge his support. Bose went on to Singapore to assume leadership of the Indian Independence League and the Indian National Army (INA)—which had become moribund. The idealistic Fujiwara Iwaichi had gone, so that the INA's founder, Mohan Singh, had fallen out with the Japanese and was in prison.

Bose's arrival electrified the INA. Although he was a civilian and a Bengali, his passion and directness convinced the soldiers that he was the man to take them where they most wanted to be: home. "It was absolutely fantastic," Lakshmi Swaminathan, a doctor who would come to head the INA's female brigade, told historian Peter Ward Fay. "They didn't get any word of command, they just stood up and put their rifles in the air—you could see a forest of rifles." Bose had a sim-ilar effect on expatriate Indian civilians. After he spoke, housewives would come up and strip their arms and necks of gold to serve the cause of freedom.[18]

A new government of Burma was about to be born, and at the in-vitation of Ba Maw, the soon-to-be head of state, Bose went to Rangoon in late July. He met local leaders, senior Japanese officers, and represen-tatives of the Indian community, and he won them all. "When Bose really got down into his subject," wrote Ba Maw, "he gave you a feeling that you were listening not to a man but to a force or something big and impersonal like that, to a long-pent, primordial force suddenly breaking through."[19]

Because he had Tojo's backing and had once headed the Indian National Congress, Bose possessed a clout and credibility that no other exiled nationalist had ever enjoyed. He also had the money and the influence to deliver the rice that he was promising for Bengal. British authorities resolved, however, to treat the offer as if it were propaganda. They recognized that since his arrival in Southeast Asia the rebel had become more potent, and "we are of course particularly anxious to discredit Subhas Bose in every possible way," wrote a senior official. Censors ensured that no mention of his offer appeared in the press.[20]

"The British must have thought his offer was genuine," opined historian Sugata Bose (and grandnephew of Subhas Bose) in an interview. "If they really thought it was a bluff they would have called it." Had the leader failed to keep his promise, he would have been destroyed as a political force. "When it came to a question of Bengalis starving to death, Subhas Chandra Bose would not have engaged in a propaganda stunt," Sugata Bose added. "When you look at his life, he was engaged in social work—plague relief and flood relief—since childhood."

The War Cabinet knew of Bose's rice offer (having received at least one of the pertinent intelligence summaries), but whether or not the issue was discussed is unclear. Although ships capable of traversing the oceans were scarce, hundreds of smaller vessels were plying along the Indian coast, most of them under government control. The proximity of Calcutta to Rangoon or other Burmese ports meant that Bose's rice could have arrived within a week or two, had the authorities chosen to collect it. Distributed at the rate of a half-kilogram per person per day, 100,000 tons would have fed 1.6 million people for four months—after which Bengalis would be harvesting their own winter crop.

To be sure, Subhas Chandra Bose was a despised enemy of the United Kingdom; he was an Axis collaborator and a target of British assassins. But when occupied Greece underwent famine in the winter of late 1941, Germany had permitted humanitarian agencies such as the International Red Cross to bring in relief and distribute it, a remarkable instance of Axis-Allied cooperation during the war. When it came to Bengal, His Majesty's Government would turn down even those offers of cereals that came not from adversaries but from friends. The dominions of Australia, South Africa, New Zealand, and Canada all asked how they could help. "Australia could supply all the wheat needed for the starving in India provided the United Kingdom could provide the ships," stated a minister in Canberra, as reported by Reuters on September 28. "Wheat was practically waiting to be loaded on boats."[21]

Virtually all dominion shipping was under the War Cabinet's control, as were seventeen merchant ships registered in India, amounting to around 80,000 gross tons, that were capable of the journey to Australia. "Almost all our ships have been taken away," Sir J. P. Srivastava later told the famine commission. (Srivastava was the member of the viceroy's executive council who was responsible for food.) At "one time I asked whether these ships could not be released to us to carry foodgrains. But nothing came of it." As a result, only highly compact foods could be loaded onto the ships that were already destined for India from the empire's ports. Amery informed the New Zealand government, which had authorized £10,000 of famine relief, that "a free gift of powdered or condensed milk to this value would be the most useful form of gift as shipping could be most easily arranged for that."[22]

Ireland sent £100,000, and Prime Minister Eamon de Valera asked his compatriots for more; meanwhile, the leader of the country's Labour Party reminded the Irish people that when their forefathers had starved under British rule in the previous century, Indians had sent help. Private charities in the United Kingdom and the United States also began to collect money. The Red Cross started operations in Calcutta, but it could provide only milk powder, vitamins, and medicines. These were valuable, but no substitute for rice or wheat.[23]

DUKHAHARAN THAKUR CHAKRABARTY, a sixteen-year-old who lived near Howrah, once went with a group of communist medical students who were distributing powdered milk and medicines they had obtained from the Red Cross. In a neighboring village, the teenager saw row after row of disintegrating huts, some missing their tin roofs, which the owners had pawned for food before abandoning them. Hearing sounds from within one hut, the students knocked. A tiny girl opened the door. Dukhaharan looked in and saw her father lying on a reed mat on the mud floor. He was sick and moaned in a continuous refrain, "Ore, ami ar banchbo na re," meaning Oh, I won't live any longer. The girl said her mother had gone somewhere, and started crying. "We gave them some milk and medicines, couldn't do much else," Chakrabarty recalled.

Another time, the teenager was about to cross a busy street near the railway station in Howrah when he saw a truck full of men come to a stop on the far side of the road. They began to grab people from the pavement and throw them onto the truck. "I didn't know who they were, but they were merciless. They were catching hold of old men, beggars, anyone they could grab. They picked up a girl, of perhaps fifteen. Her sari fell off, and I saw that she was naked under it, nothing on her but the ring in her nose. 'Hau mau kore kandchhe'"—she was howling desperately. "I stood rooted to the spot."

It was the first time Chakrabarty had seen a naked female, and the vision never left him. "I still wonder, where did they take her, what happened to her? I wish I had run forward, protested, done something to help her," he said sixty years later. "But I just stood there."

THE TRUCK WAS from a government program to cleanse Calcutta's streets. Near the end of August, Governor Herbert had come down with an inflamed ulcer and appendix. Shortly afterward, Chief Minister Nazimuddin summoned civil servant Olaf Martin to Calcutta and asked him to take charge of the relief operation. Martin had run such programs in 1936—but that year he'd "started work in January, and had found that this was not a day too soon," Martin commented in his memoir. "Here was a much bigger calamity." Eventually it dawned on the civil servant that his job was not so much to begin gruel kitchens or work-for-food programs in the countryside, for which there was not enough grain, as to rid the city of unsightly beggars "as quietly as possible. The Army was demanding this, and had the support of the Viceroy." It was a matter of morale—Calcutta being the place where soldiers billeted in the east went for recreation.[24]

With the help of politician Shyama Prasad Mookerjee, Martin rented space for relief centers just outside the city. But the refugees took to hiding when they spied the trucks that went around to collect them, because most of them were waiting for relatives who had gone in search of food. They had to be chased, grabbed, and thrown onto the trucks. The cleansing of Calcutta broke up many families, and although Martin would eventually set up a camp where those with missing relatives could go and search for lost family members, the problem of involuntary separation was never solved.

Years later, the writer Mahasweta Devi would employ a maid named Hiron who spent much of her time crying, because during the famine she had left her daughter on the pavement to go search for food and never saw her again. It was also routine to see "dead people being picked up in government trucks, tossed in like logs," Devi recalled. "*Thok thok* they would land, as if made of wood. I heard they were burned in furnaces of factories," serving the war as fuel.

MANOS BANERJEE, A seventeen-year-old student, had been jailed for participating in the Quit India movement. After his release in the summer of 1943 he arrived in Calcutta to find beggars and corpses everywhere. Dumped in a crater excavated for the construction of a movie theater were dozens of corpses that filled the environs with a horrific stench. Some months later, as he marched in a protest to the governor's palace, shouting slogans against the famine, communist thugs armed with lathis fell upon them from both sides. "A 'comrade' got my friend by the throat and was choking him," said Banerjee. "I gave him a blow, then we ran." A few of the demonstrators managed to break through the palace gate but came under police fire or were arrested.

Communists initially supported the Axis but had switched sides after Germany attacked the Soviet Union in 1941. ("Because Stalin and Churchill combined, that is fundamental," one Bolshevik would explain to the famine commission. "Churchill as a comrade in arms is

completely different from Churchill in opposition.") Thereafter the
Communist Party of India declared that it was fighting a People's War
against fascism and began to actively support the authorities. Communists were prominent among the intellectuals who chronicled the famine
in art and literature, but they placed all blame for it on speculators and
the Japanese. Consequently they stayed out of jail, prevented food stocks
from being looted, suppressed protests, helped distribute whatever relief
was available, and acquired political leverage in Bengal.[25]

THE POLICE WERE fully engaged in hunting down political sub-
versives. At one point, the teenage courier Kanu Mahapatro realized
that either the police or the Intelligence Bureau had posted men to
watch the building in north Calcutta where he had stashed copies of
Biplabi. The printed sheets were secreted in a room rented by Congress
volunteers from Burdwan district (north of Midnapore). Fearing that
a search was in the offing, Kanu decided to stage a move. Along with a
friend, he approached two streetwalkers and asked them to pose with
him as family.

The rebels from Burdwan provided pots, pans, brooms, pillows,
and other household items. These Kanu piled onto a cart, with the
newsletters hidden in a bedroll at the bottom. Acting the roles of a
householder, his wife, and his younger brother and sister, he and the
others talked and cursed volubly about water supply and other domestic
matters as they pushed the cart past the watchmen. When far enough
away, Kanu decided to stop and let the women go, and they asked what
it had all been about. "When we explained who we were, they were in
tears, so thrilled were they at having been able to help," Mahapatro said.
"They would have fallen at our feet if we'd let them. They wouldn't take
any money."

The police had been overwhelmed by duties related to war and insurgency for more than a year, as Deputy Inspector General C. J. Minister of the Criminal Investigation Department would tell the famine
commission. To begin with, he said, from early 1942 onward the police
had had to help implement the rice denial policy, which required grain

to be forcibly requisitioned from landowners and cultivators. Eventually criminals had come to realize that "they had a much greater opportunity than they had had before." Armed robbery had skyrocketed, he continued, the reason being "the steady relaxation of police surveillance over known criminals." After that, the Quit India movement had "inevitably absorbed the whole attention of the police who had no time left to take notice of anything else." The Tamluk insurgency had proved particularly onerous.[26]

On top of that, many convicts had reportedly been released from prison. The authorities remained absorbed in curbing the activities of their political adversaries, while marauders, war profiteers, child traffickers, and hucksters of all kinds roamed free. Bengali society had descended into *matsyayana*, defined as a time when big fish ate little fish.

A MADAM NAMED Durga made her fortune at the famine time. A ravishing beauty, tall and very fair of skin, she used to live with a *seth*, a powerful businessman from western India. He did not allow Durga to sell her own body; instead, she used his money to buy girls who could not get enough to eat. Famine had brought into the market females of diverse classes and castes, some of whom would normally have been cherished as daughters or wives, and who could earn large profits for brothel owners. (In the previous century, historian William Hunter had noted that famine boosted the slave trade: "Infamous women went about buying up beautiful girls.")[27]

In the old days an upper-class prostitute, as Durga had once been, would hide her face behind a fold of her sari when first encountering a potential customer. Instead she would display the heel of her foot, bordered with red paint and adorned with an anklet, so that a customer could judge her youth and class. As a madam, though, Durga dispensed with such niceties. "If you didn't get undressed right away she'd threaten to put a broken bottle up your insides," reported Kohinoor Begum, one of her former slaves. The madam would live into the twenty-first century, dying at the age of 103 and bequeathing cars, jewelry, and five brothels to her sons.

Women also sold sex of their own accord, in order to provide for themselves and their families. Historians Christopher Bayly and Tim Harper have written that, unlike the Japanese and their comfort women, the British did not need to use overt coercion to provide entertainment for their soldiers: "Free enterprise did it all for them." Officially sanctioned brothels enabled at least one enterprising military officer to put away a stash for retirement.[28]

DURING THE 1943 famine, ten-year-old Monju Patro lived with her parents and three siblings in a two-story mud house in a Midnapore village. She would line up her mug at a gruel kitchen, but sometimes it would remain empty. Her mother husked rice for a better-off family, bringing home for the children the broken rice she got in return, as well as the puffed rice they gave her for breakfast. "I never saw her eat," Patro said.

A neighbor had been working on the girl for days, telling her that he would get her a job in a babu's home. "I didn't listen," Patro related. But one day, while she was play-cooking with other children—using utensils, rice, and vegetables they had fashioned out of mud—the man drew her aside and said, "Come along, I'll buy you sweets at the train station." The girl had eagerly assented. She was wearing her only dress, "a pretty frock made of flannel—my father had given it to me for Durga Pujo," and her drawstring underpants.

When they reached the railway station, after a long trek, the man had bought her two or three *rosogolla*, cheese balls in syrup. "I was so absorbed in eating that I never realized he was putting me on the train," Patro recounted. Calcutta, which she had never seen before, had dumb-founded the young girl. The neighbor left her with a woman, who gave the girl a ruti (flat bread): "I was thrilled to get to eat." Then she cried, wondering why the man was not coming back to take her home, but to no avail. She would spend the next years drawing water, sweeping, and mopping for the madam.

After Monju menstruated, the madam said that she would arrange her marriage. "I still didn't understand," Patro recalled. "I was weeping because it didn't feel like a real wedding. Where were the guests, the music, the turmeric ceremony? She gave me something to drink, my head spun, and I went to sleep. When I woke up I was paining all over, I couldn't get up. I never saw the man." Following that initial rape, she had been made to stand on the street, wearing colorful print saris, in front of 14 Maniktola Lane—an address that, judging by her precise and bitter enunciation of it sixty-three years later, was tattooed onto her brain. "I never understood who it was I serviced—they spoke all kinds of languages. I never saw the money." Life in the brothel had been a miasma of terror. Early one morning Patro watched, through a slit that served as her window, as thugs in the lane below strangled a customer for his watch and wallet. Another time a gangster forced his way in and, laying a sword on the bed between two women, raped them all night long. "We saw a prostitute cut up and stuffed into the gutter," Patro remembered. "Couldn't do anything."

Patro eventually fled the madam, running off with a man who had fallen in love with her. She continued to sell her body, because they needed the money. Her boyfriend was a chef, but after he broke a hand he could not earn much, so they had returned to Sonagachi, Calcutta's main red-light area and fetid slum, where they lived cheaply. Years after her children were grown, Patro complained that they neglected her. "One son is a cook and lives far away," she said. "He took everything I had." Patro still remembered the faces of her own parents, whom she had never seen again. "Where will I find them now?"

PUSHPO ODHIKARI ALSO came from Midnapore but forgot the name of her village. At the famine time she had been about eight; she had a brother and a sister, and her parents were old. "My mother couldn't feed me," she remembered. "If we ate in the morning, we couldn't eat in the evening." One day, while she was playing with other boys and girls, cooking up a banquet out of mud, a stranger wearing a dhuti and vest had approached them. He offered to find her work in a babu's house, where she would eat well and even earn money to send home to her parents.

Pushpo was hungry. "I said to him, 'I'll just run in and tell my mother.' He replied, 'Don't bother, I'll tell them later.'" As had happened to Monju Patro, the man had given her sweets at the train station, brought her to Calcutta, and sold her to a madam who had first made the girl work as a maid. After Pushpo menstruated the madam put her in a room with a young man, left the door open a crack, and sat herself on a stool outside, to intimidate the child into cooperating.

After four years of prostitution, "when I got smarter," Pushpo ran off. Not knowing any other trade, she continued to work the streets of Sonagachi. She fell in love with a chauffeur, but he would beat her when she did not give him her earnings. Odhikari's son had died young. Her daughter had fortunately escaped prostitution by working as a maid in a rich household—so rich that they had security guards at the entrance. Speaking in old age of her own survival in the slums of Sonagachi, she said, "I've spent my entire life in this Hell."

BOTH THE ORPHANAGES and the brothels saved the lives of some thousands of the millions of children under ten who suffered from the famine and represented almost half the refugees on Calcutta's streets.[29]

Stationed in a Bengali town that he did not name, Clive Branson went out one evening to buy underwear and to eat in a restaurant. The food was very good and the prices astonishingly low. But walking back along the dark streets, he heard someone "sobbing her heart out" and found a little girl lying on the edge of the pavement. He gave her a few coins and tried to speak to her. Some locals gathered, explaining matter-of-factly that she was one of the starving. "At that I lost my temper completely, and told them they should be bloody well ashamed to walk past a child in her state," he related. Branson made some of them carry her to a relief center. "The whole incident upset me so much that I cannot face going into the town again, because being in the army I don't know what I can *do* to help these creatures."

Another soldier, William A. Barnes, wrote in his diary: "I have heard many homeless little children of between 5 and 10 crying bitterly and coughing terribly outside my room in the Rest Camp at Chittagong at

3 & 4 in the morning in the pouring monsoon rain. They were all stark naked, homeless, motherless, fatherless and friendless. Their sole possession was an empty tin in which to collect scraps of food. We were strictly prohibited from helping any of these refugees in any way, under heavy penalties. Many could not endure to see this suffering, though, and did help surreptitiously."[30]

Sergeant John Crout recalled that famine sufferers surrounded his army camp, because they were given the leftovers of military meals. A guard patrolled the edges of the camp to make sure any bodies were promptly removed. Once he was badly shaken by the sight of a girl, not yet dead, whose arm had been torn off and devoured by a jackal. Even battle-hardened soldiers were unnerved by such things, Crout said.[31]

Unsettling sights and sounds were all too common. The *Hindustan Standard* reported on November 15, 1943, that a stranger had guided three nuns in Islampur in eastern Bengal to an abandoned stable by a riverside. "There to their utter horror, they found about 20 babies laid in rows on the dark and unclean floor of the stable. Some of the babies were crying in agony for food, some gasping for breath and the rest in a state of utter exhaustion and stupour. On enquiry they learnt that the mothers of the babies, no longer able to carry them on their arms in their trek through the city in search of food, had left their dear little ones behind hoping to return after the day's wanderings to their babies with food for them." The odds that a mother would make it back to her baby were slim. On November 21, a doctor described women at a gruel kitchen, also in eastern Bengal: "mere skeletons covered simply with skins; some gasping for their last breath in my presence; mothers hugging their dying and dead children unable, having no strength, to weep or cry; some practically in delirium"—calling for food, only to expire within minutes or hours of eating.[32]

IN THE THIRD week of September a temporary governor, Thomas Rutherford, arrived in Calcutta. The "scenes are pretty ghastly," he reported to Viceroy Linlithgow, but he added that native ministers were being "obstructive about forcible removal to outside camps of hordes of destitutes in Calcutta." When he met the new governor, civil servant Olaf Martin was astonished to realize that he had no idea of the extent of the catastrophe. Rutherford insisted that only the few thousands who fouled the city streets were starving, whereas in fact they were just a symptom of the famine stalking almost all of Bengal's villages. Even after touring Midnapore, Rutherford assured Linlithgow that the "majority of starving are the parasitic beggars and old people hitherto maintained by private charity."[33]

The new governor seemed to have believed the official line that ordinary cultivators were causing the shortages by withholding grain from the market. These secret hoards should have kept villagers from starving, he and other officials were convinced, so the dead and dying had to belong to a small, and hopefully irrelevant, section of the population.

In truth, the worst of the hoarders were allies of the government. The administration in Bengal had issued five thousand licenses for grain procurement, and licensees could store rice with impunity. As a result, Barnes complained, "the big merchant, largely responsible in many instances for the slow and agonising death of hundreds or thousands of his fellow-countrymen, careened merrily on, unassailable and untouched in mere virtue of his wealth and connections, cornering ever more waggon-loads of life-giving produce, holding up distribution, forcing up prices, securing more Government contracts." And whereas natives "hoarded," which was at least in principle a penal offense, white men "stockpiled"—which was not only legal but recommended. British business houses were advised to store at least a month's supply of rice for their laborers. One Mr. Parker, a merchant who served on Bengal's legislature, admitted to having kept much more than he needed.[34]

That autumn, parts of Bengal that had a perennial water supply harvested a minor crop of rice. The famine commission found that the Bengal administration purchased 370,000 maunds of it in a central district, Jessore, and heaped it onto a railway platform there. The district magistrate, who was determined to preserve the stockpile, did not release any of the grain "except for small quantities in October and November, 2,400 maunds in December 1943 and about 12,000 maunds in January and February 1944," the commission stated. That is, a tiny portion of the hoard was made available for famine relief—but only after the winter harvest, reaped in late December, had reduced the necessity for stocks. Some 90,000 tons of grain were also stored under tarpaulins in the Royal Botanical Gardens near Calcutta. Although it was pressed by legislators, the administration refused to yield its stores to the starving.[35]

In 1944, witnesses testifying before the famine commission charged that part of the rice secreted by district officials had rotted and was being surreptitiously disposed of. According to contemporary accounts, the public was allowed to scavenge from the government's dumps, such as the one in the botanical gardens, only after much of the contents had decayed. Rumors also abounded of the police and military having thrown rotted rice into canals.[36]

FOR MORE THAN a year Asok Mitra, the civil servant in charge of Munshiganj in eastern Bengal, had watched the suffering increase. In August 1943 he sensed that the people were finally collapsing under the strain of starvation. "Of the people I saw on the streets, more than half had blank looks, their faces and eyes were shrunken, and their skin stuck to their bones like paper. They took a long time just to focus their eyes." Their joints poked out, and the hair on their bodies stood straight up, Mitra wrote, like "big black pins." This marker of terminal starvation, sometimes described as growth of fur, was also noted in previous Indian famines and in the Irish famine.[37]

In late September, Mitra heard that the government in Calcutta was making some of its stocks available for famine relief, and he visited the district magistrate in Dacca to see if he could get any. By the stately stairway of his superior's office he found a giant signboard, one side of which announced that the sahib would be in between 11 A.M. and 12 P.M. but would not see anyone, and the other side of which stated that he would not be in at all. Mitra finally located the district magistrate at a club, pouring himself a second pink gin before lunch. He graciously offered his subordinate a drink, but refused to discuss rice.

Mitra was subsequently able to obtain rice through a military officer. When it arrived from Calcutta it was half-rotted and gritty with gravel, but food nonetheless, and by October 20 he had opened a hundred gruel kitchens all over Munsigunj. At first the kitchens provided just soft boiled rice and phyan, but later they began to offer a nourishing mixture of rice, lentils, and bits of potato or squash, flavored with salt, turmeric, bayleaf, and a little oil. The starving would fall upon this *khichuri*, eat their fill—and swell up like balloons, their arms and legs as translucent as the whites of uncooked eggs. Their bodies having partially consumed their cell walls, the fluids they ingested had flowed into the spaces between the cells.

"If you saw the thrill in their eyes, you couldn't scold them for eating too much," Mitra said. The mixture would hasten their demise, but he felt death was inevitable for them at such a late stage of starvation. "That they got some tasty food before they died was some comfort to me." Most of those who perished in this manner were women and children; the men, he believed, had already died.[38]

AT THE TURN of the eighteenth century the marquess of Wellesley, governor-general of India, had ordered the construction of a residence grand enough for the ruler of the vast possession. The palace, built in a Greco-Roman style and surrounded by more than twenty acres of gardens, served as the seat of the British Raj for more than a century. Twelve white marble busts of Roman emperors, including those of Nero and Caligula, adorned its spacious public hall. Calcutta had long ceased to be the capital of India, but the governor's residence was still the wellspring of imperial power in Bengal.

An Englishwoman said that while driving past the edifice during the famine, she saw that someone had laid the dead and the half-dead along the walls so that they formed a circle around the kilometer-long perimeter of the palace. The wreath of corpses marked the passing of empire.[39]

CHAPTER NINE

Run Rabbit Run

In late August 1943, the mayor of Calcutta cabled to President Roosevelt, appealing to him and to Churchill for grain shipments "in the name of starving humanity." The president and the prime minister were in conference at Quebec, Canada. Churchill also received messages from the viceroy, which were seconded by the commander-in-chief in India, warning that the paucity of wheat shipments threatened all operations based in the colony. The secretary of state for India, for his part, continued to contend with the War Cabinet for grain for the remainder of that summer, as well as through the fall and the winter.[1]

At Quebec, the Allies agreed to create a collaborative military structure based in India, the South East Asia Command (or SEAC), in anticipation of an overland thrust into Burma in 1944. The forces in India were to be supplemented with troops and equipment that could be airdropped into the dense jungle of the east Himalayan foothills, and these preparations for war would further strain the Indian economy. Churchill went on from Quebec to stay at the White House for about ten days, with a break for a lecture at Harvard, but whether or not he discussed the Bengal famine with Roosevelt is unknown.

On August 23, Amery informed Leathers that the U.S. consulate in Calcutta had offered to help buy wheat in America and transport it to Bengal. The consulate had added that "shipping for 20,000 tons or so should not present serious difficulty." Amery asked Leathers, who was at the Quebec conference, to follow up on the offer with his American counterparts—but the minister had other views. "There is no wheat to spare on the East Coast of North America," a Ministry of War Transport paper noted, "owing to inland transportation difficulties." Wheat might be bought on the West Coast, but shipping from there was not straightforward. "There seems therefore little to be gained from this proposal," British officials concluded. Notwithstanding such reluctance, two U.S. military ships were loaded with 5,000 tons of Canadian wheat the following month, for transport to India.[2]

News of the Bengal famine broke in American newspapers at this time but was buried in inside pages—whereas the popular prime minister's visit filled the front pages. By then, the United Kingdom had won American hearts. The spreading of "enlightenment," as the British called their propaganda in the United States, had been assiduous, with careful attention paid to answering any U.S. criticism of British policies. For instance, when Ambassador Phillips met with a group of Harvard intellectuals and told them that democracy in India was no more than "a kind of modern frosting of the old imperial cake," a British agent took notes. These were passed to a supposedly independent Indian journalist who was to address the same gathering, so that he could counter the specific points that Phillips had raised.[3]

The U.S. State Department was, however, receiving its own reports on the condition of Calcutta's pavements. According to historian M. S. Venkataramani, on August 30 a concerned official asked the Combined Food Board, the Anglo-American agency that allocated supplies, to set aside some rice for Bengal. The British representative on the board protested that wheat was available in Australia and, after checking with London, reported that the Government of India "was coping with the situation." He insisted that His Majesty's Government alone would provide information on the famine, and he did not permit the food board to hear a representative from the Government of India's supply mission to the United States.[4]

"When a serious famine developed in Bengal in 1943, we made efforts to secure from the all too inadequate rice stocks in the Western Hemisphere an allocation of rice for India," Secretary of State Cordell Hull would write in his memoirs. "The British representatives on the Combined Food Board in Washington insisted, however, that the responsibility for Indian food requirements be left to Britain, and we perforce had to agree."[5]

Another U.S. agency, the Board of Economic Warfare, asked the War Shipping Administration, which was responsible for allocating shipping space to diverse American authorities, if some grain could be loaded onto the vessels departing for India with military stores. American soldiers in the colony were getting certain foods, such as canned meat, from home, but for wheat and rice they relied on local supplies. The shipping officials had, however, come to resent the amount of tonnage that the United Kingdom had already obtained for its domestic import program. It was up to the British to make more ships available, they replied; and if the U.S. military could find space to spare for grain, it must be in possession of more ships than it needed, in which case some would be taken away.[6]

American generals, for their part, had long been irritated by what they saw as British foot-dragging in the war against Japan. After instituting the January 1943 shipping cutback to the Indian Ocean, the British had approached the Americans with a request for 113 sailings to India (from the United States or the United Kingdom) to carry equipment for the Anakim military campaign and supplies for civilians. Subsequently, however, the British had been willing to forgo that shipping in lieu of a firm commitment of additional vessels for their domestic import program. So American general Brehon B. Sommervell had found himself pushing for a shipping allotment to India that the British themselves seemed to have lost interest in. On top of that, U.S. commanders entertained "an open suspicion" that a significant portion of the materials that the British had originally requested was intended for troops who would fight not the Japanese but the Indians.[7]

Americans were adamant that they would not help "re-build the British Empire." Yet whether the troops in India fought Indians or Japanese, they would have to eat—and if they did not get supplies from outside, then they would feed off the people. William Phillips, who was still the president's representative to India, was upset with his superior's inaction on the colony's affairs. He argued in September that the combination of British-Indian political deadlock and Bengal famine would destroy American credibility in India, and he urged the president to take steps to break the stalemate and feed the starving. Nothing came of it.[8]

MEANWHILE, AN INTELLIGENCE summary from Chittagong, the base for the upcoming jungle war, warned that soldiers were so distressed by the famine that they were "feeding beggars with their own rations, even though they are disobeying orders by so doing." Whether they were British or Indian, soldiers generally believed that the government had fallen down on its responsibilities. Recognizing the discontent in the ranks, the military leadership took up the challenge of advocating to the prime minister for increased grain shipments. On September 8, 1943, General Auchinlek wrote to the chief of the Imperial General Staff, Field Marshal Alan Brooke, asking him to use his influence. The Chiefs of Staff obliged with a memo to the War Cabinet: the situation was so grave as to threaten the prosecution of war against Japan, they asserted, and only grain imports could resolve the crisis. Amery supported their appeal by adding that "in the light of the Cabinet decision" (precisely which decision is unclear) American offers of rice and wheat had had to be "discouraged," but the situation in Bengal provided "a very dangerous handle to Japanese propaganda of which full use is being made"—an apparent reference to the offers of rice from Bose.[9]

The day before the War Cabinet was to discuss the Bengal famine for the second time, Lord Cherwell sent a memo to the prime minister, who had just returned from Washington. Once again the Prof expressed incredulity that a half-million tons, which the Government of India wanted by year-end, could make any difference. "But if conditions are really as bad as we are told it might be well, in view of the easier shipping position, to increase the loadings of grain for the time being," he suggested. Such shipments should only continue, he added, if provincial governments disgorged their supplies. Tom Wilson, the S branch researcher for Indian matters, pointed out to Cherwell that although a half-million tons of imports were indeed a small amount compared to the total crop of India, "this broad statistical comparison of orders of magnitudes is likely to be seriously misleading." The harvest was un-evenly distributed, as would be the relief, so weighing the total crop against the quantity of relief yielded a ratio with no relevance to reality. Since the deficit of grain was concentrated in certain locales, even the modest relief requested could substantially check the famine.[10]

BY THE TIME the War Cabinet revisited the issue of the famine, on September 24, 1943, Amery had obtained permission for the 50,000 tons of wheat mentioned on August 4 to go to India rather than to Ceylon. The first consignment could be loaded no earlier than October, and since the journey from Australia took a month, it must have arrived in India in November. The 5,000 tons of Canadian wheat must also have reached the colony in November and was counted as part of the 50,000 tons.[11]

At the meeting, Field Marshal Wavell, soon to be the viceroy of India, said that rations for the Indian Army had had to be cut earlier in 1943, while he was commander-in-chief, and the current situation looked much worse than it did then. According to the minutes, Leathers responded that it was now too late to relieve the famine. Although more ships were available to the British Empire, "it would not be possible to work additional ships into positions from which they could lift grain for delivery in India before the next Indian harvest." The most that he could manage before year-end was 30,000 tons of barley a month from the Balkan stockpile and 30,000 tons of wheat that were to have been sent to the Middle East but were no longer needed.[12]

The members of the War Cabinet decided, however, that Balkan stocks should not be drawn down unduly. That meant they felt no more than 50,000 tons of wheat and barley could be spared (in addition to the 150,000 tons promised earlier, which were still being processed). After the standing orders for Ceylon and the Middle East, as well as the diversions to India, were met, "up to six ships surplus to these require-ments" would present for loading at Australia in November. These would continue to transport wheat to the Balkan stockpile.[13]

Again, Amery's diaries provide an angry insight into the motives behind the proceedings. "I fought my battle for Indian food as hard as I could," he wrote. "Winston was prepared to admit that something should be done but very strong on the point that Indians are not the only people who are starving in this war and that as far as the war goes it is just as important to get food to Greece. . . . Winston may be right in saying that the starvation of anyhow under-fed Bengalis is less serious than sturdy Greeks, but he makes no sufficient allowance for the sense of Empire responsibility in this country." Wavell's account is just as revealing: "Apparently it is more important to save the Greeks and liberated countries from starvation than the Indians and there is reluctance either to provide shipping or to reduce stocks in this country." (Wavell offers the only hint that there was a discussion of supplying Bengal or southern Europe from the United Kingdom's import program.) "I pointed out military considerations and that practically the whole of India outside the rural districts was more or less engaged on war effort, and that it was impossible to differentiate and feed only those actually fighting or making munitions or working some particular railways, as P.M. had suggested."[14]

At the Quebec conference the Americans had firmly rejected a plan for an invasion of the Balkans, and Churchill did not have the military resources necessary to pursue the venture alone. That rebuff had done nothing to dull his enthusiasm for the project. According to Field Marshal Brooke, the prime minister "hated having to give up the position of the dominant partner which we had held at the start," and which the United States was inexorably assuming. "As a result he became inclined at times to put up strategic proposals which he knew were unsound purely to spite the Americans." The humiliation inflicted by multiple British defeats, at Japanese and German hands, must also have rankled him, leading Churchill to hold "in the back of his mind the desire to form a purely British theatre when the laurels would be all ours." The Balkans still held out hope for being such a front.[15]

IN OCTOBER, AT a sendoff dinner for Wavell—now elevated to the peerage to befit the Viceroyalty he was about to assume—Churchill gave a speech on India. "When we look back over the course of years we see one part of the world's surface where there has been no war for three generations," he declaimed. "Famines have passed away—until the horrors of war and the dislocations of war have given us a taste of them again—and pestilence has gone." To his profound sorrow, these accomplishments were not appreciated. "It was thought in many parts of the world that all we did was to sit on the top of India exploiting the poor unfortunate people and taking away their hard-earned sustenance in order to enrich ourselves." But should the day come, "as I pray it may not, when we cast down for ever our responsibilities there, and vanish from the scene, this episode in Indian history will surely become the Golden Age as time passes, when the British gave them peace and order, and there was justice for the poor, and all men were shielded from outside dangers. The Golden Age."[16]

Lord Wavell, a quiet man of firm convictions, had spent several frustrating months trying to get the War Cabinet to endorse some fresh political proposal so that he would not arrive in India empty-handed. He rose to respond. According to Amery, he "directly challenged Winston's whole position" by indicating that his own goal was a self-governing India. The War Cabinet subsequently discussed Wavell's proposal, which was to invite ten Indian leaders, including Gandhi and Jinnah, for discussions on the country's future. "Winston let himself go in a longish and pretty strong harangue, getting warmed up towards the end in an eloquent but irrelevant discourse on the worthlessness and probable disloyalty of India's large and well-equipped army," recorded Amery. As for Wavell, he grimly concluded that some "face-saving" formula would finally emerge from the War Cabinet discussions, "designed to carry them on and get me out there, but with every intention of blocking any progress. The more I see of politicians, the less I respect them."[17]

The next day Amery and Wavell perused a document that Churchill had drafted on India. "Peace, order and a high condition of war-time well-being" were essential for the eventual thrust against Japan, it noted. "Every effort must be made, even by the diversion of shipping urgently needed for war purposes, to deal with local shortages." The viceroy must ensure fairer distribution of resources, restore peace between Hindu and Muslim, and move toward self-government. "[Y]ou are wafted to India on a wave of hot air," Wavell wrote that Amery told him. (Amery would remember the wave as a "gentle breeze.")

When the viceroy-designate went to bid farewell to the prime minister, Churchill was "menacing and unpleasant." He "indicated that only over his dead body would any approach to Gandhi take place," Wavell recorded in his diary. Despite the sentiments he had put on paper, Churchill remained determined to stop any political advance in India.[18]

Viceroy Linlithgow, writing from Simla, the picturesque summer retreat of the colonial government, dispatched a valedictory letter to the secretary of state for India. "I can feel as I lay down this great charge that I leave the country in pretty good trim," he summed up. The leaders of Congress were "in jail and forgotten," and Gandhi "is equally out of the way of doing mischief." Linlithgow's only unresolved concerns were inflation and "the food position." A communication from Bengal's governor observed, however, that the famine "does not constitute grave menace to peace or tranquillity of Bengal or any part thereof, for sufferers are entirely submissive and emergency threatens, not maintenance of law and order, but preservation of public health and economic stability."[19]

Meanwhile, Lady Linlithgow had written to the prime minister requesting an American Liberator bomber in which to fly home, because it had twice the capacity of the one that had been assigned to her and the outgoing viceroy. Having endured seven and a half "very strenuous years" in India, she wrote, "I would like to be rewarded by a free trip home in this Liberator in which we can take quite a lot of luggage!" Churchill obliged, sending Wavell and other officers out in two civilian aircraft that would bring back the former viceroy and his wife.[20]

ARRIVING IN NEW Delhi on October 18, 1943, the new viceroy received a roundup of the colony's affairs from the departing one. No progress was possible until Gandhi died, Linlithgow advised, and in any case India would take thirty years to learn how to govern itself. As for the famine, it could have been worse. Back in July Linlithgow had anticipated a death toll of up to a million and a half, but "we looked like getting off better than he had thought possible," Wavell recorded.[21]

Days later, Viceroy Wavell flew to Bengal—and gauged that the situation was out of control. Ever since *The Statesman* had publicized the famine, wheat from the Punjab had been pouring into Calcutta, but it was still only enough for the city itself. Gruel kitchens had been opened in the rural districts, but "we simply have not the food" to give the portions prescribed by the famine code, the governor noted. Wavell mobilized the hitherto idle army to distribute relief and conduct vaccinations— an invaluable contribution, given that the military possessed the organization, the transport, the medical and other officers, and the pent-up energy that Bengal badly needed.[22]

Still, the army would need something to distribute. "This is now definitely a military as well as a charity problem since army must have a stable base," Wavell explained to Amery. "Please impress upon War Cabinet that in my view situation is most serious and that if confidence is to be restored maximum possible imports of food grains against Government of India demand must be arranged."[23]

BUT THE FAMINE had failed to temper the prime minister's fury with Indians. That October, "apropos of nothing except some stuff which that wretched Cherwell had been pouring into his ears, [Churchill] exploded again on the subject of these monstrous debts which we were incurring to India for no value received and for the piling up of a useless and unreliable army in India itself," wrote Amery. In early November, he drove with Churchill to a concert at Harrow, and on the way they talked about the colony. The prime minister reiterated that he would resist any move toward Indian self-government "as long as he lived." Amery told him that the House of Commons was "unanimous that we should send more help from here" for the famine. Churchill retorted that he "did not care what the House thought in this matter. The thing was to win the war."[24]

(The United Kingdom was releasing 500 tons of condensed milk from its stockpile. Field Marshal William Slim of the Indian Army would subsequently receive for his troops "battered, rusted tins" of milk, only half of which were still usable. The cans, he wrote, had been turned over from the United Kingdom stockpile and replaced with fresh cans from the United States.)[25]

Churchill did express sympathy to Amery for "having to bear all the kicks." The secretary of state for India had to explain the famine to the politicians and public of the United Kingdom, and it was not easy. Speaking in various forums, Amery placed responsibility for the calamity on Indians (for overpopulation, hoarding, and misgovernment), the United Nations (which controlled shipping), and the Almighty (for crop failure). His correspondence and diaries make it clear, however, that Amery saw the famine as a straightforward consequence of the war effort. "The real question of course is whether a poor country like India could ever have afforded, over and above what it has been asked to do for its own defence, to pay for its forces overseas and give as free lease-lend all the materials which we have bought from India during the war," he wrote to the head of the Indian inflation committee.[26]

Famine and sterling debt were two sides of the same coin: the exhaustive use of Indian resources for the war. Ever since Japan had reached the border, vast quantities of cash had had to be spent on military construction and provisions, explained a financial adviser to army commanders in India. "Added to this the shortage of world shipping grew more and more acute, our Far Eastern sources of supply [of rice] were lost, and imports into India of consumer goods for the civil population were reduced to a comparative trickle. So more and more money was being poured into the pockets of all classes of consumers but the goods on which they could spend their money were dwindling away, because civil stocks were being exhausted without further imports, and military demands both for India and overseas were taking a larger cut of the cake." The Government of India could not borrow or tax enough money and so had printed it, causing the prices of already scarce essentials to explode. Since the war began, the colony's expenditure on it had escalated by more than ten times, from £40.2 million (in the fiscal year that ended in March 1940) to £429.9 million (in the fiscal year that ended in March 1943). Roughly half of this outlay accrued to the United Kingdom's sterling debt—which, too, was rising steeply.[27]

"In my view the Indians have got themselves into a mess very largely through their own fault, but no one can deny that they have obtained in return for their current sacrifices altogether exorbitant sterling balances," Cherwell complained. To his mind, inflation, famine, and the sterling debt were all the fault of *the Indians*, as he had taken to calling officials of the Government of India, despite the fact that its upper echelons were almost entirely British. He may have been echoing Churchill's charge that "everyone who goes to India or the India Office becomes more anti-English than the Indians"—a reference to Linlithgow and possibly Amery. ("The suggestion that the officials here have used their position as agents of His Majesty's Government with an eye to India's interests only has caused intense resentment," Wavell would protest to Amery. "To the best of my belief there is no foundation whatever for this suggestion, and I hope you will be able to scotch it." For a British official in India to faithfully serve those who paid his salary would have been for him to betray his patriotic duty to his homeland.)[28]

Lord Cherwell despaired that his imperial nation was "losing its instinct of self-preservation" and becoming too generous. The financial agreement with India was "most unfair to us," he declared. India was not, for instance, being charged for certain military equipment that was sent from abroad. And whereas the United Kingdom paid for the early training of most of the native troops fighting in the Middle East and Africa, the colony was paying for British troops only while they were in India and not while they had trained in the U.K. (In August 1943, India was hosting 200,000 British soldiers. It had also paid for the training of 60,000 British troops in the years leading up to the war.) In one memo the Prof argued that the war in Libya was part and parcel of the defense of India, which should bear more of the cost of it. "Nothing will convince me that even under this one-sided agreement we have had value for our money," he wrote. The Indians, he believed, had contrived to make "excessive profit at our expense."[29]

Poring over the colony's accounts, the S branch discovered what it termed a "scandal": early in the war the colony had charged the United Kingdom customs duties on petrol sent for the army. As it turned out, the Government of India employed only 17 cost accountants (as opposed to 200 at the U.K.'s Ministry of Supply alone), who had made a further mistake. They had placed on India's bill the petrol imported up until March 1942—which, according to the financial agreement, should have accrued to Britain's. If that problem were also accounted for, the United Kingdom would owe the colony twice as much as it would get out of rectifying the customs error. So the Government of India suggested ignoring both mistakes.[30]

The S branch got the last word, however. It found that the reimbursement India demanded for petrol was much too high—which was the fault not of the Indians but of officials in London who had neglected to negotiate the price with sellers in the Middle East. The United Kingdom ended up repaying India only £5 million per year for the petrol, instead of the £25 million per year that the colony claimed it was owed. The upshot, as Cherwell's assistant, Thomas Wilson, triumphantly put it, was that the S branch "paid for itself with a handsome margin to spare."[31]

The inflation committee observed that the evidence "does not, in our view, sustain a general conclusion that H.M.G. has not had value for money." Even so, the United Kingdom should repudiate the debt to India, urged the Prof. "Innumerable ways can, of course, be devised of wrapping up the brute fact that we cannot and will not pay the sums in question." One was to forcibly alter the exchange rate between the rupee and the pound. (The possibility of just such a postwar devaluation of the rupee had aggravated the Bengal famine by making Punjabi peasants reluctant to exchange their grain for cash.) At the very least, Cherwell declared, India should bear the entire cost of the forthcoming campaign in Burma and Malaya.[32]

The colony would anyhow have to pay for the time being, Wilson pointed out in a paper drafted on behalf of Lord Cherwell. And whether or not the United Kingdom chose to reimburse any part of the cost in the distant future could make little difference to wartime inflation.[33]

FAMINE AND DEBT collided yet again on November 10, 1943, when Amery used Wavell's report on Bengal to schedule a third War Cabinet discussion on relief. Bengal's winter harvest of rice would not reach the market until January 1944, Amery advised. For the Government of India to have a "fighting chance" of procuring all the grain it needed from nervous cultivators, it would require another 50,000 tons of wheat by the end of December and a promise of the same quantity for each of the following twelve months. Leathers having already asserted that providing such quantities were out of the question, Amery concentrated on getting at least 50,000 tons for each of December, January, and February.[34]

The day before the meeting, the Prof wrote to the prime minister. "The quantities suggested are very small as compared with India's total consumption of over 4 million tons a month," he stated as usual. (Given Wilson's September memo, he had to know that the argument was specious.) Such imports might have the effect of thwarting hoarders, but surely enough had been done toward that end. "Strong propaganda designed to discourage hoarding can be based upon the shipments we have already decided to make." He continued: "This shortage of food is likely to be endemic in a country where the population is always increased until only bare subsistence is possible. In such circumstances small local shortages or crop failures must cause acute distress. After the war India can spend her huge hoards of sterling on buying food and thus increase the population still more, but so long as the war lasts her high birth-rate may impose a heavy strain on this country which does not view with Asiatic detachment the pressure of a growing population on limited supplies of food."[35]

CHERWELL'S ARGUMENT WAS based on the famous proposition by the Reverend Thomas Robert Malthus, who in 1798 postulated that humans multiply faster than their means of sustenance, which meant that "premature death must in some shape or other visit the human race." Those peoples whose lack of sexual restraint caused them to reproduce recklessly were especially prone to what he called "positive checks" on their population. These unhappy constraints included war, disease, vice, and "the last, the most dreadful resource of nature"—famine. Malthus's doctrine inspired no less than Charles Darwin, whose magnum opus *On the Origin of Species* is subtitled *The Preservation of Favoured Races in the Struggle for Life*. Because "more individuals are produced than can possibly survive, there must in every case be a struggle for existence," Darwin wrote. "It is the doctrine of Malthus applied with manifold force to the whole animal and vegetable kingdoms."

The entwined worldview of Malthus and Darwin provided an explanation, beguiling to Victorian elites, not only for the evolution of species but also for the ordering of society. The "evolutionist will not hesitate to affirm that the nation with the highest ideals would succeed," mused Savrola, a romantic hero that Churchill had created in the late 1890s, during his sojourn in India. Conversely, an excess of compassion could perpetuate the debilitating characteristics of defeated peoples, imperiling the greater good. An 1881 report by the Government of India on preceding famines concluded that the poorest Indians were the worst affected by such calamities, and if relief measures were to prevent their deaths they would continue to breed, making the survivors even more penurious. Death might even come as deliverance to those that nature had chosen to discard. Churchill had corroborated Malthus's perspective, writing of an 1898 Indian plague: "a philosopher may watch unmoved the destruction of some of those superfluous millions, whose life must of necessity be destitute of pleasure."[36]

In truth, Indian famines of the Victorian era cannot be fitted into Malthus's framework, because he did not envision a worldwide grain trade that would enable the people of certain nations to consume far more or far less food than they could produce. Throughout the nineteenth century Indians were harvesting enough grain to feed themselves, but the export cycle had drained grain surpluses and driven food prices beyond the reach of the poor. Great Britain, in contrast, produced far less grain than necessary to sustain its people but was free of Malthusian constraints on its population because it relied on imported food. In short, to use the language that economist Amartya Sen would introduce—in the context of the 1943 Bengal famine—the vanishing purchasing power or "exchange entitlements" of some sectors of society, having been pitted directly against the far greater entitlements of others, resulted in starvation in India.[37]

In his memo to Churchill, Lord Cherwell suggested that the Bengal famine arose from crop failure and high birthrate. He omitted to mention that the calamity also derived from India's role of supplier to the Allied war effort; that the colony was not being permitted to spend its sterling reserves or to employ its own ships in importing sufficient food; and that by his Malthusian logic Britain should have been the first to starve—but was being sustained by food imports that were six times larger than the one-and-a-half million tons that the Government of India had requested for the coming year. The memo did raise the prospect that harm would be inflicted on long-suffering Britons if help were extended to over-fecund Indians. At the War Cabinet meeting the day after the memo was promulgated, November 10, 1943, the prime minister gave his own Darwinian twist to Cherwell's Malthusian considerations. Amery made his plea, following which "Winston, after a preliminary flourish on Indians breeding like rabbits and being paid a million a day by us for doing nothing about the war, asked Leathers for his view."[38]

In his pronouncements over the years, Churchill had invented some wonderfully apt animal metaphors, with rabbits the least among them. A communist such as Stalin resembled a crocodile: "when it opens its mouth you cannot tell whether it is trying to smile, or preparing to eat you up." After a coup had done away with a pro-Axis regime in Yugoslavia, he said Hitler was in a more vicious mood than a "boa constrictor, who had already covered his prey with his foul saliva and then had it suddenly wrested from his coils." The prime minister declared that while facing Italian forces in the desert, Britannica was an "old lion with her lion cubs at her side," one of which may have been India—or at least its warlike aspect, the army. Gandhi had once been a tiger, but he had long since descended the food chain. More often than not the small, brown, fangless, and numberless Indians whom the frail old pacifist personified brought to Churchill's mind a prey species. "The British lion, so fierce and valiant in bygone days, so dauntless and unconquerable through all the agony of Armageddon, can now be chased by rabbits from the fields and forests of his former glory," he had warned during the 1930s campaign against native self-rule. During the Quit India uprising, the government had the rebels "on the run." Winston Churchill, the quintessential lion, was an excellent shot when it came to rabbits, and earlier in the war was heard to repeatedly murmur the first two lines of the ditty:[39]

> *Run rabbit, run rabbit, run run run.*
> *Run rabbit, run rabbit, run run run.*
> *Bang, bang, bang, bang! Goes the farmer's gun*
> *Run, rabbit, run, rabbit, run, run, run.*

The prey's role is to nourish the predator, and the predator's role is to keep the prey from overbreeding. Lions do not feed rabbits.

In the War Cabinet meeting that November day, Leathers said that he could do nothing to assuage India's hunger that December. He could, however, manage to send 50,000 tons for each of January and February, and that was agreed upon. As it happened, Canada had offered a free gift of 100,000 tons of wheat to India to relieve the famine, and Viceroy Wavell had accepted. Churchill had already rejected Canada's proposal because, according to a document with the Ministry of War Transport, "it would be unjustifiable to impose any additional strain on our shipping resources (especially if that involved seeking further shipping assistance from the Americans) for the sake of the wholly uneconomic prospect of shipping wheat from Canada to India." But a Canadian ship of 10,000 tons had become available at Vancouver, and Prime Minister Mackenzie King wanted to fill it with wheat for India. To Amery's consternation, Leathers and Churchill were "vehement against this" and resolved to stop the consignment. "I can only trust that they won't have begun loading before Winston's telegram arrives," Amery recorded. "The trouble is that Winston so dislikes India and all to do with it that he can see nothing but the mere waste of shipping space involved in the longer journey."[40]

At the time, a consignment of 9,000 tons of rice from Brazil was on its way to Ceylon, and shiploads of Australian wheat were circumnavigating India on their way to the Balkan stockpile. Other ships were traveling to Argentina to collect wheat for Britain—a trip twice as long as that to Canada or the United States. And as it happened, the United Kingdom already had more than enough wheat. "I hope that out of the present surplus of grain you will manage to do a little more for the domestic poultry keeper," the prime minister directed the day after this meeting. If their hens could get more grain, Britons would get more eggs.[41]

EVEN AS THE War Cabinet debated the Bengal famine that November, representatives of forty-four nations were meeting in Atlantic City, New Jersey, to hammer out the details of what would become the United Nations Relief and Rehabilitation Administration (UNRRA). India was represented by its agent-general in the United States, Sir Girija Bajpai, and by a gatecrasher named Jagjit J. Singh, a "6-foot, handsome Sikh from Kashmir," according to *Time* magazine. Singh was an entrepreneur and head of an immigrant association, the India League of America; he had earlier sent a report on the Bengal famine to Eleanor Roosevelt, who had passed it on to her husband. "This is a matter which the new UNRRA can properly take up," the president had responded.

But a key U.S. representative to the UNRRA, the diplomat Dean Acheson, stated that India was not eligible for aid. Singh protested that surely the starving in Bengal qualified, given that the organization's charter promised "relief of victims of war in any area under the control of any of the United Nations." The British representative, Colonel John J. Llewellin, announced, however, that India was not a victim of war, and its case was not taken up for discussion.

The leftist commentator I. F. Stone approved Singh's effort to give the issue of famine an airing. "I have found general agreement among officials dealing with shipping that it is nonsense to talk of a shipping shortage in connection with food for India," Stone wrote. "With some 50,000,000 tons available, much of it inadequately utilized, a few hundred thousand tons of shipping could easily be allocated to ease the famine." The problem, Stone felt, was politics: "Shipments made under pressure from public opinion would imply embarrassing admissions in British domestic policies, revive hopes of American interference in India."[42]

It was an issue on which Americans of both political parties could come together. Karl Mundt, a Republican congressman from South Dakota, met Singh and became infused with passion for his cause. Speaking in December before the House of Representatives, Mundt accused the UNRRA of harboring a "malevolent bias" against a patient ally. How did it make sense to feed former enemies and starve a friend? he asked. His appeal fell on deaf ears, so the congressman coached Singh on the tactics of lobbying on Capitol Hill. After a vigorous battle, in February 1944 the two managed to win over enough Democrats to insert an amendment to the UNRRA bill extending benefits to "any area important to the military operations of the United Nations which is stricken by famine or disease."[43]

All that effort was in vain. The War Cabinet did not permit the Government of India to apply for aid—a necessary formality before it could be sent. British authorities did, however, donate $30 million of the colony's wartime earnings to the UNRRA, making India the sixth-largest contributor to the fund.[44]

AN UNRRA ALLOTMENT of grain to India would have brought to the fore a discomfiting question: who would ferry it to Bengal? As Amery noted, the UNRRA itself was "not in a position to provide any shipping." Had any grain been sanctioned, the ships would have had to come either from the United States or from the British Empire.[45]

The War Cabinet did not intend to request further shipping from the Americans. Nor would it slow the buildup of its stockpiles by releasing ships or grain. Throughout that autumn, the United Kingdom's civilian stocks of food and raw materials continued to swell, so that by the end of 1943 they would stand at 18.5 million tons, the highest total ever. The United Kingdom imported that year 4 million tons of wheat grain and flour, 1.4 million tons of sugar, 1.6 million tons of meat, 409,000 heads of live cattle, 325,000 tons of fish, 131,000 tons of rice, 206,000 tons of tea, 172,000 tons of cocoa, and 1.1 million gallons of wine for its 47.7 million people—a population 14 million fewer than that of Bengal. Sugar and oilseeds overflowed warehouses and had to be stored outdoors in England under tarpaulins. American and Canadian grain traders complained that excessive British demand was distorting the market and worried that, after the war, the United Kingdom would use its vast stocks to manipulate world prices.[46]

Why was such a stockpile necessary? The U-boat threat had fallen away, the tide of war had turned, and a plethora of ships were available. Hitler still could, and would, launch air strikes on the United Kingdom, but the Blitz had shown that almost three-quarters of the supplies directly affected by bombing could be recovered. Air attacks threatened lives, not food supply. That fall, ships were being diverted to bring equipment for Operation Overlord, the invasion of northern France that would be launched from British soil—so it made sense to keep some extra stores at hand. But the quantities being held were far too large to be explained by the prospect of that attack alone. The War Cabinet's preoccupation with domestic stocks was in fact motivated by the economic shocks that would follow the fall of Germany. In October 1943, Churchill had informed the public that the government was preparing for the end of the war. The first of the "urgent needs" of the postwar period was to plan for smooth demobilization, and the second was the "provision of food for our island on a scale better than the wartime rations."[47]

Historian R. J. Hammond has noted that the Ministry of Food's estimates of minimum required stocks increased in tandem with actual stocks. For instance, whereas it had stated 850,000 tons of wheat as the minimum working stock in 1943, the ministry set the figure at a million tons in 1945 and represented this as a reduction from a supposed wartime minimum of 1.2 million tons. The stated minimum for oilseeds similarly swelled. "What purported to be an insurance against a breakdown of distribution was in reality something that could hardly be avowed within the Ministry of Food, and certainly not at the Combined Food Board," where Americans were all too eager to dissect British stock levels—"namely an attempt to protect the future level of United Kingdom consumption," Hammond wrote.[48]

In November 1943, Viceroy Wavell circulated a memorandum that explained to the provinces' governors why no aid could be expected for Bengal. "The Ministry of Food expect a world shortage of cereals, and although the shipping position has improved very greatly the Ministry of War Transport has to consider not merely the tonnage available but its operation as part of the general strategic plan. Thus, though foodgrains may be immediately available in Australia or North America the Ministry of Food may be reluctant to release them, and the Ministry of War Transport may be unable to deliver them to India except by diverting ships and changing loading programmes on a scale sufficient to be most embarrassing."[49]

In other words, the harvests of Australia and Canada were being regarded as part of the United Kingdom's strategic stockpile and were being conserved for postwar use—as had been recommended during the War Cabinet meeting of January 5, 1943. "Shipping [difficulty] cuts both ways," the minister of production had declared at the time. "It means [that] we are piling up stocks overseas." An undated S branch memo noted that Colonel Llewellin, who succeeded Lord Woolton as the minister of food near the end of 1943, was demanding a minimum stock of 12 million tons of wheat (presumably in the British Empire as a whole). That amount would be easy to achieve, given that "at the end of 1943/44 harvest year, stocks will amount to about 29,000,000 tons, assuming no relief shipments" to liberated areas. Still, the memo continued, it was somewhat excessive to regard "100% of the volume of trade to the 'Free World'" as a necessary minimum stock, given that 7 million tons would be ample.[50]

The extraordinary quantity of wheat stocks that the Ministry of Food regarded as essential militated against even a few hundred thousand tons being expended on famine relief in Bengal. Another reason for the paucity of aid, as Wavell had explained it, was the risk of loss of face. The diversion of a large amount of tonnage to India would possibly have been "most embarrassing" because it would have proved to Americans what they had suspected all along: the British had extracted a lot more shipping than they really needed.

WHEN THE U.S. president and the prime minister met that November in Cairo, much of the talk was about the demands of the postwar world. The Americans wanted to treat colonies, such as those of France, as "trustees" of what would be a newly organized United Nations. For the time being the colonies would remain under imperial control, but would be coached toward independence; and inspectors would visit from time to time to gauge their living conditions and political progress. Churchill refused outright to subject the British Empire to such an order.

The conference continued its work in Teheran, where the Soviets joined in. At a tête-à-tête with Stalin, Roosevelt cautioned that it was "unwise" to bring up India in the general discussions, and Stalin agreed that this was a "sore spot with the British." Sometime in the future, the president continued, he would like to discuss India at length: it would, he said, probably require Soviet-style "reform from the bottom." Stalin opined that the colony was complicated by culture and caste, but that reform from the bottom meant revolution. The Bengal famine was reaching its climax even as the world leaders met, but it appears not to have been mentioned—which is odd, given that the economics of India were discussed at some length.[51]

The U.S. military had conquered a number of Pacific islands and was determined to establish a chain of bases there. Because the islands themselves would be under international control, the president saw no contradiction in establishing such bases under the aegis of the trusteeship scheme; Stalin agreed that footholds near the Axis powers would be useful. Suspecting that the two Allied leaders sought some of the empire's possessions for these bases, Churchill angrily retorted that the British "intended to hold on to what they had" and "nothing would be taken away from England without a war." This extraordinary threat must have been directed at the president, who was displaying the most inclination to do away with old-fashioned colonies.[52]

Sometime during the conference, Stalin baited Churchill, accusing him of cowardice because of his foot-dragging on the invasion of northern France. "What happened?" he teased. "Is it advancing age? How many divisions have you got in contact with the enemy? What is happening to all those two million men you have got in India?" At one vodka-soaked banquet, Churchill was needled by Stalin so mercilessly that he stomped out in a fury.[53]

ON DECEMBER 16, at a meeting of the War Cabinet that Churchill did not attend because of illness, Leathers mentioned that Canada was "pressing very hard to allow at any rate one shipload of Canadian wheat to go to India." News of the offer had leaked in both the Indian and the Canadian media, and "the political now perhaps outweighed the shipping aspects," said Leathers. To Amery's relief, the War Cabinet acquiesced to a proposal to load a Canadian ship with wheat for India.[54]

In late July, the Government of India had requested a half-million tons of wheat to be delivered by the end of 1943. That amount was the minimum necessary for maintaining the army and the most essential war workers until the next harvest. Apart from the psychological impact of imports on hoarders (who would take substantial grain imports as a signal of falling prices and thus release grain to the market, thereby causing prices to fall in reality), the needs of rural India had not figured into this calculation. In response, the War Cabinet had authorized 130,000 tons of barley, which was of little help, and 80,000 tons of wheat, the first shipments of which reached India in November. The paucity of relief meant that for the rest of that year the soldiers and war workers in India continued to consume grain that might otherwise have been used to relieve the suffering of the people. The famine came to an end in late December, when the survivors harvested their own rice crop. According to Chitto Samonto, some in Kalikakundu died of diarrhea because they ate the creamy rice seeds long before they had had a chance to ripen.[55]

WINSTON CHURCHILL'S TRUE love was war, and it took precedence over such dreary matters as colonial economics. The chief of the Imperial General Staff, Alan Brooke, had a full-time job restraining him from headlong pursuit of whatever glittering military prize had caught his eye. "It is a wonderful character—the most marvellous qualities and superhuman genius mixed with an astonishing lack of vision at times, and an impetuosity which if not guided must inevitably bring him into trouble again and again," Brooke mused in his diary. "Perhaps the most remarkable failing of his is that he can never see a whole strategical problem at once. His gaze always settles on some definite part of the canvas and the rest of the picture is lost. . . . This failing is accentuated by the fact that often he does not want to see the whole picture, especially if this wider vision should in any way interfere with the operation he may have temporarily set his heart on."[56]

Churchill overflowed with ideas for operations and hated the lull that preceded a major undertaking. In the autumn of 1943, soldiers and supplies were being gathered for Operation Overlord, and precious little was left over for supposedly quick and easy side ventures that could turn into quagmires. Yet one day the prime minister would be pushing for an attack on the Balkans, a few days later on Sumatra or Norway, and in another week he would be back at the Balkans again. "He is in a very dangerous condition, most unbalanced, and God knows how we shall finish this war if this goes on," Brooke wrote in October.[57]

The previous year, Brooke had turned down the Middle East command so that he could stay in London and prevent the prime minister from precipitating another Gallipoli. Churchill may also have had that disaster in mind when he had appointed Brooke the chief of staff.

That is, he may have been aware that he needed containment while recognizing that, of all his generals, Brooke alone had the personality for that task. "When I thump the table and push my face towards him what does he do? Thumps the table harder and glares back at me," Churchill had said admiringly. After tremendous and exhausting battles to which he brought the full force of his conviction, lungs, vocabulary, and lachrymal glands, Churchill would eventually back down and accept Brooke's judgment—only to return to the fray the next day.[58]

When it came to civilian advisers, however, the prime minister had picked too many cronies, whose sycophantic counsel on the Indian famine he would rely on rather heavily. "All I want is compliance with my wishes after a reasonable amount of discussion," the prime minister said of the War Cabinet, and he was only half joking. Lord Woolton, Lord Leathers, and Sir Percy James Grigg owed their positions to him and deferred to him. Lord Beaverbrook, who served on the War Cabinet in a variety of positions, was an old friend and ally. Brendan Bracken, the minister of information, once circulated rumors that Churchill was his father, so enamored was he of the older man. (Bracken would personally present to Churchill preview copies of ministers' speeches due for broadcast by the BBC. One minister was shifted from his post because he intended to say that members of Parliament did much that was asked of them, but refused to shout "*Heil* Churchill!") As for Cherwell and the S branch, their allegiance was unabashedly to Churchill alone.[59]

"Churchill on top of the wave has in him the stuff of which tyrants are made," Beaverbrook had once warned. Lord Moran, Churchill's doctor, similarly noted: "when the sun shines his arrogance, intolerance and cocksureness assume alarming proportions." Ever the bumptious schoolboy, the prime minister may also have relished thumbing his nose at Leopold Amery, his lifelong rival and critic. Churchill "is instinctively inclined to disagree with anything I say," the secretary of state for India had observed two years earlier. Despite never having been to India as an adult, Amery was a far more knowledgeable and legitimate adviser on the colony than was Cherwell. Yet Amery was also long-winded and incapable of expressing himself dramatically; he had little hope of seducing the prime minister with the kind of catchy epithet Churchill relished and respected. The Prof, in contrast, knew exactly which buttons to push.[60]

The problem was that whereas Brooke served as a restraint, Cherwell acted as a goad. Lord Moran commented that the Prof's placid appearance deceived many who met him casually. Once they got into conversation with him, "men learnt with a start of surprise that the most violent views were hidden and disguised by the level tones of the Prof.'s voice." In a 1960 lecture at Harvard on Cherwell's wartime influence, physicist and writer C. P. Snow would say of Churchill's chief adviser: "He was formidable, he was savage." Snow complained that Cherwell's advocacy of area bombing of German civilian houses had prevailed over the objections of other physicists. The Prof's close relationship with Churchill had given him "more direct power than any scientist in history," Snow argued, and power so unchecked was harmful.[61]

Churchill did question Cherwell's judgment on one occasion (when the scientist dismissed evidence that the Germans were developing a rocket capable of damaging London). Yet the Prof never wavered in his personal devotion to the prime minister. The only other individuals of whom Cherwell was heard to speak admiringly were Albert Einstein and Lord Birkenhead, his biographer's father. Cherwell believed that a small circle of the intelligent and the aristocratic should run the world. "Those who succeed in getting what everyone wants must be the ablest," he asserted. The Prof regarded the masses as "very stupid," considered Australians to be inferior to Britons, advocated "harshness" toward homosexuals, and thought criminals should be treated cruelly because "the amount of pleasure derived by other people from the knowledge that a malefactor is being punished far exceeds in sum total the amount of pain inflicted on a malefactor by his punishment."[62]

Inferior as the British working class was in Cherwell's view, he nonetheless ranked it far above the black and brown subjects in the colonies. A measure of his racism can be found in his assertion that "20 percent of white people and 80 percent of coloured were immune" to mustard gas. The figures are clearly incorrect, because biology admits of no such chasm between the races, but they are in keeping with early-twentieth-century notions of eugenics.[63]

Eugenic ideas also feature in a lecture that Lord Cherwell (then known as Professor Lindemann) had delivered more than once, probably in the early 1930s. He had detailed a science-based solution to a challenge that occupied many an intellect of the time: preserving for eternity the hegemony of the superior classes. Any attempt "to force upon Nature an equality she has never admitted" was bound to lead to bloody strife, the scientist asserted in a draft of this talk. Instead of subscribing to what he called "the fetish of equality," he recommended that human differences be accepted and indeed enhanced by means of science. It was no longer necessary, he wrote, to wait for "the haphazard process of natural selection to ensure that the slow and heavy mind gravitates to the lowest form of activity." New technologies such as surgery, mind control, and drug and hormone manipulations would one day allow humans to be fine-tuned for specific tasks. Society could create "gladiators or philosophers, athletes or artists, satyrs or monks" at will—indeed, it could manufacture "men with a passion and perhaps even aptitude for any desired vocation." At the lower end of the race and class spectrum, one could remove from "helots" (the Greek word for slaves) the ability to suffer or to feel ambition.[64]

"Somebody must perform dull, dreary tasks, tend machines, count units in repetition work; is it not incumbent on us, if we have the means, to produce individuals without a distaste for such work, types that are as happy in their monotonous occupation as a cow chewing the cud?" Lindemann asked. Science could yield a race of humans blessed with "the mental make-up of the worker bee." This subclass would do all the unpleasant work and not once think of revolution or of voting rights: "Placid content rules in the bee-hive or ant-heap." The outcome would be a perfectly peaceable and stable society, "led by supermen and served by helots."

Because many people would evince an "illogical disgust" of such alterations to the nature of the human species, one might have to make do with great apes for such tasks instead of humans, the Prof conceded.

It would of course be "somewhat more difficult to make an efficient bricklayer out of a gorilla than out of a bushman," but at least no one would demand votes on behalf of an ape. As for the "unlimited number of half-witted children born of mentally defective parents," sterilization could and should ensure that society be freed of that burden. "Philosophers have failed to agree on any definition of what is good and what should be our aim is a matter of individual opinion," the professor summarized. "But unless we desire to see our civilisation perish, to see it disappear as the great eastern cultures of the Nile and Mesopotamia did, unless we wish to prepare [for] new dark ages such as followed the crumbling of the Roman empire, the fundamental cause of present day unrest will have to be removed." To consolidate the rule of supermen—to perpetuate the British Empire—one need only remove the ability of slaves to see themselves as slaves.[65]

Lindemann's utopia bears an uncanny resemblance to the science-determined dystopia that a contemporary writer, Aldous Huxley, brought to life in his novel *Brave New World*. And his talk of helots suggests inspiration from Sparta, a racially segregated city-state about which he would have learned in school. The Prof may also have derived from ancient Greece the insight that hierarchical regimes are most endangered by those who chafe under their bonds. The Spartans once offered freedom to 2,000 helots who had performed bravely in war and then killed all those who stepped forward to claim their liberty, on the assumption that, as recorded by the classical historian Thucydides, they "would be the most high-spirited and the most apt to rebel."[66]

In Lindemann's utopia, racial superiority alone would not win a high social ranking: he demanded intellectual superiority or aristocratic lineage as well. He envisioned a clique of exalted beings perched on top of a pyramid, with the rest of society ordered in caste-like layers beneath. The hierarchy resembles the terrifying society that George Orwell would sketch in his novel *1984*, in which a class of elites uses mind control to rule over a society of commoners and, below them, so inferior and distant as to be almost invisible, slaves in the colonies. The objective of the three empires chronicled in *1984* "was to arrest progress and freeze

history at a chosen moment," wrote Orwell, so that "this time, by conscious strategy, the High would be able to maintain their position per-
manently." This was the selfsame outcome that the Prof hoped to deliver.
Cherwell's utopia also recalls the predator-prey pyramid envisaged by
Darwin, in which the King of the Jungle forever reigns over forests and
fields of scurrying rabbits.[67]

CHAPTER TEN

Life After Death

As the longest year that Bengalis could remember gave way to 1944, the winter fields were golden with grain—but the villages looked deserted. When the sun rose each morning, survivors emerged from their huts to crouch on their doorsteps with vacant expressions; by afternoon many of them had gotten malarial shivers, wrapped rags around their shoulders, and gone in to lie down. The malaria virus thrives on the enfeebled frames of famine sufferers, and an epidemic began, accompanied by outbreaks of smallpox and cholera. The people had barely the strength, let alone the will, to harvest the crop. A few hunted obsessively for loved ones from whom they had become separated during their wanderings in search of food. One resident of Kalikakundu, Bhuvan Samonto, made it through the famine but lost his mind.

"The villager is undoubtedly in an extremely nervous state, probably amounting almost to panic," Lord Wavell observed. Despite a bumper crop, prices remained high—and any attempt by the government to requisition the harvest would cause it to go underground, raise prices further, and give speculators an opening. In a bid to restore confidence, the viceroy had undertaken to feed Calcutta using resources outside of Bengal, an effort that would require 650,000 tons of rice and wheat per year. On top of that, the colony was about to have to shelter and provision 20 divisions and 184 squadrons for a major attack on Burma. The expanded army, along with laborers employed on building roads and aerodromes, would require 1.1 million tons of grain. "I think Cabinet must trust man on the spot," Wavell informed Amery. "You can warn them from me that it is my considered judgment that unless we can be assured now of receiving one million (repeat one million) tons of food grains during 1944 we are heading for disaster both as regards famine and inflation."[1]

Lord Cherwell challenged Wavell's warning. "I do not think the figures presented stand up to examination or that the case has been made out for taking anything away from the U.K. import programme," he responded. If India were to receive wheat imports, it must then certainly export 120,000 tons of rice to Ceylon, he insisted. The new minister of food, Colonel Llewellin, backed him up, arguing that world stocks of wheat would likely fall to a "dangerously low level" in 1945. More immediately, Australian wheat would be needed to feed Italy and the Balkans. Should those supplies instead be used for India, the Mediterranean region would require grain from Argentina, "with a resulting increase in the strain on shipping and foreign exchange."[2]

On February 7, 1944, the prime minister refused to sanction further shipments to India, on the grounds that imports into Britain "could be further reduced only at the cost of much suffering." Instead he created a committee, comprising Cherwell, Leathers, Llewellin, and Richard A. Butler (in place of Amery, who was sick), to study the Indian food problem. Wavell was not happy: "I warn His Majesty's Government with all seriousness that if they refuse our demands they are risking a catastrophe of far greater dimensions than Bengal famine." In response, the India foodgrains committee sanctioned 50,000 tons of barley from Iraq.[3]

"I regard this as a matter of life or death for hundreds of thousands of Indians," Wavell responded. The War Cabinet should either ask the Americans for shipping or "allow India to appeal to U.N.R.R.A." He spoke to Auchinlek, the commander-in-chief in India, and to Lord Louis Mountbatten, the supreme commander of the South East Asia Command—who warned the Chiefs of Staff of "a worse famine than last year" with obvious impacts on operations. They, too, urged an approach to the Americans, while Amery, who was suffering from a kidney stone, offered to fly to Washington and ask the president for shipping, if that was the only place where it might be found. The India foodgrains committee reiterated that the British Empire stood outside the sphere of UNRRA activities, but the 50,000 tons of barley were changed to wheat.[4]

THE ARMY DISTRIBUTED quinine to civilians in Bengal to combat the threat of malaria, but it was a drop in the ocean. Exposure to the elements exacerbated the suffering from malarial fevers. The poorest villagers never could afford wool for the cold weather, and during the past year the single cotton garment that a man or woman wore, day in and day out, had fallen to pieces. "It is difficult to say whether there is more hunger or more nakedness in these parts," one traveler had written. "Obviously, both these monsters were competing with each other, with the result that the corpses in the streets were often utterly naked. I saw a mother savagely resisting her child trying to protect its naked body from the chill wind with a part of the rag she was wearing." Women could not go about nude, he added, "but the torn and dirty rags with which they tried to hide their sex made them look many times more horrible than even utter nakedness."[5]

"My mother and sister stayed inside or close to the house—only we two brothers would go places," Chitto Samonto confirmed. Ashamed of appearing unclothed before a father, brother, father-in-law, or son, many a village woman took to staying inside a room all day long, emerging only when it was her turn to wear the single fragment of cloth shared with female relatives. Some had to wait for nightfall to bathe or wash dishes, so that villages came alive after dark with shadows that looked more like ghostly skeletons than like women. A woman named Janoki Bera of Kalikakundu lost her husband to the famine but retained a small piece of land. A pair of local brothers, who were subsequently entrusted with distributing garments as a form of relief, got the field from her in exchange of a single sari and later sold off the plot.

During the war years, India produced 600,000 miles of cotton fabric—enough to girdle the earth twenty-four times. Out of this material its workshops manufactured 415 million items of military uniform and 2 million parachutes used to drop supplies. Very little cloth was being released for civilian use, and most of that in turn was ending up in the hands of speculators. The armed forces also consumed India's entire wartime production of silk (used for man-dropping parachutes), wool (used for 17 million uniforms and more than 5 million blankets), and leather (out of which was made 372,000 leather jackets, 16 million pairs of boots, and 5 million pairs of shoes). Whereas in the United Kingdom civilian needs generally had priority over military ones, in India civilians came last.[6]

In November 1943, Lord Mountbatten, the supreme commander of SEAC, asked Viceroy Wavell if the production of cotton parachutes could be doubled to 200,000 per month—"a mere trifle for India," he said, "as it only meant giving up 2% of total cloth." Wavell pointed out that 2 percent of India's population came to 8 million, "which was quite a large number to go short of clothes." Nevertheless, India did produce 200,000 parachutes per month by August 1944. By enabling vital supplies to be dropped into the jungles of the eastern Himalayas, these parachutes would make all the difference in the last battle for the British Raj.[7]

IN DECEMBER 1943, the empire's forces under Field Marshal William Slim began to hack their way through virtually impassable jungles into southern Burma. After a year of rest and training the Indian Army was in good form. Slim had built up the morale of his troops by ensuring that they were well nourished, well protected—including by daily doses of quinine—and adequately bolstered in their fighting spirit by reports of Axis atrocities. Propaganda pamphlets depicted the Indian National Army of Subhas Chandra Bose as dupes of the Japanese, or Jifs (Japanese-inspired fascists). Engineers, explosives, and teams of laborers transformed precarious mountain passes into paved roads capable of carrying tanks, so that Slim's 14th Army broke through to a valley in the Arakan peninsula.[8]

In February 1944 the Japanese commander in Burma began a counterattack in the Arakan—to draw attention away from the main thrust, which was to come in via Imphal valley in India, north of the

Arakan. After Axis forces broke through to India, the forces of Subhas Bose were supposed to enter their homeland, fight guerrilla battles, and inspire a national uprising. By that time the Indian National Army boasted roughly 20,000 former soldiers and an equal number of civilian recruits, including 500 women of the Rani of Jhansi regiment. But their Japanese allies had issued them no real weapons, which required the INA to make do with rifles and ammunition that had been surrendered by the British two years earlier. The Japanese had, however, committed to hand over all the Indian territories they would conquer to a free government of India that Bose had set up. To that end, Bose had drawn up detailed administrative plans and printed currency and stamps. The INA's bard had composed a marching song in Urdu, which began:[9]

> *Step by step let's walk along*
> *Singing songs of happiness*
> *To the land our lives belong*
> *We'll fight and fall upon its breast.*

"It is nearing zero hour," Clive Branson wrote to his wife on December 4, 1943, from Chittagong. He was finally leaving for the front. "Always remember that one is given by fate only one lifetime in which to work and live for humanity. There is no greater crime in my opinion than to renounce the world, no matter for what excuse. If anything should happen to either of us, never say, 'It is finished.' . . . What we miss we can only find in knowing humanity more deeply and not in the ever narrowing circumference of private memories. . . . And above all, whatever happens, let us never for one instant, on the slightest excuse, forget we are human beings and belong to the brotherhood of man."

Ten days later, Branson was in the jungle. The little mountain villages near the camp were deserted, so he got to peek into the huts with their airy walls of woven palm and their carved beams. "Life here glides by like a falling leaf, so that very often I don't know either day or date— but I always listen to the news," he wrote. The radio announced the end of the Bengal famine but said nothing about the malaria, he commented, or about the shortage of able-bodied men that made it hard to reap the crop.[10]

Once the soldiers went on an outing, and some of them shot a cow for the beef and took it away from a poor farmer without paying him anything. "It made me very angry," Branson related. At a distance from the camp lay a rice field, which cultivators were permitted to harvest during certain hours of the day. They had to gather a large bundle, deposit it more than a mile away, and jog back for the next load, which wore them out to the point of collapse. If they had not left the field by the military-imposed curfew, they would be shot. "I need not comment on the whole business," Branson wrote, "but it is the living result of poverty, plus peasant ownership, plus imperial army."

At other times, Branson the painter would bathe in a stream or lie in the winter sun on its sandy bank, gazing at the creatures with whom he shared the earth. "I have just seen a little fish coloured black and yellow, like a wasp—there are also other fish with horizontal lines for camouflage. Also a number of fish constructed very like a lizard—a very long body which is curled up when they rest on the sand or on a rock. . . . I have come across a common creeper with purple flowers the leaves of which are in pairs. The colour when old is gold-yellow—when fresh a green which goes golden when the sunlight shines through them. This creeper is the hunting ground of a yellow-gold butterfly whose wing shape is exactly the same as that of the leaves." Some of the men came across five graves of British soldiers, marked only by a beer bottle.[11]

On January 26, Branson wrote from a position closer to the front: "We are now only a few hundred yards away from glory." As he maintained the day's routine, making his bed, chatting, or sleeping, mortars were screaming overhead. "Here we have such complete mastery in armaments of all kinds!" The problem was that the Japanese had dug trenches deep into the sandy hills. "The bombers are just coming over— we climbed up on our tanks to have a grandstand view of 12 Liberators and dozens of Vengeance divebombers exterminating the Jap positions." One of the men caught a green snake with a salmon-colored patch behind its head, and Branson spotted "what may be the smallest moth

I've ever seen, white, with blue-black markings on wings and light brown head."[12]

Field Marshal Slim described how after the bombers had flattened the Japanese positions, "artillery took up the task and pumped shells from their accumulated dumps into the smoking, burning, spouting hillsides. Then the guns suddenly paused and the Lee-Grant tanks roared forward, the infantry, bayonets fixed, yelling their Indian war cries, following on their tails." Branson was a tank commander, and his platoon was soon to go on a dangerous assignment. He enclosed a sonnet, the last lines of which went:[13]

> *Women and children build up the only road*
> *Where overhead the shells of death whine past*
> *And cattle graze indifferent to the din.*
> *I felt perhaps I'd understood at last*
> *By close observance of all that nature showed*
> *"When life has gone, then where does death begin?"*

At some point Branson became ill and was flown to Chittagong to recover. There he met some Bengali communists with whom he had become friends during his previous stay in the city and gave them two street plays that he had written, asking that they be translated into Bengali and performed. Shortly afterward he returned to the front. On February 25, 1944, Troop Sergeant Clive Branson was killed in action at Ngakyedauk Pass in the Arakan.[14]

IN MARCH 1944 the Japanese began their main offensive, sending forces through the jungle to surround the 7th Indian Division at Imphal valley. The bulk of Allied weaponry traveled to the front on the road that ran through Imphal; after it was taken, the Indian National Army was to trek down the highway in the other direction, into the heart of India. Bose had persuaded the Japanese commanders to accept three INA battalions for the attack. Colonel Shah Nawaz Khan led one battalion on an arduous hike through dense jungles and up to a height of six thousand feet. The men lacked woolens, medicines, field radios, mortars, machine guns, and other essentials of warfare, and by the time they reached their destination, many were barefoot and a quarter suffered from malaria.

Colonel Inayat Kiani, who led an equally ill-provisioned INA battalion north toward Imphal, sent 300 soldiers across the Indo-Burmese border. A Japanese officer recalled the men "wild with enthusiasm as they walked on Indian soil, holding their rifles aloft and shouting, *Jai Hind! Chalo Delhi!" (Hail to India! On to Delhi!*—the second chant having been the cry of the sepoys during the 1857 uprising.) But they ran into an ambush, followed by enemy air strikes and more infantry attacks.[15]

By this time in the world war's eastern theater, Japan was desperately trying to hold the line in the Pacific, and Burma had become a backwater left largely to its own devices. The attackers had meager air cover and few tanks, and depended on a tenuous train of horses, mules, oxen, and elephants for such essentials as food. They trusted that once they reached India and acquired what they called "the Churchill supply," all shortages would vanish.[16]

In contrast, the British Empire's forces in the region were bolstered by Lend Lease tanks and aircraft from the United States—paid for with Indian supplies and services. Integrated SEAC operations under the overall command of Lord Mountbatten allowed American resources to be freely used against the INA. With Churchill's backing, Mountbatten diverted American Dakotas, planes that were ferrying supplies over the Hump to China, to instead reinforce the garrison in Imphal. "For a fortnight food, water and ammunition were delivered to them, like manna, from above," Churchill would write. An extraordinary airlift operation brought into the besieged valley the entire 5th Indian Division, which had returned from the Middle East and been retrained for jungle warfare. Gliders dropped 30,000 guerrillas behind enemy lines—"the largest airborne operation in the war," according to Field Marshal Slim— whose combat was to be supported by tens of thousands of parachute drops a month.[17]

In the third week of June 1944, the empire's forces broke the siege of Imphal. The Japanese retreated, with losses of more than 60,000 men. The INA battalions also fell back, their strength reduced to half, mostly by sickness. The monsoon had arrived, so that when Shah Nawaz Khan arrived at a flooded river and found no boats to cross, he had to leave behind 400 men who were too weak to ford it.[18]

It was Indian resources—and, for the most part, Indian troops—that had restored the honor of the British Empire. Most of the native soldiers killed without hesitation the compatriots whose intention it had been to make India a free country.[19]

MEANWHILE, THE VICEROY in New Delhi continued his uphill struggle to obtain food for Bengal. By March 1944, the Government of India had procured only a tenth of its target of a million tons of rice. Still, the foodgrains committee in London proposed an exchange: if India would send 25,000 tons of rice per month to Ceylon, it would get an equivalent amount of wheat, beginning some months later. "I really think they are crazy at Whitehall, or else they never trouble to read one's telegrams," Wavell vented in his diary.[20]

A fresh crisis loomed: the wheat crop was turning out poorly. If soldiers from the Punjab thought their families back home were in trouble, they would desert to return and rescue them. Beset by such worries, Auchinlek and Mountbatten offered to forgo a tenth of the military equipment being shipped to India, or 20,000 tons per month, if the shipping space could be used to bring wheat. "I think the argument is now getting unrealistic once more," the Prof grumbled, and reiterated his demand for a swap of rice for wheat.[21]

At a War Cabinet meeting on March 20, 1944, Field Marshal Brooke urged that 200,000 tons of wheat be sent right away—because not enough equipment could be found to fill the ships allocated to the military. "Winston was obviously very annoyed," according to Amery, and protested that the armed forces were overstepping their constitutional boundaries. "Brooke stood up very well over this. Winston then asked Leathers for his views, who made out as negative a case as he could." Amery warned the members of the War Cabinet "of their responsibility if the result is going to be a worse famine than the last one." After "a few monologues on the subject of the wholly worthless and possibly even dangerous Indian Army," the prime minister agreed to Brooke's proposal. He could also send a further 150,000 tons of wheat—but only in exchange for the same amount of rice for Ceylon. "This is better than nothing, but it will make Wavell very angry," Amery sighed.[22]

Tom Wilson of the S branch urged an appeal to the Americans. Even a refusal would be useful, he wrote, because "if another famine should occur it would be a good thing on political grounds to be able to say that we had asked the United States for help and that they had been obliged to turn down our request." But Leathers advised against asking the Americans—for they might actually agree. Then "they would certainly take anything away from us which they gave to India" in terms of ships.[23]

ON APRIL 6, 1944, an emissary from the viceroy pleaded with the foodgrains committee for imports. Grigg, who was present, declared that the food problem had been "largely brought about by Bengali merchants for political purposes." He insisted that it was the prerogative of His Majesty's Government, not of the viceroy, to decide whether "the available supplies in India should be applied to supply the Defence Forces or the civil population." He and Cherwell suggested hanging some wealthy natives, presumably hoarders, in order to deter speculation in grain.[24]

It was a "packed" committee, Wavell complained to Amery, "with that old menace the Professor who knows nothing of India (or very much about anything else really useful, I should say); and Leathers, an interested party, intent on holding on to all shipping he can; and Grigg, who is always inclined to be mischievous about India." As Wavell described it in his diary, the committee had pointed to three options—"(a) to supply the shipping; (b) to ask the Americans for it; (c) to tell the Viceroy to supply the Army's needs and let the Indian people starve if necessary"—and had left the choice up to the War Cabinet. "I think they would adopt course (c), if they had any real hope that the Viceroy would consent to carry it out," commented the viceroy.[25]

During these negotiations, the weather and bad luck intervened to make the situation more dire: hail wreaked havoc on the wheat ripening in the fields of the Punjab, and an ammunition-laden vessel exploded at the Bombay docks, killing 500 people, injuring 2,000, and destroying ten other ships and 40,000 tons of food. "I submit that the position is too serious to be left where it is," Amery warned the War Cabinet. This time the Prof conceded an "impasse." He eliminated what the foodgrains committee had identified as the first option—taking the required shipping out of the British import program. That left two possibilities, neither appealing. One was to ask the Americans, a choice Cherwell was not alone in resisting: "Leathers is strongly against this because he thinks any concession they might make would be taken out of us." Alternatively, should Wavell "be ordered to feed the Army even at the risk of civilian shortage?" he asked Churchill. "Amery seemed to suggest that the Viceroy might react violently to this even to the extent of resignation."[26]

The viceroy had fenced the king's first minister into a corner. Wavell's resignation would have wrought enormous damage to Churchill's standing, especially among his own armed forces: the tongue-tied warrior was a surprisingly popular man. Wavell may have known it would not come to that, having guessed that the overall shipping situation was less desperate than the War Cabinet was wont to claim. "I have never believed that the tonnage required to enable me to deal properly with our food problem would make any real difference to operations in the West or here," he explained to Amery. "A dozen ships would do the trick." Without waiting for Churchill's consent, he informed Auchinlek and Mountbatten that they could get only a limited quantity of grain from India for their troops, and that they would have to procure the rest themselves.[27]

At a subsequent meeting that was attended by Sir Firoz Khan Noon, recently appointed India's representative to the War Cabinet, Churchill "had great difficulty in holding himself in and came very near to suggesting that we really could not let Indian starvation or multiplying too fast interfere with operations" required to fight the war, Amery wrote in his diary. Still, the prime minister decided to appeal to the president for grain. A committee drafted a telegram explaining the food problem and its likely repercussions on SEAC operations, and stated that 350,000 tons of wheat were already being shipped to India. (This amount was a pleasant surprise for Wavell—until he realized that the figure included the consignments ordered in the last months of 1943.) Even more grain was needed, the telegram continued: "I am impelled to ask you to consider a special allocation of ships to carry wheat to India from Australia without reducing assistance you are now providing for us, who are at a positive minimum if war efficiency is to be maintained."[28]

In early June, the president sent a refusal: his military advisers had declined to divert American ships from current military operations. D-Day was at hand. On the 6th of that month, the Allied invasion of France began with the long-anticipated and bloody invasion of the beaches of Normandy.[29]

At All Souls, his former college at Oxford, Amery dined with Sir Arthur Salter, who had served as the United Kingdom's shipping representative in Washington. "Salter thinks it is all nonsense to say that we cannot find some ships for India," Amery recorded. The United Kingdom could always feed India out of its own quota of ships, Salter said, and if necessary "insist on the Americans giving us more to feed this country." Salter also opined that telegrams were futile. Presumably a face-to-face request was needed before the president, who was ailing, would interfere with the military's programs.[30]

The wheat situation in India deteriorated further, such that by late June the colony faced an overall shortage of 2 million tons. The War Cabinet continued to insist that the viceroy muddle through by sacrificing military imports, reducing defense requirements of food, and risking "reduced provision for the civil population with consequent possible ill effects on military performance." A second famine in India was preferable to any diminution of the British Empire's stockpile.[31]

"Without India's help the Allies would not now be in a position to invade the Continent of Europe or to threaten Japan," the viceroy wrote to the prime minister. "It would be a poor reward to condemn many hundreds of thousands of Indians to starvation." Moreover, a second famine would destroy all remnant hopes of retaining India as a dominion. The Government of India informed the secretary of state for India that, like it or not, it would announce that 400,000 tons of wheat were being shipped to the colony by September 1944. This time the War Cabinet agreed to send 200,000 tons, at the expense of military shipments.[32]

A POLITICAL CRISIS now added to the viceroy's troubles—and once again it arose from Gandhi's extraordinary ability to embody his people's torment. On February 22, 1944, his wife had died in his arms. Her death affected Gandhi profoundly, and his health gave way. "Such things we went through," one of his followers, Mira Slade, wrote to a friend. "Things that are branded on one's memory with burning fire." (Among those incarcerated with Gandhi was the daughter of a British admiral, formerly known as Miriam Slade.) Sometime that spring, the old man contracted malaria.[33]

Wavell had been commander-in-chief during the Quit India uprising; he regarded Gandhi as a "very shrewd and rather malignant politician" who had hampered him in defending India from Axis attack. Still, when early on May 4, 1944, the viceroy was woken with the news that the prisoner was at grave risk of a coronary or cerebral thrombosis, Wavell ordered his release. The acknowledged soul of the Indian nation had best not die in custody. "It is quite a different position to that of illness induced by fasting," for which Gandhi himself could be held responsible, Amery advised Churchill. Given the odds against Gandhi's survival, the War Cabinet consented to his release. Under no circumstances should the viceroy negotiate with him, the prime minister instructed: "He is a thoroughly evil force, hostile to us in every fiber, largely in the hands of native vested interests."[34]

The seventy-four-year-old Gandhi emerged from custody, broken-hearted and sick, to an India stunned by starvation, choked with in-articulate rage, and bereft of hope—except for what little could be gleaned from the fact that their leader himself was still alive, and might yet show the way. After spending a month in silence and rest, Gandhi wrote to Wavell, asking to meet with him and to consult with Congress leaders such as Nehru, who remained in jail. Gandhi was facing a se-rious problem: the ascendancy of the Muslim League, and the impli-cations for Indian unity. "Jinnah has seized the opportunity of the Congress eclipse to strengthen the position of the League, with great success," Wavell observed.[35]

An independent politician, unaffiliated with the Muslim League, chose this juncture to publish a bombshell: a proposal for the division of India to which Gandhi had agreed a year earlier, while recovering from his fast. It envisaged a Pakistan carved out of Muslim-majority areas of western and eastern India, including Bengal, provided that the people of these regions conveyed by plebiscite their wish to secede. Gandhi had espoused the principle of self-determination his entire life, and his adherence to it even in this case should not have surprised any-one. But his concession to the very idea of Pakistan shocked supporters and provoked a blast of outrage from Hindu chauvinists who feared the partition of their homeland.

Other colonies were also trying to figure out what the postwar order held for them—adding to the prime minister's distress. When the ne-cessity of granting self-government to Ceylon came up, "Winston mut-tered and growled and mumbled for a quarter of an hour or more in order to ventilate his emotions of disgust at anything that could extend self-government to brown people, but in the end subsided and gave way." All such matters, Amery observed, raised in Churchill "a wholly uncontrollable complex."[36]

In July 1944, "Winston sent me a peevish telegram to ask why Gandhi hadn't died yet!" Wavell recorded in his diary. "He has never answered my telegram about food." Gandhi also wrote to the viceroy, offering to suspend the Quit India movement and to collaborate with the war effort in exchange for an immediate declaration of independence. Military operations could continue, he wrote, but "without involving any financial burden on India." The viceroy drafted a polite reply turning Gandhi down, but offering an olive branch: if Hindus, Muslims, and the main Indian minorities agreed on a constitution, they could form a transitional government, under the tutelage of the existing one, until the war was over. In the proposed missive, Wavell also gave his blessings to private discussions scheduled between Gandhi and Jinnah.[37]

When Wavell's draft came before the War Cabinet, "the real storm broke," wrote Amery. The viceroy should not be interacting with "a traitor who ought to be put back in prison," raged the prime minister. "As for Wavell he ought never to have been appointed." The tirade lasted for a full hour: Churchill was prepared "to resign rather than betray our ancient trust, etc." A committee had rewritten Wavell's response so that it bristled with hostile legalese, but the War Cabinet sent it back for further revision.[38]

Amery's diary entry for August 4, 1944, is worth quoting at length. At the War Cabinet meeting that day, Churchill inserted into the new draft a statement of British responsibilities toward Untouchables in a land ruled by Caste Hindus. Amery pointed out that this was irrelevant to the issues that Gandhi had raised. "However, this let loose Winston in a state of great exultation describing how after the war he was going to go back on all the shameful story of the last twenty years of surrender, how once we had won the war there was no obligation to honour promises made at a time of difficulty, and not taken up by the Indians, and carry out a great regeneration of India based on extinguishing landlords and oppressive industrialists and uplift the peasant and untouchable, probably by collectivisation on Russian lines. It might be necessary to get rid of wretched sentimentalists like Wavell and most of the present English officials in India, who were more Indian than the Indians, and send out new men. What was all my professed patriotism worth if I did not stand up for my own countrymen against Indian money-lenders? Naturally I lost patience and couldn't help telling him that I didn't see much difference between his outlook and Hitler's which annoyed him no little. I am by no means sure whether on this subject of India he is really quite sane."

A Churchillian explosion followed Amery's outburst, after which a report on the sterling debt came up for discussion. The report advised that revising the financial agreement with India would be difficult, in part because of the "deprivation and starvation" that the colony had undergone—and it set the prime minister off again. "A long tirade on the worthlessness of the Indian Army was too much for me and I went for him hammer and tongs pointing out what India had done ever since it had saved the Middle East," wrote Amery. Then Churchill segued into "a long description of how he was going to present his counterclaim to India for all we have done for her defence. . . . To try and put any of the economic side of the case into his head was hopeless, but I do think I finally got him to realise the futility of raising the issue with India now when we must have what India can supply."[39]

THE CONTRETEMPS OCCURRED a year to the day since the War Cabinet had made its first, and most crucial, decision to deny meaningful relief to Bengal. It was also a year to the day since the committee on Indian inflation had been set up—the same body whose report was on the table. Perhaps the anniversary was on Amery's mind, particularly if he was apprehending another famine. Amery made the Hitler remark in the heat of argument, but clearly he stood by it. For he left much out of his diaries—notably, any hint of his Jewish heritage—and the retention of this explosive comment can be no accident. Given that Chaim Weizmann, the future premier of Israel, had recently told Amery about "the monstrous German blackmailing offer to release a million Jews in return for ten thousand lorries and other equipment, failing which bargain they proposed to exterminate them," he understood as well as anyone could in those times the implications of his remark.[40]

Amery may also have been irked by the reference to moneylenders—a hint that Churchill saw upper-class Indians, in particular Bengali babus, through the same lens as anti-Semites might perceive Jews. Others had made an explicit comparison. "All those arts which are the natural defence of the weak are more familiar to this subtle race than to . . . the Jew of the dark ages," Macaulay had written of the Bengali, who compressed into his diminutive form every loathsome aspect of the Hindu. "[A]s usurers, as money-changers, as sharp legal practitioners, no class of human beings can bear a comparison with them." The Bengali babu, another writer had joked in 1911, was "something of an Irishman, something of an Italian, something of a Jew: if one can conceive of an Irishman who would run away from a fight instead of into it, an Italian without a sense of beauty and a Jew who would not risk five pounds on the chance of making five hundred."[41]

The frustration that Amery felt that August can perhaps best be gauged by means of an extraordinary three-page typewritten draft that is to be found among his files. Entitled "The Regeneration of India: Memorandum by the Prime Minister" and appended with the initials *W.S.C.*, the manuscript appears at first glance to have indeed been written by Churchill. But a finely penciled notation reveals the paper's true author: "A skit by LSA after a harangue by WSC in Cabinet—only slightly exaggerated." The last two words are underlined.

"We have had enough . . . of shameful pledges about Indian self-government, and of sickening surrenders to babu agitation," the document asserted. "If we went even further two years ago in an open invitation to Indians to unite and kick us out of India that was only because we were in a hole." After the war was over, continued the paper, the prime minister would announce a new policy on the colony: "No more nonsense about self-government; down with all (brown) landlords and profit making industrialists, collectivise agriculture on Russian lines and touch up the untouchables." The scheme would require removing all those Englishmen, beginning with the viceroy, who "would not only appear to have taken our pledges seriously, but to be imbued with a miserable sneaking sympathy for what are called Indian aspirations, not to speak of an inveterate and scandalous propensity to defend Indian interests as against those of their own country, and a readiness to see British workers sweat and toil for generations in order to swell yet further the distended paunches of Hindu moneylenders."

The numerous babus "who infest the government offices" would also have to be disposed of, and replaced by a new force of English re-educators who would uphold "our historic right to govern India in accordance with our own ideas and interests." Every five villages would require "[o]ne English instructor in the new way of life and one English head policeman with five Indian subordinates drawn from the loyal martial races." In total, the colony would require 160,000 instructors in "regeneration," 160,000 English police officers, and 800,000 Indian policemen. Any criticism in the British Parliament of this "new Dawn over India" would be banned. "It will also be necessary, following an excellent Russian precedent, to forbid any but trusted officials to leave India or to allow any visitors from outside except under the closest supervision by an official Intourist Agency."[42]

Another penciled notation confirms that this paper was written in August 1944. Amery must have caricatured the prime minister's ramblings in order to vent his anger, and perhaps also to explain to shocked colleagues why he had compared the beloved statesman to the man who would become the most reviled figure of the twentieth century. "I have stood much during these four years which I should not have stood but for the common danger and for Winston's indispensable gifts as a war leader," Amery confided to his diary. "Now the danger is over . . . while the dangers arising from his lack of judgement and knowledge in many respects and his sheer lack of sanity over India make him increasingly dangerous."[43]

Amery's papers, which were opened to the public in 1997, decades after his death, may be seen as a plea for understanding. Amery had been an elder statesman, a gifted and respected Tory leader with more vision and liberality than most. Saddled with a thankless job for the duration of the war, he had done his best for Britain. But to the extent that posterity would remember him, it would be as the imperialist who had presided over the Bengal famine. It should not be surprising that Amery wanted to tell his side of the story, at a time when it could no longer harm anyone.

ONCE AGAIN THE prime minister crossed the Atlantic on the *Queen Mary*, consuming meals such as this one described by his personal secretary: "Oysters, consommé, turbot, roast turkey, ice with canteloupe melon, Stilton cheese and a great variety of fruit, petit fours, etc.; the whole washed down by champagne (Mumm 1929) and a very remarkable Liebfraumilch [sweet German white wine], followed by some 1870 brandy." During dinner in Quebec on September 13, 1944, the prime minister argued with President Roosevelt for an hour over India. "Churchill talked rather angrily at length about the difficulties the British were confronted with administering India and on the lack of understanding in the United States about the Indian problem," recorded an American observer. The prime minister offered his critics half of India to manage, to see if they could do any better.[44]

Churchill was determined to recapture Singapore, which he described as "the only prize that will restore British prestige in this region." India's economy was still so fragile, however, that the viceroy was reluctant to use the colony as the base for a final, massed attack against Japanese forces, scheduled for 1945. That would require the colony to serve as home base for 27 divisions and more than 200 squadrons. The Chiefs of Staff debated whether Australia or the Middle East might make for a more stable headquarters—but the S branch held otherwise.[45]

The supplies needed by the additional troops "would impose very little extra burden on the Indian economy," an S branch paper argued. "Between 1939 and 1943 total expenditure on stores, hospitals, general measures, roads, etc. has amounted to only about £50 million as compared with an annual budget deficit of £250 million. A small increase of another few millions here would make little difference." India's primary burden, to the tune of £190 million a year, was that of supplying overseas war theaters. A "very drastic cut in our expenditure will be necessary to do much good," Wilson elaborated in another memo, and that was not about to happen. Instead of forcing the Indians to deal with their problems, Wilson commented, Amery "prefers to shift the responsibility to us by telling us that we must not ask so much from India."[46]

Rather than decrease the financial load on India, the War Cabinet drastically increased it by giving all British soldiers in the east a pay raise. The viceroy was furious at not even having been consulted. General Auchinlek demanded a commensurate increase for native soldiers, who were already resentful of getting a third of what their white counterparts earned. Overall, the enhancement added £50 million to India's crippling inflationary burden. "I have found H.M.G.'s attitude to India negligent, hostile and contemptuous to a degree I had not anticipated," a weary Wavell wrote in his diary.[47]

The viceroy did, however, receive 660,450 tons of wheat in 1944— despite the fact that in the fall the Americans suddenly withdrew part of the shipping assigned for British civilian imports. Fending off a second Indian famine took the combined efforts of the secretary of state for India, the viceroy of India, the chief of the Imperial General Staff, the supreme commander in Southeast Asia, and the commander-in-chief in India. It would be beyond anyone's power, however, to win the prime minister's consent to loosening political control over the colony.[48]

CHAPTER ELEVEN

Split and Quit

On August 8, 1944, Gandhi instructed all the insurgents who had gone underground to reveal their whereabouts to the authorities. In effect, he dissolved the renegade governments that had sprung up around the country. Gandhi believed that resistance should be open, courageous, and nonviolent: he disliked secrecy. He may also have hoped that the surrender of these rebels would persuade the Government of India to release the tens of thousands of Congress members who were entering their third year in prison.[1]

"All my dreams were dashed," Sushil Dhara wrote. Gandhi's order had come on top of profound disappointment over the Indian National Army's fortunes. Throughout the previous year Dhara had listened on a makeshift radio to Axis broadcasts and dreamed of the footfall of Subhas Chandra Bose on the muktanchal, or free zone, that he and other rebels had carved out on the shores of western Bengal. In Dhara's fantasy, Netaji, or Respected Leader—as his followers called Bose—would arrive in the vicinity of Midnapore by submarine, along with his forces. Dhara would approach, flying a white flag, and with fervent humility and devotion invite the hero onto the soil of his homeland. The INA would rest and regroup in Tamluk for a week. Dhara's Lightning Brigade would meld with it, and the women's brigade would merge with the Rani of Jhansi regiment. The people of Midnapore would rise as one to welcome their savior, so that India's army of freedom would swell by more than 100,000 exalted souls.

But Bose had failed to come; and just as painful to Dhara was Gandhi's instruction, which he felt he could not disobey. The Tamluk

National Government had, after all, been born of the Congress directive that everyone should serve the cause of freedom according to his or her own conscience—but only so long as the leaders were unable to lead. The rebel government was on its fourth head of state, after the third one had also been arrested. But some of its activities, such as the courts for resolving civil disputes, were running smoothly and had become very popular. The senior members of the government did not want to disband their makeshift civil institutions, especially with independence nowhere in sight. Still, Dhara prevailed in his urging that Gandhi's wishes be respected. It was agreed that one by one the renegade government's officers would court arrest. By September 29, 1944, the second anniversary of Midnapore's march to freedom, they would have disposed of all the pending court cases, balanced their ledgers, and settled other matters. On that day Dhara himself would surface.[2]

"I assumed that I would certainly hang," he recalled. By that time, Dhara was directly or indirectly responsible for close to a hundred assassinations—of police informers, grain speculators, and others whom the Tamluk government had judged guilty of heinous crimes. He was not proud of having taken these lives, Dhara would write, nor did he regret them—with a few exceptions. Information that he received after the killings had led him to believe that three or four of those executed might actually have been innocent.[3]

One of those killed was the wealthy father-in-law of the elder sister of Kanu Mahapatro (the Tamluk government's courier). "He was a good man—he did no wrong," she later protested. As far as she knew, the victim's only faults lay in being part owner of the rice mill where the police had shot three villagers in September 1942 and in having traded in rice from Orissa during the famine. Dhara had subsequently presented the bereaved family with a cow, but no one had asked him whether it was in expiation or just in sympathy.

Biplabi, the underground newsletter, began to publish lists of the Tamluk government's officials, along with the dates on which they would surrender. Dhara spent these precious weeks of freedom touring the countryside, resolving unfinished business and trying to comfort villagers who were fearful of what would befall them once their protectors had gone. Early on September 29, he bid farewell to loved ones, including Kumudini Dakua, who had been released from jail some months earlier. The whole village seemed to be in tears, and Dhara shed some quiet ones himself. Accompanied by three close associates, he took a meandering route into Mohisadal. The police were watching the main roads, and Dhara was determined to deny these adversaries a chance to claim the reward on his head. Appearing suddenly in the bazaar, the men shouted "Freedom to India!" and displayed flags. They ended up sprinting across the bridge and into the police station, chased by policemen—who eventually concocted a tale about the capture of the terrible outlaw and shared the 10,000-rupee reward for Dhara.

Calcutta's police and intelligence officers were thrilled to find the fish jumping into their net. Within days Dhara had been sentenced to ten years' hard labor, for political offenses alone. He was also charged with twenty-nine murders, but despite their best efforts the police could not persuade a single witness to testify against him.[4]

GANDHI'S GESTURE DID not induce the Government of India to release its Congress prisoners—and his attempt to engage Jinnah was equally fruitless. The more Gandhi pondered partition, the more he feared it. Hindus and Muslims could not be nations apart, he pleaded with Jinnah at the Muslim leader's seaview mansion in Bombay. Surely religion alone could not so drastically separate peoples with almost a millennium of intertwined history.

"We are a nation of a hundred million," retorted Jinnah. Muslims, he said, had their "own distinctive culture and civilisation, language and literature, art and architecture, names and nomenclature, sense of values and proportion, legal laws and moral codes, customs and calendar, history and traditions, aptitudes and ambitions." The definition would seem to exclude the Muslims of Bengal, very few of whom spoke Urdu, the sophisticated language of Mughal courts that was favored by Muslims from northwestern India. Be that as it may, Jinnah insisted that only the Muslims of the disputed areas—and none of the other inhabitants—

should vote in any plebiscite on the partition of their provinces. Moreover, he wanted the matter settled before independence, so that the British could force the Indian National Congress to keep any promises made to the Muslim League. Gandhi, in contrast, wanted independence first. As he saw it, the very presence of the British precluded the unity that the colonizers demanded as necessary before they would leave.[5]

In the end, Gandhi and Jinnah could agree on nothing at all. "The two great mountains have met and not even a ridiculous mouse has emerged," Wavell remarked caustically when the conference was over.[6]

PERHAPS THE SECRETARY of state for India was uncomfortably aware of having inserted the partition clause into the Cripps formula that the War Cabinet had offered to the Indian National Congress in 1942. Although Amery had never wanted to break up India, he had ended up nudging events along that course. Or perhaps he was hoping to make amends for the colony's suffering during the war. For whatever reason, Amery now put forth a breathtakingly radical suggestion: the viceroy should simply declare independence. He could simultaneously release the Congress internees and invite the political parties to draw up a constitution, even as the country continued to run under the current one. Certainly Churchill would protest; but with the war drawing to a close, Labour Party members of the Cabinet were becoming more assertive and might support the idea.

As Amery saw it, the imperial presence had made Indian politicians irresponsible. "At the back of their minds they are always thinking that by stating their case in its extreme form they may get something more out of the British Government when the latter has to come to a decision," he wrote. "To that extent there is, I believe, something in Gandhi's argument that our presence in India impedes a settlement." Amery seems to have feared that the assurance of British backing would induce Jinnah to demand exorbitant terms, to which the Congress would not agree, leaving partition as the only option. Once they were actually forced to assume responsibility, Amery argued, the politicians might be less inclined to strike poses and stake claims. And without some such powerful shove forward, "the existing antagonisms only dig themselves in more deeply and the rut gets worse."[7]

If the viceroy had agreed, he would have given valuable momentum to Amery's lone attempt to spare India the slaughter to come. But Wavell dismissed the idea out of hand. "S. of S. [Secretary of State] has a curious capacity for getting hold of the right stick but practically always the wrong end of it," he opined about Amery and his idea. As Wavell saw it, agreement among the natives had to come first, and independence second. The consensus that precedes freedom is acquiescence obtained at gunpoint—a consensus the viceroy regarded as necessary to ensure a "fair" sharing of power between Hindus and Muslims.[8]

Although they agreed on a great many things, Amery and Wavell had profoundly divergent views of Indians. Both used the paternalistic lexicon of the times to describe the colony's subjects. Amery saw them as "neither parent nor child" but as young adults capable of assuming control of their own lives. Wavell, in contrast, held that the natives had reached at most the "tiresome age of adolescence" and needed tutoring in the use of freedom. He could find "hardly any sense at all of nationhood in India or of leadership likely to produce it," and searched in vain for men of vision—among the princes. He might have had more luck among his prisoners. At the very least, the viceroy believed that he would need to stand over the desks of his charges while they wrote their constitutions; only then would they be ready to graduate.[9]

There was something else. For reasons of personal history, Wavell was more inclined to sympathize with supposedly martial peoples such as Muslims than with Hindus. During World War I, he had helped conquer Palestine using Indian Muslim troops who had steadfastly guarded holy sites in Jerusalem. He had subsequently become friends with Lawrence of Arabia and sympathetic to Arabs' fears of being overwhelmed in their own land by Jewish immigrants. When it came to India, he similarly believed that valorous and loyal Muslims deserved special protection from traitorous and wily Hindus of the Congress. The warriors Wavell and Churchill could agree on this much: the malevolence of Gandhi, whose half-naked frame, hair-splitting arguments, and refusal to put up his fists encapsulated all that was repugnant to them about Hindus.[10]

Amery wrote in his diary that Wavell was refusing to see that his insistence on consensus before freedom "means Pakistan and the breakup of India." The viceroy nevertheless remained committed to breaking the political deadlock. After the war ended, prisoners who were members of Congress would have to be released, soldiers demobilized, and laborers thrown out of employment, he wrote to the prime minister in October 1944. The clamor for change would become deafening. "Indians are a docile people, and a comparatively small amount of force ruthlessly used might be sufficient; but it seems to me clear that the British people will not consent to be associated with a policy of repression, nor will world opinion approve it, nor will British soldiers wish to stay here in large numbers after the war to hold the country down."[11]

In addition to pushing for progress on the political front, Wavell requested part of the sterling balance to pay for reconstructing India after the war. At an evening meeting of the War Cabinet on November 6, 1944, Amery had what he called the "worst open row with Winston that I have yet had." The prime minister "denounced Wavell for betraying this country's interests in order to curry favour with the Indians, and went on at large about the scandal and disgrace" all around. Amery tried to control himself, "but could not help in the end exploding violently and telling him to stop talking damned nonsense."[12]

ON FEBRUARY 1, 1945, Winston Churchill was on board the HMS *Orion*, on his way to Yalta in the Crimea for a second meeting during wartime of all three Allied leaders. He wrote to his wife, recommending a book, *Verdict on India* by Beverley Nichols. "It is written with some distinction and a great deal of thought," he told her. "It certainly shows the Hindu in his true character and the sorry plight to which we have reduced ourselves by losing confidence in our mission."[13]

Verdict on India was a kind of sequel to *Mother India*—a travelogue that, two decades earlier, had detailed the sexual perversions of Hindus, and which Churchill had admired. The poverty Nichols saw in India had at first inclined him to be charitable, he wrote. "But the flock of dreadful beings that fly towards you, attracted by the clink of coins, is too great; they seem to appear from nowhere, to drop from the sky and the trees, gibbering, spitting, moaning, screaming, and pointing to their sores." The writer also saw several "QUIT INDIA" signs, proof of the government's easygoing attitude toward dissent. Of course, "no breath of democracy had ever stirred the Indian dust until we came," Nichols attested, and all such hard-fought gains would vanish with the imperialists. Should the Congress take over, the lower castes "might as well run to the nearest village well and hurl themselves into it *en masse*." Untouchability was "as integral a part of the Hindu faith as anti-Semitism of the Nazi," while the Congress party was "the only 100 percent, full-blooded, uncompromising example of undiluted Fascism in the modern world"—with Gandhi as its führer.[14]

One Indian earned Nichols's respect: "The most important man in Asia is sixty-seven, tall, thin, and elegant, with a monocle on a grey silk cord, and a stiff white collar which he wears in the hottest weather. He suggests a gentleman of Spain, a diplomat of the old school." Mohammad Ali Jinnah was as different from a Hindu politician as a surgeon from a shaman, Nichols wrote, and with a surgeon's precision he had dissected the status quo. The Muslim had nothing in common with the Hindu, Jinnah said disdainfully: "We eat the cow, the Hindus worship it." And that was the least of their differences. The skirmishing between Muslims and Hindus had produced a cancerous society, Nichols summarized. "There is only one remedy for a cancer, in its advanced stages, and that is the knife. . . . To the knife it will have to come in the end, and surely one knife, used swiftly and with precision, is better than a million knives, hacking in blind anarchy in the dark?"[15]

Thinking about India depressed him, the prime minister wrote to his wife. He received unceasing abuse for "holding on to this vast Empire, from which we get nothing." And yet he had discovered within himself "a renewed resolve to go fighting on as long as possible and to make sure the Flag is not let down while I am at the wheel. I agree with the book and also with its conclusion—Pakistan."[16]

WHEN THE THREE Allied leaders met at Yalta, the Germans were fighting on their own soil on both the Eastern and Western European fronts, and President Roosevelt had just won a fourth term. Yet the bonhomie among the men felt hollow. Roosevelt was ill—too ill, perhaps, to deal effectively with a formidable ally such as Stalin. And relations between the president and the prime minister were worse than ever. The British were upset that the Americans were not doing more to stop the Soviets from overrunning Poland, while the Americans were appalled that Churchill had met privately with Stalin to chalk out their respective spheres of influence in the Balkans—in the process, bartering several small and prostrate nations.[17]

When at Yalta the question of placing colonies under the supervision of the United Nations came up, Churchill exploded. He would never tolerate "forty or fifty nations thrusting interfering fingers into the life's existence of the British Empire." Jumping to his feet, he shouted, "Never, never, never!" He would not have "one scrap of British territory" handed over for inspection. "No one will induce me as long as I am Prime Minister to let any representative of Great Britain go to a conference where we will be placed in the dock and asked to justify our right to live in a world we have tried to save." After he had been calmed down with promises that the scheme was not going to apply to the British Empire— which was not quite true, as the fine print would later reveal—he sat down and kept muttering "never, never, never" to himself.[18]

On the president's voyage back to the United States, a reporter asked if the prime minister really wanted all his colonies back, just the way they used to be. "Yes," Roosevelt replied. "He is mid-Victorian on all things like that." In March 1945 the president reiterated his concern for "the brown people in the East." Many of them were "ruled by a handful of whites and they resent it. Our goal must be to help them achieve independence."[19]

Back in London, Churchill told his private secretary that "the Hindus were a foul race 'protected by their mere pullulation from the doom that is their due.'" (*Pullulation* means rapid breeding.) He wished that

Air Chief Marshall Arthur Harris, the head of British bomber command, could "send some of his surplus bombers to destroy them."[20]

MEANWHILE, IN OCTOBER 1944, Wavell had offered to fly home in order to consult with the War Cabinet and press it to take a decision on India. Amery had agreed: otherwise, it seemed that Churchill would stall as long as he possibly could. He appeared to be waiting not just for the end of the European war but also for the election to follow: should he become prime minister again, he would have a stronger hand to play.[21]

With Amery constantly hectoring him, Churchill had passed the matter to a committee of the War Cabinet. A Labour politician, Clement Richard Attlee, headed this so-called India Committee (to be distinguished from the Committee on India Foodgrains and the Committee on Indian Inflation). If Attlee could be trusted with the future of the British Raj, that was because he was more of an imperialist than his credentials would suggest: he was "frankly horrified" at the prospect of ceding power to a "brown oligarchy" of Indians. And although Cherwell was not on this committee, Grigg was. So Amery found little support for his idea of turning India into a dominion, if not granting actual independence, right away. Years later, he would write with sadness: "I still believe it was the only solution that might have saved Indian unity." The viceroy returned to England, but when at long last he got to meet Churchill, on March 29, 1945, the prime minister "launched into a long jeremiad about India which lasted for about 40 minutes. He seems to favour partition into Pakistan, Hindustan, Princestan, etc."[22]

Wavell also met Leathers to ask for continued wheat shipments to India, but, as always, the minister of war transport pleaded a lack of ships. "I asked where all the ships were," wrote Wavell, "and the answer seemed to be, mainly in the Pacific, where 6 to 7 million tons is absorbed in shipping used simply as storehouses." Another food crisis had come up in the colony, but Leathers "seemed indifferent to the possibility of famine in India," while the foodgrains committee, "on the basis of

Cherwell's fatuous calculations, simply tried to show that we already had enough food in India." Wavell pointed out that for several months he had received only half the wheat promised, which in turn was half of what was needed. Sitting through a routine War Cabinet meeting on April 9, he was struck by "the very different attitude towards feeding a starving population when the starvation is in Europe. In this case it is Holland which needs food, and ships will of course be available, quite a different answer to the one we get whenever we ask for ships to bring food to India."[23]

AT 3:35 P.M. ON APRIL 12, 1945, the president died in his cottage at Warm Springs, Georgia, of a stroke.

At the House of Commons, the prime minister spoke in soulful tones of the man "whose friendship for the cause of freedom and for the causes of the weak and poor have won him immortal renown," and adjourned the session as a mark of respect. But that very day, in an outright repudiation of Roosevelt's trusteeship scheme, a representative at a Commonwealth conference announced the United Kingdom's refusal to hand over its colonies to international supervision. The president's dreams for the dispossessed were buried before he was.[24]

The rift between India and the United States widened right away. The previous December, Nehru's personable sister, Vijaylakshmi Pandit, was working on famine relief and rehabilitation in Bengal when she unexpectedly heard from an American general and, days later, found herself in the bucket seat of a military transport plane, a small bag by her side, flying to New York. It could only have happened, she guessed, if the initiative had come from the president himself. She had used the American visit to campaign for Indian freedom and even lunched with Eleanor Roosevelt at the White House. When the president died, her luck changed. In June 1945, Pandit would go to a United Nations conference being held at San Francisco—but despite the best efforts of the India League she would not be allowed to represent her country. Of the major Allies, the Soviet Union alone would favorably influence Indian opinion when its delegate, Vyacheslav Molotov, expressed sympathy for nationalists.[25]

ON APRIL 30, 1945, just before Soviet troops entered Berlin, Hitler shot himself.

"I FEEL VERY lonely without a war," Churchill confided to his doctor, Lord Moran. "Do you feel like that?" On May 5, three days before the Allies accepted the surrender of Germany, Churchill had ordered a committee to review postwar security. Its appraisal identified the Soviet Union as the West's new adversary. India, which enabled access to the Middle East, Southeast Asia, and the Soviet Union, and which was also a source of fighting men, was projected to remain vital to British security. "It is of paramount importance that India should not secede from the Empire," the appraisal declared. If, however, the colony could not be held, the alternative was to keep a strategic piece of it under British control—possibly Baluchistan in the far northwest, "on the ground that it may be relatively easy to exclude this territory" from India. (Baluchistan would ultimately become the westernmost province of Pakistan.)[26]

By the end of May, Viceroy Wavell had thrashed out with the India Committee a formula to resolve the political status of the colony. Subject to War Cabinet approval, he would choose a new Viceroy's Council, or executive body, containing 40 percent each of Caste Hindus and Muslims from lists supplied by the leading political parties. Although Muslims comprised fewer than a quarter of India's population, they were to be regarded as a separate nation and by that logic were given representation far beyond their numbers. (The two or three remaining members of the council would be Sikh, lower caste, tribal, or Christian.) Such a council would inevitably safeguard British power—through the enmity between the Congress and the Muslim League. These factions were hardly likely to agree on anything, but should they do so, the viceroy proposed to retain the power to overrule his council.[27]

At the War Cabinet meeting to discuss the plan, "Winston was in his most truculent mood, and really very difficult," recorded Amery. The discussion continued into the next day, May 31, with the prime minister delivering "a long polemical statement" against any proposal to cede control to Indians. Yet when the meeting resumed that night, Wavell found to his amazement that Churchill "made just as forcible an address in favour of my proposals as he had made in their damnation." He even "exuded good will towards India and myself at every pore." The viceroy assumed that the change of heart had to do with upcoming elections: because public opinion favored easing the controls over India, Churchill could not afford to be seen as holding back progress there. "Everything ended on the happiest of happy notes," commented an equally relieved Amery.[28]

Back in India, the viceroy ordered the top eight Congress leaders to be released and invited selected politicians to the resort town of Simla to talk things over. Given that its rank and file remained in jail, the Congress had no choice but to be cooperative. Jinnah refused to be as agreeable, however: he insisted that every Muslim on the viceroy's new council belong to his League, which presented a problem because the conference included a number of prominent Muslims, one of whom was a staunch British ally but despised Jinnah. Accordingly, Wavell drew up his own list of council members. It contained five Muslims, four of whom were associated with the Muslim League, with the fifth an independent from the Punjab. The War Cabinet insisted, however, that Wavell get Jinnah's approval of the lineup. Grigg declared that it was out of the question to have a council that the Muslim League did not like: "We risked losing our friends."[29]

Jinnah refused to accept Wavell's list—he was adamant that only the Muslim League should represent Muslims—and Wavell declared that the conference had failed. He had, after all, won the War Cabinet's consent for the proceedings on the understanding that the Muslim League would be on board to counter the Congress. The prime minister "would have been outraged," wrote historian Penderel Moon, if the result of the Simla conference "had been a proposal to form a Congress-dominated council unbalanced by the League."[30]

"So ended my efforts to save a united India," Amery wrote in his diary. Churchill had missed some War Cabinet meetings, having been away campaigning for the forthcoming elections; but the diehard members of the War Cabinet, who spoke for the prime minister in his absence, had wanted the Simla talks to break down, he observed. Grigg, for instance, was "completely obsessed with his hatred of all Hindus" and accused Amery of "selling up four hundred million Indians to a handful of greedy Hindu industrialists"—who, he feared, were conspiring with the Congress to supplant British businessmen in India.[31]

Intriguingly, Wavell subsequently discovered that someone from the India Committee had gone behind his back to confer with members of his existing council who had been in London at that time. And Jinnah told a confidante that "friends in England" had communicated to him, via a member of that council, that if Jinnah held fast to his demands he "would get Pakistan." Another of his colleagues reported that a member of London's India Committee "was advising Jinnah to stand firm." To top it off, Churchill later confided to Wavell that he had let him go ahead with his attempt at an Indian settlement only because, as the viceroy wrote in his diary, "the India Committee had all told him [Churchill] it was bound to fail!"[32]

Jinnah had his own reason for rejecting the viceroy's list—the presence of an independent Muslim would have undermined his claim to represent all Muslims—and the extent to which Churchill's advisers actually influenced his decision may never be known. But it is clear that the prime minister and his supporters did their best to sabotage the Simla talks, commonly considered a major fork on the route to the creation of the nation of Pakistan. Churchill obstructed India's future as a united and peaceable nation, while simultaneously seeking to give the appearance of being progressive.

Such maneuvers were not enough to stem the slide in the prime minister's fortunes. A restless electorate was primed for change in the postwar era. In late July 1945, the United Kingdom's election results came in: a landslide victory for Labour and its party head, Clement Attlee. Churchill's tumultuous tenure as leader of the British Empire was, at least for the present, over.

The defeat shocked him. "For five years he had enjoyed the trust and affection of the whole country, and then, in a night, the confidence of his countrymen was withdrawn," Lord Moran wrote. "Why had they deserted him in the hour of victory?" Grateful as Britons were for his leadership during the war, they could not envisage Churchill as a successful peacetime prime minister. When, months after he had departed 10 Downing Street, Wavell went to visit him, Churchill's parting admonition to the viceroy was "Keep a bit of India."[33]

ON THE BRITISH Empire's far eastern border, World War II was not yet over. By the spring of 1945, British and Indian forces had traversed the foothills of the eastern Himalayas and poured into the river plains of Burma. The Americans had departed the region, because it was easier to lead an assault on Japan from islands in the Pacific than from China; the battles in Burma were now purely about restoring imperial territory.

Subhas Chandra Bose no longer hoped to liberate his homeland— at least not through conquest. He still believed that the Indian National Army had to set an example of heroism and sacrifice that would spark a spontaneous response in India. So he dispatched most of his remaining forces to resist the British advance, with the exception of the Rani of Jhansi regiment, which stayed back in a small town in the Burmese highland to tend the wounded and the sick. Lakshmi Swaminathan, its colonel, was a doctor who possessed no combat experience, and Bose had no wish to expend the regiment on a suicide mission. But airplanes bombed the hospital, killing many patients and severely injuring one of his best field commanders.

A battalion of the Indian National Army tried to oppose the enemy— the Indian Army under Field Marshal Slim—as it crossed the Irrawaddy River, but bombs sent it scattering. Another INA battalion was caught in the open, facing tanks and armored cars with rifles and bayonets, and literally crushed. The remnants of two INA divisions retired to the steep forested slopes of a dormant volcano, Mount Popa, where they could get water from natural springs, taking shelter there while their commanders directed swift, short guerrilla raids on the jungle patrols of the enemy columns passing below.

There could be no doubt who was winning the war. From their perch the INA commanders could see clouds of red dust billowing from an unending train of tanks, armored cars, and troop-laden trucks trundling by, and in July 1945 they decided to retreat before their escape route was cut off. One of their battalions emerged from the jungle by mistake and was wiped out. Another group of soldiers were sheltering in a village when airplanes circled overhead; they had been spotted. The villagers asked that the soldiers surrender, lest the homes be bombed; surrender they did. Other commanders tried to slip out of the British cordon with their troops but were surrounded and had to give up.

With the enemy approaching Rangoon, Bose gathered his remaining soldiers, including the Rani of Jhansi regiment, and began a retreat. Swaminathan opted to stay behind to look after the wounded, but after the headquarters were again bombed she dispersed her patients and fled into the jungle with a small group. She was ultimately captured by a British patrol.

Bose and his forces marched at night and rested by day for fear of being bombed. After six days they reached a railhead, where Bose sent the women ahead by train. But a rail bridge had been destroyed, and they had to disembark and set out again on foot. In the end, only a tenth of the soldiers whom Bose had brought into Burma got out. On August 6, 1945, while in Bangkok, he got news that the Americans had dropped an atom bomb on Hiroshima.

Some years later, Bose's elder brother would receive a letter in a familiar Bengali hand. "Today once again I am embarking on the path of danger," it began. "But this time towards home. I may not see the end of the road." Subhas Chandra Bose had written his farewell shortly before leaving Germany and had left the missive with his wife. "I have married here and I have a daughter. In my absence please show my wife and daughter the love that you have given me throughout your life."[34]

The fate of Subhas Chandra Bose is one of the enduring mysteries of the war. British intelligence reported in late August that he had been badly burned in an airplane crash in Taiwan on August 18, 1945, days after Japan's surrender, and had died that night. It appears that Bose had been flying from Bangkok to Tokyo, via Saigon, along with an associate and several Japanese officers. He planned to eventually reach the Soviet Union, which he hoped would aid his struggle for Indian freedom. After departing Saigon, the aircraft had halted in Taipei for an hour, and immediately after takeoff from there the left engine had broken off. The aircraft had banked and dived to the ground from a height of between twenty and thirty meters. Bose was seated near gasoline tanks, was splashed with the fuel, and caught fire.[35]

Special Operations Executive agents were all over Southeast Asia at the time, and the assassination order against Bose seems to still have been in effect—which raises the possibility that the aircraft had been tampered with. A spy in British service, known as Agent B1189, had infiltrated the Indian National Army's upper echelons. He may have been able to convey Bose's travel plans in time for SOE agents to sabotage the plane.[36]

FOR THE LONGEST time, Gandhi refused to accept that the prodigal son would never return. He hoped against hope that Bose had gone into hiding, where he was seeking a way to renew the struggle. The newspapers had already reported Bose's death in 1942, Gandhi told his associates. "Since then I have had a feeling that Netaji could not leave us until his dream [of freedom] had been fulfilled."

In July 1944, shortly after Gandhi had emerged from prison, Bose had addressed a broadcast to his former mentor in an effort to explain his controversial choice to ally with the Axis powers and raise an army. Every Indian would be happy if freedom could be won by nonviolent means, he had said. Bose believed, however, that appeals to the conscience did not work on British leaders, who were determined to retain control and, indeed, to "make good their present losses by exploiting India more ruthlessly than ever before." Indians would have to "wade through blood" to achieve their goals. "Father of our nation: in this holy war for India's liberation, we ask for your blessings and good wishes," Bose concluded.[37]

Although Gandhi deplored Bose's methods, he could not but admire his devotion to Indian independence. Moreover, the condition in which Gandhi had found India upon emerging from prison had heightened his awareness of the violence structured into a colonial society. He visited Bengal—and was heard to wonder why the starving had died in front of overflowing shops but had not looted food.[38]

On Christmas Day, 1945, Gandhi journeyed to Midnapore to investigate claims that some of his most ardent followers had committed murder. More than 100,000 men, women, and children lined the canal along which his boat traveled. They stood in notable silence, because Gandhi was feeling ill in mind and body and had asked for quiet.

Satish Samanta, who had just been released from prison, arranged for Gandhi to stay at a famine orphanage in Mohisadal. The day after his arrival, Gandhi handed his host a signed complaint that he had received from several senior Congress workers. It related the two-year campaign of extortion and assassination that the Tamluk National Government had conducted. Samanta had been behind bars for most of that period, but after consulting with subordinates he confessed that the allegations were true. The Mahatma sat as if turned to stone. After a few minutes Samanta pleaded, "Won't you hear under what circumstances we did these things?"

He told Gandhi about the police atrocities. Gandhi asked for proof, and two days later his doctor, Sushila Nayar, and his granddaughter, Abha Gandhi, went to Masuria. The men of the village were not allowed into the session that followed, but they could hear the wailing from afar. Their pain unfrozen by the empathy of their audience, dozens of women told of the terror and sobbed. "We wept with them," Nayar wrote. (Kanonbala Maity said that she had missed the meeting, because her father-in-law had forbidden her to attend.)

"If you were really nonviolent, you wouldn't be here to tell the tale," Gandhi admonished the men of Midnapore. "You would have perished defending them [the women] nonviolently." As for the Tamluk government, Gandhi acknowledged that he did not really know how he would have responded to the circumstances it had confronted: even violence was preferable to the cowardice of doing nothing, he said. Sushil Dhara, who was anxiously following events from his prison cell, heard the verdict with joy and relief. Gandhi would have been happier if the Tamluk government had stuck with nonviolence, but its achievements, he said, were nonetheless "heroic."[39]

ALTHOUGH HE PROBABLY did not live to see it, Subhas Chandra Bose's dream of inciting an Indian uprising ultimately came true. News of the Indian National Army's example of valor and sacrifice roused the country to a fever pitch. For the first time since the 1857 rebellion, an insurrection would challenge the loyalty of the sepoys.

It was Commander-in-Chief Auchinlek who unwittingly orchestrated the drama that unfolded at Delhi's Red Fort, a towering structure of red sandstone and marble redolent with the grandeur of Mughal emperors and haunted by the bloody ghosts of 1857. In November 1945 at the fort, Auchinlek placed three of the INA's surviving commanders on public trial for treason and murder. The men were Shah Nawaz Khan, Prem Kumar Sahgal, and Gurbux Singh Dhillon—a Muslim, a Hindu, and a Sikh, whose religious identities were proof of the extent of Bose's embrace. As the trial wore on and newspapers avidly reported every twist and turn of testimony, Indians came together in outrage that an occupying power should have the hubris to try for treason men who were fighting for Indian independence.

In February 1946, sailors of the Royal Indian Navy struck work and began driving around Bombay, waving Congress flags. The naval mutiny spread to several other ports and ultimately involved twenty ships. Mobs spilled into the streets in sympathy, facing off with the police and the army. The white forces in India were too small to contain a full-fledged mutiny by the military, Auchinlek gauged, and if one broke out, "nothing short of an organized campaign for the reconquest of India" would suffice to establish control. The courts ultimately found the three INA officers guilty of treason and sentenced them to deportation for life (presumably to the prison and penal colony on the Andaman Islands), but Auchinlek commuted the sentences and set them free. As he explained to furious compatriots, "any attempt to enforce the sentence would have led to chaos in the country at large, and probably to mutiny and dissension in the Army, culminating in its dissolution." For the first time since 1857, India could not be possessed by means of its own army—which meant that it could not be held at all.[40]

The three commanders had become household names. They soon learned, however, that the India for which they had fought was not the one to which they had returned. Shah Nawaz Khan appeared at political rallies to plead for unity among Hindus and Muslims. But upon emerging from a Calcutta mosque he was shocked to find Muslim League supporters stoning his car and shouting slogans favoring the separate nation of Pakistan.[41]

SO IT WAS that World War II sowed the seeds both for the independence of India and for its division. Independence became an imperative because the raw misery of the war years had sparked rage beyond the colonizer's power to subdue. Division was demanded because by exacting heavy penalties for attacks on imperial interests, the authorities could deflect the fury into internecine bloodshed that would rend Hindus apart from Muslims. During the war, the necessity of containing nationalist insurgencies had led the police to ignore criminals and, thereby, to embolden them. The same necessity, combined with the need to keep Muslim soldiers loyal, had led the authorities to empower religious separatists. As the British sought an exit from India, their primary concern would be to limit white casualties, and the forces of mayhem would run rampant.

Elections held in 1946 revealed the polarization that the war years had fostered. The Muslim League ran on a platform of partition. Before the war it had failed to get 5 percent of the Muslim vote, but it now earned 76 percent. In Bengal the famine had aided—rather than hurt—the party's fortunes because the civil administration had relied on workers of the Muslim League and the Communist Party of India to distribute relief, and as the visible faces of succor both groups had gained traction in rural areas. The Muslim League won the elections in Bengal and joined a coalition of British business interests to form the government there; the former food minister, Huseyn Shaheed Suhrawardy, became chief minister.[42]

The Indian National Congress also did well, among non-Muslims all over the country, and it won the North West Frontier Province as well. In complex negotiations with representatives of the United Kingdom's new Labour government, Congress politicians outmaneuvered the Muslim League and formed a transitional government in New Delhi. Finding himself sidelined in spite of his electoral success, Jinnah vented his frustration in a call for civil disobedience. On August 16, 1946, ominously termed Direct Action Day, Muslims would show that they were serious about establishing Pakistan. That day, at a packed Muslim League rally in Calcutta, Chief Minister Suhrawardy denounced Hindus and assured the crowd that the police would not interfere in its actions against them. The mob dispersed to burn and loot Hindu shops, and to kill.[43]

The governor of Bengal, Sir Frederick Burrows, learned that Suhrawardy was visiting the police control room in Calcutta, allegedly to ensure that the killing could continue unchecked—but Burrows did not intercede. "I had always to consider the susceptibilities of my Ministry," Burrows explained to Viceroy Wavell. When desperate residents sought the aid of Calcutta's police chief, D. R. Hardwick, the chief responded sarcastically, "Who am I to interfere in your affairs? The Hindus want us to get out. The Muslims want us to leave the country to them. I am so helpless. Why not ring up the Congress office?" Over the next two days—while the police stood aside—the criminal underworld, both Hindu and Muslim, stabbed and pillaged until the streets of Calcutta resembled, Burrows reported, the trenches of the Somme in World War I.[44]

There was one reason to be relieved, the governor informed the viceroy: not a single European had been harmed. A Muslim League official had earlier assured the authorities that the agitation would be "directed not so much at the British as at the Hindus," and an editorial published in a Calcutta newspaper on the morning of Direct Action Day had advised Muslims that attacks on "British men or women, be they civilian or military," were "against the spirit and letter of Islam." As a result, Muslim thugs had turned their fury entirely upon Hindus and Sikhs, and gangs from those two communities had retaliated—spectacularly bolstering the British claim that it was only the Raj that had kept the fractious subjects from one another's throats. Historian Rakesh Batabyal speculates that some such motive lay behind the British delay in calling out the army, which was summoned only at 8 P.M. on the second day of the killings, whereas it had intervened immediately whenever demonstrations or riots had had an anti-imperial tone.[45]

The uncontained slaughter in Calcutta, which left up to 10,000 dead in a matter of days, sparked a series of vicious religious pogroms across India, which would make partition a *fait accompli*. The killings paused for a while, but in October they began again, this time in Noakhali in eastern Bengal. There a gangster-turned-politician had long tried to mobilize peasants against landlords, with no success—until he observed the success of the Muslim League's tactics and inducted Islam as a weapon by which to achieve his political ends. The famine had eased his task, because government propaganda had already convinced Muslim peasants of eastern Bengal that their Hindu landlords were entirely to blame for their hunger. Worse, the wartime reign of the Muslim League in Bengal, in concert with the hostility toward Hindus that emanated from the highest levels of the imperial government, had thoroughly communalized the province's police and administration—both signaling and ensuring that the authorities would deal leniently with attacks on Hindus. Although the army was eventually called into Noakhali, civil servants simply freed the offenders whom the army handed over to them.[46]

In the end, the vast majority of victims in Noakhali were not landowners but villagers of the lowest castes—people who had also suffered grievously from famine, as well as from forced evacuations, rape, and other depredations by Allied forces stationed in the region.

AT THE TIME of the strife in Noakhali, Ashoka Gupta was living in Chittagong. The famine had changed her life, turning her gaze out of the home and onto the world beyond. The joy she derived from saving a child by giving her food and shelter and "bringing back a smile to her lips" was more than she had ever obtained from attending to her household chores. When the pogrom in Noakhali began, she resolved—with the help of the All India Women's Conference—to help the afflicted villagers, and in particular to rescue violated women and girls, who were being rejected by their own families after assaults by Muslim men.[47]

Gandhi arrived soon after in Noakhali, in the hope of bringing calm by trekking from village to charred village. Discouraged by the vastness of her task, Gupta went with a friend to seek his advice and found him living in a burned-down house. Gandhi was in agony; everything to which he had dedicated his life was falling apart. That religion should be used in service of violence appalled him and challenged the very foundation of his creed. But none of this turmoil was visible to Gupta. To the two women, Gandhi said that it was not enough to visit the ravaged areas: they would have to reside there. "Only if we ourselves had the courage to face the dangers of the situation, and lived continuously in the villages over an extended period of time, would the local people be assured about our commitment and return to live in their own homes," Gupta recalled him saying. "For courage, like fear, was contagious. Just a single example of a courageous deed would act like a beacon of hope and would arouse the bravery and the self-confidence of the local people."[48]

With a toddler in her arms, Gupta made a home in the terrifying ghostly hulk of what once had been a peaceable fishing village. Slowly the killings died down—but things never did return to normal. One young woman confided that she was being taken away every night by gangsters, raped, and returned the next morning to her husband. The couple dared not complain to the police for fear of reprisals.[49]

NOTHING COULD HUSH the screams that emanated from Noakhali. The outflow of terror-stricken refugees, spreading across Bengal and into Bihar in a desperate search for safety, convinced many Hindus that they could no longer coexist with Muslims. Wealthy Bengalis of both faiths began to pack up and migrate to the regions where they would be in a majority.

The pogroms of Noakhali sparked even more horrific retributions in Bihar, where Hindu landowners organized mobs to butcher poor Muslims. The toll would reach 20,000. Viceroy Wavell turned down legislators' pleas that killer mobs in Bihar be strafed by military aircraft. "Machine-gunning from the air is not a weapon one would willingly use," he noted in his diary, "though the Muslims point out, rather embarrassingly, that we did not hesitate to use it in 1942." As recently as July 1946, Wavell had ordered the destruction by bombing of villages in the North West Frontier Province—because some tribesmen had kidnapped a British consul. Compared with his resolve when imperial interests were at stake, the viceroy responded mildly to the far more lethal internecine riots. The director of the Intelligence Bureau had urged that the massacres not provoke the authorities "into action which would reintroduce anti-British agitation." If anything, he added, the religious warfare had its uses, being "a natural, if ghastly, process tending in its own way to the solution of the Indian problem."[50]

Imperial troops should stand aloof, warned the leader of the British opposition, Winston Churchill, and not become the "agencies and instruments of enforcing caste Hindu domination upon the 90 million Muslims and the 60 million Untouchables."[51]

A COLLECTION OF war-related factors had unleashed violence of a kind that India had not witnessed since 1857. But this time, Hindus and Muslims were fighting one another instead of a common enemy and, after almost a thousand years of cohabitation, could no longer see how to live together. Both independence and partition became inevitable, and were scheduled for August 15, 1947.

Gandhi arrived in Calcutta a week before that date and moved into a vacant house with Suhrawardy (who had had a change of heart) in order to symbolize reconciliation. The Muslims of Calcutta were greatly

outnumbered by Hindus and had asked Gandhi to stay in the city, so
fearful were they of being attacked; and in return, Gandhi had asked
Suhrawardy to ensure that the people of Noakhali would be safe. That
region did remain fairly quiet at this time—a hint of the influence
that politicians could wield when they so chose. But in the city the
killings went on and on, and a desperate Gandhi began a fast that he intended to end through death. "If the riots continue what will I do by
merely being alive?" he asked in anguish. "If I lack even the power to
pacify the people, what else is left for me to do?"[52]

Over the next days, as Gandhi began to waste away, the massacres
came to a halt—amazingly, not even murderers wanted *his* blood on
their hands. The weary leader was persuaded to stop fasting. "He was
now a broken man, lost, his faith in human beings destroyed," mourned
Gupta, who witnessed the old man's torment. Gandhi never did celebrate
the independence of India, which bore no resemblance to the idyll of
freedom and fellowship to which he had dedicated his life. Instead he
left for the Punjab, where the slaughter had reached a staggering scale,
hoping to diminish the violence there.[53]

Although India and Pakistan had just been born, in part by dividing
the provinces of Bengal and Punjab, the exact borders between the nations had not been announced. As a result, blood-crazed men sought to
separate the Siamese twins by slashing at the flesh that held them together. The gutters of cities ran red, murder and rapine emptied entire
districts, and trainloads of refugees became trainloads of corpses. The
carnage was much the worse in the northwest of the subcontinent because this region was home to hundreds of thousands of demobilized
soldiers. Bands of infantrymen, trained and brutalized by participation
in a world war, regrouped into the same clans in which they had earlier
fought. (The Indian Army used kinship ties to foster loyalty, with blood
relatives assigned to the same platoon and men from the same village
joining the same battalion.) They took the machine guns, rifles, hand
grenades, bombs, mortars, signaling systems, and other contemporary
technology of warfare they had picked up in distant deserts and jungles

and turned them upon their neighbors. Some even donned their former khaki or olive uniforms. At least 1 million people were killed and 10 to 15 million displaced.[54]

"The fearful massacres which are occurring in India are no surprise to me," Churchill declaimed in September 1947. "We are, of course, only at the beginning of these horrors and butcheries, perpetrated upon one another, with the ferocity of cannibals, by the races gifted with capacities for the highest culture, and who had for generations dwelt, side by side, in general peace, under the broad, tolerant and impartial rule of the British Crown and Parliament. I cannot but doubt that the future will witness a vast abridgement of the population throughout what has, for sixty or seventy years been the most peaceful part of the world and that, at the same time, will come a retrogression of civilization throughout these enormous regions, constituting one of the most melancholy tragedies that Asia has ever known."[55]

Some time after elections had removed him from power, Churchill had initiated a covert correspondence with Mohammad Ali Jinnah. Speculation abounds as to the contents of the communications between the two men. In one missive dated August 3, 1946—two weeks before the carnage on Direct Action Day—Churchill appears to have suggested that Pakistan could in future invade a defenseless India. But since very few of these letters have been found, and because Jinnah left virtually no record of his personal reflections, the extent to which Churchill had continued to influence events in India cannot be properly gauged. Yet even without the evidence the letters might provide, there can be no doubt that if someone more sympathetic to Indians had been prime minister during the war years—someone less inclined to derail the independence movement by any means possible, whether through incarcerating nationalists or inciting separatists or tolerating starvation—the colony's freedom would have been attained with far more modest loss of life.[56]

So it was that the sun set on the British Empire. Turning their backs on a horizon red with flame and blood, Britannica's soldiers trudged toward the ships that would carry them home, some marching to this chant:[57]

Land of shit and filth and wogs
Gonorrhea, syphilis, clap and pox.
Memsahib's paradise, soldiers' hell
India, fare thee fucking well.

On January 30, 1948, a Hindu fanatic shot Mohandas Karamchand Gandhi dead during an open-air prayer meeting in Delhi.

CHAPTER TWELVE

The Reckoning

In 1947, Winston Churchill hired a team of researchers and ghost-writers to formulate the definitive history of World War II. As historian David Reynolds has detailed, the treatise was in actuality a memoir of epic proportions, one in which fact often fell victim to selective memory. When Churchill read out loud parts of the history he was writing, Lord Moran, who remembered the events differently, would wonder, "Could it be that he had come to believe what he wanted to believe?" The Bengal famine received but fleeting mention, in a document that happened to make it into an appendix. Despite their distortions, the six massive volumes became the primary reference for a generation of historians—which may explain why the famine is almost totally absent from the tens of thousands of tomes since written about the war.[1]

Behind the scenes, Leopold Amery had done his best to ensure that all the blame for the calamity would fall within India. In late 1943, Viceroy Wavell had faced a vociferous demand from Bengal's politicians for an enquiry into the famine. The secretary of state for India had advised against any "definite commitment" to that end. When it became impossible to stave off the inquiry, he had helped the viceroy select the members of the famine commission and to impose "specific limitations of kinds of topic which the enquiry is permitted to consider." These would include an avoidance of "strategical and other circumstances as may have contributed to internal transportation difficulties or affected H.M.G.'s decisions in regard to shipping of imports." Nor was the commission permitted to summon testimonies from anyone who had since left India (such as Linlithgow).[2]

So it was that the famine commission, which began its secret hearings in July 1944, would elucidate all the local factors that had led to the catastrophe—and avoid every lead that pointed back to London. For instance, although the commission deplored the policy of food and boat denial, it heard nothing about scorched earth orders issued by the War Cabinet. The commission also left the impression that only imports of rice, not wheat, would have broken the famine, which was far from having been the case. Nor did it discuss any of the international offers of aid that were rejected.[3]

Hints of a cover-up abound. Amery's diaries do not contain any mention of scorched earth, and his papers are missing the pertinent correspondence with India. The testimonies submitted to the famine commission were reportedly to have been destroyed (except for one copy that survived as the Nanavati Papers). Civil servant Leonard G. Pinnell stated in his unpublished memoir that he had retained his own set of testimonies, but its location is unknown. The unpublished memoir of civil servant Olaf Martin, written some time after the war, is missing pages that appear to have dealt with his refusal to serve as chief secretary of Bengal. "At that time I had to be careful what I said," Martin recalled of 1943, "just as, at present, I have to be careful what I write."[4]

At least one India Office file, on rice exports to Ceylon, has been destroyed and another one, on Canada's offer of wheat for Bengal, is missing. No figures could be located for rice exports from India in the fiscal year 1943–1944. In the minutes of a meeting of the Chiefs of Staff, available on microfilm at the National Archives of the United Kingdom, a section dealing with shipping to India is blacked out. The cabinet secretaries' notes on War Cabinet discussions, which were released in January 2006, stop abruptly in mid-1943—just before Churchill, Cherwell, Leathers, and Grigg made their August decision to deny relief to famine-stricken Bengal. Among the papers of Lawrence Burgis, who informally transcribed War Cabinet meetings, no notes on India are available for August 4, 1944, when Churchill's tirade on the colony induced Amery to compare him with Hitler, but other discussions on that date are recorded. References to Subhas Chandra Bose are conspicuous by their absence in War Cabinet minutes, although the assassination order shows how seriously he was taken as an enemy.[5]

IT ALSO APPEARS that the famine commission suppressed the results of a government-sponsored survey on famine mortality. Instead, it provided its own estimate of the death toll—a figure that remains controversial to this day. The public health department had recorded 1,873,749 deaths during 1943. Subtracting from this total the average number of deaths per year (as recorded during the preceding five years), the commission got 688,846 excess deaths during the famine year.[6]

This count, the commission noted, did not include those who had died on the roads or in distant towns during their search for food. The death registration figures were highly unreliable for another reason, however: in Bengal the usually illiterate village chowkidar collected all such information. One observer had commented that officials of the Government of India were "very keen on amassing statistics—they collect them, add them, raise them to the nth power, take the cube root and prepare wonderful diagrams. But what you must never forget is that every one of these figures comes in the first instance from the *Chowkydar* (village watchman), who just puts down what he damn pleases." Even in normal times, a discrepancy of 30 percent showed up between death statistics collected by the chowkidar and the more reliable figures compiled during decennial census operations.[7]

Moreover, thousands of chowkidars were unpaid in late 1941, and given the progressive breakdown in civil administration as war reached India's borders and the Quit India movement erupted, there is no reason to suppose that they were paid in 1943. The chowkidar's salary of 6 rupees a month—plus a "special bonus" of an eighth of a rupee for helping with cyclone relief—was in any case too low for his family's survival at the prices that prevailed during the famine. Recall that Giribala Malakar of Kalikakundu said that her first husband, a chowkidar, had carried relief materials during the famine and had still starved to death. It is inconceivable that all through 1943 these functionaries were faithfully discharging their manifold duties to the empire. When the famine inquiry committee asked relief commissioner Olaf Martin about the registration figures, he replied, "I know that they are exceedingly bad."[8]

It is even possible that the figures supposedly compiled by the chowkidars were actually filled in by higher-level officials who had little idea of the toll the famine took and perhaps little interest in recording a disturbingly high number of casualties. After the famine Richard Symonds, a charity worker, was employed by the governor of Bengal to help with relief and rehabilitation. In an effort to learn the number of children orphaned by the famine, he sent forms around to the district offices. On a subsequent tour he discovered why the results he'd gotten had made little sense: "At the very bottom of the Government pyramid, the circular would come to an officer who might be less concerned with accuracy than with the consequences for his career." One functionary might suppose that a small number of orphans would speak to his zealousness in supplying relief; another might figure that a large number of orphans would lead to generous funds arriving for their support. In sum, the figure either man would put down would be fictitious.[9]

Demographers Tim Dyson and Arup Maharatna noted a peculiar pattern in the registration data for West Bengal (the piece of Bengal province that went to India after the partition). During the years 1941 to 1946, the proportion of deaths in certain districts remained exactly the same—a sign that the numbers had been manufactured from the figures for undivided Bengal. Had village-level registration data been available, such manipulation would not have been necessary.[10]

Be that as it may, the famine commission declared that "there was no universal breakdown in 1943 in the system of recording deaths." After introducing a correction for the usual shortfall in death registrations and for roadside deaths, it concluded: "The number of deaths in excess of the average in 1943 was of the order of one million—that is, some 40 percent, in excess of the officially recorded mortality. We have found no valid reason for accepting estimates in excess of this figure. On the other hand, the high excess mortality in 1944 must be added to the toll of mortality. On this basis we must conclude that about 1.5 million deaths occurred as a direct result of the famine and the epidemics which followed in its train."[11]

Diverse authors have applied equally diverse corrections to the raw numbers supposedly collected by the chowkidars to obtain other estimates for the mortality. Economist Amartya Sen took the registered deaths for West Bengal, extended them to East Pakistan (nowadays Bangladesh), and applied corrections to get around 3 million for the famine toll. Dyson and Maharatna used figures that they unearthed for undivided Bengal, argued that the system of data collection had remained essentially intact during the famine, and got 2.1 million.[12]

Intriguingly, historian Paul Greenough discovered that a careful statistical survey of famine mortality had been presented to the famine commission but was never published or publicized. Calcutta was home to one of the world's foremost statisticians, Prasanta C. Mahalanobis, who had founded the Indian Statistical Institute in 1931. By means of exploratory projects in Bengal, Mahalanobis had developed the sample survey, which permits reliable results for the many to be inferred from those for the appropriately chosen few. To that end he had devised pilot surveys (preliminary studies that help refine the design of the final, exhaustive one), overlapping samples, and other means of reducing error. Mahalanobis would go on to become a Fellow of the Royal Society and to run the United Nations statistics bureau.[13]

In late 1943 and early 1944, Mahalanobis and his team designed and carried out an elaborate survey, at government expense, of the famine victims. The researchers interviewed the members of 13,358 households in a representative spectrum of districts and villages to estimate a total number of deaths during 1943 of 3.1 million. (This is not the famine toll, as will presently become clear.) The death rate in Bengal in 1943 came out to be 5.3 percent. The worst-affected subdivision was Bhola in the southeast, with a death rate of 14.79 percent.[14]

The survey had its own shortcomings, but these were precisely defined, allowing for a more solid grasp of the problem than the squishy registration data would allow. To begin with, Mahalanobis did not include the deaths of children less than one year old because the respondents were unreliable on that figure. Second, the survey depended on the reports of relatives, and so could not account for individuals who were missing—some of whom must have died—or for families that had perished in their entirety. (In Kalikakundu at least one family, consisting of Behari and Duari Das and their teenage son, died out.) Third, Mahalanobis did not get to repeat the survey to account for deaths from famine-related disease during 1944 and later. Fourth—and this is the most difficult problem—in order to calculate the famine toll, one has to subtract from the total number of deaths those that would have occurred in the absence of famine.

The "normal" rate of death is very hard to determine, because the death rate varies from time to time and from place to place. The mortality rate for India as a whole is believed to have been 2.1 in 1942, but no data specific to Bengal are available. Compared to the politically favored northwest, the state of nutrition and health in Bengal was miserable, and Mahalanobis assumed a normal death rate of 4 percent for the province, based on the census of 1931.[15]

One can gauge the applicability of this death rate to the early 1940s by reviewing how mortality in Bengal might have evolved during the 1930s. The rate of land sales offers strong evidence that economic distress increased all through that decade. (This kind of data is reliable because land sales, unlike deaths, had to be registered in order to take effect.) The number of land sales in Bengal in 1929 had been 79,929, but the frequency of such transactions increased steadily so that in 1938 the figure was three times as high. The next year—when the war began—the sales doubled, and they continued to rise until in 1942 the number was 749,495. In 1943, the famine year, the figure doubled again, to 1,532,241. Since an owner parted with land only as a last resort—to save his life and that of his family—these figures indicate that the suffering in Bengal, and in all likelihood the mortality rate, increased throughout the depression and war years and reached a peak with the famine.[16]

The easiest way to begin estimating the number of famine deaths is to picture a pyramid representing a pile of corpses that towers over a flat expanse—as would be the norm. But with the 1943 Bengal famine, one is forced to try and separate a peak from the mountain upon which it sits. Where should a determination be made between the two? What level of mortality should be regarded as normal? It becomes as much a matter of inclination as of science.

Beginning with Mahalanobis's figure for the total number of deaths in 1943, Greenough corrected for infant deaths (which were 18 percent of the deaths in normal times) and subtracted the estimate of normal deaths provided by Sen to estimate a famine toll of 2 million for 1943. To that he added Sen's estimate of mortality during 1944 and 1945 to get between 3.5 and 3.8 million as the number of deaths attributable to famine.[17]

A more consistent approach is to stick with mortality rates for the entire calculation. Mahalanobis's mortality rate of 5.3 percent, when corrected for infant deaths, yields a total mortality rate of 6.5 percent for 1943. The population of Bengal in January 1943 was 61.8 million, which gives a total of 4 million deaths for 1943. From this figure must be subtracted 2.5 million baseline deaths (calculated by using the normal death rate of 4 percent that Mahalanobis preferred). That gives 1.5 million for the famine toll in 1943. Doubling this figure, because death registrations were roughly symmetric around December 1943, provides a famine toll of around 3 million.[18]

None of these estimates for famine mortality account for starvation deaths during 1942—although in coastal Bengal, scorched earth and cyclone had caused the famine to begin by at least the last quarter of that year. And it remains unclear how, if at all, Mahalanobis accounted for those individuals and families who had simply vanished. On the other hand, it is possible that the normal death rate was even higher than 4 percent, which would tend to reduce the famine toll. One thing is clear: the figure of 3 million does not include all fatalities from shortage of food, because deaths from malnutrition were undoubtedly occurring even in so-called normal years. If for comparison we were to use the death rate of 2.1 percent that was the norm for India (rather than Bengal) in 1942, the famine toll would be 5.4 million. Nor do these figures include famine deaths in the rest of the rice belt, such as in Orissa and Madras.

IN 1949, A session of the Geneva Convention extended the guidelines for civilized warfare and included a prohibition against starving civilians in occupied territories. "To the fullest extent of the means available to it, the Occupying Power has the duty of ensuring the food and medical supplies of the population; it should, in particular, bring in the necessary food-stuffs, medical stores and other articles if the resources of the occupied territory are inadequate," the convention declared. In 1977, additional protocols strengthened the injunction against starvation, prohibiting the removal or destruction of "objects indispensable to the survival of the population." If the application of an economic blockade resulted in starvation, the convention further mandated the provisioning of essential supplies to the civilian population. In fact, depriving civilians of an occupied territory of vital foods and failing to supply them with adequate relief constitute war crimes as understood today.[19]

Given that the War Cabinet enjoyed absolute control over shipping to and from India, that tens of thousands of nationalists were in prison, that in the estimation of military intelligence India was "an occupied and hostile country," and that the War Cabinet spoke for Indians—by, for instance, turning down offers of grain on their behalf—India was presumed by the United Kingdom to be an occupied territory. If such provisions protecting civilians had been in place before the war, the Denial Policy and the failure of His Majesty's Government to relieve the famine could conceivably have been prosecuted as war crimes.

ALTHOUGH THE ACTIONS of the War Cabinet can be traced with some accuracy (mainly through documents of the Ministry of War Transport), its motives for denying adequate grain to India in the summer and fall of 1943 remain too various and intertwined to tease apart. One reason it chose not to relieve the famine derived from its determination to meet the target of 27 million tons of civilian imports for the United Kingdom. To Cherwell, at least, that meant no ships could be released from the import program. A second reason was the Balkan stockpile, close to Churchill's heart, and also close to Cherwell's because that reserve could take some of the pressure of feeding liberated Europe off the U.K. stockpile. A third reason appears to have been the avoidance of embarrassment, as in having to admit to American officials that the British Empire controlled enough ships and grain to send substantial relief to a colony imperiled by hunger.

Saving face might seem to be a peculiarly trivial reason for permitting a famine to run its course, but perhaps it was not too trivial, given that the English government deemed the lives of Bengalis to be inconsequential. Churchill's broad-brush loathing of the natives might have added impetus to the other rationales for failing to aid them, as might have the continued defiance of Subhas Chandra Bose, who was wildly popular among Bengalis. (The mere existence of the Indian National Army was a source of humiliation to the British, because it advertised the fact that armies of subjects in British colonies had chosen to fight alongside the Japanese, whereas the reverse was true in the Philippines, an American possession.) The War Cabinet's shipping assignments made in August 1943, shortly after Amery had pleaded for famine relief, show Australian wheat flour traveling to Ceylon, the Middle East, and southern Africa—everywhere in the Indian Ocean area but to India. Those assignments suggest a will to punish.

Fiercely evident through almost every War Cabinet discussion on India in 1943 is Churchill's inchoate rage: rage because the colony was slipping out of his grasp, and rage because in violation of the laws of nature and man it had turned from being a debtor to a major British creditor. As late as 1947, Churchill would write in a draft of his war history that India was "the greatest war profiteer." (A similar charge could be made of His Majesty's Government. It stockpiled food during famine, and by selling such liquid assets "must have made a considerable profit on the rising market after the war," according to historian R. J. Hammond.) Churchill and Cherwell were convinced that for the United Kingdom to owe money to India was a "monstrous" injustice, and that the colony should be forced to bear the entire burden of war expenses.

All the evidence points to the prime minister and his closest adviser having believed that Indians were ordained to reside at the bottom of the social pyramid, such that their financial ascendancy as creditors during the war became a source of frustration and fury. Long after India had obtained independence, the Prof would describe "the abdication of the white man" as the worst calamity of the twentieth century—more deplorable than two world wars and the Holocaust.[20]

In the end, it is not so much racism as the imbalance of power inherent in the social Darwinian pyramid that explains why famine could be tolerated in India while bread rationing was regarded as an intolerable deprivation in wartime Britain. Cherwell, for instance, did not think much of the British working class either, but he was deeply engaged in feeding it and placating it. Economist Amartya Sen observes that famine has never occurred in a functioning democracy—a form of government that inverts the traditional power structure by making rulers accountable to those whom they rule.[21]

If Cherwell lavished attention on British civilians, that was no doubt because all of his considerable power derived from his friendship with Churchill, whose own power and popularity would be tested in postwar elections in the United Kingdom. References to public opinion are frequent among the S branch papers. While urging the shipping cut to the Indian Ocean, for instance, the Prof had warned of "political repercussions" unless his advice was heeded. Remonstrating against promises of food for postwar Europe, he had asserted that if these pledges were "fulfilled at the expense of U.K. rations we shall be blamed at home." During the war, Cherwell protected Churchill's domestic flank with the single-minded devotion and ferocity of a guard dog. Indians did not vote in British elections.[22]

The central evil of imperialism is the inability of subject peoples to hold their rulers accountable—and all the rest, even the racism, may flow from that essential powerlessness. In her classic treatise on totalitarianism, Hannah Arendt distinguished between "race-thinking," the categorization of humans by perceived characteristics, and racism, the ranking of these categories into high and low. She argued that racism was a direct consequence of imperialism, which "would have necessitated the invention of racism as the only possible 'explanation' and excuse for its deeds, even if no race-thinking had ever existed in the civilized world." The British imperial need to demonize Hindu males vanished overnight with India's independence—which points to the accuracy of Arendt's observation.[23]

ONE PERSON WHO emerges from the famine with remarkably clean hands is Leopold Amery. True, he had urged ruthlessness in implementing the War Cabinet's scorched earth policy, had initially hoped that the viceroy would muddle through without grain imports, and had relayed Churchill's demands for continued rice exports from India. And given that Amery appears to have orchestrated a cover-up—by, for instance, ensuring that the famine commission would refrain from discussing shipping constraints, and (probably) issuing the order to destroy certain India Office documents relating to grain exports from the colony—it is imaginable that in some other way, which may never be known, he had aggravated the famine. But after mass starvation was reported to the government, he did urge upon the Ministry of War Transport and the War Cabinet the necessity of sending grain.

Amery's willingness to endure opprobrium for the Bengal famine may have been a form of atonement for the actions of his son. John Amery had been in France when the Nazis invaded, and after Hitler attacked the Soviet Union he had gone to Berlin to offer his help. Convinced that the United Kingdom should oppose the Soviets instead of aiding them, he had tried to recruit his countrymen to what he called a British Legion of St. George that would fight the Russians on the eastern front.

John Amery was captured in April 1945 and brought back to England for trial. He protested that he was an anti-communist rather than a Nazi, but he pleaded guilty to treason, apparently to spare his family further pain. He was executed that December. At the time his father circulated among friends a poignant note explaining why John had acted as he did. He had spent so much time on the Continent that he thought himself more European than English. He was also rather psychologically disturbed, had a broken marriage, suffered a bankruptcy that he blamed on Jewish bankers, and claimed to have seen atrocities in Spanish concentration camps that had given him a horror of communism. Amery gave him this epitaph:[24]

> At end of wayward days he found a cause.
> 'Twas not his Country's—Only time can tell
> If that defiance of our ancient laws
> Was treason—or foreknowledge. He sleeps well.

Leopold Amery's patriotism was never in question, but the stanza perhaps hints at his own subterranean affinities—in particular, his deep empathy for Jews, which motivated at least in part his lifelong support for the cause of a Jewish homeland in Palestine. After his tenure as secretary of state for India ended in 1945, Amery never returned to political life. Behind the scenes, he continued to urge that Britain discourage a partition of India. A secret patron of Israel, he visited that new nation in 1950, where President Chaim Weizmann received him. Amery also embarked on an autobiography. He had written three large volumes without getting much into discussions of the war when he died in 1955, at the age of eighty-one.[25]

IN THE SPRING of 1949, Prime Minister Jawaharlal Nehru declared that India would like to remain within the Commonwealth. To Churchill that meant that the British Empire might endure in spirit, and it thrilled him. Meeting Nehru in London, he said with emotion that he had done him great wrong, hailing the Indian leader as a "prodigal who has returned to the fold of the family." Nehru was on his way to Washington, D.C., and Churchill said he would have liked to introduce him to America as having "conquered two great human infirmities: you have conquered fear and you have conquered hate."[26]

Churchill was clearly thinking of himself. A "tyrant" when at the top of a wave, as Beaverbrook had once observed, after the wave crashed he could be a remarkably introspective man. "Now the arrogance and self-assertion have gone, and there is left a deep humility," Moran had observed of him after the Tory loss in postwar elections.[27]

The war memoirs turned Churchill into a hero, and in 1951 he was elected prime minister. In that capacity he had cause to interact further with Nehru, with whom he had something in common: they were both graduates of Harrow. These encounters prompted Churchill to revise some more of his long-standing prejudices. "When you learn to think of a race as inferior beings it is difficult to get rid of that way of thinking; when I was a subaltern the Indian did not seem to me equal to the white man," he confided to his doctor.[28]

In June 1953, after witnessing the coronation of Queen Elizabeth, Churchill found himself standing next to Nehru's daughter, Indira Gandhi, while they both waited for their cars to drive up. "You must have hated the British for the treatment meted out to your father," Churchill said. "It is remarkable how he and you have overcome that bitterness and hatred."

"We never hated you," she responded.

"I did, but I don't now," he replied.[29]

Not long after, Churchill suffered a debilitating stroke. Believing that he was about to die, he told Moran, albeit with a great many reservations, "that he had been wrong about India." What exactly he regretted, the doctor's account gives no clue.[30]

Lord Cherwell suffered no such qualms. He continued to complain bitterly to friends that Indians and Egyptians "had defrauded us" during the war. After Churchill became prime minister for the second time, Cherwell moved into 11 Downing Street, from where he could stroll into Number 10 through an interconnecting door. He was the prime minister's adviser on nuclear warfare. From time to time, with what economist Roy Harrod called an "expression of extreme severity," the Prof would express his profound dismay at the demise of the colonial system. He hated the cold of winter and longed to retire to a warm place, such as Jamaica, but he was deterred by his phobia of blacks. Eventually he returned to Oxford to live in his former rooms and in 1957 died in his sleep.[31]

Churchill lived for seven years longer, slipping inexorably into the sort of depression that had beset him previously in his life. He would sit for hours in front of a fire brooding on the past. "If Winston has believed in anything at all in the course of his long life it has been in the British Empire and all that it stands for," Moran wrote. "Some of his happiest hours as a young subaltern were spent in India—and India was gone." In the memoirs that Churchill had written about the war, he had tried to justify all that he had done, and managed to convince almost everyone of the rightness of his actions. "But have there been black hours when he has not been so sure?" the doctor mused. "There was the sinking of the *Prince of Wales* and the *Repulse* and the lives of the English sailors lost in that unhappy affair. And there was——. But the mind of the man of action does not work like that. When he has taken a decision on which thousands of lives depend, he puts it away from him. How otherwise could he keep sane?" The blank that Moran left in his memoir cannot be filled in until at least the 2020s, when some of his draft manuscripts will be opened to the public. Moran continued: "And yet, when all this is said, my doubts remain. Does the artist, for that is what Winston is, really escape so lightly?"[32]

On January 24, 1965, Winston Spencer Churchill died at his home in London, at ninety years of age.

A MONTH BEFORE Indian independence, Sushil Dhara was released from prison and came home to a hero's welcome. Asked to address the crowd, he broke down in tears. He cried for the youths he had led to their deaths in September 1942, who had not gotten to enjoy the liberty they craved.

Kumudini Dakua's husband had also been released from prison. He took to traveling extensively in connection with his social work, which led Dakua to draw ever closer to Dhara. When Dhara's sister-in-law perished in childbirth, leaving three young children, Dakua joined the household as their surrogate mother.

Dhara's last sojourn in prison had given him time to read and reflect, and had turned him back into a Gandhian. Entrusted with all the cash that remained after the Tamluk government's books were balanced, he used it to build a maternity hospital—a venture aided by Chitto Samonto. Samonto also helped Dhara with other projects inspired by Gandhi's ideas for restoring self-sufficiency to villages, such as perfecting a formula for soap made of local ingredients.

SOON AFTER INDEPENDENCE, Samonto walked to a high school owned by Mohisadal's zamindars and, summoning up all his courage, asked to see the headmaster. The great man was seated on a chair mounted high on a platform, like a judge, and asked in a booming voice what the youth wanted. "Free schooling," Chitto replied.

The headmaster glanced over his old grade reports, regarded the young man carefully, and agreed. Chitto would, however, have to pay 5 rupees for the first three months, after which his fees would be waived. His brother came up with the money, and Chitto was admitted. All the other boys in the school were from wealthy families and would spend their time smoking and lazing around, but Chitto did not even have the money to buy textbooks. He had an idea. "In those days you could get thin paperbacks, mostly biographies, for a quarter of a rupee. Whatever money I could collect, I would spend on buying one of these. I started a library service, would lend to the boys. With the money I earned, I bought more for my library and kept some aside to buy my own books." Chitto also cooked and sold food at fairs. "My classmates bought snacks from me, and sometimes helped me out at the stall. I used to walk every day from here to Mohisadal and come back the same way. In winter it would be dark by the time I got back."

Much against Chitto's wishes, his mother had subsequently arranged his marriage. The angry young man had left home with the idea of becoming a wandering sadhu, or holy man. It was Dhara who had found him, sheltered him, and persuaded him to return to his bride. "I wronged her," Samonto said in 2005, looking at the woman who had since been his uncomplaining partner. Throughout their long marriage, she worked from dawn to dusk, mopping the walls of the two-story mud house so that they would not crumble into dust, tending the cows and the vegetable gardens, and, later, helping her daughter-in-law in the kitchen.

In middle age Chittobabu, as he came to be known to all, served as the *prodhan* (chief) of Kalikakundu. At the time he acquired government funding for an irrigation canal that now gave the village three crops of rice a year. More recently, he had organized villagers to rebuild a shrine for the stone image of Kali that had given the village its name. Even better, his elder sister had saved up all the money she had earned as a nurse and bought her brother a field by the family home. A local landlord gave him another as a gift. Since then, Chitto Samonto, his wife, and their children had been able to grow all the food that they needed and were even able to donate the occasional bowl of rice or an eggplant to their poorer neighbors.

Samonto's grandchildren did not work in the fields but had the lightest chores, such as sweeping, because they were expected to study. Samonto's eldest son, Ashok, had planted the field in front of the house with protein-rich kolai peas, just for the children to eat. "They can pick and eat all they want," he said proudly. When the peas are gone, it is the cows who chew the stringy plants that had once helped save his father.

Acknowledgments

Not everyone I wanted to thank for helping me with this book lived to see it finished. I discussed the project often with Laura van Dam, who published my first book, until one day I suddenly realized I was no longer hearing from her. I miss her. The incredibly courageous and sharp-witted Ashoka Gupta, who was already in her nineties when I first met her, became a source of information and inspiration; I miss her too. I mourn the passing of the feisty Kumudini Dakua, whose eyes would light up like those of a mischievous schoolgirl when she related her past exploits; and of Phulrenu Guha, another of the remarkable women I encountered in the course of my research. And I would have dearly loved to gift the book to Bimal K. Ghose, the grandfatherly neighbor I called Dadu, who sparked my curiosity about the famine several decades ago when he became the first person to tell me about it.

Among the sources of inspiration and information who, thankfully, are still with us are Mahasweta Devi, who described the famine to me in awful detail, and who continues her lifelong battle against injustice. Radhakrishna Bari's comprehensive history of Midnapore proved to be an invaluable resource. Dukkhaharan Chakrabarty helped me find research materials, while Ela Mitra, Ranjit Bhattacharjee, and others described their experiences of the 1940s. Nayan and Bishu Chatterjee made me welcome in London. Amal Das introduced me to the elderly people of his village in Burdwan, and Dilip Mondal drove me around on my field trips. Amit Bhattacharya introduced me to Moni Nag, who introduced me to the Durbar Mahila Samanyaya Samiti, the sex workers' collective in Sonagachi, which in turn introduced me to Kohinoor Begum, who in *her* turn introduced me to famine victims who lived in the slum. I thank them all. I am deeply grateful to the women of Sonagachi, as well as to the villagers of Kalikakundu, Makarda, and elsewhere, for sharing their stories with me.

On the academic front, I am indebted to Dietmar Rothermund, Kevin Smith, Dilip Menon, Alex Danchev, Tirthankar Roy, and Vinay Lal for taking the time to provide detailed comments on a voluminous early draft of the book. Amartya Sen was kind enough to critique the book proposal. I have also enjoyed very helpful interactions with Sugata Bose, Dipesh Chakrabarty, Indivar Kamtekar, Mike Davis, Paul Greenough, Dipankar Chakrabarti, Arup Maharatna, Barun De, Bikramjit De, William Rubinstein, Gautam Bhadra, Manu

Bhagavan, Milan Hauner, Tim Dyson, Ramakrishna Mukherjea, Rila Mukherjea, Nazes Afroz, Erin Weir, Sumit Guha, Debraj Ray, Narayani Gupta, Douglas Kerr, Adam Jones, and Nikhil Sur; I thank them for giving me generously of their time and expertise. I am grateful to Sita Venkateswar for suggesting books that helped me learn the basics of world history; to Eric Werthman, for helping me search for a publisher; and to Daniel Gordon for trying to tell me—many years ago, when I was too young and too full of science to understand—that history matters.

I offer heartfelt thanks to my friend, Angelika Fahimi, librarian at the Johann Christian Senckenberg-Frankfurt University Library, for not only finding books that I needed but borrowing them on my behalf. She made my research infinitely easier. Another friend and librarian, Rani Sinha, helped me locate documents. I thank the Warden and Fellows of Nuffield College for access to the Cherwell Papers, and librarians Elizabeth Martin and Clare Kavanaugh for their unstinting assistance. The efficient staff at the British National Archives at Kew made the task of finding and perusing documents thoroughly enjoyable. Katharine Thomson of the Churchill Archives Centre and Judy Nokes of the Office of Public Sector Information patiently answered my endless questions about British copyright law. Professor Paul Greenough of the University of Iowa kindly supplied me with a digitized copy of a microfilm made of Mahalanobis' original typed notes. Greenough obtained the microfilm in 1971 through the kindness of Dr. M. Mukherjee, at that time the Director of the Research and Training Branch of the Indian Statistical Institute, Calcutta. Pramod Mehra at the National Archives of India also helped me immensely. But I found the Nanavati Papers, invaluable records of wartime India, to be in sorry shape; I would love to see copies made and distributed to at least the major libraries in India, if nowhere else.

I would like to thank my publisher, Lara Heimert, and my agent, Anna Ghosh, for their commitment to the project; and my gifted editor, David Groff, for slicing up a large and unwieldy manuscript and helping me put it back together into a book. Patricia Wynne rendered the maps with painstaking accuracy.

Last but not least, I want to acknowledge the contributions of my family. My husband, Stefan, put food on the table while I indulged my private passion of researching and writing; and from time to time he was called upon to provide technical and emotional assistance. My mother-in-law, Wera, faithfully relayed to me the volumes that Angelika brought home, returned the same, and helped care for my son when my investigations required travel. My son, Robi, spotted an error in one of the maps; and it is because of him that I possess an inkling of how a mother might feel when she cannot feed her child. I am grateful for the moral support and feedback of my sister, Nandini, my brother, Dhrubo, and my niece Anandi. My mother, Sabita, shared with me details of the famine, which she had witnessed, painful though they were for her to recall. And my father, Biren, remained as ever an invaluable source of wisdom and succor.

Bibliography

Archives

AMEL	Amery Papers, Churchill Archive Centre, Churchill College, Cambridge
BRGS	Burgis Papers, Churchill Archive Centre, Churchill College, Cambridge
CAB	War Cabinet Papers, The National Archives, Kew
CAB 195/1&2	Cabinet Secretaries' Notebooks from World War II, available online at http://www.nationalarchives.gov.uk/documents/cab_195_1_transcript.pdf and http://www.nationalarchives.gov.uk/documents/cab_195_2_transcript.pdf
CHAR, CHUR	Churchill Papers, Churchill Archive Centre, Churchill College, Cambridge
Cherwell Papers	Nuffield College, Oxford University
CO	Colonial Office Papers, The National Archives, Kew
CSAC	Cambridge South Asia Collection (William Barnes Papers, Olaf M. Martin Papers, L. G. Pinnell Papers), Cambridge
IOR	India Office Records, British Museum, London
HS	Special Operations Executive War Diaries, The National Archives, Kew
Linlithgow Collection	India Office Records, National Archives of India, New Delhi
Moran Papers	Wellcome Library, London
MT	Ministry of Transport papers, The National Archives, Kew
Nanavati Papers	Memoirs and oral proceedings of the famine commission, 1944–1945, National Archives of India, New Delhi
T	Treasury Papers, The National Archives, Kew
WO	War Office Papers, The National Archives, Kew

Publications

Amery, Leopold S. *My Political Life.* In 3 volumes. London: Hutchinson, 1953–1988.

Anonymous. "Ba Maw, the Great Asian Dreamer." *The Oracle* 2, no. 1 (January 1980): 8.

Anonymous. "Bengal Famine: Mr. Amery on Relief Measures." *The Times* (London), October 16, 1943.

Anonymous. "Cyclone Havoc in Bengal." *The Statesman*, November 3, 1942.

Anonymous. "Gandhi's Goat." *Time*, November 2, 1931. Available online at http://www.time.com/time/magazine/article/0,9171,753085,00.html.

Arendt, Hannah. *The Origins of Totalitarianism.* San Diego: Harvest.

Atkinson, Fred J. "Rupee Prices in India, 1870 to 1908." *Journal of the Royal Statistical Society* 72, no. 3 (September 1909): 496–573.

Baker, Nicholas. *Human Smoke.* New York: Simon & Schuster, 2008.

Bandopadhyay, Ranjan. *Monikanchon.* Kolkata: Ananda, 2005.

Bari, Radhakrishna. *Tamrolipto Jatiyo Sorkar.* Kolkata: Sushil Kumar Dhara, 2000.

Barnes, John, and David Nicholson, eds. *The Empire at Bay: The Leo Amery Diaries 1929–1945.* London: Hutchinson, 1988.

Basu, Major B. D. *The Ruin of Indian Trade and Industries.* Calcutta: Prabasi, 1935.

Batabyal, Rakesh. *Communalism in Bengal: From Famine to Noakhali, 1943–7.* New Delhi: Sage, 2005.

Bayly, Christopher, and Tim Harper. *Forgotten Armies: The Fall of British Asia 1941–45.* London: Allen Lane, 2004.

———. *Forgotten Wars: The End of Britain's Asian Empire.* London: Allen Lane, 2007.

Baynes, Norman H., ed. *The Speeches of Adolf Hitler, April 1922–August 1939.* In 2 volumes. New York: Howard Fertig, 1969.

Behrens, C.B.A. *History of the Second World War: Merchant Shipping and the Demands of War.* London: HMSO, 1955.

Bera, Anjan, ed. *Janajuddha Patrika: Sondhikshaner Mukhopatro.* Kolkata: National Book Agency, 1995.

Bernier, François. *Travels in the Mogul Empire AD 1656–1668.* New Delhi: Munshiram Manoharlal, 1992.

Berthon, Simon, and Joanna Potts. *Warlords.* Cambridge, Mass.: Da Capo, 2006.

Bhatia, B. M. *Famines in India: A Study in Some Aspects of the Economic History of India with Special Reference to Food Problem*, 1860–1990. New Delhi: Konark,1991.

Bhatt, P. N. Mari. "Mortality and Fertility in India 1881–1961: A Reassessment." In *India's Historical Demography*, edited by Tim Dyson. London: Riverdale, 1989.

Bhattacharya, Chittoprasad. *Hungry Bengal.* Bombay: Peoples' Publishing, 1943.

Bhaumik, Mani. *Code Name God: The Spiritual Odyssey of a Man of Science.* New Delhi: Penguin, 2006.

Birkenhead, Earl of. *The Professor and the Prime Minister.* Boston: Houghton Mifflin, 1962.

Blake, Robert, and Wm. Roger Louis. *Churchill: A Major New Assessment of His Life in Peace and War.* New York: Norton, 1993.

Bose, Sarmila. "Love in the Time of War." *Economic and Political Weekly*, January 15, 2005.

Bose, Sisir Kumar, ed. *A Beacon Across Asia: A Biography of Subhas Chandra Bose.* London: Sangam Books, 1996.

Bose, Sisir Kumar, and Sugata Bose, eds. *Netaji: Collected Works*. In 12 volumes. Delhi: Permanent Black, 1995–2006.

Bose, Sugata. *Agrarian Bengal: Economy, Social Structure and Politics 1919–1947*. Cambridge: Cambridge University Press, 1986.

———. *Peasant Labour and Colonial Capital: Rural Bengal Since 1770*. Cambridge: Cambridge University Press, 1993.

Bose, Sugata, ed. *South Asia and World Capitalism*. Delhi: Oxford University Press, 1990.

Bose, Sugata, and Ayesha Jalal. *Modern South Asia: History, Culture, Political Economy*. London: Routledge, 2002.

Branson, Clive. *British Soldier in India: The Letters of Clive Branson*. London: Communist Party, 1944.

Brennan, Lance. "Government Famine Relief in Bengal: 1943." *Journal of Asian Studies* 47, no. 3 (August 1988): 541–566.

Buchanan, Patrick J. *Churchill, Hitler, and the Unnecessary War*. New York: Crown, 2008.

Butler, Lord. *The Art of the Possible: The Memoirs of Lord Butler*. Harmondsworth: Penguin 1973.

Caldwell, John C. "Malthus and the Less Developed World." *Population and Development Review* 24, no. 4 (December 1989): 675–696.

Carter, Violet Bonham. *Winston Churchill: An Intimate Portrait*. New York: Harcourt Brace, 1965.

Chakrabarti, Dilip K. "Archeology of Coastal West Bengal: Twenty-four Parganas and Midnapore Districts." *South Asian Studies* 10 (1994): 135–160.

Chakravarty, Suhash. *The Raj Syndrome: A Study in Imperial Perceptions*. New Delhi: Penguin, 1991.

Chandra, Bipan, Mridula Mukherjee, Aditya Mukherjee, K. N. Pannikar, and Sucheta Mahajan. *India's Struggle for Independence*. New Delhi: Penguin, 1989.

Charmley, John. *Churchill: The End of Glory*. New York: Harcourt Brace, 1993.

Chattopadhyay, Boudhayan. "Notes Towards an Understanding of the Bengal Famine of 1943." *Cressida Transactions* 1, no. 1 (Summer 1981): 112–153.

Chaudhuri, Nani Gopal. *Cartier: Governor of Bengal*. Calcutta: Firma Mukhopadhyay, 1970.

Chowdhury-Zilly, Aditee Nag. *The Vagrant Peasant: Agrarian Distress and Desertion in Bengal 1770 to 1830*. Wiesbaden: Franz Steiner Verlag, 1982.

Churchill, Randolph, and Martin Gilbert. *Winston S. Churchill 1874–1965*. In 8 primary volumes and 13 companion volumes. London: Heineman, 1966–1988.

Churchill, Winston Spencer. *India: Speeches*. London: Thornton Butterworth, 1931.

———. *Lord Randolph Churchill*. In 2 volumes. London: Macmillan, 1906.

———. *My Early Life: A Roving Commission*. London: The Reprint Society, 1944.

———. *Savrola*. New York: Random House, 1956.

———. *The Second World War: Closing the Ring*. London: Penguin, 1985.

———. *The Second World War: The Hinge of Fate*. Cambridge: Houghton Mifflin, 1950.

———. *The Story of the Malakand Field Force*. London: Mandarin, 1990.

Clive, Robert. "Speech in Commons on India, 1772." *Internet Modern History Sourcebook*. Available online at http://www.fordham.edu/halsall/mod/1772clive-india.html.

Colville, John. *The Fringes of Power: Downing Street Diaries*, Vol. 2. London: Sceptre, 1987.

Connell, Arthur K. "Indian Railways and Indian Wheat." *Journal of the Statistical Society of London* 48, no. 2 (June 1885): 236–276.

Connell, John. *Wavell: Supreme Commander 1941–1943*. London: Collins, 1969.

"Convention IV Relative to the Protection of Civilian Persons in Time of War." International Humanitarian Law: Treaties and Documents. Available online at http://www.icrc.org/ihl.nsf/FULL/380?.

Danchev, Alex, and Daniel Todman, eds. *War Diaries 1939–1945: Field Marshal Lord Alanbrooke*. London: Weidenfeld & Nicholson, 2001.

Das, Tarakchandra. *Bengal Famine (1943) as Revealed in a Survey of Destitutes in Calcutta*. Calcutta: University of Calcutta Press, 1949.

Davis, Mike. *Late Victorian Holocausts: El Niño Famines and the Making of the Third World*. London: Verso Press, 2002.

De, Bikramjit. "Imperial Governance and the Challenges of War: Management of Food Supplies in Bengal, 1943–44." *Studies in History* 22, no. 1 (2006): 1–43.

Denney, Joseph Villiers, ed. *Macaulay's Essay on Warren Hastings*. Boston: Allyn and Bacon, 1907.

Denniston, Robin. *Churchill's Secret War: Diplomatic Decrypts, the Foreign Office and Turkey 1942–44*. Stroud: History Press, 2009.

Devi, Mahasweta. *The Queen of Jhansi*. Calcutta: Seagull, 2000.

Dhara, Sushil Kumar. *Probaho*. Janakalyan Trust, Kolkata, Bengali Year 1389.

Digby, William. *"Prosperous" British India: A Revelation from Official Records*. London: T. Fisher Unwin, 1901.

Dilks, David, ed. *The Diaries of Sir Alexander Cadogan*. New York: Putnam, 1972.

Dirks, Nicholas B. *The Scandal of Empire: India and the Creation of Imperial Britain*. Delhi: Permanent Black, 2006.

Dutt, Romesh Chander. *Ancient India*. Delhi: Butala, 1980.

———. *Indian Trade, Manufactures and Finance*. Calcutta: Elm, 1905.

———. *Speeches and Papers on Indian Questions*. Calcutta: Elm, 1902.

———. *The Economic History of India*. In 2 volumes. Ministry of Information and Broadcasting, Government of India, New Delhi, 1989.

Dutt, R. Palme, *India To-day*. Calcutta: Manisha, 1979.

Dyson, Tim, ed. *India's Historical Demography*. London: Curzon, 1989.

Dyson, Tim, and Arup Maharatna. "Excess Mortality During the Bengal Famine: A Re-evaluation." *Indian Economic and Social History Review* 28, no. 3 (1991): 281–297.

Farren, William, and George P. Thomson. "Frederick Alexander Lindemann, Viscount Cherwell." *Biographical Memoirs of Fellows of the Royal Society* 4 (November 1958): 60.

Fay, Peter Ward. *The Forgotten Army: India's Armed Struggle for Independence 1942–45*. Daryaganj: Rupa, 2005.

Fort, Adrian. *Prof: The Life of Frederick Lindemann*. London: Jonathan Cape, 2003.

Gallagher, John. *Decline, Revival and Fall of the British Empire*. Cambridge: Cambridge University Press, 1982.

Gandhi, Mohandas Karamchand. *Collected Works of Mahatma Gandhi*. In 98 volumes. (Electronic Book.) New Delhi: Government of India Publications Division, 1999. Available online at http://www.gandhiserve.org/cwmg/cwmg.html.

———. *Satyagraha in South Africa*. Ahmedabad: Navajivan Publishing House, 2003.

———. *The Story of My Experiments with Truth*. New York: Dover, 1983.

Gandhi, Rajmohan. *Ghaffar Khan: Nonviolent Badshah of the Pakhtuns*. New Delhi: Penguin, 2004.

Ghose, Ajit K. "Food Supply and Starvation: A Study of Famines with Reference to the Indian Sub-Continent." *Oxford Economic Papers* 34, no. 2 (July 1932): 368–389.

Ghosh, Kali Charan. *Famines in Bengal*. Calcutta: Indian Associated, 1944.

Ghosh, Tusharkanti. *The Bengal Tragedy*. Lahore: Hero Press, 1944.

Gilbert, Martin. *Churchill and America*. London: Simon & Schuster, 2005.

Gilbert, Martin, ed. *The Churchill War Papers*. In 3 volumes. London: Heinemann, 1995.

Gopal, Sarvepalli, "Churchill and India." In *Churchill*, edited by Robert Blake and Wm. Roger Louis. New York: Norton, 1993.

Gordon, Leonard. *Brothers Against the Raj: A Biography of Indian Nationalists Sarat and Subhas Chandra Bose*. New York: Columbia University Press, 1990.

Graham, Gordon, and Frank Cole, eds. *The Burma Campaign Memorial Library: Descriptive Catalogue and Bibliography*. London: School of Oriental and African Studies (SOAS), 2001.

Greenough, Paul. "Political Mobilization and the Underground Literature of the 'Quit India' Movement." *Modern Asian Studies* 17, no. 2 (August 1983): 353–386.

———. *Prosperity and Misery in Modern Bengal*. New York: Oxford University Press, 1982.

Guha, Sumit. *Health and Population in South Asia: From Earliest Times to the Present*. New Delhi: Permanent Black, 2001.

Gupta, Ashoka. *In the Path of Service: Memories of a Changing Century*. Kolkata: Stree, 2005.

Gupta, Partha Sarathi, ed. *Towards Freedom: Documents on the Movement for Independence in India 1943–44*. In 3 parts. Delhi: Oxford University Press, 1997.

Gupta, Saibal Kumar. *Kichhu Smriti Kichhu Kotha*. Kolkata: Manshi Press, 1998.

Habib, Irfan. *Essays in Indian History*. New Delhi: Tulika, 1995.

Hammond, R. J. *History of the Second World War: Food*. In 3 volumes. London: HMSO, 1951.

Hancock, W. K., ed. *Statistical Digest of the War*. London: HMSO, 1951.

Hancock, W. K., and M. M. Gowing. *History of the Second World War: British War Economy*. London: HMSO, 1949.

Harrod, R. F. *The Prof: A Personal Memoir of Lord Cherwell*. London: Macmillan, 1959.

Hauner, Milan. *India in Axis Strategy: Germany, Japan and Indian Nationalists in the Second World War*. Stuttgart: Klett-Cotta, 1981.

Herman, Arthur. *Gandhi & Churchill: The Epic Rivalry That Destroyed an Empire and Forged Our Age*. New York: Bantam Dell, 2008.

Hess, Gary R. *America Encounters India, 1941–47*. Baltimore: Johns Hopkins Press, 1971.

Hill, Ronald Paul, and Elizabeth C. Hirschman. "Human Rights Abuses by the Third Reich." *Human Rights Quarterly* 18 (1996): 848–873.

Hitler, Adolf. *Mein Kampf*. New Delhi: Adarsh Books, 2005.

Hull, Cordell. *The Memoirs of Cordell Hull*. In 2 volumes. London: Hodder & Stoughton, 1948.

Hunter, William W. *Famine Aspects of Bengal Districts*. London: Trübner, 1874.

———. *The Annals of Rural Bengal*. New York: Leypoldt and Holt, 1868.

———. "The Bengal Famine of 1866." *North British Review* 46, no. 91 (March–June 1867): 242–276.

Huq, Fazlul. *Bengal Today*. Calcutta: Gupta Rahman and Gupta, 1944.

Iyer, Raghavan. "Utilitarianism and All That." In *St. Anthony's Papers No. 8 (South Asian Affairs, No. 1)*, edited by Raghavan Iyer. London: Chatto and Windus, 1960.

Jablonsky, David. *Churchill, The Great Game and Total War*. London: Frank Cass, 1991.

James, Lawrence. *Raj: The Making and Unmaking of British India*. New York: St. Martin's Griffin, 1997.

James, Robert Rhodes. *Churchill: A Study in Failure 1900–1939*. Harmondsworth: Penguin, 1973.

Jeffrey, Keith, ed. *The Military Correspondence of Field Marshal Sir Henry Wilson*. London: The Army Records Society, 1986.

Jennings, Louis. *Speeches of the Right Honourable Lord Randolph Churchill*. In 2 volumes. New York: Kraus Reprint Co., 1972. Original printing 1889.

Johnson, Louis. Telegram to Secretary of State, April 11, 1942, Franklin D. Roosevelt Presidential Library. Available online at http://www.fdrlibrary.marist.edu/psf/box3/a34f03.html.

Jones, Adam. *Genocide: A Comprehensive Introduction*. New York: Routledge, 2006.

Jones, R. V. "Lindemann beyond the Laboratory." *Notes and Records of the Royal Society of London* 41, no. 2 (June1987): 191–200.

Kamtekar, Indivar. "A Different War Dance: State and Class in India 1939–1945." *Past and Present*, no. 146 (August 2002).

———. "The Military Ingredient of Communal Violence in Punjab, 1947." *Proceedings of the Indian History Congress*, Calcutta (1995): 568–572.

———. "The Shiver of 1942." *Studies in History* 18, no. 1 (2002).

Kerr, Douglas. "Orwell's BBC broadcasts: colonial discourse and the rhetoric of propaganda." *Textual Practice* 16, no. 3 (2002): 473–490.

Khosla, G.D. *Stern Reckoning: A Survey of the Events Leading Up To and Following the Partition of India*. Reprinted in David Page et al., *The Partition Omnibus*. New Delhi: Oxford University Press, 2006.

Kiernan, Ben. *Blood and Soil: A World History of Genocide and Extermination from Sparta to Darfur*. New Haven: Yale University Press, 2007.

Kirby, Major-General S. Woodburn. *The War Against Japan*. In 2 volumes. London: HMSO, 1958.

Knight, Sir Henry. *Food Administration in India 1939–47*. Stanford: Stanford University Press, 1954.

Kumar, Dharma, and Tapan Raychaudhuri, eds. *The Cambridge Economic History of India*. In 2 volumes. Hyderabad: Orient Longman, 2004.

Law-Smith, Auriol. "Response and Responsibility: The Government of India's Role in the Bengal Famine, 1943." *South Asia* 12, no. 1 (1989): 49–65.

Leighton, Richard M., and Robert W. Coakley. *Global Logistics and Strategy, 1940–43*. Washington, D.C.: Office of the Chief of Military History, Department of the Army, 1955.

Lewis, Julian. *Changing Direction: British Planning for Post-War Strategic Defence, 1942–47*. London: Frank Cass, 2003.

Loewenheim, Francis, Harold Langley, and Manfred Jonas, eds. *Roosevelt and Churchill: Their Secret Wartime Correspondence*. New York: Saturday Review Press, 1975.

Louis, Wm. Roger. *Imperialism at Bay: The United States and the Decolonization of the British Empire*. New York: Oxford University Press, 1978.

———. *In the Name of God, Go! Leo Amery and the British Empire in the Age of Churchill*. New York: Norton, 1992.

Loveday, A. *The History and Economics of Indian Famines*. New Delhi: Usha, 1985.

Macaulay, Thomas Babington. *Lord Clive*. Cambridge: Cambridge University Press, 1914.

MacDougall, Donald. *Don and Mandarin: Memoirs of an Economist*. London: John Murray, 1987.

MacMunn, Major G. F. *The Armies of India*. London: Adam & Charles Black, 1911.

Mahalanobis, Prasanta K. "Mortality in Bengal in 1943." Microfilm obtained by Paul Greenough from M. Mukherjee of the Indian Statistical Institute, Calcutta, in 1971.

Mahapatro, Srikrishna Chaitanya. "Ananya Sushilda." *Chiro Tarun Biplobi Sushilkumar*. Kolkata: Sushil Kumar Dhara Asititama Janmyotsab Udyog Committee, 1991.

Maharatna, Arup. *The Demography of Famines: An Indian Historical Perspective*. Delhi: Oxford University Press, 1996.

Maity, Pradyot Kumar. *Quit India Movement and the Tamralipta Jatiya Sarkar*. Kolkata: Purvadri Prakashani, 2002.

Majumdar, R. C. *History of Mediaeval Bengal*. Calcutta: Bharadwaj, 1973.

Mansergh, Nicholas, ed. *The Transfer of Power 1942–7*. In 12 volumes. London: Her Majesty's Stationery Office, 1970–1982.

Marcus, David. "Famine Crimes in International Law." *American Journal of International Law* 97, no. 2 (April 2003): 245–281.

Mayo, Katherine. *Mother India*. London: Jonathan Cape, 1938. Original printing 1927.

Metcalf, Barbara D., and Thomas R. Metcalf. *A Concise History of India*. Cambridge: Cambridge University Press, 2003.

Metcalf, Thomas. *Ideologies of the Raj*. Cambridge: Cambridge University Press, 1994.

Mill, James. *The History of British India*. Abridged and with an Introduction by William Thomas. Chicago: University of Chicago Press, 1975.

Mitra, Asok. *Tin Kuri Dash*, Vol. II. Calcutta: Dey's Publishing, Bengali Year 1407.

Moon, Penderel, ed. *Wavell: The Viceroy's Journal*. Oxford: Oxford University Press, 1973.

Moore, R. J. *Churchill, Cripps, and India, 1939–1945*. Oxford: Clarendon Press, 1979.

Moran, Lord. *Churchill: The Struggle for Survival 1940–1965*. Boston: Houghton Mifflin, 1966.

Naoroji, Dadabhai. *Poverty and Un-British Rule in India*. New Delhi: Government of India, 1996.

Narayan, Shriman, ed. *The Selected Works of Mahatma Gandhi*. In 6 volumes. Ahmedabad: Navajivan, 1995.

Narayanan, T. G. *Famine over Bengal*. Calcutta: The Book Company, 1944.

Nash, Vaughan. *The Great Famine and Its Causes*. London: Longmans, Green and Co., 1900.

Nayar, Sushila. "Satish Samanta Da." In *Sarbadhinayak*. Tamluk: Tamralipta Swadhinata Sangram Itihas Committee, 1982.

Nichols, Beverley. *Verdict on India*. New York: Harcourt Brace, 1944.

Ó Gráda, Cormac. *Famine: A Short History*. Princeton: Princeton University Press, 2009.

O'Malley, Kate. *Ireland, India and Empire*. Manchester: Manchester University Press, 2009.

Orme, Robert. *Historical Fragments of the Mogul Empire, of the Morattoes, and of the English Concerns in Indostan*. London: Wingrave, 1805.

Orwell, George. *Burmese Days*. New York: Penguin, 1980.

———. *1984*. New York: Signet, 1990.

———. *The Collected Essays, Journalism and Letters*. In 4 volumes. London: Secker & Warburg, 1968.

Page, David. *Prelude to Partition: The Indian Muslims and the Imperial System of Control 1920–1932*. Reprinted in David Page, Anita Inder Singh, Penderel Moon, and G. D. Khosla, *The Partition Omnibus*. New Delhi: Oxford University Press, 2006.

Page, David, Anita Inder Singh, Penderel Moon, and G. D. Khosla. *The Partition Omnibus*. New Delhi: Oxford University Press, 2006.

Palmer, The Hon. R. *A Little Tour in India*. London: Edward Arnold, 1913.

Pati, Biswamoy S., ed. *Turbulent Times: India 1940–44*. Mumbai: Popular Prakashan, 1998.

Phillips, William. *Ventures in Diplomacy*. London: John Murray, 1955.

Ponting, Clive. *Churchill*. London: Reed, 1994.

Prest, A. R. *War Economics of Primary Producing Countries*. Cambridge: Cambridge University Press, 1948.

Rai, Anuradha. "Ponchaser Mannontar O Banglar Silposahityo." *Anushtup*, 13, no. 4 (1989): 1–85.

Rao, C. R. "Prasantha Chandra Mahalanobis 1893–1972." *Biographical Memoirs of Fellows of the Royal Society*, 19 (December 1973): 454–492.

Read, Anthony, and David Fisher. *The Proudest Day: India's Long Road to Independence*. London: Pimlico, 1998.

Reynolds, David. *In Command of History: Churchill Fighting and Writing the Second World War*. New York: Random House, 2005.

Risley, Herbert. *The People of India*. New Delhi: Asian Educational Services, 1999.

Roberts, Andrew. *Hitler and Churchill: Secrets of Leadership*. London: Weidenfeld & Nicholson, 2003.

———. *Masters and Commanders*. London: Penguin, 2008.

Roosevelt, Elliott. *As He Saw It*. New York: Duell, Sloan and Pearce, 1946.

Roskill, Stephen. *Churchill and the Admirals*. London: Collins, 1977.

Rothermund, Dietmar. *An Economic History of India*. New Delhi: Manohar, 1989.

———. "A Vulnerable Economy: India in the Great Depression, 1929–1939." In *South Asia and World Capitalism*, edited by Sugata Bose. Delhi: Oxford University Press, 1990.

Roy, Kaushik. "Military Loyalty in the Colonial Context: A Case Study of the Indian Army During World War II." *Journal of Military History* 73, no. 2 (April 2009): 497–529.

Rubinstein, William. "The Secret of Leopold Amery." *Historical Research* 73, no. 181 (2000).

Russell, Sharman Apt. *Hunger: An Unnatural History*. New York: Basic, 2006.

Salter, Arthur. *Slave of the Lamp: A Public Servant's Notebook*. London: Weidenfeld & Nicholson, 1967.

Santhanam, K. *The Cry of Distress: A First-Hand Description and an Objective Study of the Indian Famine of 1943*. New Delhi: Hindustan Times, 1943.

Sarila, Narendra Singh. *The Shadow of the Great Game: The Untold Story of India's Partition*. New Delhi: HarperCollins India, 2005.

Sbrega, John J. "The Anticolonial Policies of Franklin D. Roosevelt." *Political Science Quarterly* 101, no.1 (1986): 76.

Schofield, Victoria. *Wavell: Soldier & Statesman*. London: John Murray, 2006.

Sen, Amartya. *Development as Freedom*. Oxford: Oxford University Press, 2001.

———. *Poverty and Famines: An Essay on Entitlement and Deprivation*. New Delhi: Oxford University Press, 2004.

———. "Wars and Famines: On Divisions and Incentives." *Peace Economics, Peace Science and Public Policy* 6, no. 2 (Spring 2000).

Sen, Ranjit. *Economics of Revenue Maximization in Bengal, 1757–1793*. Calcutta: Nalanda, 1988.

Sengupta, Kalpataru. *Smritir Somoy Somoyer Smriti*. Kolkata: Nikhilbanga Prathamik Sikkhak Samiti, 2001.

Sengupta, Nitish. *History of the Bengali-Speaking People*. New Delhi: UBS Publishers, 2001.

Sengupta, Sukharanjan. *Bangosanghar Ebong*. Kolkata: Naya Udyog, 2002.

Sherwood, Robert E. *Roosevelt and Hopkins: An Intimate History.* In 2 volumes. New York: Bantam Books, 1950.

Singh, Anita Inder. "Imperial Defence and the Transfer of Power in India, 1946–1947." *The International History Review* 4, no. 4 (November 1982): 568–588.

———. *The Origins of the Partition of India 1936–1947.* Reprinted in David Page, Anita Inder Singh, Penderel Moon, and G. D. Khosla, *The Partition Omnibus.* New Delhi: Oxford University Press, 2006.

Sinha, Narendra K. *The Economic History of Bengal.* In 3 volumes. Calcutta: Firma KLM Pvt. Ltd., 1981.

Sinha, N. C., and P. N. Khera, *Indian War Economy: Supply, Industry and Finance.* New Delhi: Government of India, 1962.

Slim, Field-Marshal Sir William. *Defeat into Victory.* London: Landsborough, 1958.

Smith, Kevin. *Conflict over Convoys: Anglo-American Logistics Diplomacy in the Second World War.* Cambridge: Cambridge University Press, 2002.

Snow, C. P. *Science and Government.* Cambridge, Mass: Harvard University Press, 1961.

Srivastava, Hari Shanker. *The History of Indian Famines 1858–1918.* Agra: Sri Ram Mehra, 1968.

Stephens, Ian Melville. *Monsoon Morning.* London: Ernest Benn, 1966.

Stevenson, Richard. *Bengal Tiger and British Lion.* Xlibris, 2005.

Stone, I. F. "The Indian Skeleton at Atlantic City." *The Nation,* December 11, 1943.

Sur, Nikhil. *Chiattorer Monnontar O Sannyasi-Fakir Bidroho.* Kolkata: Subarnarekha, 1982.

———. "The Bihar Famine of 1770." *Indian Economic and Social History Review* 13, no. 4.

Symonds, Richard. *In the Margins of Independence.* Karachi: Oxford University Press, 2001.

Tauger, M. B. "Enlightenment, Shortage and the 1943 Bengal Famine: Another Look." *Journal of Peasant Studies* 31 (2003): 45–72.

Taylor, A.J.P., Robert Rhodes James, J. H. Plumb, Basil Liddell Hart, and Anthony Storr. *Churchill: Four Faces and the Man.* Harmondsworth: Pelican, 1973.

Tendulkar, D. G. *Mahatma: Life of Mohandas Karamchand Gandhi.* In 8 volumes. New Delhi: Government of India, 1990.

Trevor-Roper, Hugh, ed. *Hitler's Table Talk 1941–1944: Hitler's Conversations Recorded by Martin Bormann.* Oxford: Oxford University Press, 1988.

Tucker, Todd. *The Great Starvation Experiment.* New York: Free Press, 2006.

Tunzelmann, Alex. *Indian Summer: The Secret History of the End of an Empire.* New York: Henry Holt, 2007.

Venkataramani, M. S. *Bengal Famine of 1943: The American Response.* Delhi: Vikas, 1973.

Venkataramani, M. S., and B. K. Shrivastava. *Roosevelt Gandhi Churchill: America and the Last Phase of India's Freedom Struggle.* New Delhi: Radiant, 1983.

Voigt, Johannes H. *India in the Second World War.* New Jersey: Humanities Press, 1988.

Weinberg, Gerhard L., ed. *Hitler's Second Book: The Unpublished Sequel to* Mein Kampf. New York: Enigma, 2006.

Weir, Erin. "German Submarine Blockade, Overseas Imports, and British Military Production in World War II." *Journal of Military and Strategic Studies 6*, No. 1 (2003).

Welch, Steven R. "'Our India': Nazi Plans for the East." In *Genocide, History and Fictions.* Melbourne: University of Melbourne, 1997.

West, W. J. *The Larger Evils: 1984, the Truth Behind the Satire.* Edinburgh: Canongate, 1992.

West, W. J., ed. *Orwell: The War Broadcasts.* London: Duckworth, 1985.

Wiesel, Elie. *Night.* New York: Bantam, 1982.

Wilson, Thomas. *Churchill and the Prof.* London: Cassell, 1995.

Wolf, Eric R. *Europe and the People Without History.* Berkeley: University of California Press, 1997.

Wolpert, Stanley. *Gandhi's Passion: The Life and Legacy of Mahatma Gandhi.* Oxford: Oxford University Press, 2001.

Woodham Smith, Cecil. *The Great Hunger.* Sevenoaks: New English Library, 1984.

Woodhead, Sir John. *Famine Inquiry Commission: Report on Bengal.* Delhi: Manager of Publications, 1945.

Woods, Frederick, ed. *Young Winston's Wars.* London: Sphere, 1972.

Yadav, K. C., and Akiko Seki, eds. *Subhas Chandra Bose: The Last Days.* Delhi: Hope India, 2003.

Miscellaneous

Bengal Famine: 1943. Produced by Nazes Afroz. British Broadcasting Corporation World Service, Bengali Radio Service, 1997. CD.

Biplabi. Nimtouri: Iamralipta Swadhinata Sangram Itihas Committee, 1991.

Lives of a Bengal Lancer. Directed by Henry Hathaway. Paramount Films, 1935.

The Forgotten Famine: Bengal Famine 1943. Produced by Patrick Uden. Uden Associates for United Kingdom Channel 4, August 12, 1997.

Notes

Prologue

1. Churchill, *The Second World War: The Hinge of Fate*, 204. See also chapter 12 of the present volume for a discussion of the famine mortality.

2. Clive, "Speech in Commons on India, 1772."

3. Bernier, *Travels in the Mogul Empire*, 437–438, 442; Majumdar, *History of Mediaeval Bengal*, 177–178.

4. Majumdar, *History of Mediaeval Bengal*, 184; Bernier, *Travels in the Mogul Empire*, 438–439.

5. Majumdar, *History of Mediaeval Bengal*, 183, 187; Sinha, *The Economic History of Bengal*, Vol. I, 4, and Vol. II, 111–113; Sen, *Economics of Revenue Maximization in Bengal*, 300–302; quoted in Chowdhury-Zilly, *The Vagrant Peasant*, 11–12.

6. Dirks, *The Scandal of Empire*, 39.

7. Majumdar, *History of Mediaeval Bengal*, 123–124; Dutt, *The Economic History of India*, Vol. I, 21.

8. Majumdar, *History of Mediaeval Bengal*, 133; James, *Raj*, 40; quoted in Dutt, *The Economic History of India*, Vol. I, 28.

9. Majumdar, *History of Mediaeval Bengal*, 138–142; quoted in Dutt, *Indian Trade*, 10.

10. Dutt, *Indian Trade*, 16, 20; Dutt, *The Economic History of India*, Vol. I, 21; James, *Raj*, 42.

11. Dirks, *The Scandal of Empire*, 53; James, *Raj*, 50; Sur, *Chiattorer Monnontar*, 11; quoted in Dutt, *The Economic History of India*, Vol. I, 18.

12. Metcalf and Metcalf, *A Concise History of India*, 51, 53; Hunter, *The Annals of Rural Bengal*, 304; Dutt, *The Economic History of India*, Vol. I, 31.

13. Hunter, *The Annals of Rural Bengal*, 306.

14. Bose, *Peasant Labour and Colonial Capital*, 18.

15. Hunter, *The Annals of Rural Bengal*, 26; Kumar and Raychaudhuri, *The Cambridge Economic History of India*, Vol. II, 299.

16. Chaudhuri, *Cartier*, 51–53; quoted in Ghosh, *Famines in Bengal*, 26.

17. Chaudhuri, *Cartier*, 62; Sur, *Chiattorer Monnontar*, 24.

18. Quoted in Dutt, *The Economic History of India*, Vol. I, 30; quoted in Sur, "The Bihar Famine of 1770"; quoted in Hunter, *The Annals of Rural Bengal*, 37, 381. At the time, one sterling pound equaled about ten rupees.

19. Hunter, *The Annals of Rural Bengal*, 63–64.

20. Ibid., 71.

21. Sinha, *The Economic History of Bengal*, Vol. II, 57; quoted in Chaudhuri, *Cartier*, 44.

22. Quoted in Dutt, *The Economic History of India*, Vol. I, 32; James, *Raj*, 49–51; Dirks, *The Scandal of Empire*, 48.

23. Dirks, *The Scandal of Empire*, 59; Sinha, *The Economic History of Bengal*, Vol. II, 276–284; Dutt, *The Economic History of India*, Vol. I, 48–50.

24. Dirks, *The Scandal of Empire*, 111, 85.

25. Dutt, *The Economic History of India*, Vol. I, 61–62; Metcalf and Metcalf, *A Concise History of India*, 70–71. At the time, the region that came to be called the North West Frontier Province belonged to Afghanistan.

26. Dutt, *The Economic History of India*, Vol. I, 245; quoted in Nash, *The Great Famine and Its Causes*, 242.

27. Several of the Madras famines lasted two years or longer, so that different sources give slightly different dates for their occurrence. See Digby, *"Prosperous" British India*, 125–127; Greenough, *Prosperity and Misery in Modern Bengal*, 281–283; and Mill, *The History of British India*, 241–243.

28. Mill, *The History of British India*, 245, 326.

29. Metcalf and Metcalf, *A Concise History of India*, 57.

30. Mill, *The History of British India*, 247. Mill was not the first to find Indians unmanly, however; see Orme, "On the Effeminacy of the Inhabitants of Indostan," in *Historical Fragments of the Mogul Empire*, 455–472.

31. Jennings, *Speeches of the Right Honourable Lord Randolph Churchill*, Vol. 1, 212.

32. Chandra et al., *India's Struggle for Independence*, 43.

33. Metcalf and Metcalf, *A Concise History of India*, 78; Devi, *The Queen of Jhansi*, 191.

34. Bose and Jalal, *Modern South Asia*, 95.

35. Quoted in Bose and Jalal, *Modern South Asia*, 98.

36. Metcalf, *Ideologies of the Raj*, 104–106, 205–207.

37. Mill, *The History of British India*, 326; Metcalf, *Ideologies of the Raj*, 127, 210–212, 165–167; Chakravarty, *The Raj Syndrome*, 127; Macaulay, *Lord Clive*, 70.

38. Quoted in Chandra et al., *India's Struggle for Independence*, 125.

39. Bose and Jalal, *Modern South Asia*, 120.

40. Quoted in Metcalf and Metcalf, *A Concise History of India*, 159; The Hon. R. Palmer, *A Little Tour in India*, 152.

41. Mayo, *Mother India*, 29–34, 99; Churchill and Gilbert, *Winston S. Churchill*, Vol. V, Companion 2, 309.

42. T 160/1263, "India's Sterling Balance," January 22, 1942. Estimates for deaths in India from Spanish flu range from 10 million to 17 million.

43. Gandhi, *Satyagraha*, 191, 106.

44. Gandhi, *The Story of My Experiments with Truth*, 17.

45. Ibid., 19; Gandhi, *Satyagraha*, 85.

46. James, *Raj*, 473.

47. Jeffrey, *The Military Correspondence of Field Marshal Sir Henry Wilson*, 187; Churchill, *India*, 19, 28.

48. Quoted in Louis, *In the Name of God*, 68–70.

49. Gandhi, *The Story of My Experiments with Truth*, 430.

50. Chandra et al., *India's Struggle for Independence*, 189–191.

51. Gandhi, *Satyagraha*, 295; quoted in Iyer, "Utilitarianism and All That," 26; Churchill, *India*, 95; CHAR 20/165/43, May 27, 1944.

52. Gilbert, *The Churchill War Papers II*, 368; Taylor et al., *Churchill*, 109.

53. Churchill and Gilbert, *Winston S. Churchill*, Vol. V, Companion 3, 828; CAB 121/11, "War Cabinet: Overseas Defence Committee," January 22, 1942.

54. Quoted in James, *Raj*, 571.

55. Birkenhead, *The Professor and the Prime Minister*, 11.

Chapter One

1. Churchill and Gilbert, *Winston S. Churchill*, Vol. V, 480–481.

2. Singh, "Imperial Defence and the Transfer of Power in India," 569–570; Hauner, *India in Axis Strategy*, 124; Gilbert, *The Churchill War Papers*, Vol. I, 188. India's defense budget was £38.5 million in 1937–1938.

3. Moran, *Churchill: The Struggle for Survival*, 827; Gilbert, *The Churchill War Papers*, Vol. I, 1290, and Vol. II, 22.

4. Louis, *In the Name of God*, 30, 121–122.

5. Barnes and Nicholson, *The Empire at Bay*, 617; Louis, *In the Name of God*, 120–124; Gilbert, *The Churchill War Papers*, Vol. II, 368.

6. Barnes and Nicholson, *The Empire at Bay*, 620; quoted in Louis, *In the Name of God*, 129.

7. Gilbert, *The Churchill War Papers*, Vol. II, 397.

8. Sinha and Khera, *Indian War Economy*, 58; Kamtekar, "A Different War Dance," 194–195, 198; Prest, *War Economics of Primary Producing Countries*, 31. Of India's war expenditure of £2.054 billion, £1.042 billion was recoverable from the United Kingdom.

9. Barnes and Nicholson, *The Empire at Bay*, 606.

10. Narayan, *The Selected Works of Mahatma Gandhi*, Vol. VI, 343–345, 377–379.

11. Barnes and Nicholson, *The Empire at Bay*, 48; Churchill and Gilbert, *Winston S. Churchill*, Vol. V, 586.

12. Bose and Bose, *Netaji*, Vol. 9, 30.

13. Ibid., 65, xxii.

14. Gordon, *Brothers Against the Raj*, 114; Bose and Bose, *Netaji*, Vol. 9, 93, 145.

15. Nehru, *The Discovery of India*, 472.

16. Chandra et al., *India's Struggle for Independence*, 266, 450; Nehru, *The Discovery of India*, 475.

17. Singh, *The Origins of the Partition of India*, 48, 53.

18. Chandra et al., *India's Struggle for Independence*, 431.

19. Gilbert, *The Churchill War Papers*, Vol. I, 715–716.

20. Churchill, *India*, 14; Churchill and Gilbert, *Winston S. Churchill*, Vol. V, Companion 3, 827.

21. Churchill and Gilbert, *Winston S. Churchill*, Vol. V, Companion 3, 827.

22. Gilbert, *The Churchill War Papers*, Vol. I, 1038.

23. Barnes and Nicholson, *The Empire at Bay*, 634; Gilbert, *The Churchill War Papers*, Vol. II, 528–529.

24. Gilbert, *The Churchill War Papers*, Vol. II, 506–507, 529(footnote); Barnes and Nicholson, *The Empire at Bay*, 608.

25. Dilks, *The Diaries of Sir Alexander Cadogan*, 316; Barnes and Nicholson, *The Empire at Bay*, 637.

26. Gilbert, *The Churchill War Papers*, Vol. II, 584. Nowadays, *Anglo-Indian* indicates people of mixed European and Indian ancestry.

27. AMEL 1/6/21, India Office to Prime Minister, April 8, 1941.

28. Barnes and Nicholson, *The Empire at Bay*, 49–50.

29. Churchill, *India*, 35, 46–47; Churchill and Gilbert, *Winston S. Churchill*, Vol., V, 595; James, *Churchill*, 259. By some accounts, Churchill intended *shame* rather than *sham*.

30. Churchill, *Lord Randolph Churchill*, Vol. 1, 561, 564; Jennings, *Lord Randolph*, Vol. I, 272–273; Churchill, *My Early Life*, 71; quoted in Ponting, *Churchill*, 25.

31. Churchill, *My Early Life*, 21, 25.

32. Ibid., 52–53.

33. Ibid., 113.

34. Ibid., 114, 121.

35. Ibid., 126; Martin Gardiner, quoted in James, *Churchill*, 36; Carter, *Winston Churchill*, 20.

36. Churchill, *My Early Life*, 133–134; Bhatia, *Famines in India*. For a detailed account of these two famines, see Davis, *Late Victorian Holocausts*.

37. Churchill, *My Early Life*, 135.

38. Churchill, *The Story of the Malakand Field Force*, 2.

39. Woods, *Young Winston's Wars*, 44; quoted in Ponting, *Churchill*, 26.

40. Woods, *Young Winston's Wars*, 93, 77; Churchill, *My Early Life*, 158; Churchill, *The Story of the Malakand Field Force*, 165.

41. Churchill, *My Early Life*, 166.

42. Quoted in Woods, 27; Churchill, *My Early Life*, 69.

43. Mansergh, *The Transfer of Power*, Vol. I, 878.

44. Chandra et al., *India's Struggle for Independence*, 454.

45. Barnes and Nicholson, *The Empire at Bay*, 667. The modern hunger strike was invented by English suffragettes and adopted by, among others, Irish nationalists. See Russell, *Hunger*, 74–79.

46. Bose and Bose, *Netaji*, Vol. 10, xi.

47. Macaulay, *Clive*, 70, 35; Bose and Bose, *Netaji*, Vol. 2, 336.

48. Bose and Bose, *Netaji*, Vol. 10, 197; Gordon, *Brothers Against the Raj*, 417–418.

49. Bose and Bose, *Netaji*, Vol. 11, 35.

50. SOE War Diaries: HS7/214–217, 319, 626–627, 672, 1045, 1057.

51. Dhara, *Probaho*, 93, 107.

52. Ibid., 98–101.

53. Ibid., 40; Sengupta, *History of the Bengali-Speaking People*, 380–383.

54. Bari, *Tamrolipto Jatiyo Sorkar*, 53.

55. Gupta, *Kichhu Smriti Kichhu Kotha*, 60.

56. Chandra et al., *India's Struggle for Independence*, 273–276; Gandhi, *Ghaffar Khan*, 86.

57. Churchill, *India*, 94, 97, 120.

58. The deliberate fostering of divisions between Hindus and Muslims by such measures as separate electorates would ultimately lead to the partition of India. See Page, *Prelude to Partition*, 260.

59. Anonymous, "Gandhi's Goat"; Rothermund, *An Economic History of India*, 107; Churchill and Gilbert, *Winston S. Churchill*, Vol. V, 432.

60. Dhara, *Probaho*, 55.

61. Ibid.

62. Rothermund, *An Economic History of India*, 105; Rothermund, "A Vulnerable Economy," 324.

63. Chandra et al., *India's Struggle for Independence*, 288; Nehru, *The Discovery of India*, 401–403.

64. Dhara, *Probaho*, 102.

65. Ibid., 103, 95, 67.

Chapter Two

1. Quoted in Hauner, *India in Axis Strategy*, 28.

2. During World War I, India had donated more than £100 million to the war effort. But that "gift" had aroused great resentment, so during World War II it was replaced in part by a loan, to be repaid after the war. See Kamtekar, "A Different War Dance," 197.

3. Dutt, *Ancient India*, 12.

4. Risley, *The People of India*, 53; quoted in Metcalf, 127. The scholar was G. F. MacMunn, writing in *The Armies of India*.

5. Baynes, *The Speeches of Adolf Hitler*, Vol. II, 1258–1259, 989.

6. Weinberg, *Hitler's Second Book*, 160–163.

7. Baynes, *The Speeches of Adolf Hitler*, Vol. I, 792–795.

8. Trevor-Roper, *Hitler's Table Talk*, 69, 33–34, 42, 198–199, 24; Baynes, *The Speeches of Adolf Hitler*, Vol. I, 800; Welch, "'Our India,'" 35–36.

9. Trevor-Roper, *Hitler's Table Talk*, 33; Hauner, *India in Axis Strategy*, 33.

10. Amery, *My Political Life*, Vol. I, 97.

11. Barnes and Nicholson, *The Empire at Bay*, 380, 397; Louis, *In the Name of God*, 115–116.

12. Rubinstein, "The Secret of Leopold Amery."

13. Louis, *In the Name of God*, 72–73.

14. Amery, *My Political Life*, Vol. I, 28–31, 49; William Rubinstein, email communication.

15. Churchill, *My Early Life*, 25–26.

16. Amery, My *Political Life*, Vol. I, 63, and Vol. III, 278; Rubinstein, "The Secret of Leopold Amery,"184; Barnes and Nicholson, *The Empire at Bay*, 517.

17. Sengupta, *History of the Bengali-Speaking People*, 354; Hitler, *Mein Kampf*, 597; Hauner, *India in Axis Strategy*, 62.

18. Bose and Bose, *Netaji*, Vol. 11, 45–47.

19. Hauner, *India in Axis Strategy*, 479; Bose, "Love in the Time of War." But Bose's wife, Emilie Schenkl, told historian Leonard Gordon that she and Bose were secretly married in 1937.

20. Baynes, *The Speeches of Adolf Hitler*, Vol. II, 1623, 1688.

21. Baker, *Human Smoke*, 178, 191–192, 226.

22. Churchill and Gilbert, *Winston S. Churchill*, Vol. VI, 1059.

23. Hammond, *Food*, Vol. I, 15, 47.

24. Gilbert, *The Churchill War Papers*, Vol. III, 1430; Birkenhead, *The Professor and the Prime Minister*, 222.

25. Harrod, *The Prof*, 5, 198–199; MacDougall, *Don and Mandarin*, 26.

26. Harrod, *The Prof*, 193.

27. Gilbert, *The Churchill War Papers*, Vol. III, 1431.

28. Cherwell Papers A93/f8.

29. Birkenhead, *The Professor and the Prime Minister*, 124; Moran, *Churchill: The Struggle for Survival*, 777.

30. Birkenhead, *The Professor and the Prime Minister*, 11; Churchill and Gilbert, *Winston S. Churchill*, Vol. V, 391.

31. Harrod, *The Prof*, 29, 97; Cherwell Papers A91/f2,f3.

32. Quoted in Farren and Thomson, "Frederick Alexander Lindemann, Viscount Cherwell," 60.

33. Gilbert, *The Churchill War Papers*, Vol. III, 802; Harrod, *The Prof*, 195, 204; MacDougall, *Don and Mandarin*, 21.

34. Fort, *Prof*, 217.

35. Hammond, *Food*, Vol. I, 102, 235; Kamtekar, "A Different War Dance," 213.

36. Hancock and Gowing, *British War Economy*, 263; Harrod, *The Prof*, 201; Birkenhead, *The Professor and the Prime Minister*, 228–229; MacDougall, *Don and Mandarin*, 31.

37. Barnes and Nicholson, *The Empire at Bay*, 762.

38. Mansergh, *The Transfer of Power 1942–7*, Vol. II, 505; Sinha and Khera, *Indian War Economy*, 73.

39. Prest, *War Economics of Primary Producing Countries*, 31; Bose and Jalal, *Modern South Asia*, 157.

40. Kamtekar, "A Different War Dance," 191.

41. De, "Imperial Governance and the Challenges of War," 20; William A. Barnes, CSAC, Box 8.

42. Tendulkar, *Mahatma*, Vol. VI, 46–47; Mansergh, *The Transfer of Power 1942–7*, Vol. II, 590.

43. Quoted in Digby, *"Prosperous" British India*, 123–131; Loveday, *The History and Economics of Indian Famines*, 136–138; Greenough, *Prosperity and Misery in Modern Bengal*, 278–285; Rothermund, *An Economic History of India*, 36; Dutt, *India To-day*, 133.

44. Quoted in Digby, *"Prosperous" British India*, 31; Habib, *Essays in Indian History*, 305–306; Rothermund, *An Economic History of India*,18.

45. Wolf, *Europe and the People Without History*, 261.

46. Jennings, *Speeches of the Right Honourable Lord Randolph Churchill*, Vol. II, 266–267; quoted in Dutt, *The Economic History of India*, Vol. I, 172–173; Bose, *South Asia and World Capitalism*, 214.

47. Basu, *The Ruin of Indian Trade and Industries*, 7, 124; Dutt, *The Economic History of India*, Vol. I, 202, 192, and Vol. II, 69.

48. Quoted in Dutt, *The Economic History of India*, Vol. I, 172; Bhatia, *Famines in India*, 22.

49. Rothermund, *An Economic History of India*, 37; Kumar, *The Cambridge Economic History of India*, Vol. II, 873; Dutt, *Speeches and Papers on Indian Questions*, 48.

50. Rothermund, *An Economic History of India*, 33; Naoroji, *Poverty and Un-British Rule in India*, 214–216; Bhatia, *Famines in India*, 9; Shrivastava, *The History of Indian Famines*, 360–361.

51. Bhatia, *Famines in India*, 38–39; Kumar, *The Cambridge Economic History of India*, Vol. II, 850–851.

52. Hunter, *Famine Aspects of Bengal Districts*, 15–17; Naoroji, *Poverty and Un-British Rule in India*, 216; Connell, "Indian Railways and Indian Wheat," 242–247, 256.

53. Bhatia, *Famines in India*, 106, 122; Nash, *The Great Famine and Its Causes*, 139.

54. Kumar, *The Cambridge Economic History of India*, Vol. II, 873; Atkinson, "Rupee Prices in India," 530.

55. Digby, *"Prosperous" British India*, 130, 128; Maharatna, *The Demography of Famines*, 15; Bhatt, "Mortality and Fertility in India," 111.

56. Churchill and Gilbert, *Winston S. Churchill*, Vol. II, 102; Churchill, *India*, 82; James, *Churchill*, 259.

57. Ghose, "Food Supply and Starvation," 376; Chattopadhyay, "Notes Towards an Understanding of the Bengal Famine of 1943," 124–125; Nanavati Papers, Vol. I, 226; Bose, *Agrarian Bengal*, 23–24.

58. Ghosh, *Famines in Bengal*, 31.

59. Chakrabarti, "Archeology of Coastal West Bengal," 135–160.

60. Majumdar, *History of Mediaeval Bengal*, 183.

Chapter Three

1. Quoted in Connell, *Wavell: Supreme Commander*, 31, 19.

2. Sinha and Khera, *Indian War Economy*, 323; Hauner, *India in Axis Strategy*, 268; Connell, *Wavell*, 30; Gilbert, *The Churchill War Papers*, Vol. II, 758; Barnes and Nicholson, *The Empire at Bay*, 641.

3. WO 208/819A; Bayly and Harper, *Forgotten Armies*, 304.

4. Roosevelt, *As He Saw It*, 37.

5. Ibid., 34–39; Reynolds, *In Command of History*, 54. Elliot Roosevelt's book has been described as unreliable because some remembered conversations were rendered as actual speech, but the information it contains on India is consistent with that from other sources.

6. Barnes and Nicholson, *The Empire at Bay*, 710; Hess, *America Encounters India*, 28; AMEL 7/36, Diary, January 8, 1942.

7. Churchill, *The Second World War: The Hinge of Fate*, 209.

8. Schofield, *Wavell: Soldier & Statesman*, 256; Bayly and Harper, *Forgotten Armies*, 142.

9. Bayly and Harper, *Forgotten Armies*, 147; Barnes and Nicholson, *The Empire at Bay*, 725.

10. Barnes and Nicholson, *The Empire at Bay*, 722.

11. Ibid., 751; Bayly and Harper, *Forgotten Armies*, 167.

12. Sinha and Khera, *Indian War Economy*, 55.

13. Hess, *America Encounters India*, 37; Mansergh, *The Transfer of Power*, Vol. I, 310, 328; Churchill, *The Second World War: The Hinge of Fate*, 209–210.

14. Barnes and Nicholson, *The Empire at Bay*, 729, 769; Mansergh, *The Transfer of Power*, Vol. I, 166, 239.

15. Barnes and Nicholson, *The Empire at Bay*, 676, 776.

16. Quoted in Roy, "Military Loyalty in the Colonial Context," 503.

17. CAB 113/1, Prime Minister's Personal Minute, Serial No. M. 1044/1; CAB 121/111, "War Cabinet: Oversea Defence Committee," January 22, 1942; WO 193/137, "Secretary of State to Government of India, Defence Dept.," January 30, 1942.

18. WO 106/3796, "Plan for the Defence of North-East India," February 12, 1942; WO 193/137, "Secretary of State to Government of India," March 27, 1942; WO 193/137, "Govr. General, Defence Dept., to S. of S. for India," March 31, 1942.

19. WO 106/3796, "Fifth Column in India," April 23, 1942; CSAC, Olaf M. Martin Papers, Memoir, 233, 241; Nanavati Papers, Vol. I, 39.

20. Nanavati Papers, Vol. II, 544, 547; Bari, *Tamrolipto Jatiyo Sorkar*, 94.

21. Nanavati Papers, Vol. II, 545–546; Woodhead, *Famine Inquiry Commission*, 26.

22. Nanavati Papers, Vol. II, 543, 546; Bera, *Janajuddha Patrika*, 98; Gupta, *Towards Freedom*, Vol. II, 1831.

23. Mitra, *Tin Kuri Dash*, 140–141; Afroz, *Bengal Famine 1943*; Sengupta, *Bangosanghar Ebong*, 35.

24. Huq, *Bengal Today*, 12; Mansergh, *The Transfer of Power*, Vol. III, 211.

25. MT 59/657, "Imports of Cereals into India"; Woodhead, *Famine Inquiry Commission*, 28.

26. Loewenheim, Langley, and Jonas, *Roosevelt and Churchill*, 191–192.

27. Mansergh, *The Transfer of Power*, Vol. I, 395, 400.

28. Ibid., 396; Barnes and Nicholson, *The Empire at Bay*, 783; Tendulkar, *Mahatma*, 72.

29. Moore, *Churchill, Cripps, and India*, 111–112.

30. Ibid., 116, 119; Mansergh, *The Transfer of Power*, Vol. I, 722; Barnes and Nicholson, *The Empire at Bay*, 794.

31. Johnson, Telegram to Secretary of State; Loewenheim, Langley, and Jonas, *Roosevelt and Churchill*, 202–203.

32. Hess, *America Encounters India*, 40; Sherwood, *Roosevelt and Hopkins*, Vol. 2, 109.

33. Loewenheim, Langley, and Jonas, *Roosevelt and Churchill*, 204.

34. Hess, *America Encounters India*, 82.

35. Churchill, *The Second World War: The Hinge of Fate*, 219–220.

36. WO 193/127, Armindia to Air Ministry, April 14, 1942; Connell, *Wavell*, 223–224.

37. Churchill, *The Second World War: The Hinge of Fate*, 186; CAB 195/1, W.M. (42) 56th Meeting, 25.

38. WO 106/3796, C. in C. India to War Office, May 1, 1942; WO 106/3796, "C. in C. India to War Office," May 29, 1942; Barnes and Nicholson, *The Empire at Bay*, 822; CAB 195/1, W.M. (42) 96th Meeting, 82.

39. Churchill, *The Second World War: The Hinge of Fate*, 363.

40. Hauner, *India in Axis Strategy*, 389, 435.

41. WO 106/3796, C. in C. India to War Office, May 1, 1942; WO 193/127, "Chiefs of Staff Committee, Meeting to be Held on 4th February, 1942," February 3, 1942; Kirby, *War Against Japan*, Vol. II, 47.

42. Branson, *British Soldier in India*, 9, 16.

43. Ibid., 11.

44. Ibid., 16.

45. Ibid., 12, 34–35.

46. Ibid., 71.

47. Ibid., 30–31, 84.

48. Tendulkar, *Mahatma*, 75, 105, 81.

49. Mansergh, *The Transfer of Power*, Vol. II, 363, 376–377; James, *Raj*, 563.

50. Mansergh, *The Transfer of Power*, Vol. II, 532–533; quoted in Hess, *America Encounters India*, 79.

51. Mansergh, *The Transfer of Power*, Vol. II, 621–624.

52. Quoted in Moore, *Churchill, Cripps, and India*, 37; Greenough, "Political Mobilization," 359–360; Mansergh, *The Transfer of Power*, Vol. II, 557–558.

53. Branson, *British Soldier in India*, 18–19.

54. Ibid., 23, 26.

55. Mansergh, *The Transfer of Power*, Vol. II, 747, 908; Voigt, *India in the Second World War*, 166; Louis, *Imperialism at Bay*, 33; Barnes and Nicholson, *The Empire at Bay*, 830.

56. Mansergh, *The Transfer of Power*, Vol. III, 3.

57. CHUR 2/43 A "India: Government Policy," 2, 3; Branson, *British Soldier in India*, 29; Mansergh, *The Transfer of Power*, Vol. II, 961, 978.

58. Churchill, *The Second World War: The Hinge of Fate*, 509.

Chapter Four

1. Dhara, *Probaho*, 112–113, 120; Greenough, "Political Mobilization," 362–364.

2. Dhara, *Probaho*, 114–115.

3. Ibid., 115–116; *Biplabi*, "Donipurer gulir kese saja," 203.

4. Bari, *Tamrolipto Jatiyo Sorkar*, 133.

5. Ibid., 134.

6. Ibid., 135–136.

7. Ibid., 138–139.

8. Ibid., 137–138, 162–163.

9. Also see ibid., 152. His account has a single aircraft dropping two bombs.

10. Dhara, *Probaho*, 121.

11. Ibid., 122.

12. Bari, *Tamrolipto Jatiyo Sorkar*, 146.

13. Ibid., 147; Dhara, *Probaho*, 123–124.

14. Bari, *Tamrolipto Jatiyo Sorkar*, 159–160.

15. Ibid., 165.

16. Maity, *Quit India Movement*, 35.

17. Bari, *Tamrolipto Jatiyo Sorkar*, 168–70, 327; Brennan, "Government Famine Relief in Bengal," 549; Bose, *Agrarian Bengal*, 248.

18. Stephens, *Monsoon Morning*, 71; Mitra, *Tin Kuri Dash*, 148; India Office Records, R/3/2/37, October 26, 1942.

19. *Biplabi*, "Mohisadal thana," 40.

20. Anonymous, "Cyclone Havoc in Bengal," *The Statesman*, November 3, 1942; Bari, *Tamrolipto Jatiyo Sorkar*, 167–170.

21. Dhara, *Probaho*, 132; Bari, *Tamrolipto Jatiyo Sorkar*, 179.

22. Dhara, *Probaho*, 133; Maity, *Quit India Movement*, 33.

23. Dhara, *Probaho*, 141–142.

24. Branson, *British Soldier in India*, 40–43.

25. CSAC, Pinnell Papers, Memoir, 98.

26. Ibid., 99; Nanavati Papers, Vol. II, 441, 447.

27. Nanavati Papers, Vol. II, 442–444; CSAC, Martin Papers, Memoir, 250.

28. Nanavati Papers, Vol. III, 834; Bose, *Agrarian Bengal*, 24.

29. Nanavati Papers, Vol. II, 441; Nanavati Papers, Vol. V, 1333.

30. Nanavati Papers File 6B; quoted in Law-Smith, "Response and Responsibility," 61; pictured in the documentary *The Forgotten Famine*, Uden Associates for U.K. Channel 4, 1997.

31. De, "Imperial Governance and the Challenges of War," 10; *Biplabi*, "Annabhabe mrityu" and "Khudar jalay atmohotya," 179–180; quoted in Brennan, "Government Famine Relief in Bengal," 542–567; Nanavati Papers, Vol. II, 445.

32. Mahalanobis, "Mortality in Bengal in 1943."

33. *Biplabi*, "Bhogini senar sotsahos," 51.

34. *Biplabi*, "British sobhyotar sreshtho nidarshon,"109–113; Maity, *Quit India Movement*, 108.

35. Maity, *Quit India Movement*, 27–29.

36. Linlithgow Collection 2336, Telegrams from Governor of Bengal to Viceroy, February 2, 1943, and February 22, 1943; Huq, *Bengal Today*, 26.

37. Sengupta, *Bangosanghar*, 35; Huq, *Bengal Today*, 15–16; Linlithgow Collection 2336, Telegram from Governor of Bengal to Viceroy, February 11, 1943; Nanavati Papers, Vol. IV, 1104. According to Sengupta, soldiers posted on the coast of Noakhali had landed by night at a shoreline village, Sanoa, while the men were fishing at sea, and raped the women. In the early morning the fishermen had returned, chanced upon the rapists, and rushed to attack with knives; they were mowed down by machine-gun fire. Huq had tried to visit the village but was barred by the district magistrate, acting on Herbert's orders.

38. Huq, *Bengal Today*, 30–32; Linlithgow Collection 2336, Telegram from Governor of Bengal to Viceroy, April 7, 1943.

39. Gallagher, *Decline, Revival and Fall of the British Empire*, 183; Mansergh, *The Transfer of Power*, Vol. III, 320, 893.

40. Mitra, *Tin Kuri Dash*, 161–162; Linlithgow Collection 2336, May 4, 1943; AMEL 1/6/21 file 2, Secretary of State to Prime Minister, March 4, 1943.

Chapter Five

1. CHAR 23/11, W.P. (43) 106, "Demands on Shipping Resulting from Overseas Cereal Requirements."

2. Behrens, *Merchant Shipping and the Demands of War*, 320; MT 59/621, "Supply of Food Grains to East Africa," March 4, 1943.

3. Mansergh, *The Transfer of Power*, Vol. I, 425–426, and Vol. II, 506–507; MT 59/621, "Supply of Food Grains to East Africa," March 4, 1943.

4. Barnes and Nicholson, *Empire at Bay*, 833, 836.

5. Mansergh, *The Transfer of Power*, Vol. III, 21–23, 37, and Vol. II, 998.

6. Mansergh, *The Transfer of Power*, Vol. II, 590.

7. Rothermund, *An Economic History of India*, 119; Barnes and Nicholson, *Empire at Bay*, 836.

8. Hess, *America Encounters India*, 94–95; Phillips, *Ventures in Diplomacy*, 218. British sensitivities precluded the naming of Phillips as ambassador to the colony.

9. Quoted in Louis, *Imperialism at Bay*, 200; Barnes and Nicholson, *Empire at Bay*, 842.

10. MT 59/657, "Imports of Cereals into India"; Mansergh, *The Transfer of Power*, Vol. III, 333–334, 357, 394.

11. MT 59/631, "With Sir William Croft's Compliments: India's Foodgrains Supply," July 19, 1943. Also see Sen, *Poverty and Famines*, 57–63; Tauger, "Entitlement, Shortage and the 1943 Bengal Famine," 45–72; Nanavati Papers, Vol. II, 440, and Vol. IV, 1104; and De, "Imperial Governance and the Challenges of War," 34. Economist Amartya Sen used official harvest projections to argue that the rice shortfall in 1943 was not in itself enough to cause famine, but Tauger points out that crop infestations greatly reduced the actual harvest in Bengal. A contemporary peasants' association gauged three-eighths of the crop to have failed; the director of

agriculture estimated 30 percent failure, while Pinnell estimated a 20 percent shortfall in Bengal.

12. Mansergh, *The Transfer of Power*, Vol. III, 358–362, 437.

13. Knight, *Food Administration in India*, 130.

14. Woodhead, *Famine Inquiry Commission*, 21; Nanavati Papers, Vol. II, 339.

15. WO 208/810, Weekly Intelligence Summary No. 81.

16. Mansergh, *The Transfer of Power*, Vol. IV, 301.

17. Linlithgow Collection 2336, Governor of Bengal to Viceroy, January 2, 1943.

18. WO 208/810, Weekly Intelligence Summary 63, January 15, 1943; Mansergh, *The Transfer of Power*, Vol. III, 373, 421–422; WO 208/809, "Copy of telegram from Secretary of State for India to Government of India, Food Department, dated 15th December 1942"; WO 208/809, "Copy of telegram from Viceroy to Secretary of State for India dated 26th December, 1942."

19. Mansergh, *The Transfer of Power*, Vol. III, 476–477.

20. Barnes and Nicholson, *Empire at Bay*, 867.

21. WO 208/809, "Government of India, Food Department to Secretary of State for India," January 10, 1943; Mansergh, *The Transfer of Power*, Vol. III, 479–480.

22. Smith, *Conflict over Convoys*, 130.

23. CAB 195/2, W.M. (43) 7th Meeting, 57; Mansergh, *The Transfer of Power*, Vol. III, 492, 510.

24. Sinha and Khera, *Indian War Economy*, 55.

25. WO 208/809, Extract from the Conclusions of the 3rd (43) meeting of the Lord President's Committee, January 15, 1943; CO 852/427/2, From Secretary of State for India to Governor General, January 16, 1942; Mansergh, *The Transfer of Power*, Vol. III, 515.

26. MT 59/621, Government of India, Food Department to Secretary of State for India, January 20, 1943; WO 208/809, "Background Note on the Food Situation," September 24, 1943; Mansergh, *The Transfer of Power*, Vol. III, 581.

27. Behrens, *Merchant Shipping and the Demands of War*, 313–315.

28. Hancock and Gowing, *British War Economy*, 206; Smith, *Conflict over Convoys*, 242–243.

29. MacDougall, *Don and Mandarin*, 32.

30. Smith, *Conflict over Convoys*, 130; MT 59/108, "The United Kingdom Import Situation in 1943," February 9, 1943; MT 62/73, Prime Minister from Cherwell, January 2, 1943.

31. MacDougall, *Don and Mandarin*, 26. There would have been ninety-two sailings in February, so the cut was actually to 43 percent.

32. As paraphrased in Behrens, *Merchant Shipping and the Demands of War*, 320. The original Ministry of War Transport document could not be located.

33. Behrens, *Merchant Shipping and the Demands of War*, 340–342.

34. Plaque at Keoladeo Bird Sanctuary.

35. Mansergh, *The Transfer of Power*, Vol. III, 439–440.

36. Ibid., 536, 558–559.

37. Ibid., 589–590, 469, 632; quoted in Roberts, *Masters and Commanders*, 350; Barnes and Nicholson, *Empire at Bay*, 872.

38. Phillips, *Ventures in Diplomacy*, 231, 234; Mansergh, *The Transfer of Power*, Vol. III, 652–653, 687–688.

39. Mansergh, *The Transfer of Power*, Vol. III, 690; CHAR 20/107, For Lord Halifax from Prime Minister, February 21, 1943.

40. Mansergh, *The Transfer of Power*, Vol. III, 659, 669, 730, 718, 770–771; Churchill, *The Second World War: The Hinge of Fate*, 736.

41. Mansergh, *The Transfer of Power*, Vol. III, 737–738.

42. Quoted in Smith, *Conflict over Convoys*, 159.

43. Mansergh, *The Transfer of Power*, Vol. III, 473–478.

44. Nanavati Papers, Vol. II, 356.

45. WO 208/809, "Shipping—Indian Wheat Requirements," January 21, 1943; MT 59/377, British Merchant Shipping Mission from Ministry of War Transport, January 22, 1943, and March 1, 1943; Cherwell Papers H137/20; AMEL 1/6/14 File 1, Secretary of State to Viceroy, February 18, 1943; CAB 195/2, W.M. (43) 32nd Meeting, 91.

46. AMEL 1/6/14 File 1, Viceroy to Secretary of State for India, February 21, 1943; MT 59/621, "Supply of Food Grains to East Africa," March 4, 1943.

47. MacDougall, *Don and Mandarin*, 32; Behrens, *Merchant Shipping and the Demands of War*, 325; Hancock and Gowing, *British War Economy*, 267.

48. Cherwell Papers F231/36; MT 59/108, "The United Kingdom Import Situation in 1943: Table III," February 9, 1943.

49. Hancock and Gowing, *British War Economy*, 431, 424–425; CAB 195/1, W.M. (42) 98th Meeting, 84.

50. Hammond, *Food*, Vol. I, 75–76, 185–186; CAB 195/1, W.M. (42) 89th Meeting, 75.

51. Hancock and Gowing, *British War Economy*, 422–423; Hammond, *Food*, Vol. III, 534.

52. CAB 195/1, W.M. (42) 98th Meeting, 85.

53. Hammond, *Food*, Vol. I, 268–269, and Vol. III, 613, 615.

54. Kevin Smith, private communication; Hancock and Gowing, *British War Economy*, 357; Behrens, *Merchant Shipping and the Demands of War*, 325. Total stocks of food and raw materials were 15.8 million tons in December 1942 and 15.5 million tons in June 1943. Imports in this period were 10.8 million tons plus about 0.15 million tons from Eire. Consumption, being imports plus stock used, was therefore 11.3 million tons. So excess of stock over consumption was 4.5 million tons.

55. Cherwell Papers, F255/1 and F255/3/1, 2; CHAR 23/11, "The Shipping Position." Also see Appendix LIV in Behrens, *Merchant Shipping and the Demands of War*, 325. Stocks totaled 15.8 million tons in December 1942 and 15.2 million tons in January 1943.

56. MT 59/108, "The United Kingdom Import Situation in 1943," February 9, 1943; Cherwell Papers F255/1; Smith, *Conflict over Convoys*, 174–176.

57. Leighton and Coakley, *Global Logistics and Strategy*, 694, 702; Cherwell Papers F255/3/2. Kevin Smith states that Gross's estimate of essential British imports was based less on actual calculation than on political considerations (personal communication).

58. CAB 195/1, W.M. (42) 98th Meeting, 84.

59. Cherwell Papers, H298/21.

60. CAB 195/2, W.M. (43) 2nd Meeting, 45–46.

61. Cherwell Papers, F255/1; Smith, *Conflict over Convoys*, 130.

62. Smith, *Conflict over Convoys*, 196; Behrens, *Merchant Shipping and the Demands of War*, 325; Hammond, *Food*, Vol. I, 274.

63. Hammond, *Food*, Vol. I, 169(footnote), 277, and Vol. III, 544; CHAR 23/10, "Home Food Production," December 24, 1942; Cherwell Papers F255/1; Hancock and Gowing, *British War Economy*, 433.

64. Hancock and Gowing, *British War Economy*, 357–358; Hammond, *Food*, Vol. III, 534, and Vol. I, 276; Behrens, *Merchant Shipping and the Demands of War*, 325. Stock of wheat and flour totaled 1.8 million tons in December 1942 and 2.2 million tons in June 1943. So 0.4 million tons of stock were built up in these six months, while imports were 1.9 million tons. Consumption, being imports minus stock increase, comes to 1.5 million tons. Thus wheat consumption per month was 250,000 tons, which amounts to stocks in December 1942 of about seven months.

65. CAB 79/59, March 9, 1943, and April 9, 1943; Cherwell Papers F255/3/2.

66. WO 208/809, Government of India to Secretary of State for India, April 17, 1942, and May 2, 1943.

67. MT 59/631, "Indian Wheat Requirements"; Nanavati Papers, Vol. II, 341.

68. MT 59/694, Mance to Anderson, December 29, 1942; MT 59/694, Note by H. S. Mance, April 8, 1943.

69. Cherwell Papers F255/3/2; Mansergh, *The Transfer of Power*, Vol. III, 515, 581.

70. Gupta, *Towards Freedom*, Part II, 1843; Nanavati Papers, Vol. II, 353.

71. MT 59/621, "Brief for Shipping Committee"; MT 59/694, "Brief for the Shipping Committee"; Ghosh, *Famines in Bengal*, 18, 3; Gupta, *Towards Freedom*, Vol. II, 1829; WO 208/818, Weekly Intelligence Summary 76, April 16, 1943. In total, about 80,000 tons were received, but India was also forced to re-export some 20,000 tons.

72. Nanavati Papers, Vol. IV, 1013; Gupta, *Towards Freedom*, Vol. II, 1837–1838; Ghosh, *Famines in Bengal*, 17; Narayanan, *Famine over Bengal*, 61.

73. Nanavati Papers, Vol. V, 1372; CSAC, Pinnell Papers, Memoir, 97; Mansergh, *The Transfer of Power*, Vol. III, 544.

74. Nanavati Papers, Vol. II, 513; CAB 195/1, W.M. (42) 153rd Meeting, November 16, 1942, 181–182.

75. Nanavati Papers, Vol. II, 552.

76. Nanavati Papers, Vol. I, 216–217; Ghosh, *Famines in Bengal*, 31; Sinha and Khera, *Indian War Economy*, 4; MT 59/631, "Exports from India by Sea"; India Office Records R/3/2/37, August 31, 1942; MT 59/621, "Area Outside Jurisdiction of M.E.S.C.," April 22, 1943.

77. Famines in nineteenth-century India and Ireland were aggravated by the British authorities' adherence to free-market policies; see Woodham Smith, *The Great Hunger*, 127, 408. A half-kilogram of cereal a day may not be enough to save an adult, but almost half the famine victims were children under ten years of age. So a ration scale varying around such an average would suffice.

78. MT 59/631, Government of India to Secretary of State for India, July 21, 1943.

Chapter Six

1. Phillips, *Ventures in Diplomacy*, 240–244, 250.

2. Mansergh, *The Transfer of Power*, Vol. III, 909–910.

3. Ibid., 954, 978, 1022–1023.

4. Phillips, *Ventures in Diplomacy*, 251.

5. Ibid., 253–254.

6. Butler, *The Art of the Possible*,112–113.

7. Churchill, *My Early Life*, 145.

8. Gandhi, *Ghaffar Khan*, 167; Mansergh, *The Transfer of Power*, Vol. IV, 186.

9. Quoted in James, *Raj*, 571; Mansergh, *The Transfer of Power*, Vol. IV, 104.

10. *Biplabi*, "British sobhyotai," 110–11; Dhara, *Probaho*, 136.

11. Maity, *Quit India Movement*, 56; Dhara, *Probaho*, 139–140.

12. Dhara, *Probaho*, 148–153.

13. Ibid., 158–169.

14. Mansergh, *The Transfer of Power*, Vol. III, 1014; Gupta, *Towards Freedom*, Vol. II, 1843.

15. De, "Imperial Governance and the Challenges of War," 31, 14.

16. Mansergh, *The Transfer of Power*, Vol. III, 1016–1019.

17. Mansergh, *The Transfer of Power*, Vol. IV, 44, 112; quoted in Venkataramani, *Bengal Famine of 1943*,16.

18. Cherwell Papers H290/13; Santhanam, *The Cry of Distress*,166.

19. MT 59/631, "With Sir William Croft's Compliments: India's Foodgrains Supply," July 19, 1943; Nanavati Papers, Vol. I, 216–217; Mansergh, *The Transfer of Power*, Vol. IV, 76–79.

20. Mansergh, *The Transfer of Power*, Vol. IV, 5.

21. Ibid., 135–137.

22. Wilson, *Churchill and the Prof*, 132.

23. Cherwell Papers H290/1,2.

24. Mansergh, *The Transfer of Power*, Vol. IV, 155–157.

25. Danchev and Todman, *War Diaries*, 537; Moran, *Churchill: The Struggle for Survival*, 478; Churchill and Gilbert, *Winston S. Churchill*, Vol. VI, 1084.

26. Mansergh, *The Transfer of Power*, Vol. IV, 158, 169.

27. MT 59/631, "Wheat for India."

28. Wilson, *Churchill and the Prof*, 132–134. Wilson further argued that India had harvested a large rice crop in 1942, and should have possessed "substantial stocks to carry over into 1943" because the shortfall in imports from Burma and the exports to war theaters were small in comparison to the colony's total production. No such stocks were in evidence. Notably, such statistical comparisons are similar to those that Wilson himself described, in a September 1943 memo to Cherwell, as misleading.

29. Leighton and Coakley, *Global Logistics and Strategy*, 704; Smith, *Conflict over Convoys*, 192–193, 197; Cherwell Papers H290/14; Salter, *Slave of the Lamp*, 196.

30. CHAR 23/11, "Forecast of Monthly Loss Rates of Dry Cargo Ships," July 13, 1943; Hammond, *Food*, Vol. I, 272.

31. James, *Churchill*, 48–49, 70, 117; Taylor et al., *Churchill*, 42–44.

32. Denniston, *Churchill's Secret War*, 110, 121–123; Roskill, *Churchill and the Admirals*, 222.

33. Wilson, *Churchill and the Prof*, 133–134; MT 59/631, "Indian Food Situation," September 17, 1943; Behrens, *Merchant Shipping and the Demands of War*, 348; Bayly and Harper, *Forgotten Armies*, 285.

34. CSAC, Martin Papers, Memoir, 261.

35. Nanavati Papers, Vol. IV, 1157, and Vol. II, 348–349.

36. Cherwell Papers H123/4; Mansergh, *The Transfer of Power*, Vol. IV, 178; Barnes and Nicholson, *The Empire at Bay*, 933.

37. Schofield, *Wavell: Soldier & Statesman*, 286; Voigt, *India in the Second World War*, 216–217; Moon, *Wavell*, 12–13; Mansergh, *The Transfer of Power*, Vol. IV, 125, 131.

38. Mansergh, *The Transfer of Power*, Vol. IV, 157, 163; Barnes and Nicholson, *The Empire at Bay*, 934.

39. BRGS 2/17, August 4, 1943.

40. MT 59/631, "Wheat for India." A small portion of the Balkan stockpile was also to be used for feeding Greek and Yugoslav guerrillas.

41. MT 59/631, "Note of a Meeting held to discuss Cross Trade Programme Requirements," August 11, 1943; Mansergh, *The Transfer of Power*, Vol. IV, 318.

42. MT 59/631, India Office to Leathers, October 27, 1943.

43. Nanavati Papers, Vol. IV, 1153.

44. Ibid., 1150–1152; Davis, *Late Victorian Holocausts*, 39; Hill and Hirschman, "Human Rights Abuses by the Third Reich," 850.

Chapter Seven

1. *Biplabi*, "Jibonto kawbor," 284.

2. Ghosh, *Famines in Bengal*, 80–81; *Biplabi*, "Durbhikkho," 325.

3. Tucker, *The Great Starvation Experiment*, 124, 139, 148; Das, *Bengal Famine*, 9.

4. Rai, "Ponchaser Monnontor o Banglar Silposahityo," 13; Ghosh, *Famines in Bengal*, 75.

5. Bhaumik, *Code Name God*, 48, 52; Bandopadhyay, *Monikanchon*, 48–50, 55.

6. Narayanan, *Famine over Bengal*, 170–171.

7. Ghosh, *Famines in Bengal*, 83; Nanavati Papers, Vol. V, 1368.

8. Nanavati Papers, Vol. II, 446. Food riots occur during relatively mild shortages, or they precede famines. See Ó Gráda, *Famine: A Short History*, 56.

9. Tucker, *The Great Starvation Experiment*, 170; Wiesel, *Night*, 108, 57.

10. Tucker, *The Great Starvation Experiment*, 8.

11. Orwell, *The Collected Essays, Journalism and Letters*, Vol. IV, 467.

12. Ghosh, *Famines in Bengal*, 87; *Biplabi*, "Durbhikkho," 263.

Chapter Eight

1. Branson, *British Soldier in India*, 52, 69.

2. Ibid., 70–72, 81, 90, 94.

3. Ibid., 100.

4. Ibid., 101.

5. Durga Pujo refers to the worship of the goddess Durga, which takes place in the autumn. An image of the goddess, depicted as riding a lion and slaying the buffalo demon, is typically worshipped for five days; the rituals may include animal sacrifice. Durga Pujo is also a time for dancing, feasting, and giving gifts of clothing.

6. Gupta, *In the Path of Service*, 77.

7. Santhanam, *The Cry of Distress*, 33.

8. Bera, *Janajuddha Patrika*, 100; Ghosh, *The Bengal Tragedy*, 9.

9. Stephens, *Monsoon Morning*, 176–179.

10. AMEL 7/36, Diary, May 13 and August 11, 1942; Stephens, *Monsoon Morning*, 248, 197, 176.

11. Stephens, *Monsoon Morning*, 181–182.

12. Bhattacharya, *Hungry Bengal*. Pages from the surviving copy are pictured in the documentary *The Forgotten Famine* (Uden Associates, 1997). See also Venkataramani, *Bengal Famine of 1943*, 31.

13. WO 208/809, "Extract from G.H.Q. India W.I.S. No. 94 dated 20 Aug 1943," "Indian Famine: Bose Offers 100,000 Tons of Rice," August 25, 1943.

14. WO 208/818, "Extract from GHQ India Weekly Intelligence Summary 97, Dated 10 September 1943."

15. Hauner, *India in Axis Strategy*, 479.

16. Ibid., 486. The meeting may instead have been on May 29. See Gordon, *Brothers Against the Raj*, 484.

17. Bose, *A Beacon Across Asia*, 134–137.

18. Fay, *The Forgotten Army*, 203.

19. Anonymous, "Ba Maw, the Great Asian Dreamer," 8.

20. India Office File No. 114/43-Poll (I), September 1, 1943. Courtesy of Sugata Bose.

21. MT 59/631, "Wheat 1," September 28, 1943.

22. WO 298/809; Nanavati Papers, Vol. II, 461, 468–470; AMEL 1/6/14 File 2, Secretary of State to Viceroy, October 15 and 22, 1943.

23. O'Malley, *Ireland, India and Empire*, 145.

24. Mansergh, *The Transfer of Power*, Vol. IV, 194; CSAC, Olaf M. Martin Papers, Memoir, 252–253.

25. Nanavati Papers, Vol. IV, 1038; Rai, "Ponchaser Mannontar O Banglar Silposahityo," 53–59.

26. Nanavati Papers, Vol. IV, 1092–1093; Mansergh, *The Transfer of Power*, Vol. IV, 973.

27. Hunter, "The Bengal Famine of 1866," 272.

28. Bayly and Harper, *Forgotten Wars*, 300.

29. Das, *Bengal Famine*, 34.

30. CSAC, William Barnes Papers, Box 8, Diary, 125.

31. *The Forgotten Famine* (Uden Associates, 1997).

32. Quoted in Ghosh, *Famines in Bengal*, 80, 76.

33. CSAC, Olaf M. Martin Papers, Memoir, 256; Mansergh, *The Transfer of Power*, Vol. IV, 284, 331.

34. Nanavati Papers, Vol. IV, 1038; CSAC, William Barnes Papers, Box 8, Diary, 127; Ghosh, *Famines in Bengal*, 50, 176; Gupta, *Towards Freedom*, Part II, 1915.

35. Woodhead, 224–225; De, "Imperial Governance and the Challenges of War," 27.

36. Nanavati Papers, Vol. V, 1328–1329.

37. Woodham Smith, *The Great Hunger*, 191.

38. Mitra, *Tin Kuri Dash*, 161–163. Men are more likely than women to die during famines; see Ó Gráda, *Famine: A Short History*, 99.

39. Sheila Chapman-Mortimer, in *The Forgotten Famine* (Uden Associates, 1997).

Chapter Nine

1. Venkataramani, *Bengal Famine of 1943*, 19; Mansergh, *The Transfer of Power*, Vol. IV, 169, 177; Barnes and Nicholson, *The Empire at Bay*, 935.

2. MT 59/631, W.C.O to QUADRANT, August 23, 1943; MT 59/631, "Grain for India."

3. Louis, *Imperialism at Bay*, 9–10; Venkataramani and Shrivastava, *Roosevelt Gandhi Churchill*, 162–163.

4. Venkataramani, *Bengal Famine of 1943*, 19–21.

5. Hull, *The Memoirs of Cordell Hull*, Vol. II, 1496.

6. Leighton and Coakley, *Global Logistics and Strategy*, 548; Venkataramani, *Bengal Famine of 1943*, 22.

7. Leighton and Coakley, *Global Logistics and Strategy*, 544, 537.

8. Quoted in Bayly and Harper, *Forgotten Armies*, 363; Venkataramani and Shrivastava, *Roosevelt Gandhi Churchill*, 301–302.

9. Mansergh, *The Transfer of Power*, Vol. IV, 273, 217, 304–306; WO 208/809, Weekly Intelligence Summary 98, September 17, 1943.

10. Cherwell Papers, H290/3, 4, 5.

11. Mansergh, *The Transfer of Power*, Vol. IV, 317; MT 59/631, "Grain for India."

12. Mansergh, *The Transfer of Power*, Vol. IV, 318–319.

13. MT 59/631, "Middle East," October 6, 1943.

14. Barnes and Nicholson, *The Empire at Bay*, 943; Moon, *Wavell*, 19.

15. Danchev and Todman, *War Diaries*, 473.

16. Mansergh, *The Transfer of Power*, Vol. IV, 375–376.

17. Ibid., 377; Barnes and Nicholson, *The Empire at Bay*, 946; Moon, *Wavell*, 23.

18. Moon, *Wavell*, 23; Barnes and Nicholson, *The Empire at Bay*, 947.

19. Mansergh, *The Transfer of Power*, Vol. IV, 349, 396.

20. CHAR 20/97A/39, 46–48.

21. Moon, *Wavell*, 32–34.

22. Mansergh, *The Transfer of Power*, Vol. IV, 362–363.

23. Ibid., 415–416.

24. Barnes and Nicholson, *The Empire at Bay*, 948, 950.

25. MT 59/631, "Indian Food Situation," September 17, 1943; Slim, *Defeat into Victory*, 143.

26. Narayanan, *Famine over Bengal*, 100; Anonymous, "Bengal Famine: Mr. Amery on Relief Measures"; Mansergh, *The Transfer of Power*, Vol. IV, 445; Barnes and Nicholson, *The Empire at Bay*, 933, 950.

27. WO 208/810, "Address by the Financial Adviser, Military Finance at the Army Commanders' Conference," July 9, 1943; Sinha and Khera, *Indian War Economy*, 345; Prest, *War Economics of Primary Producing Countries*, 31. The rupee was fixed at 1 shilling and 6 pence.

28. Cherwell Papers H130/6; Barnes and Nicholson, *The Empire at Bay*, 835; Mansergh, *The Transfer of Power*, Vol. IV, 594.

29. Cherwell Papers H123/10, H124/4, H125/10, and H132/6,7,8; Singh, "Imperial Defence and the Transfer of Power in India," 569.

30. Cherwell Papers H127/1,2,29,35 and H128/4,7.

31. Wilson, *Churchill and the Prof*, 180, 228(endnote 16).

32. Cherwell Papers H136/15–19 and H129/1–4.

33. Cherwell Papers H128/12.

34. Mansergh, *The Transfer of Power*, Vol. IV, 465, 470.

35. Cherwell Papers H290/10.

36. Churchill's biographers believe that Savrola was endowed with traits, such as valor and wisdom, to which the youthful author himself aspired: his opinions were Churchill's own. See Churchill, *Savrola*, 81–82; Caldwell, "Malthus and the Less Developed World," 683; quoted in Ponting, *Churchill*, 24; Taylor et al., *Churchill*, 219–222.

37. Ghose, "Food Supply and Starvation," 376.

38. Barnes and Nicholson, *The Empire at Bay*, 950.

39. Danchev and Todman, *War Diaries*, 516; quoted in Roberts, *Hitler and Churchill*, 122; quoted in Gilbert, *Churchill and America*, 226; Churchill, *India*, 84; Gilbert, *The Churchill War Papers*, Vol. II, 337.

40. Mansergh, *The Transfer of Power*, Vol. IV, 465–466; MT 59/631, From Canada (Govt.) to D.O., November 13, 1943; MT 59/631, copy of note signed D. Gibbs, November 3, 1943; Barnes and Nicholson, *The Empire at Bay*, 951.

41. MT 59/637, "India and Ceylon Cereals Requirements"; Cherwell Papers F247/15.

42. Stone, "The Indian Skeleton at Atlantic City," 686–687.

43. Venkataramani, *Bengal Famine of 1943*, 43, 47–52.

44. Hess, *America Encounters India*, 134.

45. Cherwell Papers H291/11.

46. Behrens, *Merchant Shipping and the Demands of War*, 325; Hancock, *Statistical Digest of the War*, 167; Cherwell Papers, H137/20; Hancock and Gowing, *British War Economy*, 436.

47. Hammond, *Food*, Vol. I, 159–160; Hancock and Gowing, *British War Economy*, 436; Churchill, *The Second World War: Closing the Ring*, 151.

48. Hammond, *Food*, Vol. III, 544–545, 481.

49. Mansergh, *The Transfer of Power*, Vol. IV, 418.

50. CAB 195/2, W.M. (43) 2nd Meeting, 47; Cherwell Papers, H307/1.

51. Louis, *Imperialism at Bay*, 283.

52. Louis, *In the Name of God*, 285.

53. Dilks, *The Diaries of Sir Alexander Cadogan*, 582.

54. MT 59/631, "Canadian Wheat for India," December 17, 1943; Barnes and Nicholson, *The Empire at Bay*, 957.

55. Mansergh, *The Transfer of Power*, Vol. IV, 678. The army alone needed 250,000 tons for six months.

56. Danchev and Todman, *War Diaries*, 451.

57. Ibid., 458–459.

58. Ibid., xvi.

59. Quoted in Jablonsky, *Churchill, The Great Game and Total War*, 92; West, *The Larger Evils*, 87.

60. Quoted in James, *Churchill*, 379; Moran, *Churchill: The Struggle for Survival*, 321; Barnes and Nicholson, *The Empire at Bay*, 758, 953.

61. Moran, *Churchill: The Struggle for Survival*, 778–779; Snow, *Science and Government*, 65, 63.

62. Snow, *Science and Government*, 12; Harrod, *The Prof*, 80, 73, 77.

63. Cherwell Papers F29/33.

64. Harrod, *The Prof*, 78. As late as October 1937, Cherwell remained fascinated by the possibility of creating "Sub men or supermen." See Cherwell Papers, E39/1–13.

65. Cherwell Papers E1/3–6 and E2/1–11.

66. Weinberg, *Hitler's Second Book*, 20; quoted in Kiernan, *Blood and Soil*, 47.

67. Orwell, *1984*, 203.

Chapter Ten

1. Sinha and Khera, *Indian War Economy*, 54; Mansergh, *The Transfer of Power*, Vol. IV, 475–476, 679, 558, 590.

2. Cherwell Papers H291/2; Mansergh, *The Transfer of Power*, Vol. IV, 695.

3. Mansergh, *The Transfer of Power*, Vol. IV, 701–702, 706–707, 719.

4. Ibid., 734–735, 741, 744, 750.

5. Santhanam, *The Cry of Distress*, 34.

6. Sinha and Khera, *Indian War Economy*, 286, 288, 290, 420–421; Ghosh, *Famines in Bengal*, 46.

7. Moon, *Wavell*, 37; Sinha and Khera, *Indian War Economy*, 286.

8. Slim, *Defeat into Victory*, 186–192.

9. Ibid., 193; Fay, *The Forgotten Army*, 259. The original first stanza of the song: *Kadam kadam badaye ja/Khusi ke geet gaye ja/Ye zindagi hai kaum ki/Ye kaum pe lutaye ja.*

10. Branson, *British Soldier in India*, 109–112.

11. Ibid., 113–114.

12. Ibid., 116–117.

13. Ibid., 118; Slim, *Defeat into Victory*, 191.

14. Sengupta, *Smritir Somoy Somoyer Smriti*, 45–46; Graham and Cole, *The Burma Campaign Memorial Library*, 101.

15. Fay, *The Forgotten Army*, 286–290.

16. Bayly and Harper, *Forgotten Armies*, 382.

17. Churchill, *The Second World War: Closing the Ring*, 496; Slim, *Defeat into Victory*, 443; Sinha and Khera, *Indian War Economy*, 286.

18. Fay, *The Forgotten Army*, 302–303.

19. Bayly and Harper, *Forgotten Armies*, 379.

20. Mansergh, *The Transfer of Power*, Vol. IV, 801(footnote), 808; Moon, *Wavell*, 59.

21. Cherwell Papers, H291/19, 24, 28; Mansergh, *The Transfer of Power*, Vol. IV, 776, 818.

22. Mansergh, *The Transfer of Power*, Vol. IV, 827; Cherwell Papers H291/28; Barnes and Nicholson, *The Empire at Bay*, 972.

23. Cherwell Papers, H291/30.

24. Cherwell Papers H292/2; Mansergh, *The Transfer of Power*, Vol. IV, 863–864; Barnes and Nicholson, *The Empire at Bay*, 976.

25. Mansergh, *The Transfer of Power*, Vol. IV, 925; Moon, *Wavell*, 81, 68; Cherwell Papers H292/2, 3.

26. Mansergh, *The Transfer of Power*, Vol. IV, 925; Cherwell Papers H292/4, 10, and F235/31.

27. Mansergh, *The Transfer of Power*, Vol. IV,1034, 900.

28. Barnes and Nicholson, *The Empire at Bay*, 979; Mansergh, *The Transfer of Power*, Vol. IV, 941, 939, 964.

29. Barnes and Nicholson, *The Empire at Bay*, 985; Mansergh, *The Transfer of Power*, Vol. IV, 999.

30. Barnes and Nicholson, *The Empire at Bay*, 987–988.

31. Mansergh, *The Transfer of Power*, Vol. IV, 1044; Barnes and Nicholson, *The Empire at Bay*, 989; Cherwell Papers H292/13.

32. Mansergh, *The Transfer of Power*, Vol. IV, 1045–1046, 1056.

33. Quoted in Read and Fisher, *The Proudest Day*, 346.

34. Moon, *Wavell*, 88; AMEL 1/6/21, File 1, Secretary of State's Minute to Prime Minister, May 4, 1944; CHAR 20/165/43, May 27, 1944.

35. Mansergh, *The Transfer of Power*, Vol. IV, 962–963.

36. Moon, *Wavell*, 78; Barnes and Nicholson, *The Empire at Bay*, 988.

37. Mansergh, *The Transfer of Power*, Vol. IV, 1100, 1136–1138.

38. Barnes and Nicholson, *The Empire at Bay*, 992; Mansergh, *The Transfer of Power*, Vol. IV, 1152–1154, 1147.

39. CAB 66/52/48, "Report of Committee on Indian Financial Questions," July 19, 1944; Barnes and Nicholson, *The Empire at Bay*, 992–993.

40. Cherwell Papers J68/20; Barnes and Nicholson, *The Empire at Bay*, 986.

41. Denney, *Macaulay's Essay on Warren Hastings*, 36; quoted in Chakravarty, *The Raj Syndrome*, 127.

42. AMEL 1/6/34, "The Regeneration of India: Memorandum by the Prime Minister."

43. Barnes and Nicholson, *The Empire at Bay*, 995.

44. Colville, *The Fringes of Power*, Vol. II, 139; Loewenheim, Langley, and Jonas, *Roosevelt and Churchill*, 74.

45. Quoted in Ponting, *Churchill*, 635; Sinha and Khera, *Indian War Economy*, 54.

46. Cherwell Papers, H126/1, 2, and H124/22.

47. Moon, *Wavell*, 93; Roy, "Military Loyalty," 511; Mansergh, *The Transfer of Power*, Vol. V, 128.

48. MT 59/657, "Import of Food Grains into India," January 1945.

Chapter Eleven

1. Dhara, *Probaho*, 172–175. Bose did send small parties of INA operatives by submarine, but almost all were captured.

2. Ibid., 176.

3. Ibid., 176–179.

4. Ibid., 182–184.

5. Quoted in Read and Fisher, *The Proudest Day*, 350; Mansergh, *The Transfer of Power*, Vol. II, 106.

6. Moon, *Wavell*, 91.

7. Mansergh, *The Transfer of Power*, Vol. V, 81–82, 258, 371, 375.

8. Moon, *Wavell*, 111.

9. Ibid., 108.

10. Ibid., 260–261, 368, 236; Schofield, *Wavell: Soldier & Statesman*, 115.

11. Barnes and Nicholson, *The Empire at Bay*, 1023; Mansergh, *The Transfer of Power*, Vol. V, 130–131.

12. Barnes and Nicholson, *The Empire at Bay*, 1018.

13. Churchill and Gilbert, *Winston S. Churchill*, Vol. VII, 1166.

14. Nichols, *Verdict on India*, 15–17, 23, 36–39, 184, 188–189.

15. Ibid., 216–224.

16. Churchill and Gilbert, *Winston S. Churchill*, Vol. VII, 1166.

17. Berthon and Potts, *Warlords*, 268.

18. Sbrega, "The Anticolonial Policies of Franklin D. Roosevelt," 76; Louis, *Imperialism at Bay*, 458–460.

19. Louis, *Imperialism at Bay*, 486.

20. Colville, *The Fringes of Power*, Vol. II, 203.

21. Barnes and Nicholson, *The Empire at Bay*, 1015; Mansergh, *The Transfer of Power*, Vol. V, 126, 1070.

22. Mansergh, *The Transfer of Power*, Vol. V, 765; Moon, *Wavell*, 120; Barnes and Nicholson, *The Empire at Bay*, 1031 (footnote).

23. Moon, *Wavell*, 121–123.

24. Louis, *Imperialism at Bay*, 509–510.

25. Venkataramani and Shrivastava, *Roosevelt Gandhi Churchill*, 256–259.

26. Moran, *Churchill: The Struggle for Survival*, 273; Lewis, *Changing Direction*,157–160; Sarila, *The Shadow of the Great Game*, 22, 181–182.

27. Barnes and Nicholson, *The Empire at Bay*, 1013; Mansergh, *The Transfer of Power*,Vol. V, 826.

28. Barnes and Nicholson, *The Empire at Bay*, 1044–1045; Moon, *Wavell*, 135–136; Mansergh, *The Transfer of Power*, Vol. V, 1073–1077, 1083–1086.

29. Mansergh, *The Transfer of Power*, Vol. V, 1222–1225.

30. Ibid., 1128; Moon, *Wavell*, 157–158.

31. Mansergh, *The Transfer of Power*, Vol. V, 1229.

32. Sarila, *The Shadow of the Great Game*, 186; Moon, *Wavell*, 310, 168.

33. Moran, *Churchill: The Struggle for Survival*, 331; Moon, *Wavell*, 168.

34. Bose and Bose, *Netaji*, Vol. 7, 228.

35. Yadav and Seki, *Subhas Chandra Bose*, 120–125.

36. WO 208/3812, "The Last Movements of S. C. Bose." The spy appears to have been S. C. Goho, a Malayan of Indian origin. See WO 203/4673, War Dept. to HQ SEAC: "Confidential 12166," October 1945.

37. Bose and Bose, *Netaji*, Vol. 12, 212–222.

38. Related to the author by former Congress worker Manos Banerjee.

39. Nayar, "Satish Samanta Da," 86; Mahapatro, "Ananya Sushilda," 207.

40. James, *Raj*, 595; Fay, *The Forgotten Army*, 516–517.

41. James, *Raj*, 591.

42. Batabyal, *Communalism in Bengal*, 133, 136.

43. Read and Fisher, *The Proudest Day*, 393–396; Sarila, *The Shadow of the Great Game*, 224; Mansergh, *The Transfer of Power*, Vol. VIII, 106–107; Singh, *The Origins of the Partition of India*, 592.

44. Batabyal, *Communalism in Bengal*, 253; Singh, *The Origins of the Partition of India*, 185; Khosla, *Stern Reckoning*, 58–59; Mansergh, *The Transfer of Power*, Vol. VIII, 298, 303.

45. Batabyal, *Communalism in Bengal*, 250–253, 316, 322; Khosla, *Stern Reckoning*, 58; Singh, *The Origins of the Partition of India*, 182–183, Mansergh, *The Transfer of Power*, Vol. VIII, 302.

46. Batabyal, *Communalism in Bengal*, 281, 321, 78–79, 293, 305–308.

47. Gupta, *In the Path of Service*, 77, 93.

48. Batabyal, *Communalism in Bengal*, 345; Gupta, *In the Path of Service*, 96.

49. Gupta, *In the Path of Service*, 108.

50. Moon, *Wavell*, 374; 322–23; quoted in Sarila, *The Shadow of the Great Game*, 225.

51. Churchill and Gilbert, *Winston S. Churchill*, Vol. VIII, 294–295.

52. Wolpert, *Gandhi's Passion*, 242.

53. Gupta, *In the Path of Service*, 116.

54. Kamtekar, "The Military Ingredient of Communal Violence in Punjab, 1947," 568–572; Singh, "Imperial Defence and the Transfer of Power in India," 569.

55. Quoted in Gandhi, *Collected Works*, Vol. 97, 6.

56. Gilbert, *Winston S. Churchill*, Vol. VIII, 248; Tunzelmann, *Indian Summer*, 127–128; Page et al., *The Partition Omnibus*, 305.

57. James, *Raj*, 597.

Chapter Twelve

1. Reynolds, *In Command of History*, 39, 103, 125, 190, 195, 380, 399; Moran, *Churchill: The Struggle for Survival*, 112; Churchill, *The Second World War: Closing the Ring*, 587.

2. Mansergh, *The Transfer of Power*, Vol. IV, 461, 468, 725.

3. Ibid., 1139.

4. CSAC, Olaf M. Martin Papers, Memoir, 247 (pages 312–331 are missing); Mitra, *Tin Kuri Dash*, 167.

5. Mansergh, *The Transfer of Power*, Vol. III, 509(footnote), and Vol. IV, 445(footnote); CAB 79/59, C.O.S. (43) 38th meeting, March 9, 1943.

6. Woodhead, *Famine Inquiry Commission*, 108.

7. Knight, *Food Administration in India*, 20; Dyson and Maharatna, "Excess Mortality During the Bengal Famine," 290.

8. Pati, *Turbulent Times*, 41; Ghosh, *Famines in Bengal*, 105–106; Gupta, *Towards Freedom*, Part I, 272; Nanavati Papers, Vol. II, 540. According to Ghosh, the chowkidar served as night watchman of his village; informer on the whereabouts of political fugitives and habitual criminals; office boy, domestic servant, and courier for local officials; shepherd for police officers' cattle; guard for the neighborhood railway track when it conveyed dignitaries; caretaker and cook for the government guesthouse in the locale; guarantor of land rights and safe harvesting of crops; material witness for the Crown; compiler "of all official statistics relating to acreage and yield of all principal crops, livestock, carts and vehicles, sugar-cane crushers, ploughs and tractors, date and palm trees for production of molasses"; reporter of all market prices; and registrar for births and deaths.

9. Symonds, *In the Margins of Independence*, 23.

10. Maharatna, *The Demography of Famines*, 284–286.

11. Woodhead, *Famine Inquiry Commission*, 109–110.

12. Sen, *Poverty and Famines*, 202; Maharatna, *The Demography of Famines*, 147; Dyson and Maharatna, "Excess Mortality During the Bengal Famine," 297.

13. Rao, "Prasantha Chandra Mahalanobis 1893–1972," 472; Greenough, *Prosperity and Misery in Modern Bengal*, 305.

14. Mahalanobis, "Mortality in Bengal in 1943."

15. Guha, *Health and Population in South Asia*, 90.

16. Bose, *Agrarian Bengal*, 151.

17. Greenough, *Prosperity and Misery in Modern Bengal*, 309.

18. Maharatna, *The Demography of Famines*, 143–144; Woodhead, *Famine Inquiry Commission*, 113. If infant deaths are 18 percent of the total, the remaining deaths must be 82 percent of the total. Since 82 percent of the mortality is 5.3, then 100 percent is 6.5.

19. Marcus, "Famine Crimes in International Law," 245–281; "Convention IV relative to the Protection of Civilian Persons in Time of War," August 12, 1949.

20. Reynolds, *In Command of History*, 195; Hammond, *Food*, Vol. I, 281–282; Harrod, *The Prof*, 261–262; Mansergh, *The Transfer of Power*, Vol. III, 49.

21. Sen, *Development as Freedom*, 16; Sen, *Poverty and Famines*, 80; Sen, "Wars and Famines." Sen mistakenly believed, however, that the Government of India had no reason to anticipate the Bengal famine. He quoted the official estimate of the rice shortage as 140,000 tons, whereas the document to which he refers states 1.4 million tons.

22. Cherwell Papers H305/9.

23. Arendt, *The Origins of Totalitarianism*, 183–184.

24. Barnes and Nicholson, *The Empire at Bay*, 1071, 1075.

25. AMEL 1/6/32, File 2, April 30, 1947.

26. Gopal, "Churchill and India," 469.

27. Moran, *Churchill: The Struggle for Survival*, 333.

28. Ibid., 394.

29. Gopal, "Churchill and India," 469.

30. Moran, *Churchill: The Struggle for Survival*, 195.

31. Harrod, *The Prof*, 261; Birkenhead, *The Professor and the Prime Minister*, 11, 291, 279–280.

32. Moran Papers, PP/CMW/K.1–5; Moran, *Churchill: The Struggle for Survival*, 499–500, 621.

Index